A Contextual Approach

PAUL
& THE
LAW

FRANK THIELMAN

IVP Academic

An imprint of InterVarsity Press
Downers Grove, Illinois

InterVarsity Press
P.O. Box 1400, Downers Grove, IL 60515-1426
World Wide Web: www.ivpress.com
E-mail: email@ivpress.com

©1994 by Frank Thielman

InterVarsity Press® is the book-publishing division of InterVarsity Christian Fellowship/USA®, a student movement active on campus at hundreds of universities, colleges and schools of nursing in the United States of America, and a member movement of the International Fellowship of Evangelical Students. For information about local and regional activities, write Public Relations Dept., InterVarsity Christian Fellowship/USA, 6400 Schroeder Rd., P.O. Box 7895, Madison, WI 53707-7895, or visit the IVCF website at <www.intervarsity.org>.

Quotations from the Old Testament are from the New Revised Standard Version of the Bible, copyright 1989 by the Division of Christian Education of the National Council of the Churches of Christ in the USA. Used by permission. All rights reserved. New Testament quotations are the author's own translation.

ISBN 978-0-8308-1854-9

Printed in the United States of America ∞

Library of Congress Cataloging-in-Publication Data

Thielman, Frank.
 Paul and the law: a contextual approach/Frank Thielman.
  p. cm.
 Includes bibliographical references and index.
 ISBN 0-8308-1854-5
 1. Bible. N.T. Epistles of Paul—Theology. 2. Law (Theology)—
Biblical teaching. I. Title.
BS2655.L35T46 1994
241'.2'092—dc20   *94-31571*
                            CIP

P	25	24	23	22	21	20	19	18	17	16	15	14	13	12	11	10	9	8	7
Y	25	24	23	22	21	20	19	18	17	16	15	14	13	12	11	10	09		

For Abby

A Note on Translations and Abbreviations

Quotations from the Old Testament follow the renderings of the New Revised Standard Version, and quotations from Josephus are from the Loeb Classical Library edition of Josephus's works. Translations of other Greek texts are my own. The following abbreviations are used:

Comm. Gal.   John Calvin's commentary on Galatians in *Commentarii in Quatuor Pauli Epistolas: Ad Galatas, ad Ephesios, ad Philippenses, ad Colossenses*

Comm. Phil.   John Calvin's commentary on Philippians in *Commentarii in Quatuor Pauli Epistolas: Ad Galatas, ad Ephesios, ad Philippenses, ad Colossenses*

Comm. Rom.   John Calvin, *Commentarius in Epistolam Pauli ad Romanos*

Inst.   John Calvin, Institutio Christianae religionis

LW   Luther's Works

SCG   Thomas Aquinas, *Summa contra Gentiles*

ST   Thomas Aquinas, *Summa Theologica*

WA   The "Weimarer Ausgabe" of Luther's works

Preface

New Testament theology as a credible discipline has fallen on hard times. The difficulties began over two centuries ago when theologians themselves began to question the scientific legitimacy of their discipline. Was it defensible to limit New Testament theology to the study of the twenty-seven canonical documents even though those documents had been chosen, and others rejected, on nonscientific and religious grounds? Was it rational to speak of "New Testament theology" at all, given that an objective investigation of the documents contained in the New Testament seemed to reveal numerous, often contradictory, theologies with little relationship to one another?

The answer given then by a few voices, and today by far more, is that New Testament theology may be carried on in the church, where people are accustomed to thinking unscientifically; but it has no place within the rigorously objective sphere of academic inquiry and little role to play in life as most people experience it. One eminent New Testament scholar has therefore called for an end to the attempt to identify within the New Testament a consistent core of teaching that could be called "the theology of the New Testament." Such a theology quite simply, he says, does not exist, and outside of churches, which have an interest in keeping alive the myth of a New Testament theology, the search for such a theology serves no purpose.[1]

Paul, once considered the New Testament theologian par excellence, has not surprisingly been a central figure of contention in the debate over the legitimacy of New Testament theology. An increasing number of scholars are concluding that this or that aspect of Paul's theology, once thought important, hopelessly contradicts the rest, and a few have decided that nothing in Paul's letters is worth salvaging.[2] One influential study, for example, concludes by asking the apparently rhetorical question, "Can a Paul who devotes his energies to the creation and maintaining of sectarian groups hostile to all non-members . . . still be seen as the bearer of a message with profound universal significance?"[3]

At the center of this negative evaluation of New Testament, and particularly Pauline, theology lies the recent cross-examination of Paul's view of the Jewish law. It would be hard to imagine a more fundamental principle of Protestant theology than Paul's dictum that salvation comes by faith alone, apart from works of the law. Martin Luther's understanding of this statement lay at the heart of his protest against the Roman Catholic Church, and a variety of theologians, both Protestant and otherwise, came to agree that the great Reformer's interpretation of this statement was both historically correct and theologically necessary. During the past several decades, however, Luther's reading of Paul's statements about the Jewish law has come under devastating attack. The attack has concentrated on showing that Luther's interpretation of Paul is based on a caricature of the place of the law in Judaism, and that this incorrect and demeaning stereotype of the central symbol of the Jewish religion has been reproduced by, and propagated with the blessing of, the highest levels of Christian scholarship over the past two centuries. With a few notable exceptions, many Pauline scholars believe that insofar as this attack was directed against Luther's view of Judaism, it has proved its point.[4]

If this is true, they have asked, then what did Paul mean by his famous statement that salvation comes by faith and not by works of the Jewish law? Was it an unfortunate rhetorical device, reflecting more the bluster of the moment than what Paul's Jewish opponents really believed about the law?[5] Was it the self-contradictory musing of a troubled person?[6] Was it a disingenuous way of distancing Paul's new, predominantly Gentile congregations from the synagogue?[7] Or does it form part of a coherent, reasonable and profound theological insight? In response to the new perspective on Paul, many scholars have denied that an unbiased reading of the apostle will produce anything but a negative response to this last question.[8] Paul's statements about the law, they claim, are simply too peculiar and inconsistent to be part of a carefully worked out theology.

The following pages argue that this final question *can* receive a positive answer if we follow three methodological procedures. First, we should examine Paul's view of the law not only topically or systematically but also within the context of each letter. Perhaps the most important hermeneutical conclusion about Paul's letters in the last century has been that they are not systematic treatises but real letters, written to address a variety of practical problems within churches for which Paul felt some pastoral responsibility. Most of the book-length examinations of Paul's view of the law, however, examine it topically, as a glance at their chapter headings shows.[9] It would be unfair to say that this procedure prevents the authors of these learned monographs from understanding Paul's statements about the law contextually: these are meticulous books produced by first-rate exegetes. Yet the reader of these books never gains a feel for how Paul applied his understanding of the law to the problems that faced his churches or an understanding of how this application varied from church to church. A progression through Paul's letters, taking into account the contingencies that each letter addressed, may help to bring clarity to Paul's statements about the law by allowing the reader to see why Paul says what he does in each situation.[10]

Second, we should give as much attention to those letters in which the law is not a bone of contention as to those in which it is, and as much attention to Paul's allusive references to the law as to his explicit statements. Letters in which Paul refers to the Mosaic law infrequently or allusively, because it is not the main topic of debate, provide "controls" by which to evaluate what he says about the law in other letters where it is the central issue in a fight for the loyalty of his churches. If what he says about the law in passing matches up with what he says about the law in the more heated and law-oriented letters, then it seems reasonable to conclude that Paul's view of the law is self-consistent and deserves serious consideration. Moreover, the ideas about the law that he repeats implicitly in some letters and explicitly in others can lay reasonable claim to being central to his thinking about the law.

Third, we should pay careful attention both to our own theological context and to the wider cultural contexts in which Paul's understanding of the law took shape. Understanding our own theological presuppositions makes us aware of the interpretive conclusions that we are most likely to draw, and understanding Paul's presuppositions helps us to know whether those conclusions are correct. Presuppositions are not bad, and they are in any case unavoidable, but knowing what they are, both in our own case and in Paul's, can only help us to understand Paul on his own terms. The first two chapters of this study, therefore, are devoted to sorting out the theological climate in which we interpret Paul's view of the law and to understanding the theological climate in which Paul's view took shape.

The term *law*, of course, can refer to many things, as Paul's own use of it shows. It can refer generally to a norm that guides the conduct of those under its influence, to the Hebrew Scriptures, to the first five books of those Scriptures or to the commandments contained in those books.[11] This study is not a lexical analysis of Paul's use of the word *law* but an attempt to describe Paul's understanding of the covenant that God made with Israel during its wilderness wanderings and whose story and stipulations appear in the Torah, the first five books of the Hebrew canon. For Paul and for Jews of his time, this "law of Moses" was "the law" in the quintessential sense.

Because this is the task, limiting the scope of the study to the passages in which Paul explicitly refers to "the law" would be unwise. The Mosaic covenant contains certain broad themes, such as the election of God's people and the importance of their sanctity, which reappear in Paul's letters in more subtle ways than a study only of Paul's explicit statements about the Mosaic covenant would detect. This study tries to show that the way Paul uses and transforms these thematic patterns of the Mosaic covenant reveals important assumptions about the Mosaic law which complement his more explicit statements and make them more intelligible.

If I have succeeded in this effort at all, it is in large measure because of those who have worked with me to make this book possible. I am profoundly grateful to several friends who sacrificed time from their own scholarly endeavors to help me with this one. T. David Gordon, Rollin G. Grams and my colleague Gerald Bray read portions of the manuscript and saved me from more than one gaffe. Douglas Moo, professor of New Testament at Trinity Evangelical Divinity School, read through a draft of the entire book and offered a series of valuable suggestions for its improvement. He sent me back to the text at many points, and although we continue to disagree on some issues, his salutary influence is evident at several critical junctures in the argument. Daniel G. Reid, academic and reference book editor for InterVarsity Press, provided the insightful assistance that only an editor who is also an accomplished Pauline scholar could give to such a study. I am grateful for his encouragement, practical advice and illuminating exegetical observations. Finally, my student assistant Eric Mason read through the entire manuscript in a busy time after his graduation and before his wedding. The kind efforts of each of these friends have improved the book significantly.

This book was written in the corners of time available to a full-time teacher and father: between classes, late at night, early in the morning. During this time my parents, Calvin and Dorothy Thielman, and two close friends, Steve and Tracy Whitner, prayed faithfully for my work and helped in other practical ways too numerous to recount. More than from anyone else, however, the time and energy to write this book were a gift from my wife, Abby. Her constant love and unselfish concern for the advancement of the gospel make my work possible. If the book clarifies to any extent the shape of Paul's theology, it is largely because Abby's unselfish help with my other responsibilities gave me the time to think about Paul and the law. We will both be satisfied that the long hours were worthwhile if the result edifies the church and brings glory to its King and Head.

CHAPTER ONE

PAUL, THE LAW & JUDAISM:
The Creation & Collapse of a Theological Consensus

The thoughts of those who have read Paul before us have molded the way we think about the apostle to the Gentiles. Some in ancient times who claimed to be Christians rejected him as an evil influence; others believed that he was the only faithful apostle. But those of us who see him as "the blessed apostle Paul" alongside the other apostles do so because people like Ignatius, Clement, Polycarp, Irenaeus and Tertullian embraced him as an authority alongside other canonical authorities.[1] The influence of these ancient authorities helps to explain why we accept Paul at all, but the *way* we understand Paul at the turn of the twentieth century is due in large measure to the quiet revolution that took place in the newly founded urban universities of the late Middle Ages and to the earthshaking events that revolution eventually brought about. The story of these events and the intellectual forces they unleashed has filled many books much longer than this one. The roots of the modern understanding of Paul's view of the law, however, can be seen when we take a brief look at three important thinkers in this intellectual revolution: Thomas Aquinas, Martin Luther and John Calvin.

Thomas Aquinas is important for at least two reasons. First, he is the greatest representative of the interpretive tradition that helped bring about the Protestant Reformation, a tradition known as Scholasticism. Second, in the years following the Reformation, Thomas's reading of Paul continued to enjoy a wide reception among Roman Catholics, and their responses to Luther were often formulated in Thomistic terms.[2]

The first and greatest of the Protestant Reformers, Martin Luther, grounded not only his challenge to the Roman Catholic Church but also his understanding of the entire world in his understanding of Paul's statements about the law. If, said Luther in introducing Galatians, "the doctrines of works and of human traditions" should dominate the church, then "the whole knowledge of truth, life, and salvation is lost" (LW 26:3). Even during Luther's own lifetime, this understanding of Paul's view of the law was "by the grace of God . . . very well known." In later centuries, as we shall see below, it became an extraordinarily powerful influence on the way both humble Christians and erudite scholars interpreted not only Paul but also the whole Jewish religion.

Part of the reason for this was the wide influence of John Calvin. Calvin understood better than any who preceded him that in order to apply the Bible properly to his own age, it was first necessary to understand it within its own cultural and historical context. Thus he frequently used whatever lexical, historical and geographical reference works were available to him as he worked to explain the meaning of Scripture.[3] When applied to Paul's letters, this method had the effect of placing Luther's understanding of Paul, with a few modifications, on an even more impressive intellectual footing than Luther had provided.

These great thinkers built an interpretive framework for Paul's statements about the law which stood for centuries. In the last hundred years, however, and especially in the last three decades, the pillars of understanding that they provided for interpreters of Paul have, like the Porch of the Maidens on the Athenian Acropolis, been slowly disintegrating. Out of the resulting confusion a new hermeneutical tradition is rapidly forming, whose convictions about Paul we must understand if we are to grasp our own interpretive context clearly.

Law, Grace and Merit in Thomas Aquinas

What the faith-works antithesis was to Luther, Aristotle was to Thomas: the great philosopher made sense of the world, especially the theological world to which Thomas had devoted his life and his considerable intellectual powers. His mammoth *Summa Theologica* was an attempt to place Christian belief on the rational basis that Aristotle provided for understanding reality. In it the classic themes of Christian theology are scrutinized in unrelenting Aristotelian syllogisms to produce a monumental theological and intellectual achievement.

Aristotle's influence on Thomas is plain in the treatises in the *Summa Theologica* on law and grace (1a2ae.90-114). Aristotle believed that everything must act in accordance with its own inherent nature and that human and divine nature are qualitatively different, for human nature is temporal and divine nature eternal. This posed an immediate problem, however, for Christian theology, which regarded the purpose of human nature to be undisturbed communion with an eternal God.[4]

Thomas believed that grace solves this problem. Grace was created to serve human nature by elevating it to a supernatural level, so enabling it to attain both eternal life and union with God. Prior to the Fall, people lived perfectly and in accordance with their natural state, which God had intended for them. Even in this unfallen state, however, Adam and Eve could not have attained eternal life on their own, because human nature and eternal life, like human nature and God himself, are qualitatively different entities. Therefore, in order to step from the level appropriate to their status as people up to the level appropriate to God, Adam and Eve needed God's grace even prior to the Fall.[5] The need for grace became even more acute, of course, after the Fall, for now human nature itself was corrupt and required the restorative powers that only supernatural grace could provide. Thomas believed, then, that fallen people occupied a place two removes from eternal life: they were corrupt because of the Fall, but even in their uncorrupted state they could not have risen to eternal life and to God himself without the aid of God's grace (*ST* 1a2ae.109.2; compare *SCG* 3.147).

The help of God's grace, supplied by the Holy Spirit, was absent during the period when the law of Moses was in effect. Although the Old Law was good, and although it originated with God, discouraged idolatry and foreshadowed Christ's coming (*ST* 1a2ae.98.1-2), it was unable to lead people to the goal of eternal life for which God had created them. Like a medicine administered for the purpose of helping to restore a person's health, but which cannot accomplish the task by itself, the Old Law was both good and necessary, but imperfect (*ST* 1a2ae.98.1). This is why, Thomas explains, the law was given through angels rather than directly from the hand of God (*ST* 1a2ae.98.3; compare Gal 3:19).

The restorative task was completed, however, by the New Law, which, given directly from God and accompanied by the grace of the Holy Spirit, rescues people from sin and transfers them into an uncorrupted state (*ST* 1a2ae.98.3). Because the New Law was accompanied by the transforming power of God's grace, people can now please God from a simple and free desire to act in accord with their own newly constituted nature. In this regard, as in many others, the New Law stands in stark contrast to the Old. The Old Law had forced people into virtuous action against their own desires through the harsh instruments of threats and punishments. The New Law, however, supplies the grace that changes the human heart and enables people to do virtuous acts not from fear but from their own desire to love and please God (*ST* 1a2ae.108.1).

The grace supplied by the New Law, then, releases people from the condemnation of the Old Law and allows them to perform meritorious works worthy of eternal life (*ST* 1a2ae.111.2; 112.1; 114.1-9; *SCG* 3.147-50). Thomas is careful to say that since God and human beings are not equals, it is inappropriate to speak of people "meriting" anything from God in the common use of the term. He is also careful to distinguish between two different roles that grace plays in justification. The first role is to supply the necessary change in human nature which elevates the person to the supernatural level of God. This action comes not as a reward from God for any good work but "by grace" (and here Thomas quotes Rom 11:6).[6] Once that grace has been given, however, it takes on a second role as it enables people to perform works that merit God's reward. In this second role it is even possible, according to Thomas, that God would grant the request of a virtuous person—virtuous of course because of the grace God had given—that another person be saved. The granting of this request could, Thomas believed, come as a result of the merit that the virtuous person has in God's eyes (*ST* 1a2ae.114.6).

In summary, Thomas believed that human nature needs the transforming action of God's grace in order to receive eternal life. This transformation is needed not only because of human sin but also simply because human nature is qualitatively different from God's nature. Human sin only made the problem worse, and attempts to control human sin by means of the Old Law, as laudable as they were, could not be successful. Grace, which accompanied the giving of the New Law, provides the necessary transformation of human nature to the divine level and supplies the change of heart needed for humanity to act both freely and virtuously. Although the grace that supplies the ability to act virtuously comes as a free gift from God and is not the reward of any work, the virtuous action that results can merit eternal life both for oneself and for others.

Luther and the Law

It was over this last concept—that grace aids us in performing the works that merit eternal life for ourselves and at times for others—that Luther came into serious conflict with Thomas and the Scholastic method that Thomas represented. Prior to his protest against the Roman Catholic Church, Luther feared that neither his own good works, even if done out of love for Christ, nor the merits of his monastic order could save him from God's dreadful righteousness. He passed through a period of extreme pain and anxiety that drove him to the brink of mental collapse and, by his own confession, to hatred of the God who seemed to torture him so:

> Though I lived as a monk without reproach, I felt that I was a sinner before God with an extremely disturbed conscience. I could not believe that he was placated by my satisfaction. I did not love, yes I hated the righteous God who punishes sinners, and secretly, if not blasphemously, certainly murmuring greatly, I was angry with God, and said, "As if, indeed, it is not enough, that miserable sinners, eternally lost through original sin, are crushed by every kind of calamity by the law of the decalogue, without having God add pain to pain by the gospel and also by the gospel threatening us with his righteousness and wrath!" Thus I raged with a fierce and troubled conscience. (*LW* 34:336-38)

At the same time that Luther was experiencing this dark night of the soul, however, he was lecturing on Paul's epistles in the university at Wittenberg and was captivated especially by Paul's letter to the Romans. There he found that God's righteousness is revealed in the gospel (1:17), a terrible thought for someone convinced that God's righteousness means God's wrath. After meditating on the letter at length, however, Luther discovered that rather than God's wrath, "the righteousness of God" refers to God's willingness to give life to all who have faith in him. Suddenly it seemed that God had ceased to be his angry accuser and instead had become his rock of refuge and mighty fortress: "I felt that I was altogether born again and had entered paradise itself through open gates. There a totally other face of the entire Scripture showed itself to me" (*LW* 34:337).

This experience informed Luther's reading of the entire Bible, but especially of Paul's letters. In Galatians, for example, he found extensive evidence that no human activity, or "active righteousness," no matter how sincere or vigorous, could save people from God's wrath. Such salvation could come only through "passive righteousness"—a righteousness provided in its entirety by God himself and appropriated by faith in Jesus Christ. Luther claimed that if, as Paul said in Galatians 2:16, the excellent law of God himself could not justify, then surely no works "chosen by self-righteous people" can justify either (*LW* 26:141). The demands of the law and the attempt to keep them, he understood Paul to be saying, could not save but only condemn and inspire terror. "No matter how wise and righteous men may be according to reason and the divine Law," he says in commenting on Galatians 2:16, "yet with all their works, merits, Masses, righteousness, and acts of worship they are not justified" (*LW* 26:140), for the law was not designed to justify the sinner and therefore cannot provide salvation.

The primary role of the law, Luther never tired of saying, was to terrify the sinner, much as Luther himself had been terrified before discovering God's grace. "The law," he asserted, "only shows sin, terrifies, and humbles; thus it prepares us for justification and drives us to Christ" (*LW* 26:126). It does this not only by forbidding sins that everyone recognizes to be sin, as in the Ten Commandments, but also by forbidding a host of activities that are not in themselves sinful, as in the purity laws of Leviticus. The reason for forbidding both, Luther said, was so that people might be overwhelmed by sin, that sin "might simply become numerous and be heaped up beyond measure" and the human conscience might be afflicted and fly for refuge to the gospel (*LW* 35:244). This, said Luther, is what Paul meant when he called the law "an agent of sin" (Gal 2:17), a "dispensation of death" (2 Cor 3:7) and a revealer of the "knowledge of sin" (Rom 3:20); and this is why the apostle said that "by works of the law no one becomes righteous before God" (Rom 3:20; *LW* 35:242).

This function of the law, unpleasant as it may be, is nevertheless essential according to Luther. Without it people would remain in the worst kind of deception, because they would be unable to recognize sin. Strolling blithely through a respectable life, they would believe that the occasional good work was all that God required, that periodic lapses into bad behavior were only natural. Such people would be unaware that sin is the real enemy. It was the great task of Moses to dispel this fog of self-deception and to open human eyes to the awful face of death, which stands "ready to devour such a sinner and to swallow him up in hell" (*LW* 35:243).

In the sphere of justification, therefore, the law and "human effort" have no place. Doing good and exercising love are necessary activities for the Christian, and their performance should receive ample attention, but when the subject under examination is justification, any work that originates from the human side, even love, should not enter the discussion. Salvation comes simply and purely by faith, and faith is the belief that one's sins have been shifted onto Jesus Christ at his crucifixion (*LW* 26:132). Therefore when justification is under discussion, it is proper to speak of faith alone and to banish discussion of works to another day. The Christian must be alone with Christ, without the nuisance of good works interfering in their communion (*LW* 26:137-38), for by putting faith in Christ, the Christian has climbed up into heaven and left the law far away on the earth below (*LW* 26:156-57).

When the time came to discuss good works, Luther was ready to say that the law serves to teach and discipline the Christian's flesh (*LW* 26:158; 27:232). He could even say that after the accusing work of the law has been accomplished in the believer, and the believer has come "under Christ," the law should then "be fulfilled through the Spirit" (WA vol. 39, pt. 1, p. 249).[7] These statements are not typical of Luther, however, and he never worked out systematically how it could be that Christ was the end of the law yet the believer still must fulfill the law through the Spirit. Far more typical is Luther's claim that each Christian is a new Decalogue by virtue of the Holy Spirit's guidance (*LW* 34:112-13) and that whatever is still useful in the law has been written on the Christian's heart (*LW* 35:168; compare *LW* 35:244).[8] It was on this point that Luther's younger contemporary John Calvin made certain modifications.

Calvin and the Law

Calvin placed less emphasis than Luther on the role of the law in terrifying the sinner and greater weight on the law as the revelation of God's will in all its holiness and perfection. This, Calvin felt, was the law's principal function, and its role as accuser was only made necessary by the Fall (*Comm. Rom.* 7:10). Calvin divided the law into three parts: the moral, the ceremonial and the judicial. The ceremonial law foreshadowed Christ and, although sacred and important for instruction, was fulfilled by Christ's death and resurrection. When Paul said in Galatians 3:24 that the law functioned as a tutor, Calvin believed he was referring to the ceremonial law's anticipation of Christ's redemptive work. The judicial law provided for justice and equity in the civil government of Israel but, like the ceremonial law, was peculiar to Israel and not normative for other peoples. It too had come to an end (*Inst.* 4.20.15; compare 2.7.1).

The moral law, however, has not been terminated, for it simply reflects God's will, and God's will is unchanging. Relying primarily on his reading of

Paul's epistles, Calvin believed that the moral law serves three functions. First, like Luther, Calvin believed Paul's teaching implies that the law makes sin, which might otherwise go undetected, explicit and therefore leads people to seek God's grace. This is the point, says Calvin, of Romans 7:7, where Paul claims that he would not have known covetousness had it not been for the commandment forbidding it. It is also what Paul means when he seems to speak negatively of the law in such passages as Romans 3:20, 4:15, 5:20 and 2 Corinthians 3:7. Like Luther, Calvin believed that such passages do not detract from the excellence of the law—they only show that the law forces people to face the truth about their own righteousness (*Inst.* 2.7.6-9).

Second, said Calvin, the law serves as a check on unbelievers, since they often restrain themselves from evil on the basis of some knowledge, however partial, of God's law and its sanctions.[9] Paul refers to this partial submission of unbelievers to the law when he says that "the law is not laid down for the just but for the lawless and rebellious" (1 Tim 1:9). Calvin also maintained that this function of the law serves to restrain unbelievers who will eventually believe from becoming utterly contemptuous of God. Paul is, at least in part, referring to this use when he speaks of the law as a "tutor" in Galatians 3:24 (*Inst.* 2.7.10-11).

Third, the law serves believers as a guide to God's will. Calvin vigorously opposed the claim, already advanced by some during Luther's lifetime, that since the law was part of the "dispensation of death" (2 Cor 3:7), the believer is in no sense obligated to its commands. Such passages in Paul's letters, he said, referred to the law's ability to condemn believers and to the ceremonial law, but not to the law as the revelation of God's moral will (*Inst.* 2.7.12-17). Thus as long as the believer is still encumbered by the flesh, the law is useful for discovering the will of God more accurately and for avoiding sin. This use, said Calvin, "pertains more closely to the proper purpose of the law" (*Inst.* 2.7.12).

Nevertheless, Calvin did not think that the believer, even with the help of the Spirit, can keep the law perfectly in this life. When God justifies the believer, he grants the blessings promised in the law for the obedient, but he does this because Christ's obedience has been imputed to us, not because the Spirit somehow enables us to keep the law and so receive its blessings (*Inst.* 2.7.4). Thus Calvin read Romans 8:3-4 ("God . . . condemned sin in the flesh in order that the just requirement of the law might be fulfilled in us") as a reference to Christ's righteousness, now imputed to the believer, and not as a reference to righteousness that characterizes the believer's behavior (*Comm. Rom.* 8:4).

The difference between Luther and Calvin in their interpretation of Paul's view of the law, therefore, lay in each Reformer's view of the proper purpose of the law. Luther viewed its proper purpose as condemnation, whereas Calvin viewed its proper purpose as the revelation of God's will. For Calvin, the condemning function of the law was not inherent in it from the beginning but was an incidental result of the Fall.[10]

Law, Grace, Merit and Judaism in Luther and Calvin

When one is reading Luther and Calvin, it is easy to become caught up in the depth of their theological insight and to miss the significance of a subtle hermeneutical step that each has taken. Often in the course of discussing Paul's letters, these Reformers place the Roman Catholic Church, its scholars, such as Thomas, and its hierarchy in the role that Judaism occupies in Paul's statements about the law. Paul's statements about justification by faith apart from works of the law are taken, without hesitation, to be statements about the medieval system of salvation by meritorious works. A brief example from each Reformer will illustrate how this happens.

In the lectures on Galatians that Luther delivered in 1535, when the battle lines between Protestant and Roman Catholic were clearly drawn, he included an extensive comment on Galatians 2:16 ("knowing that a person is not justified by works of the law but through faith in Jesus Christ"). His explanation of the meaning of this verse centers on two propositions: that the law, both ceremonial and moral, is a unity and therefore is denied any place in justification, and that the works of the law themselves, whether performed before or after justification takes place, play no role in justification (*LW* 26:122-24). From these two principles Luther draws a conclusion that will occupy his attention for the rest of his extensive comment on this verse:

> Therefore the dangerous and wicked opinion of the papists is to be condemned. They attribute the merit of grace and the forgiveness of sins to the mere performance of the work. For they say that a good work performed before grace can earn a "merit of congruity"; but once grace has been obtained, the work that follows deserves eternal life by the "merit of condignity." If a man outside a state of grace and in mortal sin performs a good work by his own natural inclination—such as reading or hearing Mass, giving alms, etc.—this man deserves grace "by congruity." Once he has obtained grace this way, he goes on to perform a work that merits eternal life "by condignity." (*LW* 26:124)

Luther is here responding to the Scholastic teaching that although the

22

ceremonial law has been abrogated in the gospel, the moral law is still in effect and plays a role in justification both before and after the actual moment in which justification takes place.[11] Prior to justification, the performance of a righteous act, because it corresponds to or is "congruous" with what God desires, results in God's free granting of justification. He is not bound by any obligation to reward these deeds, since they are performed by people who are not justified and whose nature has not therefore been transformed; nevertheless, because these acts correspond to acts that please him, he does in fact graciously reward them with justification. After justification, good deeds are truly "condign" or "deserving," since they are performed by people whose nature has been transformed by the infusion of divine grace and who can genuinely act in a way that pleases God. God is therefore obliged to reward these acts with eternal life, and so it is proper to speak of those who perform them as earning eternal life by what they do. The phrase "works of the law" in Galatians 2:16, therefore, has become for Luther a cipher for the system of merit that he found in the church's medieval Scholastic writers.

Later, in his infamous tractate *On the Jews and Their Lies* (1543), Luther assumes that the Jews always believed that the act of circumcision itself, separated from the Word of God, would save them. Like "the papists," they divorced an outward ritual—"merely a human work"—from God's Word and so believed that their own effort would make them pleasing to God. The law drives them, like "the barefoot friars," not to the feet of God to beg for his mercy but to point boastfully to their own holiness and to claim that they possess such an excess of it "that they can use it to help others to get to heaven, and still retain a rich and abundant supply to sell" (*LW* 47:172; compare 47:159-76). Like the papists, theirs is an external religion emphasizing nothing but "deeds, works, and external show"; they have forgotten that God is a God of mercy and grace (*LW* 47:175). For Luther, then, Paul's statements about salvation through faith rather than by works of the law were leveled not only against the Roman Catholic Church of the sixteenth century but against Judaism as well.

Calvin, although more careful in his exegesis, occasionally makes the same hermeneutical shift from the Judaism of the first century to the Roman Catholicism of the sixteenth century. For example, in commenting on Paul's statement in Philippians 3:5 that he was "as touching the law, a Pharisee," Calvin claims that Paul uses the term *law* to refer generally to the corrupt religion of the day. Calvin then compares this general religious corruption to the way Christianity had been corrupted in his own day by "the Papacy"

(*Comm. Phil.* 3:5).[12] Later, when commenting on Paul's willingness to consider his own righteousness "loss and dung," Calvin refers to Roman Catholics of his own time as "present-day Pharisees" who believed they could uphold "their own merits against Christ" (*Comm. Phil.* 3:8).

The hermeneutical shift that both Luther and Calvin make in these passages is troubling because of the ease with which, especially in Luther, the Jewish understanding of the law is identified with the Roman Catholic understanding of the role that works play in justification. There is no attempt to examine carefully what Paul was opposing and no argument to support the assumption that works of the law in Paul's context were analogous to works of the law in medieval Scholasticism. Instead, Luther and, to a lesser extent, Calvin take Paul's contrast between faith and works of the law to mean that although the Jew and the Scholastic differed on the validity of the ceremonial law, their attitude toward the moral law was similar: Jews, like the medieval Scholastics, earned their way to heaven by acquiring merit. Thomas Aquinas has, at least implicitly, become a Jew, and Thomas's teaching on merit, somewhat attenuated at that, has been woven into the fabric of Jewish teaching on the law.

The Establishment of a Paradigm

In the centuries after Luther and Calvin, and especially in the hundred years from the mid-nineteenth to the mid-twentieth century, this equation between the enemies of the Reformers and Judaism would become a standard feature of Protestant biblical scholarship. Old Testament scholars frequently portrayed Judaism as having degenerated from a strong set of convictions about national unity and community in which the law played a subsidiary role to a religion concerned with the individual's relationship to the law. The highly influential nineteenth-century Old Testament scholar Julius Wellhausen believed that the publication of Deuteronomy under Josiah in the seventh century B.C. and the publication of the priestly code under Ezra in the fifth represented "an immense retrogression" from the spontaneous, natural relationship between God and people in Israel's early history.[13] Some sixty years later, Martin Noth argued similarly that Israel's religion had spiraled downward from its emphasis prior to the exile on divine initiative and corporate responsibility to an obsession with the individual's ability to earn a reward from God by keeping the law's commandments. After the exile, said Noth, the law became "an absolute entity," a "definite unit" that the individual could fulfill in its externals and so " 'exhaust' his religion in it."[14] Although it would be unwise to attribute these attitudes wholesale to

Luther, there is a similarity between these comments on the demise of Judaism and Luther's belief that one of the law's most dangerous aspects was its ability to deceive people into thinking that by keeping it in part they had fulfilled God's will in full.

The influence of Luther's evaluation of the law and Judaism was even more pronounced, however, in Protestant New Testament scholarship. Here knowledge of Judaism was often mediated through handbooks that were themselves the product of an interpretive bias reminiscent of Luther's. One of the most widely used of these handbooks was Ferdinand Weber's *Jewish Theology on the Basis of the Talmud and Related Writings*.[15] Weber's book, comprising over four hundred pages of text, was a summary of passages chosen from the extraordinarily complex and massive rabbinic writings. The summaries were arranged systematically under headings, subheadings and subsubheadings, preceded by a brief evaluation and strung together with a running commentary. Weber believed that "legalism," by which he meant the study and fulfilling of the law, was the primary goal of the religion depicted in these writings.[16] They portrayed a stern God whose relationship with humanity was mediated through the law on a strictly economic basis: payment of reward for fulfilling commandments and punishment for failing to do so. God appeared as a bookkeeper whose business is to assess and reckon the number of merits and demerits that belong to each person and to reward each one accordingly with eternal life or eternal punishment.[17] As in the Roman Catholic Church, said Weber, in rabbinic Judaism it was possible for some individuals to have a treasury of excess merits that could be shared with those who did not have enough, but it was frequently considered impossible to know just where one stood with God, and so the typical Jew lived in uncertainty about the eternal future and in fear of death.[18]

Although Weber's book claimed to be a description of relatively late Jewish writings, interpreters of the New Testament frequently used it as a summary of Jewish religious conceptions during the time of Jesus and Paul.[19] It seems to have been at the right hands of William Sanday and Arthur C. Headlam, for example, as they composed their influential commentary on Romans. Sanday and Headlam considered Weber's book so authoritative that they cited his summaries, complete with parenthetical references to the German in order not to lose the correct nuance of Weber's words, as proof of what the rabbis believed.[20] Weber was also used to construct a summary at second hand of rabbinical teaching about the role of merit in salvation, and this summary in turn served as a foil for Paul's position.[21]

Many scholars whose evaluation of the place of the law in Judaism is reminiscent of Luther's also drew on Emil Schürer's *A History of the Jewish People in the Time of Jesus Christ.*[22] In a section titled "Life Under the Law," Schürer described how in the time of Jesus the governing principle of Jewish religion was the belief that God would judge each Israelite strictly on the basis of legal performance. The result, he said, was "an incredible external-izing of the religious and moral life," with the further consequence that "the whole religious and moral life was drawn down into the sphere of law."[23] Schürer considered this a "grievous error" because it burdened each person with countless specific commandments and stifled the individual's ability to make free moral choices.[24] There was virtually no true piety, therefore, in Judaism, as demonstrated by the formalized prayers and the ritualized practice of fasting ("in the most public manner possible"). The emphasis on external fulfillment of the law's commandments choked genuine morality and prevented obedience to the law's real intention.[25]

Symptomatic of the problem that plagued New Testament studies in this era is the way Weber's bleak picture of Judaism was perpetuated from scholar to scholar with apparently little effort to examine the bewildering mass of rabbinic literature for themselves. As a corroborating authority for some of his most severe judgments, Schürer cites Ferdinand Weber's *Jewish Theology.*[26] Similarly, one of the twentieth century's most influential New Testament scholars, Rudolf Bultmann, obtained his understanding of first-century Judaism not only from Schürer but also from Wilhelm Bousset—who, even more than Schürer, was dependent on Weber.[27] Luther's original hermeneu-tical error, by this time no doubt mixed with other traditions such as German Romanticism and existentialism, was being perpetuated from scholar to scholar while little effort was being expended on understanding the Judaism of Paul's time, or of any time, on its own terms.

A paradigm for understanding Paul's antithesis between law and faith or grace had been established: when Paul said that believers were no longer under law but under grace, he meant that they had been rescued from thinking that their duty to God was exhausted if they fulfilled a lengthy checklist of often silly commands. The more detailed this checklist could be made to appear and the more remote and mechanical the God who adjudi-cated it, the more brightly could Paul's understanding of grace and faith be made to shine in contrast.

The pervasiveness and persistence of this understanding of Judaism cannot, however, be attributed to a misreading of Weber or even to the influence of Luther alone. Part of the reason it was so successful was that the theological insight on which it was based was valid, not as an insight into the "grievous error" of Judaism (as Schürer put it) but as an insight into the implications of Paul's comments about boasting in the law. This insight, moreover, met the theological needs of the times in which it was perceived. In the context of the problems faced by the sixteenth-century Roman Catholic Church, it was important to emphasize Paul's convictions about the danger of placing confidence in human ability, as it has been in nearly every epoch since. The problem lay not in the validity of the theological insight, nor in drawing that insight from Paul, but, as a few scholars have pointed out, in regarding Judaism as the great symbol of the problem before attempting to understand it on its own terms.

The Dismantling of a Paradigm

No one protested this injustice more vigorously than the distinguished Jewish reformer and theologian Claude G. Montefiore (1858-1938).[28] In an article that was based on a lecture to England's St. Paul Association in 1900 and that has, unfortunately, remained buried in an old issue of the *Jewish Quarterly Review*, Montefiore took Weber's book to task for both its method and its substance.[29] At the level of method, Montefiore claimed that Weber had made the grave error of trying to present a systematic theology of the rabbinic writings. These writings, he pointed out, are massive and complex, and frequently engage in sober exegesis in one breath and playful jest in another. Outright contradiction is not infrequent, and opinions are frequently expressed which cover a wide range of subject matter. The result is that the scholar can obtain an accurate feel for them only after reading them all, and reading them with a measure of scholarly detachment and sympathy. They simply do not lend themselves to organization in a neat system.[30] "The Rabbinic literature," said Montefiore, "contains almost every conceivable variety of opinion. One has to ask: what is the *usual* opinion, what is the prevailing or predominating note?"[31] Weber had failed to ask these questions. Instead he had imposed a systematic grid on the rabbinic literature, derived from what he felt must be true about it, and then taken passages out of context to fit the grid.[32]

The picture of Judaism that emerged, Montefiore argues, is a caricature. The place of the law in rabbinic Judaism did not typically produce self-righteous Jews who could think of nothing but earning their way to heaven by means of meritorious works and who trembled in fear of death lest on the appointed day their evil works outweigh their good ones. The law was not a burden for Jews, said Montefiore, but a benefit and a delight.[33]

The elevated place of the law in rabbinic religion, moreover, did not lead inevitably to hypocrisy or externalism. Over and over the rabbis emphasized that works are not to be done for external show but that intentions as well as actions are important.[34] When the law went unfulfilled, a gracious and merciful God stood ready to forgive at the slightest movement of the offending party toward repentance, and if good deeds did not outweigh evil ones on the day of judgment, God could and would graciously forgive the sinner and open the gates of paradise.[35] Consequently, a morbid fear of death was relatively rare in Judaism and certainly was not a logical consequence of Jewish belief about the law.[36] The sense of God's grace and mercy among the rabbis was too strong, the doctrine of repentance too important, and the belief that the law was a blessing too deeply implanted for terror and fear to be the result of rabbinic religion.[37]

A second round of protest against the Protestant consensus on the character of Jewish religion came from the American rabbinics scholar George Foot Moore. In a lengthy article in the *Harvard Theological Review,* Moore produced a withering critique not only of Weber's work but of the books by Schürer and Bousset as well.[38] On the basis of a careful comparison between Weber and the polemical Christian works on Judaism of a bygone era, Moore concluded that Weber's "research" consisted largely of culling quotations from the rabbinic sources which he found in old Christian apologetic works on Judaism.[39] Moore demonstrated that in places Weber had even relied on a notorious eighteenth-century anti-Semitic treatise by Johann Andreas Eisenmenger, a work so inflammatory that its publication was delayed for years by the civil authorities for fear that it would generate public disturbances.[40] Moore believed that Weber's work itself originated from apologetic, and even missionary, motives but, unlike its predecessors, concealed these motives beneath the veneer of an apparently objective evaluation of Judaism's basic theological ideas.[41] Thus, said Moore, Weber imposed the grid of Lutheran dogmatics on rabbinic material—material that is ill-suited to any kind of systematic evaluation, but especially to a Lutheran one.[42] As if all this were not bad enough, Moore pointed out several serious blunders in Weber's interpretation of specific passages in the rabbinic literature.[43] He concluded that Weber had little firsthand acquaintance with his subject and that his level of ignorance was matched by the fervor of his desire to demonstrate the inferiority of Judaism to Christianity.

The same malady infected the works by Schürer and Bousset where they dealt with the character of Jewish religion, and especially where they commented on the place of the law in Judaism. Their books, unlike Weber's, retained some usefulness, however, because they had other purposes than to describe the religion of the rabbis. In Schürer's case, most of the work offers helpful historical and geographical information on Palestine in the time of Jesus, and at least the second edition of Bousset's book constitutes a reasonably good analysis of Judaism's older and off-beat literature such as the apocalypses.[44] Nevertheless, both Schürer and Bousset were plagued, in Moore's view, with a lack of firsthand knowledge of normative (that is, rabbinic) Jewish literature and with a lack of scholarly sympathy for the religion they sought to describe.[45]

Unlike Montefiore, Moore was a widely respected authority on ancient Judaism, a professor at a distinguished American university, and was not Jewish. It would have been reasonable, therefore, to expect his essay, published in an influential scholarly journal, to put an end to Protestant reliance on tendentious handbooks and send Christian students of "Jewish backgrounds" scurrying to the original sources. Strangely, this did not happen. With some notable exceptions, the majority opinion among interpreters of Paul for the next half-century continued to be that ancient Judaism was simply sixteenth-century Roman Catholicism in different dress.[46] In an ironic twist, moreover, Moore's own work on Jewish theology during the first Christian centuries was sometimes quoted—despite Moore's clear protest within the work itself against such an interpretation of Judaism—as evidence for a pejorative evaluation of ancient Judaism as a legalistic religion concerned primarily with earning one's way to heaven by means of good works.[47]

Like a massive train laden with freight, all of this has screeched to a halt since the appearance in 1977 of the momentous work by E. P. Sanders, *Paul and Palestinian Judaism: A Comparison of Patterns of Religion*. This book is more about Judaism during Paul's era than it is about Paul, and like the work of Montefiore and Moore, it attempts to describe the Judaism of the period of Christian beginnings in its own terms. Its conclusions about the belief among New Testament scholars that ancient Judaism was a religion of works-righteousness are similar to those of Montefiore and Moore: such an account of Judaism is a travesty that, although it is believed by many to rest on solid evidence, is ultimately based on erroneous descriptions of Judaism that force it into the role of Christianity's foil. Sanders succeeded where Montefiore and Moore had failed primarily because he wrote self-consciously from the perspective of a New Testament scholar and incorporated his account of Judaism within a book that was also about Paul.[48]

Sanders's purpose in *Paul and Palestinian Judaism* was to compare the pattern of religion in Paul's letters with the pattern of religion in Jewish literature between 200 B.C. and A.D. 200. By "pattern of religion" Sanders means the way the followers of a particular religion understand "getting in" and "staying in" their religion.[49] Comparing two religions in this way is better than comparing their "essences," Sanders argues, because reducing an entire religion to an essence like "legalism" or "grace" results in oversimplification of complex matters and is frequently fraught with polemical overtones concerning the superiority of one religion over another.[50] Comparing religious patterns is also better than simply comparing "motifs," because the motifs are usually selected according to what is important to one religion rather than what is important to the other. Such comparisons, moreover, lend themselves to the mistake of taking "motifs" out of context and distorting them. By comparing patterns of religion, on the other hand, Sanders believes that he has discovered a way both to describe the relationship between Paul and Judaism and to learn something about each of them individually by means of the comparison.[51]

Most of Sanders's book turns out to be a description of the pattern of religion in ancient Judaism during the four centuries from 200 B.C. to A.D. 200: only 125 of the book's 556 pages are devoted to Paul.[52] Two crucial conclusions emerge from this enormous undertaking. First, Sanders concludes that Montefiore and Moore were correct in their charges against non-Jewish New Testament scholars. Sanders takes up roughly where Moore left off and documents in detail the unchecked continuation of Ferdinand Weber's and Wilhelm Bousset's inaccurate evaluation of ancient Judaism in some of the most influential works of New Testament scholarship. This section of Sanders's work makes painful reading because he demonstrates all too clearly the unconscionable misrepresentation of Judaism within some of the most influential works of modern New Testament scholarship.[53] Second, Sanders finds that although Judaism is worked out in different ways in the early rabbinic literature, the Dead Sea Scrolls, the Apocrypha and the Pseudepigrapha, the religious expressions described and presupposed by these documents rest on a common pattern of religion.[54]

Sanders calls this pattern "covenantal nomism." Covenantal nomism, he says, is "the view that one's place in God's plan is established on the basis of the covenant and that the covenant requires as the proper response of man his obedience to its commandments, while providing means of atonement for transgression."[55] God's choice to enter into a covenant relationship with Israel is, in all of this literature, a free act of God's grace, and the salvation that membership in that covenant implies is also by God's grace. Getting into the covenant people of God, then, was a matter of God's grace. It is true that maintaining one's place in the covenant involved obedience, but God had provided means of atonement and opportunity for repentance as ways of dealing with the transgression of his people. Thus "election and ultimately salvation are considered to be by God's mercy rather than human achievement."[56] Judaism from Ben Sira (about 200 B.C.) to the Mishna (about A.D. 200), therefore, was, despite all its diversity, a religion of grace that kept works on the "staying in" side of the religious pattern and did not allow them to intrude on questions of "getting in."[57]

Seldom in the history of New Testament scholarship has a single book effected such a dramatic change. When confronted with Sanders's chronicle of the misrepresentation of Judaism in many influential works in their field and when faced with his carefully sifted and analyzed evidence, many New Testament scholars found his conclusions about the gracious character of ancient Judaism difficult to resist. The pleas of Montefiore and Moore, largely unheeded in their time, were answered sympathetically in this new form by many New Testament scholars.

The problem for those who accepted Sanders's proposal now became what to make of Paul. Paul, after all, sums up the cause of Israel's failure as its choice of "works" over "faith" (Rom 9:32) and in terms of its quest to establish its own righteousness rather than to submit to the righteousness of God (Rom 10:3). This is the wrong way to proceed, he continues, "because Christ is the end of the law as a way to righteousness for all who believe" (10:4). What did Paul mean by these statements if the picture of Judaism that we find in Luther and in much of the Protestant tradition is not accurate?

In Search of a New Paradigm

In the decades prior to Sanders, those who opposed the standard Protestant view of Judaism often explained Paul's argument with Judaism by adopting some form of Montefiore's theory. In an essay that he called "The Genesis of the Religion of St. Paul," Montefiore claimed to have found the solution to the puzzle of Paul's polemical statements about the law.[58] Paul's pessimistic view that evil pervaded the world, his belief that the law was created by God to intensify sin, his neglect of the Jewish emphasis on repentance and his anxiety over the salvation of Gentiles could all be attributed to Paul's origins in the Jewish Diaspora. Montefiore contended that unlike Palestine, where the pleasant religion of the rabbis flourished, in the Diaspora of Paul's day Judaism was "poorer, colder, less satisfying and more pessimistic than Rabbinic Judaism."[59] Diaspora Judaism in the first century had come into contact with Greek philosophy, had experienced the heckling of a Greco-Roman majority who thought the legal observances of the Jews were silly, and had become more defensive in its posture. Under these conditions, God had become more remote, questions about the purpose of the law's more peculiar requirements arose, and the feasibility of belief in a God who chose Israel rather than the huge numbers of Gentiles came into doubt.[60] Sin began to loom larger, and talk of repentance receded.[61]

The stage was set for the entrance of Paul, who, under the influence of Greco-Roman mystery religions, experienced in a flash the answer to all the problems posed by the grim religion of Diaspora Judaism and insisted that his insight provided the only solution for everyone else as well.[62] This scenario, Montefiore argued, is responsible for the understanding of Judaism implied in Paul's letters. Paul's polemic against the law, therefore, completely bypasses the Judaism of first-century Palestine and its rabbinic successor of later centuries and instead focuses on the "poorer" religion of Diaspora Judaism.

This thesis, albeit in revised form, has persisted in the decades since Montefiore. Hans Joachim Schoeps, for example, although he criticized Montefiore for uncritically describing rabbinic Judaism as a monolithic religion, for ignoring the influence of apocalyptic notions within rabbinic Judaism and for uncritically assuming that he could describe "the theology of the Pharisaic Diaspora," nevertheless was confident that Montefiore's theory held great promise.[63] Hellenistic Judaism (as Schoeps called it), particularly as it is revealed in the Greek translation of the Scriptures that Paul used, could explain Paul's argument against Jewish legalism and show that his polemic was "directed much less against the rabbinical than against the Hellenistic Judaism of his origins."[64] Samuel Sandmel similarly suggested that representatives of Hellenistic Judaism sometimes saw value in the law only as a guide to other religious ideals and so played down the importance of its literal observance. Paul, as a product of this brand of Judaism, was predisposed to devalue the law.[65]

The attraction of this thesis is obvious. It allows the authoritative documents of Christianity and Judaism both to be right, and it provides this peaceful solution at the expense of a type of Judaism about which no one is any longer concerned. Who cares if Paul accused Hellenistic Judaism of legalism? There are no Hellenistic Jews left. The Judaism of today, derived as it is from rabbinic Judaism, and Paul's critique of the Judaism on which so much Protestant theology is based are allowed to pass like ships in the night, and both are left in peace.

Unfortunately, most scholars of early Christian and middle Jewish history have not found the thesis convincing. The foundation on which it rests—that the Palestinian Judaism and the Diaspora Judaism of the first century were marked by fundamentally different theological convictions—cannot, as it turns out, bear the weight of the evidence. The evidence points instead to a far-reaching influence of Greek language and culture within Palestine *and* to a thorough acquaintance with and interest in Palestinian Judaism among Jews of the Diaspora. The body of relevant material that supports this conclusion is massive and has been the subject of several detailed studies, but perhaps one small piece of evidence will demonstrate the point. In the early twentieth century, archaeological excavations near the Temple Mount in Jerusalem turned up the following Greek inscription from a synagogue built prior to A.D. 70:

> Theodotus, son of Ouettenos, priest and synagogue ruler, son of a synagogue ruler and grandson of a synagogue ruler, built the synagogue, whose foundation the fathers and elders and Simonides laid, for the reading of the law and for the teaching of the commandments, [and built] the guest room, the accommodations, and the facilities for water as an inn for those in need from abroad.[66]

The person who built this synagogue was a devout Jew. He wanted to perpetuate the reading and exposition of the law, was himself a priest and spent considerable funds to build a synagogue under the shadow of the temple itself. Yet the language he chose for the synagogue's dedicatory inscription was not Hebrew but Greek, the language of the Diaspora. Moreover, his inclusion of guest facilities for travelers from abroad demonstrates that it was common for Greek-speaking Jews of the Diaspora to make pilgrimages to Jerusalem. Both realities—that Palestinian Jews felt as comfortable with Greek as with Hebrew and that Greek-speaking Diaspora Jews regularly visited Palestine—are confirmed in numerous other Greek inscriptions, accounts of pilgrimages to Jerusalem and the remarkably faithful financial support given to the Jerusalem temple by Diaspora Jews.[67] There were differences between Jewish belief and practice within Palestine and outside it, but in the view of most scholars, the evidence points to enough common ground to rule out both the simple dichotomy between the two branches of Judaism proposed by Montefiore and the more sophisticated refinements of Montefiore's theory proposed by others.

Sanders: Paul Worked from Solution to Plight
Sanders recognized the fundamental problems with Montefiore's thesis and, taking a hint from George Foot Moore, chose a different explanation for Paul's relationship to Judaism. Although Moore was not a New Testament

scholar and therefore made no attempt to explain Paul in any detail, he made several brief comments in his analysis of ancient Jewish theology which revealed how he thought Paul's critique of Israel and the law could be explained. Paul's idea that works of the law do not justify, he said, resulted from his prior conviction that salvation can come to no one except through faith in Jesus Christ. The reason Paul felt so strongly about this, said Moore, was that he believed expiation to be a necessary requirement for the forgiveness of sin. By focusing on individual rather than national salvation, and by neglecting the Jewish understanding of human repentance and divine forgiveness, Paul missed entirely the significance of the law in Judaism.[68] In other words, a prior conviction about Jesus, itself unrelated to Judaism as we know it from the rabbinic literature, led Paul to say what he did about the Jewish law. Paul's starting point, then, was different from the Jewish starting point, and it inevitably followed from this that his "critique" of Judaism and the law was based on presuppositions that no Jew would accept.

What Moore expressed only in passing, however, Sanders worked out in detail. Sanders's principal treatments of Paul are found in three books, all of which contend that Paul's statements about getting into the group of the saved and staying there (his "soteriology") did not originate with abstract speculation about the plight of humanity. Instead they originated with the insight that Jesus Christ is the universal Savior and then moved in various directions, as the persuasive urgencies of the moment demanded, to show that people needed saving. In other words, when Paul speaks soteriologically in his letters, his argument runs from solution to plight, not from plight to solution. Paul's primary conviction is that Jesus Christ is the Savior of all, and any reference to the human plight is simply the necessary corollary of this central, and dogmatically held, conviction.[69]

The classic statement of Sanders's position is in *Paul and Palestinian Judaism*. Here he marshals detailed evidence that even though Paul sometimes argues from a human plight to the solution in Jesus Christ (as in Romans), these moments in Paul's letters do not mean he arrived at his convictions about Christ by pondering the human dilemma. A close look at the letters shows the direction of Paul's thinking. When Paul speaks of himself prior to his conversion, when he summarizes the content of his preaching and when he offers a synopsis of what Christians believe, the human plight plays no role. Paul was blameless with respect to the law prior to his conversion (Phil 3:6); Paul preached the "word of the cross" or "the word of reconciliation" (1 Cor 1:18; 2 Cor 5:19); and Christians believed "that

34

Jesus died and rose again" (1 Thess 4:14).[70]

The crowning argument in Sanders's case that Paul thought backwards from the solution of faith in Christ to the human plight that this solution demanded, however, is a careful evaluation of Paul's statements about the Jewish law.[71] This investigation turns up neither a pre-Christian dissatisfaction with the law nor a post-Christian accusation that Judaism is legalistic.[72] Instead, it consistently finds Paul's fundamental conviction to be that since salvation comes to both Jew and Gentile by means of participation in Jesus' death, then salvation by any other means, including the way of the law, is necessarily excluded.

This is a dogmatically held conviction, said Sanders, which Paul knew to be true because of his own call to preach the gospel to the Gentiles, and it is the basis again and again of Paul's critique of the law. In Galatians 2 and 3 the burden of Paul's argument does not rest on statements that keeping the law is impossible or that human effort leads to sinful pride but on the conviction that if righteousness came through the law, then Christ died in vain (2:21; compare 3:21).[73] Paul's argument in 2 Corinthians 3:7-18 likewise assumes that the old dispensation was glorious, not a part of some predicament. It has simply been surpassed by a more glorious dispensation.[74] Philippians 3:6-9 contains no critique of the law or of zeal for the law but says that Paul cast these off as worthless when he found Christ. In fact, in Philippians 3:9 Paul admits that pursuing the law leads to *a* righteousness; the problem is that it leads to the wrong kind of righteousness.[75]

Even in Romans, where Paul seems to speak explicitly of failure to keep the law, of boasting and of death through the law, a close analysis of the relevant passages produces the real reasons for Paul's argument against the law: he was convinced that salvation could not come by means of the law because if it did, (1) Gentiles would be excluded and (2) Christ's death would be in vain.[76] Paul's negative statements about works of the law therefore form one way among many others of saying that humanity can be saved only through Christ and, like those other summaries of the human plight, are simply the "reflex" of Paul's conviction that salvation can come through no other means than Jesus Christ.[77]

The "reflex" character of Paul's statements about the law can also be seen in their frequently contradictory character. Romans 2, for example, holds out the possibility of righteousness on the basis of doing the law in the course of an argument that everyone is sinful and therefore needs the salvation that Christ offers.[78] Paul variously claims that God intended that the law should condemn sin, that sin intended that the law should lead people into transgression, and that an inner law prevents people from obeying God's law.[79] These disorganized ruminations on the law demonstrate that Paul did not work toward the solution of salvation in Christ by first thinking about life "under law." His thought instead ran the other way.

Sanders's comments on Paul's view of the law as well as his exhaustively argued case that Paul knew the answer to the human dilemma before he could articulate what the dilemma was are both part of a still larger argument that the pattern of religion we find in Paul and the pattern we find in ancient Judaism are fundamentally different.[80] There are similarities between the two patterns—ironically, salvation by grace but judgment according to works is one of the similarities—and there are substantial parallels between Pauline and Jewish ethics, but in the course of a comparison many incongruities between Paul and Judaism emerge.[81] Paul's view of transgression as setting up incompatible unions, his idea that sin was a power that enslaved, his consequent neglect of repentance, his talk of a new creation, his conviction that salvation comes only to those who participate in Christ's death and resurrection, and his use of the term *righteous* to indicate entry into the religious community rather than, as in Judaism, the conduct of those who are already members all demonstrate that Paul's religion was structurally different from ancient Judaism as we know it.[82] Consistent with this is the affirmation that Paul's fundamental criticism of Judaism is not that it encourages boasting in one's merits before God but rather that it cannot provide salvation, which must come through Christ. "In short," says Sanders in a now-famous statement, "*this is what Paul finds wrong in Judaism: it is not Christianity.*"[83]

Paul can still speak the language of Judaism, especially on ethical issues, but on the fundamental matters of getting in the group of the elect and staying there, Paul and Judaism occupy different orbits. Not only do Paul and rabbinic Judaism pass one another by in effective silence, but the same can be said of Paul and *any* of the ancient expressions of Judaism still available for us to examine.[84]

It will illumine the course of the debate over Paul after Sanders if we pause briefly at this point to compare Sanders's explanation of Paul with Montefiore's. As we have seen, both were faced with the same problem: Paul's critique of Judaism, particularly of the Jewish law, did not seem to correspond to the function of the law in Judaism. The answers that Montefiore and Sanders gave to this dilemma have a point of similarity and a point of difference, both of which prove significant for the debate after Sanders. On the similarity side of the ledger, the explanations Montefiore and Sanders offer for the origin of Paul's theology both allow Paul and modern Judaism to pass by one another in effective silence. For Montefiore, Paul offers valid criticisms of a real form of Judaism, but that form of Judaism has died along with the ancient world, and so for the modern Jew Paul's voice is simply crying in the wilderness. For Sanders, Paul's statements about the law have suffered misinterpretation at the level of Paul's real reasons for making them. Paul did not intend to articulate a profound theological case for the inferiority of existence under the law; he really intended to convince his readers, by whatever means, that since Judaism saw no need for salvation exclusively by Christ, it was wrong. Hence Paul's statements about the law are really loud assertions that salvation comes only through faith in Christ. Like Montefiore, Sanders believes that Paul and modern Judaism, at least at the level of soteriology, speak entirely different languages.

The dissimilarity between Montefiore and Sanders lies in their different explanations of the ultimate origin of Paul's statements about the Jewish law. Montefiore believes that they can be explained as reactions to developments within the Judaism of Paul's time. Sanders, however, believes that they originated in Paul's own experience with Christ and with the outworking of that experience in Paul's mission to the Gentiles. Since some commandments of the law were particularly difficult for Gentiles to adopt, and since the really crucial thing was to believe in Christ, Paul broke with Jewish Christianity's view that Gentiles must observe the law. There was therefore nothing within any form of Judaism current during Paul's time that would cause a dispassionate observer to sympathize with Paul's statements about the law. The reasons for them lie ultimately within Paul's own experience with Christ and within his call to take the gospel to the Gentiles.[85] With remarkable regularity, scholars who have tried to make sense of Paul's view of the law in the light of Sanders's portrait of Judaism have either, like Montefiore, attempted to explain Paul in the light of developments within the Judaism of Paul's day or, like Sanders, focused instead on Paul's own peculiar Christian experience.

Räisänen: Paul Was Inconsistent

Among the assessments of Paul indebted to Sanders, the most widely discussed is that of Heikki Räisänen.[86] Räisänen concurred entirely with Sanders's exposé of the Protestant caricature of Judaism, with the summary of Jewish religion as covenantal nomism and with the conclusion that Paul thought backwards from a predetermined solution to a rhetorical human plight.[87] He goes beyond Sanders, however, in four directions. First, he mounts an unrelenting assault on the consistency of Paul's view of the law. Sanders made a similar case in a second book on Paul, but Räisänen's *Paul and the Law* takes this as its primary theme. He argues that Paul's position fluctuates between diametrically opposed extremes on such crucial issues as who possessed the law, who fulfills the law, whether the law is still valid, how much of the law is still valid, who gave the law and what effect the law had on those to whom it was given. The attempt to make all of this fit into some coherent, much less profound, view of the law is hopeless, for it all adds up to the unavoidable conclusion that Paul was arguing backwards. He knew the conclusion that his personal convictions demanded and then sought arguments in every direction for why his convictions must be true.[88]

Second, unlike Sanders, Räisänen crowned his attack on Paul's consistency with the thesis that Paul not only had failed to sustain a convincing and coherent argument about the origins, effect and observance of the law but had also misrepresented the role of the law in Judaism. The many passages in Galatians and Romans that contrast the law with faith in Christ, he says, give the impression that in Judaism the law served as a "gateway to salvation."[89] In fact, argues Räisänen, in Judaism salvation came by grace, and the law, as Sanders had argued, simply provided a statement of God's will for the conduct of his covenant people. The disorganized appearance of Paul's statements about the law and his miscalculation about the role of the law in Judaism, said Räisänen, once again demonstrate the artificial nature of Paul's argument: his conclusion that Christ was the exclusive Savior of the world was firmly in mind before he was forced to articulate reasons that this should be the case.

Third, Räisänen went beyond Sanders by drawing conclusions about the theological consequences of this understanding of Paul. In *Paul and Palestinian Judaism* Sanders had been willing to say that Paul's backwards thinking occasionally resulted in a penetrating analysis of the human plight, and Sanders had avoided negative general conclusions about Paul's stature as a theologian.[90] Räisänen felt none of Sanders's inhibitions at this point: "It is certainly no common experience that a penetrating analysis of anything (except for a mathematical problem!) should follow, when the analyst has a rigidly fixed point of departure and a predetermined goal."[91] Moreover, Paul's misrepresentation of Judaism, although it was probably not intentional, should give pause to everyone who believes the apostle to be a profound theologian.[92]

Finally, Räisänen explores in much more detail than Sanders the possible historical and psychological reasons for Paul's strangely inconsistent comments about the Jewish law.[93] He proposes that Paul was converted to the open Christianity practiced among the group of Hellenistic Jewish Christians who developed the church at Antioch on the principle that Gentiles as well as Jews could be saved through faith in Christ. This group, Räisänen argues, probably felt no hostility toward the law but gave legal customs such as circumcision and dietary restrictions a spiritual rather than literal meaning. This meant that Gentiles did not have to accept literal circumcision or change their eating habits in order to belong to the community of believers.

Paul supposedly shared this approach to the law and for many years carried on his Gentile mission without observing the law himself or requiring that his Gentile converts observe it. Eventually, however, a group of conservative Jewish Christians attempted to impose literal observance on Paul's converts. To make matters worse, they produced a persuasive series of straightforward arguments from Genesis that circumcision was an eternal sign of God's covenant people. Paul's statements about the law in his letters, then, were the result of his bitter opposition to this group and his desperate attempts to justify his longstanding practice from Scripture. The result was a series of conservative statements about the law, reflecting Paul's Hellenistic Christian past, as well as a series of statements claiming the abolition of the law and reflecting the polemical urgencies of Paul's current situation. As with Sanders, and in contrast to Montefiore, Paul's view of the law was ultimately rooted not in any characteristics of ancient Judaism open to the disinterested observer but in Paul's own strategy for preserving the integrity of his mission to the Gentiles.

Beker: Contextualizing Paul's Theological Method

At the same time that Räisänen's views were first appearing in print, J. Christiaan Beker published an important work on Paul's theology which, although he was fully aware of Sanders's *Paul and Palestinian Judaism*, moved in a different direction from either Sanders or Räisänen.[94] Beker's book is primarily an investigation of Paul's theological method rather than a comparison of Paul with Judaism or a study of Paul's view of the law, but it addresses issues of profound significance for the debate over the relationship between Paul and Judaism and the coherence of Paul's view of the law. To a greater extent than either Sanders or Räisänen, Beker emphasized the importance of understanding Paul's theological statements within the context of the specific historical situations to which his letters were addressed. When these situations are taken into account, said Beker, Paul's theology emerges as the interaction between a central conviction—the approaching cosmic triumph of God—and the specific historical concerns of the communities to which Paul wrote. Paul's theological method is distorted, he claimed, when the central convictions are separated from the contingencies in which they were expressed or when Paul is viewed primarily as a "thinker" rather than as someone whose thinking, as a matter of conviction, always expressed itself in dialogue with the problems of his churches.[95]

Moreover, because Paul expressed his central convictions within often urgent historical situations, his theological statements are not always smooth or perfectly logical. In Galatians 3:10-29, for example, Paul argues for a radical opposition first between faith and the law (3:10-14) and then between the promise to Abraham and the law (3:15-29). The opposition is so radical that the law seems to slip from God's grasp and to take on a role of its own, a role that is antithetical to God's purposes. Paul rescues himself from this dualistic solution to the origin and purpose of the law by bringing the law back within the sphere of God's purposes in a few corrective verses (3:10, 13, 19, 21-25), but his escape is narrow.[96] What drove Paul to such extremes? The origin of Paul's position on the law in Galatians, says Beker, was the historical situation facing Paul's churches in Galatia. Judaizing Christians had arrived on the scene and produced convincing arguments that Gentiles should add circumcision to faith in Christ. In response, Paul's argument about the law overshot the mark. In Paul's letter to the Romans, where the historical situation demanded a nuanced treatment of the law, we find a more positive and complete evaluation of the law's place in salvation history.[97] This interplay between the contingent situation and the coherent center of Paul's gospel, Beker argued, "constitutes Paul's particular contribution to theology."[98]

When Beker attempts to summarize Paul's coherent convictions about the law, he is much more optimistic than either Sanders or Räisänen about Paul's consistency. Beker begins with a warning against forcing Paul's view of the law into a series of logical propositions divorced from the contexts in which he first expressed them.[99] Having said this, however, he is not afraid to argue that the coherent center of Paul's contingent statements about the law lies in his radical view of the nature of sin. Paul rejected the Jewish notion that repentance and sacrifice were completely effective against sin. Instead, Jesus' death on the cross for sin demonstrated that transgressions were only surface expressions of the deeper power of sin.[100] Christ's death for our sins meant that he was cursed by the law, since the law curses anyone hung on a tree (Deut 21:23), and God's vindication of Christ in spite of this curse meant that the law's mission was complete.[101]

None of this implies that the Jews of Paul's day attempted to earn salvation by meritorious works. Romans 7, Beker argues, cannot be interpreted as a picture of the struggle of the Jew to rely on self rather than on God for salvation.[102] Nevertheless, Sanders's belief that Paul argues backwards from salvation in Christ to a necessary plight under the law that no Jew would understand is exaggerated. Paul's argument in Romans 1—5 is that the Jews have transgressed the law, are therefore subject to the power of sin and so are in need of Christ's redeeming death. By constructing his argument in this way, Paul is trying to convince Jews of their need for faith in Christ on their own ground and is not simply arguing abstractly from his prior convictions.[103]

For Beker, therefore, Sanders had neither paid enough attention to the contingent situations that called forth Paul's letters nor given enough weight to the actual method of Paul's argumentation in Romans 1—5. Paul's occasional inconsistency resulted not from a backwards direction of thinking but from the turbulence caused by the confluence of his central convictions with various historical situations in his churches. Paul's argument about the Jewish plight under the law, moreover, would have been intelligible to Jews of his day, since it centered not on the theme of earning salvation by meritorious works but on the thesis that all Jews have transgressed the law. Like Montefiore, and in contrast to Sanders and Räisänen, Beker argued that Paul's view of the law would have been intelligible to Jews of his time.

Dunn: Paul and the Social Function of the Law

Beker's book, however, is primarily about Paul's theological method and barely touches on the Jewish culture from which Paul and his letters emerged.[104] The same need not be said of James D. G. Dunn, whose extensive writing on Paul's view of the law attempts at every turn to relate Paul's statements to attitudes that were prevalent within first-century Judaism.[105] Dunn agrees heartily with Sanders and Räisänen that the old Protestant picture of Judaism as a religion of works-righteousness must be abandoned, and he endorses the description of Judaism as "covenantal nomism."[106] He believes, however, that neither Sanders nor Räisänen has understood correctly the "new perspective" on Paul that Sanders's own picture of Judaism provides. Instead of attempting to understand Paul against the background of Jewish covenantal nomism, he says, Sanders and Räisänen have attributed Paul's view of the law to the apostle's own idiosyncrasies. Paul emerges from their writings as an enigma whose personal experience with Christ propelled him out of first-century Judaism into a different world.[107]

Dunn's own explanation of Paul's attitude toward the Jewish law attempts to avoid both the old Lutheran caricature of Judaism against which Sanders and Räisänen protested and the description of Paul as an eccentric, inconsistent thinker which the Sanders-Räisänen approach has embraced. He does this by bringing into focus what he describes as the "social function" of the law within the Judaism of Paul's time.[108] During the era in which Paul lived, he argues, Jews viewed the law as a unique sign that God had graciously chosen their nation as his special possession and had entered into an eternal covenant with their race alone. The law, therefore, was viewed both as a badge of Israel's special relationship with God and as a boundary marker between them and others.[109] This social function of the law, says Dunn, is fully consistent with the concept of "covenantal nomism," for it highlights the covenant as the sign of God's gracious favor and obedience to the law as the means of maintaining one's place in the covenant. The social function of the law is precisely what Paul rejects when he says that "we have believed in Christ Jesus in order that we might be justified by faith in Christ and not by works of the law" (Gal 2:16).[110]

In statements such as this Paul does not fault the law because it cannot be kept, nor does he claim that the law leads to the attempt to earn salvation by works. Paul does not, in fact, fault the law at all. Instead he takes issue with the *use* of the law as a racial barrier to exclude Gentiles from entrance into the people of God.[111] The phrase *works of the law*, says Dunn, refers primarily to this use of the law within the Judaism of Paul's time. Paul's antithesis, therefore, does not oppose "good works" to faith but instead denies that using the law to limit God's special favor to ethnic Israel is an appropriate expression of faith.[112] Such a limitation is actually a violation of the law itself, since it "puts too much weight on physical and national factors, on outward and visible enactments, and gives too little weight to the Spirit, to faith and love from the heart."[113] Those who use the law in this way are therefore subject to the curse that the law pronounces on all who violate it (Gal 3:10; compare Deut 27:26).[114]

The uniqueness of Dunn's position lies in its ability to explain Paul's view of the law within the matrix of "covenantal nomism" as Sanders describes it. Instead of passing like ships in the night, Paul and first-century Judaism enter into vigorous dialogue with one another, in terms that each participant in the dialogue understands. Neither Sanders nor Räisänen found a way to do this, with the result that Paul emerged from their studies as something of a crank. Beker perceived the problem in their approach, but since his own book was an attempt to tie Paul's thought more closely to the immediate context of his letters, he did not attempt to describe the place of Paul within the broader context of first-century thought and so left the problem unsolved. The strength of Dunn's work is that not only is it based on a close exegesis of the letters in which Paul's view of the law is articulated, but at every step it seeks to relate what Paul says to the broader context of Jewish "covenantal nomism" as Sanders, and many others working in the field, describes it.[115]

Westerholm: Back to Luther

The question that persists after one reads Dunn is whether his thesis can withstand the glare of exegetical scrutiny. Will Paul's negative statements about the law, particularly those referring to "works of the law," consistently fit the framework that Dunn's "social function" theory builds for them? Can it be true that when Paul opposes "works of the law" and "faith" he is saying nothing about the role of human activity or good works in salvation, as Luther thought, and is instead simply saying that salvation is no longer limited to those who possess the law? Stephen Westerholm, in an elegant monograph on Paul's view of the law, contends that a straightforward look at what Paul says will reveal that Dunn's proposal cannot be correct and that Luther, in spite of his unreliable view of Judaism, is a master when it comes to reading Paul.

Westerholm argues that in Paul's letters the term *law* refers most frequently to the Mosaic legislation given to Israel at Mount Sinai. Paul recognized, moreover, that this legislation was given to Israel in order that they might "do" it or "keep" it (Rom 2:13, 25, 27; Gal 5:3; 6:13; and so on).[116] Because the primary demand of the law was that it be "done," Paul contended that the law was based on "doing" rather than on "faith" (Gal 3:11-12; compare Rom 4:14, 16). The phrase *works of the law*, then, is most naturally understood as "the doing of the law," not as Israel's misuse of the law to limit the people of God to their own national boundaries.[117]

Paul's argument in Romans 2:17—3:20, according to Westerholm, confirms this. The point of that passage, he says, is that the law requires works, Israel has transgressed the law instead of supplying the required works, and because of this "by works of the law shall no flesh be justified" (Rom 3:20).[118] This understanding of the phrase is confirmed a few verses later when Paul contrasts Abraham's faith not with a nationalistic misuse of the law, nor even with the Jewish law in general, but with the far broader category of human activity (Rom 4:1-5). This passage, says Westerholm, is "positively fatal to Dunn's proposal," for in it the real problem with the law is clearly identified:

the law is based on the principle of human activity, and human activity cannot save.[119] Luther, then, was right when he understood Paul's antithesis of works of the law to faith as an antithesis between human activity and God's grace.[120]

If this is true, however, where does that leave Judaism? Are we not forced back into saying that Paul believed Judaism to be a graceless religion of works-righteousness and then having to choose between Paul's witness to Judaism and Judaism's witness to itself? Westerholm is far from unaware of the problem. Nearly half of his book is devoted to describing the twentieth-century debate over Paul's view of the law. The proposals of Montefiore and Schoeps, he says, are not convincing, nor is Räisänen's theory that Paul misrepresented the place of works in Jewish soteriology. As noted above, he does not view Dunn's position as satisfactory, nor is he convinced that Paul's statements about the law are unreflective attempts to justify Paul's own soteriology to the exclusion of all others.[121]

Instead, Westerholm says, the proper solution rests in recognizing that if the Old Testament is taken to be representative of Judaism, and Paul took it that way, then works do play some role in Jewish "soteriology." Who can deny that the Old Testament promises life to those who do the commandments of the law (Lev 18:5; Deut 4:1; 5:33; and so forth)? This is not to say that Judaism is a religion devoid of grace—it did, as Sanders and others argue, articulate a balanced view of the relationship between works and grace. It is to acknowledge, however, that works play some role in salvation according to the Old Testament, and therefore according to Judaism.

If we recognize this, then the difference between Paul and Judaism comes into bold relief: Paul, as Luther correctly saw, insisted that human activity played no role in salvation, for human activity had only resulted in transgression and wrath; Judaism, on the other hand, did not conclude from Israel's failure that obedience to the law was an impossible task and balance the attempt to obey with belief in a merciful God who would continue to forgive transgression.[122] This is one of Westerholm's most important points, because it argues against what was so often assumed after Sanders—that in Judaism works played no role in salvation and that, as Sanders put it, "on the point at which many have found the decisive contrast between Paul and Judaism—grace and works—Paul is in agreement with Palestinian Judaism."[123]

Westerholm agreed with Sanders, however, that Paul came to his conclusions about the Jewish law on the basis of his experience with the risen Christ and not because prior to that experience he labored under a religious system that he thought to be inadequate. Therefore, the reasons for the inadequacies of the law that Paul gives are, as Sanders insists, Christian reasons and quite understandably draw only puzzled looks from the Jew who simply does not believe that law and grace, law and faith, or law and God's promise are incompatible.[124] Nevertheless, they are not theologically inconsequential to the Christian theologian for that reason. Rather, as Luther perceived, they represent a profound achievement worthy of study and admiration. So unlike Sanders, who concentrated on showing that Paul's statements about the law are secondary rationalizations of a more basic, and dogmatically held, conviction, Westerholm acknowledges this insight and then dwells on what Sanders would call Paul's "secondary argumentation." Despite their secondary nature, says Westerholm, such arguments constitute a monumental theological insight.[125]

A Summary of Paul and the Law Since Aquinas

Stephen Westerholm brings the interpretation of Paul's view of the law back to Luther and Luther's unwillingness, in reaction to Scholasticism, to let human activity encroach even an inch on the Pauline view of grace. The journey has been a long one and has passed through the dark valley of Judaism's vilification at the hands of leading New Testament scholars, but it has much to teach the Christian student of Paul's writings who looks to them not merely because of their important place in history but also in order to learn what to believe and how to live.

The clearest lesson the journey teaches is that an awareness of our own theological context will help to rescue us from the assumption that Paul, who wrote within a different context, must mean whatever our own traditions teach that he means. Aquinas should have been more keenly aware that the link between his own time and Paul was not Aristotle. Luther and Calvin should have been more sensitive to the differences between ancient Judaism and the Scholasticism of their era. Ferdinand Weber, as George Foot Moore pointed out, should have understood that Paul was not a nineteenth-century German pietist. If more of these influential figures in the history of interpretation had tried to allow Paul to speak to his own context before announcing how he spoke to their own, Christians might have worked harder to resist the anti-Semitism that so tragically scars the hermeneutical history of Paul's statements about the law and might have been more profoundly obedient to the Word of God.

No one, however, should be able to get away with the claim that after the destruction of the old Lutheran-Weberian consensus on Judaism, scholarship on Paul's view of the law has reached some enlightened, bias-free plane. It is probably not accidental that Claude G. Montefiore's thesis about Paul's view of the law was developed within the context of late-nineteenth-century liberalism, for the Hellenistic Judaism to which Paul was supposedly reacting becomes, in Montefiore's hands, almost a distillation of all that Montefiore believed was wrong with the practice of both Judaism and Christianity in his own day.

The books of Sanders and Räisänen, similarly, have been produced within a context in which theological truth is increasingly viewed as elusive and many from Christian traditions are trying to come to terms with the shameful treatment of Jews by "Christians" throughout the history of the church. Painting Paul as a relatively eccentric Jew whose polemical punches at "the works of the law" fail to land fits comfortably into this intellectual and theological landscape.[126] Dunn's reading of Paul's statements about the law were produced, similarly, in a climate in which the intellectual world has become increasingly concerned with the problems of racism, nationalism and the plight of the oppressed, and Dunn is quick to demonstrate how his understanding of Paul helps to address these issues.[127]

The point, of course, is not that allowing our traditions to influence our understanding of Paul leads necessarily to error, nor that all readings of Paul are culturally conditioned and no true reading of Paul is therefore possible. It is instead the rather simple point that being aware of our traditions while we interpret Paul will help us to avoid reading them into Paul where they do not exist. In order to discern Paul's meaning, we must be aware not only of his context but of our own as well.

A second lesson that Paul's past interpreters teach is the importance of treating the traditions of others honestly. The story of the misinterpretation of Judaism by New Testament scholars should cause every Christian interpreter of Paul to wince and should stand as a warning of the immense harm that comes when we wrench the traditions of others out of shape in order to pillory them. This warning should stand out in especially bold relief for Christians who, because of their interest in Paul, must know something about Judaism, for the history of the Christian misinterpretation of Judaism is too grim not to make an accurate understanding of Judaism on its own terms a top priority.

On the other hand, as Westerholm reminds us, the pendulum has now swung so far the other way that scholars stand in danger of pillorying Luther and the Protestant tradition in retaliation for what they did to Judaism.[128] Luther's bad handling of Paul's relationship to Judaism does not necessarily mean that the great Reformer misinterpreted Paul.

The modern student of Paul's theology therefore sits at a particularly complicated—and heavily traveled—intersection of viewpoints. Given the number of signboards, each flashing its own message or warning, it seems all too easy to make a wrong turn. Understanding the theological context in which we are traveling, however, will help enormously, as will understanding the context in which Paul made his theological journey.

CHAPTER TWO

OPPRESSION, ELECTION & SALVATION: The Law of Moses & the Hope of Israel in the Time of Paul

Prior to his conversion, Paul was devoted to the accurate interpretation and blameless observance of the Mosaic law. "I am a Jew," he tells a crowd assembled at the temple, "born in Tarsus of Cilicia but reared in this city and accurately taught the ancestral law at the feet of Gamaliel" (Acts 22:3). The picture is confirmed in Paul's letters where he reveals that his parents were devout Jews and that prior to his conversion he observed the law blamelessly (Phil 3:5-6). Paul's statements about the law in his letters therefore do not come from an outsider but from one who understood the convictions about the law which Jews of his period commonly held. Without clear evidence to the contrary, it seems reasonable to assume that Paul's statements about the law in his letters should be interpreted against these common convictions.

What were they? Both the primary and the secondary literature on the subject is vast, but for understanding Paul's statements about the law, three convictions are particularly important. First, the Jews of Paul's time believed that the foreign domination under which they lived was a result of their disobedience to the Mosaic law. Second, they believed that their observance of the Mosaic law signified their status as God's chosen people. Third, many Jews trusted God to intervene on their behalf to rescue them from their disobedience to the law and the oppression of foreign domination.

The Curse of the Law and the Story of Israel

Among the most prominent themes of the Old Testament is that Israel's suffering at various points in its history is a result of its disobedience to the terms of the Mosaic covenant. The theme pulses through Deuteronomy and the historical books, emerges clearly at the conclusion of Leviticus and appears frequently in the Prophets. In both Deuteronomy and Leviticus, Moses describes the blessings that will come to Israel if they obey the law and the curses that will come to them for disobedience. The curses, however, quickly outpace the blessings in number and specificity until the reader realizes that Moses is prophesying the future course of Israel's history. Defeat at the hands of foreign powers and the scattering of God's people among the nations of the earth become, in this prophecy, God's punishment for disobedience to the Mosaic law (Deut 28:1—31:29; Lev 26:3-39). In 2 Kings the prophetess Huldah declares to the emissaries of Josiah that the Lord will destroy Jerusalem and its inhabitants because of their idolatry (22:14-17). Jeremiah prophesies similarly that many other nations will pass by Jerusalem after it has been destroyed and ask why God has dealt it such a severe blow. The answer, he says, will be, "Because they abandoned the covenant of the LORD their God, and worshiped other gods and served them" (Jer 22:9; compare Deut 29:24-27). These are only brief examples of a theme that functions as a leitmotif of the entire Bible.[1]

But was it a widely understood way of viewing Israel's situation during Paul's time? A wealth of evidence shows that it was indeed an important means by which both educated scribe and common synagogue worshiper made sense of Israel's suffering.[2] The prominence of the theme in four confessional prayers that were probably used in synagogues throughout the second temple period (Ezra 9:6-15; Neh 9:5-37; Dan 9:4-19; Baruch 1:15-3:8) shows that the common worshiper during this period was aware of it.[3] The prayer in Nehemiah 9:5-37 recounts in an almost rhythmic pattern Israel's ungrateful refusal to obey God's law, God's punishment of Israel for disobedience, and God's faithfulness to his people even though they had received the covenant's curses (vv. 16-31). The prayer concludes by pleading with God to look kindly on the sufferings of his people, since even under the relatively benevolent hand of the Persians, the Israelites remain "slaves" in the land of their forefathers (vv. 32-37).

Daniel 9:4-19, Ezra 9:6-15 and Baruch 1:15-3:8 follow an almost identical pattern. Each prayer laments Israel's cycle of disobedience to God in spite of God's graciousness, mourns the curses of the covenant that have come upon Israel as a result of its sin and expresses the hope that God will be merciful to his people again.[4] The prayer in Baruch, for example, confesses that from the days of the exodus the people of Israel have neglected God's voice. Because of this "there have clung to us the disasters and the curse which the Lord commanded through his servant Moses" (1:20).[5] These three prayers and the prayer in Nehemiah follow Deuteronomy's explanation of the oppression that Israel experiences at the hands of foreign powers: it is the result of Israel's disobedience to the Mosaic law.[6]

This theme is also prominent in the tale of Judith, probably written during the reign of John Hyrcanus, Hasmonean high priest of the now independent state of Israel (134-105 B.C.).[7] Judith's motivation for single-handedly defending Jerusalem and the temple against the wicked king Nebuchadnezzar and his general Holofernes is her conviction that Israel cannot escape God's judgment if, in violation of the covenant, it compromises with Gentile oppressors. When the magistrates of the besieged city contemplate surrendering to Holofernes in response to a plea from the starving populace, Judith is incensed:

> There has not arisen either in our generation or at this time a tribe or family or people or town from among us which worships hand-made gods, as happened in former times. It was because of this that our fathers were given over to the sword and plunder and fell before our enemies in a great disaster. (Judith 8:18-19)

Judith understands that any measure of success that Israel has enjoyed over the previous few years has resulted from its renewed commitment to learn the lesson of the past and to keep God's covenant (compare 5:17-21), and she is so determined not to turn back to the days of disobedience that she daringly infiltrates the enemy camp and, through a ruse, slays the evil Holofernes.

Unlike the book of Judith, which appears to be appreciative of Hasmonean rule over Israel, 2 Maccabees was written some time after the death of John Hyrcanus and represents a voice of protest against the Hasmoneans.[8] Nevertheless, the thesis that God punishes his people when they sin against him is as strong in this book as it was in Judith. The author believes that the sack of Jerusalem in 169 B.C. by Antiochus IV Epiphanes of Syria was a direct result of the high priest's encouragement of Greek customs within Jerusalem several years earlier (4:16). "It is no light matter," he explains, "to deal impiously with the divine laws" (4:17; compare 6:12-17; 7:18, 32; 10:4). The great hero of the story, Judas Maccabeus, punctiliously observes the law, and he goes from victory to victory over the impious generals and kings of the Syrians despite the small numbers who fight with him (8:27; 12:31, 38; compare 12:39-45; 13:7). The "thrice-accursed" general Nicanor, walking dejected and alone back to Antioch after Judas has scattered his army, exemplifies what will happen to all who repeat his mistake. Nicanor's blunder, the author reminds us, is that he refused to recognize that "the Jews had a Champion, and that therefore the Jews were invincible, because they followed the laws laid down by him" (8:36).[9]

So the literature of the establishment (Judith) and the literature of protest (2 Maccabees) agree that the curse of the law falls on those who disobey its stipulations. This agreement shows that at least in the second century the idea was common currency among Jews who may have differed widely from one another in other ways.

Josephus's Interpretation of Jewish History

The most valuable evidence for the prominence of the theme during the time of Paul comes from the Jewish historian Josephus. The authors of Judith and 2 Maccabees lived a century before Paul, but Josephus was a young man during the time that Paul wrote most of his letters. His two great works, *The Jewish War* and *The Antiquities of the Jews*,[10] provide a wealth of information about the theology and practice of Judaism during Paul's time, and the idea that Israel's suffering is a result of its violation of the Mosaic law emerges as a prominent theme in both.[11]

In *The Jewish War* Josephus adopts the theme as a way of making theological sense of the tragic defeat of his people in their great war against Rome: Jerusalem has been destroyed, the temple has been burned, and worst of all for Josephus, who was himself a priest, the sacrifices prescribed in the law have ceased. Thus at the outbreak of hostilities, Herod Agrippa tries to dissuade the Jews from pursuing their cause by pointing out that it will necessitate the violation of the law, and once that happens God will no longer stand with them:

> Consider . . . the difficulty of preserving your religious rules from contamination, even were you engaging a less formidable foe; and how, if compelled to transgress the very principles on which you chiefly build

your hopes of God's assistance, you will alienate Him from you. If you observe your sabbath customs and refuse to take any action on that day, you will undoubtedly be easily defeated, as were your forefathers by Pompey, who pressed the siege most vigorously on the days when the besieged remained inactive; if, on the contrary, you transgress the law of your ancestors *[ton patrion nomon]* I fail to see what further object you will have for hostilities, since your one aim is to preserve inviolate all the institutions of your fathers. (2.391-93)

Tragically, the Jews did not heed Agrippa's advice. Josephus frequently observes in his narrative of the ensuing war that the Jews, caught up in the fury of their cause, not only fought against the Romans on the sabbath (2.518; compare 4.97-105, 151-54, 157) but also repeatedly violated the traditions of their ancestors by persecuting their own people and profaning the temple.[12] Because of these impieties, God led the insurrectionists to commit atrocities that were not even in their immediate best interest. Thus they slaughtered the more reasonable members of their group and made strategic blunders that led inexorably to destruction (4.297, 323, 573; 5.343, 559, 572). Josephus tells his readers that just as God had used Nebuchadnezzar to punish his people for their sins, so during the Jewish war he used Vespasian and Titus as instruments of his wrath (4.370; 5.368; 6.215, 411; compare *Ant.* 10.139), a fact splendidly confirmed for Josephus by his belief that the date on which the Romans burned the temple corresponded exactly to the date on which Jerusalem had fallen to the Babylonians six centuries earlier (6.250, 268). He believed that the pattern of sin against God's law which had culminated in the burning of the first temple had been repeated in his own time.

The theme appears most clearly in a speech that Josephus claims to have shouted to Jewish insurgents gathered on top of the city wall during the siege of Jerusalem. He had long since defected to the Romans, and Titus, who was in charge of the siege, had asked him to try to persuade those inside the city to surrender. In an effort to comply with the general's request, Josephus walked around the wall pleading with his countrymen to recognize the foolishness of their resistance to Roman might and the wisdom of suing for peace (5.362-419).

Josephus's first attempt to make this point failed immediately. No people had successfully resisted the Romans, he argued, "for what was there that had escaped the Romans, save maybe some spot useless through heat or cold?" (5.366). The Romans were simply stronger than the Jews, such a situation must be God's will, and the insurgents should follow the example of their ancestors who had recognized Rome's strength and yielded to them long ago (5.367-69). His rebellious audience did not find this logic compelling, and they answered it with a shower of insults and stones (5.375).

Forced to change the basis of his argument, Josephus urged those gathered at the top of the wall to consider the history of their people. Never, Josephus contends, had the Jews successfully resisted an enemy by taking matters into their own hands and trusting in their military prowess to lead them to success. When they had succeeded in overcoming an enemy, they had trusted God rather than the weapons of war. At those times, God had fought for them and the enemy had been defeated. Sadly, this was not Israel's present situation. Their present plight resembled the Babylonian siege of Jerusalem. Comparing himself to Jeremiah, Josephus contended that just as the nation had refused to heed the warnings of the prophet to submit to their Babylonian conquerors and suffered the destruction of their temple as a result, so now the Jewish insurgents would lose both city and temple unless they listened to Josephus and came to terms with their Roman captors (5.391-94).

Here the biblical theme of divine retribution for covenant breaking entered Josephus's argument. The transgressions of the people had made Roman domination inevitable, he said, just as the transgressions of Israel in former days brought the wrath of the Babylonians. Chastisement for transgression must therefore come; the only question was whether it would come peacefully or with slaughter and destruction (5.392). The impiety of Jerusalem's inhabitants during the days of Hyrcanus and Aristobulus had delivered the city into Roman hands in the first place, and resistance to Roman rule thirty years later was unsuccessful because God intended to punish the Jews for their sins (5.398; compare *Ant.* 14.176). The present insurgents, however, had violated the law of Moses more completely than any of these ancestors and should, therefore, confess their sins, repent, throw down their weapons and surrender. Only in this way could they preserve their city, their temple and their families (5.401-19). The speech, of course, did not succeed, and Jerusalem was destroyed, but Josephus's audience apparently heard him out, unwilling to dismiss his point out of hand, because they shared with him an understanding of this theme.

The indelible impression that the stubbornness of the insurrectionists and the fall of Jerusalem left on Josephus is probably one reason that in his later work *Antiquities of the Jews,* he elevated the deuteronomic principle to a description of the way God deals with all people.[13] Josephus knew from his own experience that God brings destruction to those who violate his commands, and in the *Antiquities* he uses the Jewish people as an example of this principle in relentless operation. He clearly states his purpose in his preface:

> The main lesson to be learnt from this history by any who care to peruse it is that men who conform to the will of God, and do not venture to transgress laws that have been excellently laid down, prosper in all things beyond belief, and for their reward are offered by God felicity; whereas, in proportion as they depart from the strict observance of these laws, things [else] practicable become impracticable, and whatever imaginary good thing they strive to do ends in irretrievable disasters. (1.14)

Although the work runs to twenty volumes in length, Josephus never loses sight of this purpose. From the account of the flood in Genesis (1.72) to the burning of the temple in the war with Rome (20.166), he points out at every opportunity that God blesses those, whether individuals or nations, who keep his laws and punishes all who stray from them. As we might expect, the theme is especially prominent in Josephus's paraphrase of Deuteronomy and the historical books of the Bible, but he often makes it more explicit than it appears in Scripture and on occasion plants it in his sources when he finds it missing from them. One example, which could easily be multiplied, will illustrate the point.

Josephus begins his account of the Israelite apostasy to the Moabite gods in Numbers 25 with a nonbiblical speech of the prophet Balaam to the Moabite king Balak. In this speech Balaam informs Balak that he will be unable to inflict any lasting punishment on the Israelites because God is protecting them against any calamity that might destroy them completely. Nevertheless, he says, Balak can inflict temporary damage on Israel by enticing the Israelites to abandon the law. The best way to do this is to tempt Israelite men to marry Moabite women (4.126-30).[14] This advice, although it has some basis in Numbers 31:16, is an invention of Josephus, calculated to introduce the story that follows of how Moabite women persuaded the young Israelite men to "transgress the traditions" by convincing them to eat impure food and to worship idols (4.139).

The story itself is an elaborate reshaping of the account in Numbers 25 to bring out the principle that those who violate God's law can only expect destruction. In Numbers 25:6-8, for example, only Phineas takes up the spear against those who had married the Midianites, and his reasons for doing so are merely said to be his zeal on God's behalf (v. 11). In Josephus, however, a group of young men join Phineas and ensure that the wrath of God falls upon many of the transgressors of the law *(paranomēsantōn)*. The rest are destroyed by a plague, presumably the same one that, according to Numbers

25, Phineas's solitary action brought to an end (v. 8; *Ant.* 4.154-55).

Josephus, then, made sense of the often tragic history of his people with the understanding of the covenant articulated in Deuteronomy. The periods of prosperity under Moses, David and a few others were marked by obedience to the stipulations of the covenant, and the much more numerous periods of plague, siege, defeat and exile came because of transgression of "the traditions of the fathers." The disastrous events of A.D. 66-73 provided only the most recent illustration of this unremitting principle of God's dealings with his people.

In summary, the biblical notion that God would bring the blessings of the covenant on those who obeyed the law and the covenant's curses on those who transgressed it provided an important framework to Jews in Paul's time for understanding the historical suffering of God's people. Violation of the law of Moses, the covenant that God had made with his people at Sinai, had brought Assyria, Babylon and Rome into God's land and had scattered the land's inhabitants among the nations. This conviction was not the private notion of the literate and sophisticated but was shared by many common people who attended worship in synagogue and temple. It seems safe to say that at the time when Paul wrote his letters, most Jews, whether common laborer or sophisticated priest, understood the scattering of their people throughout the world and the Roman domination of their land to be a result of Israel's violation of the covenant that God had made with them at Sinai.

The Law as the Sign of Israel's Election
Jewish existence during the period in which Paul wrote his letters would have been bleak indeed if the belief that it had suffered the curses of the covenant had stood alone. The harshness of this notion was alleviated, however, by the firm conviction that the Mosaic covenant itself continued to testify to Israel's status as the chosen people of God. According to the Old Testament, God gave the law to set Israel apart from the surrounding nations as God's special possession. Thus Exodus 19:5-6 proclaims that although the whole world is God's, Israel is his "treasured possession" and that the covenant God is about to make with them will be the sign of their special status. It will mark them off as "a priestly kingdom and a holy nation," distinct from the other peoples of the world (19:6; compare 22:31).

Leviticus and Deuteronomy return again and again to this purpose as they lay out the various stipulations of God's covenant with Israel. The distinction between clean and unclean foods in Leviticus 11 stands parallel to the distinction between Israel and the surrounding nations, and God's insistence that Israel abstain from eating unclean animals is, accordingly, a sign that they are "holy" or set apart from all other nations as his elect people (Lev 11:44-45; 20:25-26).[15] Similarly, Deuteronomy 7 forbids the Israelites from marrying into the families of the people whom they will conquer once they cross the Jordan, for if they do, these people will lead them into idolatry and cause them to lose their distinctiveness as God's "treasured possession" and "people holy to the LORD" (v. 6; compare 28:9).

According to Ezekiel, the destruction of Jerusalem and the deportation of Israelites into exile under the Babylonians in the late sixth century was a direct result of Israel's transgression of these laws and implicit renunciation of its position as God's holy, elect people.[16] Judgment will come to Israel, says the prophet, because instead of obeying the law contained in God's covenant with them, the Israelites chose to obey the laws of the surrounding nations (5:6; compare 11:12). When Ezekiel spells out the specific laws that Israel has disobeyed he uses the "Holiness Code," a section of Leviticus (17—26) whose theme is that the holiness of God's people should reflect the holiness of God himself.[17] Echoing the language of this section, Ezekiel 18:5-18 implies that Israel has engaged in idolatry (compare Lev 19:4), adultery (compare Lev 20:10), unlawful marital intercourse (compare Lev 18:19), robbery (compare Lev 19:13) and usury (compare Lev 25:35-37). Similarly, in 22:6-12 Ezekiel claims that judgment for Jerusalem is imminent because its inhabitants have dishonored their parents (compare Lev 19:3), the alien (compare Lev 19:34; 24:22), the orphan and the widow. They have also profaned the sabbaths and committed slander, murder (compare Lev 19:16), idolatry (compare Lev 19:4) and a number of sexual improprieties (compare Lev 18:8-9, 19-20; 20:10-12, 17).[18]

It is natural, then, for Ezekiel to prophesy that the first step in God's future rescue of his people from the plight of their exile will be a purification of their impurity and a reestablishment of their holiness. The priests had defiled the holy things of God, had refused to distinguish between what is holy and common, had failed to teach the people the difference between pure and impure, and had not observed the sabbaths described in the law (22:26). In the future restoration of Israel, however, God would make his people ritually pure and provide them with a new heart and a new Spirit so that they would follow his statutes and carefully perform his ordinances (36:25-27).

When the exiles began to return to Jerusalem in the late sixth and early fifth centuries, their leadership seems to have taken Ezekiel's perspective on the nation's experience under the Babylonians. Israel's leaders took steps, therefore, to ensure that all who returned to the land from exile and married foreign wives divorced them and spurned the children born to such marriages (Neh 13:23-29; Ezra 9:1—10:44; compare Neh 10:30). They also banned foreigners from the temple (Neh 13:4-9), enforced the laws of tithe (Neh 10:37-39; 13:10-14) and mandated sabbath observance (Neh 10:31; 13:15-22). Ezekiel would have been pleased with Nehemiah's admonition to the returned exiles who were conducting daily commercial business with non-Israelites from Tyre on the sabbath:

> What is this evil thing that you are doing, profaning the sabbath day? Did not your ancestors act in this way, and did not our God bring all this disaster on us and on this city? Yet you bring more wrath on Israel by profaning the sabbath. (Neh 13:17-18)

If the origins of Israel's destruction at the hands of the Babylonians lay in their disregard of the laws that set them apart from other nations, then the first step in rebuilding the nation was the enforcement of precisely those laws.

In the book of Tobit, written about a century and a half after Nehemiah's time but set during the Assyrian exile, the emphasis on the laws that set Israel apart as God's holy and treasured possession is as strong as ever. In the first two chapters Tobit describes the meticulous piety of his life prior to and after the Assyrian defeat of Israel. In contrast to other Jews whose commitment to the Jewish way of life diminished before the Assyrian exile, Tobit claims that he was conscientious about avoiding pagan worship. He dutifully traveled from his home to Jerusalem for the Jewish festivals, paid firstfruits and tithes on all crops and income as prescribed by the law, and married within his family (1:5-9).

This commitment to the law continued after he was forced to move to Nineveh, the capital of Assyria. There, in contrast to many of his compatriots, he refused to eat food that was forbidden to Jews in Moses' law (1:10-11). He also provided charity to the destitute and burial for Jews who had died but whose bodies had been treated carelessly (1:16-17). In addition, he observed the prescribed rules for cleansing from corpse impurity (2:9), refused to receive stolen property (2:13) and admonished his son to marry an Israelite woman (4:12). If this tale reflects the common elements of Jewish piety around the beginning of the second century, then the emphasis of Ezra and Nehemiah on observance of the law as a boundary between Israel and the other nations was still firmly in place.

The Jews Under the Seleucids

Only a few years after Tobit was composed, the Jews of Palestine faced their most serious crisis since the destruction of the temple in the sixth century. In 200 B.C. the great military strategist and ruler of the Seleucid empire Antiochus III ("the Great") defeated Ptolemy V ("Epiphanes") of Egypt in the fateful battle of Panion, and over eighty years of nearly uninterrupted Egyptian rule of Palestine ended. The Seleucids now had control of the crucial buffer zone between Antioch and Alexandria and, eager to live on peaceful terms with the subdued inhabitants, granted them a wealth of gifts and concessions.

Under pressure from Rome, the Seleucid empire began to break apart over the next three decades, and as a result of this instability its relationship with the Jews of Judea began to change. In the eyes of Antiochus IV Epiphanes, ruler of the Seleucid empire from 175-163 B.C., Judea needed to be closely controlled not only because of the wealth it could supply for tribute to the Romans but also because it separated the Seleucid empire from its age-old enemy, Egypt.[19]

Wealthy Jews eager to compromise with Greek customs as an avenue to power were willing to aid Antiochus in his efforts as their ancestors had been willing to compromise Jewish ways years earlier under Ptolemaic rule.[20] One such self-promoter, Jason, offered to buy the right to the high priesthood from Antiochus and insisted as part of the arrangement that he be allowed to establish Greek institutions in Jerusalem, thereby securing for himself and for those within his circle the privileges that Antiochus IV reserved for Greeks. Antiochus agreed, only to find a little while later that a certain Menelaus was willing to offer more money than Jason for the same privileges. After his installation as high priest, however, Menelaus was unable to produce the necessary payment. Antiochus, on his way back from a military foray into Egypt, lost patience and confiscated the temple treasury. Pious Jews were horrified at this sacrilege. But the worst was yet to come.

After a second attempt to invade Egypt had been cut short by a humiliating encounter with Rome, Antiochus set out for Antioch, only to discover on his way back that Jerusalem was in turmoil. Jason had mustered an army and attempted to wrest the high priesthood from Menelaus by force. Antiochus responded to what he viewed as an insurrection by sacking Jerusalem and slaughtering a number of its citizens. Once the king returned to Antioch, he followed these measures with the imposition of an oppressive tax burden on Judea and by establishing a contingent of Seleucid soldiers and Hellenistic Jews in the old City of David, which was then fortified to protect its inhabitants from harassment.[21] Perhaps because so much of his trouble with Judea to this point had revolved around the high priest and the temple, Antiochus took a still more drastic step a few weeks later: the Jewish religion would be dismantled and replaced with a polytheistic cult whose chief deity would be Zeus Olympius, a figure with whom Antiochus identified himself.[22]

The procedure Antiochus followed to accomplish this task is instructive. The most detailed ancient account of Antiochus's policies claims that the Seleucid king not only forbade worship of Israel's God in the Jerusalem temple (2 Macc 6:1-5) but also made illegal the observance of the sabbath and Jewish festivals (2 Macc 6:6, 11), forbade circumcision (2 Macc 6:10) and embarked on a cruel campaign to force Jews to violate the Jewish law's dietary stipulations (2 Macc 6:18-7:41).[23] It seems natural to conclude that Antiochus believed that these elements of Jewish observance were the most obvious religious boundary markers of the Jewish people. If the Jews of Palestine were to become as submissively Hellenistic as his other subjects, he must have thought, Jewish worship in the Jerusalem temple had to be transformed into pagan worship, and the distinctive Jewish practices of observing a special religious calendar, circumcising male children and abiding by the dietary stipulations of the law had to be abolished.

On the Jewish side, literature composed or popularly read during and shortly after this difficult period of persecution emphasizes one or more of these elements of Jewish religion as points on which pious Jews were unwilling to compromise. The date of *Jubilees* is uncertain, but good arguments can be made for placing it just prior to Antiochus's decrees forbidding the practice of the Jewish religion and during the time when Jason and a significant number of other Jews were compromising with their Hellenistic masters in order to advance their own status.[24] This book urges Jews to be especially careful about the observance of the sabbath (2:17-33; 50:1-13), Jewish festivals (6:17-31; 17:28-31), circumcision (16:25-34) and eating meat whose blood has not been properly drained (6:4-16; 7:28-33; 21:18). Violating these laws, says *Jubilees,* is tantamount to apostasy (2:27; 6:12; 7:28; 16:26, 34; 50:8, 13).

Although Daniel was written earlier, it became popular during the reign of Antiochus and features a hero who, along with his friends, refuses to violate the biblical boundaries between pure and impure food (1:8-16). It also expresses horror at the violation of the temple by someone designated symbolically as "the little horn," probably a reference to Antiochus IV Epiphanes (8:9-13; compare 9:27; 11:31; 12:11).

The tale of Judith, written somewhat later, features a heroine who places herself in dangerous and compromising situations in order to rescue her people (8:21, 24) but who nevertheless goes to great lengths not to eat the impure food in the Gentile camp that she has infiltrated (10:5; 12:1-4).

The Revolt and Its Aftermath

From the earliest days of the Jewish revolt against Antiochus, Jewish leaders compelled those who lived in areas under their control to be circumcised. The original leader of the revolt, Mattathias, instituted the practice when he and his fellow insurrectionists "forcibly circumcised all the uncircumcised boys that they found within the borders of Israel" (1 Macc 2:46). Several decades later, after Israel had achieved political independence, it continued the policy of forcing the people within its expanding borders to accept circumcision. Josephus says that John Hyrcanus (134-105 B.C.) conquered the Idumeans and "permitted them to remain in their country so long as they had themselves circumcised and were willing to observe the laws of the Jews" (*Ant.* 13.257), and Aristobulus adopted the same policy toward the Itureans (*Ant.* 13.318).

The tradition of the temple was also enhanced during this period. Its rededication by Judas Maccabeus early in Israel's revolt against the Seleucids was a crucial event for Israel both politically and religiously. The importance of this moment to Jews of various religious and political persuasions is clear from its celebration in both 1 Maccabees, which is the official court history of Judas's Hasmonean successors (4:52-59), and in 2 Maccabees, which is an alternative account produced by outsiders (10:5-8).[25] Its universal religious importance for Jews is also plain from the first of two letters that form the preface to 2 Maccabees. This letter admonishes the Jews of Egypt to join the Jews of Palestine in celebrating the newly founded festival of the rededication of the temple on the twenty-fifth day of Chislev (1:9). It seems safe to conclude that the desecration of the temple under Antiochus and its restoration to God's service under Judas were events of profound religious significance to most Jews, even those who lived outside of Palestine.

During the next two centuries these aspects of the Jewish law—regulation of the temple cult, sabbath keeping, circumcision and dietary observance—continued to receive emphasis as especially important symbols of Israel's distinctiveness. They demonstrated both to those within Israel and to those outside that the Jews considered themselves a special people, God's "treasured possession" among the nations. Once again, the evidence from Josephus is particularly valuable because of its close chronological proximity to Paul. Josephus quotes from a number of official edicts of the Roman government issued during the first century before Christ which grant special privileges to the Jews. In these documents, sabbath keeping and dietary restrictions are frequently cited as Jewish customs that local magistrates should tolerate. Thus in a decree directed to Ephesus in 43 B.C., the Jews are to be excused from military service since their law forbids them to bear arms on the sabbath and the rigors of military life would not allow them to "obtain the native foods to which they are accustomed" (*Ant.* 14.226). In another decree issued to nearby Miletus sometime after 46 B.C., the "magistrates, council, and people" are ordered to stop forbidding the Jews either to observe the sabbath or to handle their produce according to their laws (*Ant.* 14.245).[26] Moreover, during the Jewish war against Rome over a century later, Jewish forces quickly adopted the policy of their Maccabean predecessors and required circumcision of all who lived in areas under their control, regardless of whether they were Jews (*War* 2.454; *Life of Flavius Josephus* 112-13).

At this point the objection might reasonably be raised that this intense level of concern with the laws that distinguished Jews from Gentiles existed principally among the leaders of the Jewish revolt, their zealous followers and their Hasmonean successors. After all, both 1 and 2 Maccabees have to admit that many common Jews compromised with their Hellenistic overlords and many wealthy Jews actually participated in Antiochus's Hellenistic reforms in an effort to advance their own political power. It is not unusual to read modern descriptions of the persecutions of Antiochus which claim that "the majority of the people bowed to the inevitable and complied with the king's order" to abandon their ancestral religion.[27] In light of this, can we believe that most Jews in the years after the persecutions of Antiochus viewed the law as the inviolable sign that God had chosen them?

Josephus provides a wealth of information for answering this question. It must be handled carefully, because he was predisposed to place his people in the best light possible for his Roman patrons and readers. His tendency, therefore, is to exaggerate the commitment of the common Jew to "the traditions of the fathers," a loyalty that Josephus's readers would have found attractive.[28] It is not surprising to find in Josephus extravagant claims about the Jews' loyalty to the law: Jews regard their Scriptures as the Word of God from the day of their birth and will happily die rather than say anything against them (*Apion* 1.42-43). They believe the most fundamental task in life is to keep the "laws and pious practices based on them" (1.60). The law is straightforward enough in its essentials that anyone can understand it (2.190-92). "A transgressor is a rarity" (2.175). Despite all this, parts of Josephus's writings do not display this tendency, and in those places Josephus gives us enough information to justify the conclusion that these claims contain a kernel of truth.

Offhand comments from two stories designed to make a different point illustrate the level of commitment that most Jews felt, for example, to observance of the sabbatical year.[29] In the first, Josephus says that after Ptolemy, son-in-law of Simon Maccabeus, had killed Simon and imprisoned the rest of Simon's family, Simon's third son, John Hyrcanus, escaped Ptolemy's clutches. John was able to muster an army to attack his enemy, and he successfully besieged the fortress where Ptolemy was hiding. John's advantage was complicated, however, since Ptolemy still held John's mother and brothers and periodically brought them to the top of the fortress wall and tortured them in full view of John and his forces. Josephus tells us that during these trials John's mother urged her son not to give in to Ptolemy's schemes, for "to her, death at Ptolemy's hands would be better than immortality, if he paid the penalty for the wrongs which he had done to their house" (War 1.58; Ant. 13.232).

This moving story is Josephus's main interest, and he reveals almost as a parenthesis both that the siege eventually failed and the reason for its failure:

> The siege . . . dragged on until the year of repose came round, which is kept septennially by the Jews as a period of inaction, like the seventh day of the week. Ptolemy, now relieved of the siege, put John's brethren and their mother to death and fled to Zeno, surnamed Cotulas, the despot of Philadelphia. (War 1.60; compare Ant. 13.235)

In other words, even the torture of his own family did not persuade John to lift his siege of Ptolemy's fortress, but when the seventh year arrived, he and his military forces understood that they must cease making war and observe the mandated "idle year" (to argon etos).

The second account is equally remarkable. Josephus says that after Herod had defeated his Hasmonean rival Antigonas and captured Jerusalem, he "plundered" the population of Judea and lavished Anthony and his other Roman allies with the stolen wealth. This created great hardships for the common people, but these difficulties were compounded by their observance of "the seventh year," which "compelled the land to remain uncultivated since we are forbidden to sow the earth in that year" (Ant. 15.7). Although impoverished by war and oppressed by a ruthless king, the Jews increased their suffering rather than violate the law and sow their crops in the sabbatical year. Josephus's primary interest is elsewhere—he wants to portray Herod as a cruel overlord—but in the process he reveals that most Jews, even under extreme duress, attempted to keep Moses' command to observe the sabbatical year.[30]

Josephus also reveals that many Jews kept the dietary laws, even at great personal cost. In the *Life,* for example, Josephus tells a story whose primary intention was to discredit his nemesis John of Gischala but which implies that many Jews observed the law's dietary requirements. After hostilities against Rome were in full swing, he says, Herod Agrippa II sequestered the Jews in the important city of Caesarea Philippi in order to prevent their participation in the war. According to Josephus, John of Gischala told the king that the Jews of Caesarea Philippi had petitioned him to secure "pure" oil for them so that they would not have to resort to "Grecian" oil. John, says Josephus, knew that in Gischala he could buy pure oil for a tenth of the price for which it would sell in Caesarea Philippi, so he could get rich by means of this scheme. The king, himself a pious Jew, consented, and the Jews of Caesarea Philippi made John a wealthy man (74-76). Enough Jews were willing, then, to pay a high price for oil that had been kept pure according to Jewish dietary custom to make for John "an immense sum of money" (76).

Most Jews apparently showed the same tenacity in observing the laws of temple sacrifice. When Herod and the Roman general Sossius together besieged Jerusalem to force the surrender of the Hasmonean prince Antigonas, Josephus describes how the besieged people fought valiantly against their attackers, boldly venturing outside the city walls to set fire to the Roman siege engines and maintaining their position within the city even under severe hardship from famine. When the Romans finally broke through the city's defenses, Antigonas's forces gathered within the temple complex and continued to keep the Romans at bay. Astonishingly, while in this vulnerable position, Antigonas's forces sent an embassy from within the temple enclosure to the Romans outside to plead with them that they might be allowed to bring into the temple "only sacrificial animals" (*Ant.* 14.477). They had run short of victims for sacrifice and were horrified at the thought of allowing the daily sacrifice to cease.

During the great war against Rome over a century later, this commitment to the temple cult emerged again, this time in the action of the common people. Josephus says that many Jews risked life and limb to observe Passover in Jerusalem and to perform the prescribed sacrifices (*War* 5.99; 6.421).[31] What was true of the valiant few who fought against Herod also appears to have been true of the common Jew: keeping the laws of cultic sacrifice was worth risking death.

This is confirmed by another passing comment in Josephus's *Life.* Here we learn that Josephus was commissioned to serve as the commander of the Jewish forces in Galilee during the war with Rome and that once he had arrived in Tiberius in Galilee, he was to ally himself with as many of his priestly colleagues as were willing to stay in Tiberius and help him. Josephus says that they wanted to return home, however, because they had "amassed a large sum of money from the tithes which they accepted as their priestly due" (63). Clearly, even in the midst of hostilities with Rome, people were dutifully paying tithes to the priests.[32]

This conscientiousness about the temple and its priests, moreover, was not restricted to Jews who lived close enough to the temple to visit it regularly. It was equally true of many Jews who lived in the Diaspora. These Jews, although many miles distant from the Holy City and its temple, converged on Jerusalem during the three major festivals (Pentecost, Booths and Passover) and dutifully paid the annual two-drachma temple tax. The massiveness of the crowd assembled in Jerusalem at Pentecost in Acts 2 vividly illustrates the devotion of Diaspora Jews to the temple (compare *Ant.* 17.214). Josephus claims that the reason the temple treasury was so luxuriously supplied with funds is that "all the Jews throughout the habitable world" contributed to it (*Ant.* 14.110).[33]

Keeping the Jewish law, therefore, was important not merely to a select group of purists but to most Jews of Paul's time. Many of these were willing to endure great personal sacrifice in order not to compromise the law's precepts. Moreover, by the time Paul wrote his letters, the reforms of Ezra and the persecutions of Antiochus IV Epiphanes had solidified a commitment on the part of most Jews to certain elements of the law: devotion to the temple cult, observance of the Jewish calendar, circumcision and dietary customs.[34] It seems safe to assume that the reason Jews from all walks of life and in great numbers observed precisely these elements of the law so conscientiously is that they viewed them as especially clear indications of Israel's election. The law, and particularly these elements of it, demonstrated that out of all the nations of the earth, Israel was God's treasured possession.

The Law and Israel's Restoration

Did these Jews also believe that their diligent obedience to the law would reverse the curse and bring about the eschatological restoration of their fortunes? And did some believe that, whatever might become of the nation, they individually could attain salvation by their piety?

The law itself places obedience within the framework of God's gracious act of deliverance at the exodus. The first sentence of the Decalogue is, "I am the LORD your God, who brought you out of the land of Egypt, out of the house of slavery" (Ex 20:2; compare Deut 5:6). Deuteronomy says repeatedly that Israel's election is a result not of its worthiness but of God's unconditional love (7:7-8; 8:14-18; 9:4-5). Leviticus urges Israel to imitate the holiness of God because of God's great act of deliverance in the exodus (11:45). Here and elsewhere, obedience is a response to God's grace, not the means of earning his goodwill.[35]

These same Scriptures, moreover, prophesy that Israel's eschatological restoration will come at God's initiative, as a result of God's purification of Israel and re-creation of the people's hearts, not through their own efforts to win God's favor. Israel's repeated violation of the terms of the covenant, recounted so poignantly in Jeremiah, Ezekiel, and the prayers of confession in Ezra 9, Nehemiah 9 and Daniel 9, stands as a preface to the hope that God will take the initiative and do for his people what their wayward hearts cannot accomplish. Thus Deuteronomy offers life for obedience (30:11-20) but surrounds the offer with prophecies that Israel will not obey and must therefore depend on God's gracious intervention for deliverance from sin and its consequences (28:15—30:10; 31:16-29; 32:1-38). Jeremiah and Ezekiel look forward to a time when God will remake the hearts of his people (Jer 31:31-34) and send his purifying Spirit among them so that they will obey him (Ezek 11:19; 36:22—37:14). Daniel 9:16-19 similarly holds out the hope that God will not deal with his people as their stubborn wickedness deserves but will once again look down in mercy on the suffering into which their sin has led them and restore to them his goodwill (9:18).

Despite all this, some Jews of Paul's time did not read their Scriptures this way. They saw Deuteronomy 30:11-20 as a simple statement that obedience to the law results in life, disobedience in death, and that the choice between the two lies in the hands of the individual. "Choose life," Moses says, "so that you and your descendants may live" (v. 19).[36] Ben Sira, writing in the second century B.C., echoes these words and lays particular stress both on the freedom of the individual either to keep the law or to disobey it and on the life or death that the individual will receive as a result:

If you wish, you will keep the commandments, and to act faithfully is a matter of free choice [eudokias]. He has placed before you fire and water. Stretch out your hand for the one you wish. Life and death are before each person, and whatever each chooses [eudokēsē] will be given him. (Sirach 15:15-17)

Psalms of Solomon, produced about a century and a half later, expresses a similar conviction:

Our works are in the choosing and authority of our own souls. To do righteousness and wickedness is in the works of our hands, and in your righteousness, you pass human beings in review. The one who does righteousness will treasure up for himself life with the Lord, and the one who does wickedness will be the cause of his own soul's destruction. (9:4-5)[37]

These texts do not betray an unwillingness to rely on God, a boastful spirit or a fear that bad deeds will outweigh good ones at the final judgment. Nevertheless, they express unambiguously the idea that salvation from God's wrath depends at least to some extent on the human choice to do good and human success at doing it.

This was not the position of all Jews, however. Many appear to have understood the biblical stress on obedience as a response to God's gracious acts of redemption, on Israel's wickedness and on their need for a gracious act of God to deliver them from their inclination to sin. The prayer of confession in Baruch 1:15—3:8, for example, acknowledges the indelible stain of Israel's wickedness (2:8, 10, 12, 24; 3:4-8) and that any future return of God's favor to his people would be wholly undeserved (2:19; compare 3:4-5). It also affirms that if the Israelite people are to obey God's commands, God himself must grant them "a heart that obeys and ears that listen" (2:31; compare 3:7; Deut 30:6; Jer 24:7). These convictions were not, moreover, restricted to the national and corporate level. Many Jews understood that they individually were sinners in need of God's mercy. Baruch's confessional prayer speaks of the failure of "each" member of the nation to turn away from "the thoughts" of their "evil hearts" (2:8). In a similar way, Daniel describes his prayer of repentance as a confession not only of the sins of the nation but also of his own sins (9:20).

The best example of this kind of piety, however, is the Prayer of Manasseh. The prayer was composed by a Jew sometime prior to the destruction of Jerusalem in A.D. 70 and represents an imaginative reconstruction of the confession that, according to 2 Chronicles 33:12-13, the wicked king Manasseh uttered from his Babylonian imprisonment.[38] The prayer speaks of God's anger against sin (5) but then affirms that God in his "gentle grace" has "appointed repentance for sinners as the [way to] salvation" (7). It then shifts to the first person:

I have sinned, O Lord, I have sinned; and I certainly know my sins. I beseech you; forgive me, O Lord, forgive me! Do not destroy me with my transgressions; do not be angry against me forever; do not remember my evils; and do not condemn me and banish me to the depths of the earth! For you are the God of those who repent. In me you will manifest all your grace; and although I am not worthy, you will save me according to your manifest mercies. (vv. 12-14)[39]

The author of this prayer appears to have understood that he was no better than the most evil of Judah's kings, that his works could not even cooperate with God's grace to effect salvation and that salvation was entirely a matter of God's grace.[40]

The Evidence of the Gospels

The Gospels provide evidence that both ways of understanding sinful humanity and God's grace were abroad in the first century. Jesus told the parable of the Pharisee and the tax collector "to some who had confidence in themselves, that they were righteous" (Lk 18:9). This confidence apparently led some to believe that they were not "sinners," despite their neglect of the weightier matters of the law (Mt 23:16-36; Lk 11:37-52). In the parable, therefore, the Pharisee believes that because he is innocent of robbery, wickedness and adultery and because he fasts and tithes, he will be justified (Lk 18:11-12). Unlike the tax collector, he is unwilling to acknowledge his need for repentance, for he does not view himself as a sinner (v. 13).

The Gospels identify this self-trust as the reason that some rejected Jesus' preaching of repentance: they erroneously believed themselves to be "righteous" and criticized Jesus for associating with "sinners" (Mt 9:10-13; Mk 2:15-17; Lk 5:27-32; 7:36-47). The belief that righteousness before God depended on the human choice to cooperate with God's grace by producing good works did not necessarily lead to this kind of self-trust, but the Pharisee's conduct in the parable shows that it happened often enough to serve as the subject of an illustrative story.

Nevertheless, the tax collector in the parable was also a Jew, and as the Prayer of Manasseh shows, his plea, "God be merciful to me, the sinner!" (Lk 18:13), was no less typical of Jewish piety than the Pharisee's self-trust.[41] Moreover, the Gospels affirm that many first-century Jews maintained both a commitment to the law and the conviction that they were sinners in need of God's eschatological act of redemption. Thus Zechariah, although upright before the Lord and blameless in his observance of the law (Lk 1:6), affirms that God's people need both forgiveness for their sins (1:77) and God's intervention so that they might "serve him without fear in holiness and righteousness before him" forever (1:74-75). Simeon, similarly, was upright and devout but looked for the consolation of Israel and the time of God's salvation (Lk 2:25, 30). Undoubtedly the same could be said of Elizabeth, Anna, Joseph and Mary, all of whom observed the law faithfully and valued the temple as the house of God (Lk 1:6; 2:22, 24, 27, 37, 39, 41, 49).

During Jesus' ministry, much opposition came from Pharisees and scribes who refused to acknowledge their need of repentance, but others helped Jesus (Lk 13:31) and received his commendation (Mk 12:34). Even those who opposed him fell under Jesus' censure less because of their teaching about the law than because their conduct failed to match what they taught (Mt 23:2-3, 23; compare Lk 10:28).

First-Century Diversity

As we might expect in a religious movement as large and geographically diverse as Judaism in the first century, then, a common base of commitment to the law expressed itself in a variety of ways. Most Jews believed that the Mosaic covenant distinguished Israel from the surrounding nations, and virtually all Jews believed that it was a gracious sign of God's election. Many believed that Israel lived in a period of punishment for disobedience to the law and awaited a time when God would intervene powerfully to remake the rebellious hearts of his people, live among his people by his Holy Spirit and restore his people's fortunes. Some felt that acquittal before God on the final day would come to those who freely chose to obey God's laws; others believed humanity to be so sinful that true obedience would come only as a result of God's prior work in the human heart.

All of these convictions about the law are addressed in Paul's letters. Some of them he affirms, some he reshapes, and some he rejects. Do his choices reflect some consistent theological principle, a touchstone that guides his decisions about what to affirm, transform and reject? Paul wrote no treatise "On the Law of Moses," and so the evidence must be pieced together from his occasional letters, each written to address concrete pastoral problems within specific churches. When the historical contexts of these letters, the literary contexts of Paul's statements and assumptions about the law, and the cultural context of common Jewish convictions about the law are taken into account, an answer to this question begins to unfold.

CHAPTER THREE

SANCTIFIED GENTILES IN THESSALONICA: A Paradox in the Thessalonian Letters

Paul's letters to the Thessalonians go virtually unaddressed in contemporary studies of the apostle's attitude toward the Jewish law. Other than a few references to his Jewish-sounding ethical admonitions in 1 Thessalonians 4:1-8 and occasional mention of his statements about Jewish opposition to his mission to the Gentiles in 1 Thessalonians 2:14-16, the standard treatments of Paul's view of the law pass over the Thessalonian correspondence in silence. At one level this silence is understandable, since the term *law (nomos)* never appears in the letters and their purpose seems to have been both to encourage the young church in the face of persecution and to correct a misunderstanding that arose because of Paul's hasty exit from the city. With the far more complex and controversial material in Galatians and Romans clamoring for attention, it has no doubt seemed unwise to devote much energy to 1 and 2 Thessalonians.

Can we so quickly assume, however, that simply because Paul does not use the term *law,* the phrase *works of the law* or the idea of "justification" in these letters that they are virtually irrelevant to the discussion of his view of the law? A careful examination of 1 and 2 Thessalonians in light of the historical circumstances that prompted Paul to write them shows that to dismiss them from the discussion too quickly is unwise.[1] The Thessalonian letters are important for painting an accurate picture of Paul's view of the law because although the law is not explicitly addressed in them, Paul alludes to it, and his allusions reveal a pattern of thinking about the law which will reappear frequently in his other letters. If we are to understand the significance of these allusive references, however, it is first necessary to consider the circumstances that prompted them.

The Thessalonian Correspondence in Context

If anything is clear about the nature of the Thessalonian church from Paul's two letters, it is that former pagans with no previous attachment to the synagogue and no apparent familiarity with Judaism made up the vast majority of the community. The evidence for this is straightforward and comes from two distinct sections of the first letter. In 1:9 Paul briefly recalls the ready welcome he received from the Thessalonians when he came to the city. The result of this response was that the Thessalonians "turned to God from idols—to serve the living and true God." Paul would hardly have written this way if Jewish Christians or Gentiles who had previously attended the synagogue were uppermost in his mind.[2] Similarly, the admonition to avoid sexual immorality in 4:3-5 would not have been appropriate for a Jewish Christian community or for a congregation of God-fearing Gentiles. Both of these groups would have been familiar with the sexual standards Paul upholds in this passage from their exposure to the Scriptures and to the teaching of the synagogue.[3] Some Jews and God-fearers were part of the church, as Acts 17:1-4 indicates, but at least by the time Paul wrote 1 Thessalonians, the number of converts made during Paul's three sabbath sermons in the Thessalonian synagogue must have been small in comparison to the number of pagans who responded to the gospel as Paul labored beside them in the workshop (1 Thess 2:9; compare 2 Thess 3:7-9).[4]

In addition, when Paul wrote the first letter no serious problems seem to have arisen in the congregation, and by the time he felt compelled to write the second letter, its only serious difficulty involved a misunderstanding about the nature of Christ's Second Coming. This reading of the evidence is not uncontroversial, but it is based on what is arguably the most straightforward understanding of Paul's references in the letter to the Thessalonian situation.[5] Thus, although Paul was distressed about the ability of the Thessalonians to persevere under hardship (1 Thess 3:2), he was relieved to discover from his emissary Timothy that they were standing firm "in the Lord" (3:8). The letter opens, then, with a description of the Thessalonians' productivity in faith and love and of their endurance in the hope "of our Lord Jesus Christ" (1:3).

Paul's admonitory comments in 4:1-12 and 5:4-11, accordingly, are not meant to correct deviant behavior but to emphasize particularly important aspects of Paul's previous teaching while with the Thessalonians. The Thessalonians, moreover, are presently following this teaching, as three passages in chapters 4 and 5 reveal:

Finally therefore, brothers, we request and encourage you in the Lord Jesus that *just as you received from us* how it was necessary for you to live and to please God—*just as you also are living*—you excel in this more and more. (4:1)

But concerning brotherly love *you have no need for me to write to you,* for you yourselves are taught by God in order that you might love one another, *and you are doing it* to all the brothers throughout Macedonia. But we encourage you, brothers, to excel in this more and more. (4:9-10)

Therefore admonish one another and each of you edify the other, *just as you are doing.* (5:11)

In at least the areas covered by these descriptions, the Thessalonians are doing well, and Paul writes only to encourage them to continue their progress.[6] Even Paul's careful defense of his conduct while in Thessalonica in 1 Thessalonians 2:1-12 is probably an effort to distinguish himself from the well-known philosophical hucksters of the day rather than a response to any specific charges of chicanery from the Thessalonian community.[7] This seems to be the best way of reconciling Paul's apology in 2:1-12 with his claim in 3:6 that Timothy has just arrived with the good news that "you always remember us fondly, longing to see us, just as we long to see you."

The only point in the first letter where Paul clearly corrects a misunderstanding is when he addresses the question of what will happen to those who have died before the return of Christ (4:13-18). Paul begins this section with the phrase "But we do not want you to be ignorant, brothers" (v. 13), a phrase that in other letters he reserves for the introduction of an especially weighty matter, often a subject whose neglect in the community has led to some inappropriate behavior or attitude.[8] Paul clearly uses the phrase in that way here. Perhaps because of his hasty and unexpected departure from Thessalonica (2:17; compare Acts

17:10), his teaching about eschatological matters was cut short. This section of the letter, therefore, is intended to fill the gap in the Thessalonians' understanding (3:10) and to correct the discouragement that has resulted from this deficiency (4:13; compare 4:18).[9]

The Thessalonians' preoccupation with the elements of Paul's eschatological teaching that they did understand (5:1), including the idea that Christ's coming might happen at any time (5:2), had probably already led to some trouble with "idlers" by the time Paul wrote the first letter (5:14).[10] This trouble then became worse and prompted Paul in a second letter to provide a more detailed explanation of his position on the imminence of Christ's coming (2 Thess 2:3-12) and the impropriety of idleness (2 Thess 3:6-15).[11]

Paul, then, although concerned that the Thessalonians continue down the straight road on which they had begun (1 Thess 3:11-13; 4:1, 10), was generally pleased with their condition at the time he wrote the first letter. The one problem present at that time, and which eventually became serious enough to prompt a second, sterner letter, was a defective understanding of the nature and time of Christ's Second Coming. As a consequence, 1 Thessalonians is a valuable guide to those points in Paul's teaching that he considered important enough to reiterate even when the situation in the church to which he wrote did not require it. When we look at this material carefully, we discover that although he was writing to a group composed almost entirely of converts from pagan religions, Paul chose to emphasize the continuity between believers in Jesus Christ, whatever their previous background, and the people of God as they are defined in the Mosaic law.

Members of God's Covenant People

As we saw in chapter two, one of the primary purposes of the Mosaic law in the eyes of Jews who lived at the time of Paul was to distinguish Israel as God's special people. When God gave the law to Israel at Sinai and constituted them as a people, he stated this purpose in unambiguous terms:

> If you should obey my voice and keep my covenant you shall, out of all the nations, be to me a peculiar people, for the earth is mine. And you shall be to me a priestly kingdom and a holy [hagion] nation. (Ex 19:5-6 LXX)

Leviticus reiterates this purpose by stating that the laws that it contains not only urge Israel to imitate God's holiness (11:44-45; compare 19:2; 20:26; 22:32) and to avoid defiling the dwelling place of his presence (15:31) but also mark the boundary between Israel and the people of the land that Israel is shortly to inherit (20:22-26; compare Deut 4:5-8). Israel's sanctity, and hence its election, was jeopardized when its people broke the law and went into exile, and God's restoration of his people would involve the restoration of this sanctity.

From the perspective of first-century Jews familiar with all of this, the most astonishing characteristic of the Thessalonian letters would have been Paul's assumption that the collection of uncircumcised Gentiles together with some God-fearers and Jews in Thessalonica stood in continuity with God's chosen people as they are described in the Old Testament. Thus when Paul addresses both letters "to the church of the Thessalonians in God the Father and the Lord Jesus Christ" (1 Thess 1:1; 2 Thess 1:1), he uses a phrase similar to the term "assembly of the LORD" *(ekklēsia kyriou)* found in Deuteronomy to designate the gathering of Hebrews at the time of the covenant's ratification and Israel's designation as God's special people (Deut 23:1, 4, 9 LXX).[12] Moreover, when Paul reminds the Thessalonians of their "election" and that they are "brothers beloved by God" (1 Thess 1:4; 2 Thess 2:13-14; compare 1 Thess 2:12; 2 Thess 1:11), he recalls the frequently repeated statement in Deuteronomy that God "loved" Israel and demonstrated his love for them by "electing" their ancestors and eventually the Israelites themselves, among all the peoples of the earth, to be his own possession (Deut 4:37; 10:15; compare 7:8; 23:5). Paul also frequently says that God "calls" or "has called" the Thessalonians much in the same way that the second part of Isaiah refers to God's election of Israel as his "call" to them. Just as God would call Israel from the ends of the earth (Is 41:9; compare 42:6) and had called Israel's ancestors (Is 48:12) in order to bless them and make them a great nation (Is 51:2), so Paul tells the Thessalonians that God calls them "into his kingdom and glory" (1 Thess 2:12; compare 2 Thess 2:14), that he has called them in sanctification (1 Thess 4:7; compare 2 Thess 1:11) and that he will be faithful to the Thessalonians because of his role as the One who calls them (1 Thess 5:24).

Taken individually, Paul's application of these terms to the Thessalonians would not be particularly significant. After all, the term *ekklēsia* had been used in Greek literature for centuries prior to Paul to refer simply to an assembly of people for a particular purpose. Paul certainly could have referred to the Thessalonians as "chosen" and "loved by God" without thinking specifically of the use of that language to describe Israel in the Bible. The term *call* is found much more frequently in the Bible in an innocuous sense, absent the connotations of God's original call to Israel, than it is found carrying those connotations.[13]

Yet Paul's use of these terms together and his use of them to describe the transformation of the Thessalonian believers from people who once worshiped idols to people who "serve the living and true God" (1 Thess 1:9) show that he views the conversion of the Thessalonians as analogous to—perhaps even a recapitulation of—what happened to Israel at the foot of Mount Sinai.

Once we realize Paul's purpose in using this language, it should come as no surprise that in spite of the Thessalonians' good behavior (1 Thess 4:1), Paul emphasizes their "sanctification" in the two letters. Just as in Leviticus Israel's pursuit of sanctification is a response to God's election, so in the Thessalonian correspondence the believers' election and their sanctification go hand in hand (1 Thess 4:7; 5:23-24; 2 Thess 2:13-14). Moreover, just as in Leviticus the purpose of sanctification is to separate Israel from the surrounding people, so in the Thessalonian correspondence it is intended to distinguish "the assembly of the Thessalonians in God and in our Lord Jesus Christ" from "those outside" who do not belong to the community (1 Thess 4:5; compare 4:12).

This last parallel between the sanctification of Israel in Leviticus and the sanctification of the Thessalonian believers in 1 and 2 Thessalonians is especially clear in Paul's admonition about sexual purity in 1 Thessalonians 4:1-8. In the course of his admonition, Paul gives a lucid statement of its purpose:

> For this is the will of God—your sanctification [hagiasmos]—that you abstain from sexual immorality, that each of you know how to control his own sexual urges in sanctification [hagiasmos] and in honor, not in lustful passion as the Gentiles do who do not know God.[14] It is God's will that no one transgress against and take advantage of his brother in this matter, because God is the avenger of all these things, just as we told you and warned you before. For God did not call us to uncleanness [akatharsia] but in sanctification. (4:3-6)

In other words, Paul wants the Thessalonian community to be particularly careful not to commit sexual improprieties because he wants them to be distinct from the Gentiles. Since Paul is writing to people who in the eyes of most first-century Jews, perhaps even most first-century Jewish Christians, were Gentiles, this is an extraordinary statement indeed.[15] It matches well, however, the emphasis on sexual purity in Leviticus as a mark of distinction for Israel and therefore a vital component in Israel's sanctification.

In Leviticus 18 and 20 the Lord gives his people laws to govern their sexual conduct. The burden of these chapters is the careful definition and prohibition of incest, but they cover a wide range of other sexual offenses as well.[16] Although Paul does not refer to the particulars of these laws but speaks generally of abstaining from sexual immorality and controlling one's sexual passions, the purpose for Paul's admonition and the purpose for the laws in Leviticus are parallel.[17] In Leviticus 18 the laws are introduced with the statement that God's people are not to follow either the customs of the Egyptians or those of the Canaanites but are instead to keep the laws of God (vv. 1-5). If the Israelites do slip into the sexual customs of the nations around them, they will be sent into exile as assuredly as the Lord is about throw the sexually immoral Canaanites out of the land and replace them with Israel (18:24-25; 20:22-23). The reason the Lord takes sexual purity so seriously is that it serves as a boundary marker between Israel and the nations, and consequently as a sign of Israel's election:

> I am the Lord your God who has marked you off from all the Gentiles. ... You shall be holy [hagios] to me; for I the Lord your God am holy, and I have distinguished you from all the Gentiles to be mine. (Lev 20:24, 26 LXX)

Paul's understanding of the identity of the Thessalonian community, therefore, is patterned after the understanding of Israel's identity revealed in the Mosaic law. Just as the people of Israel were the chosen people of God and were required to demonstrate their special status by observances that set them apart from "the Gentiles," so the Thessalonians are chosen by God and are therefore required to live sanctified lives, distinguished from "the Gentiles" by their sexual purity.[18]

Any first-century Jew familiar with the Greek translation of Scripture would have understood immediately what Paul was doing. The pictures of Israel in solemn assembly at the foot of Mount Sinai entering into a covenant with God and then receiving instruction from Moses on their election and sanctification while poised at the border of the Promised Land were deeply etched in the Jewish religious consciousness. How Paul thought he could legitimately use such language of uncircumcised Gentiles who only a few months earlier had worshiped idols is another question entirely. From Paul's perspective, what had happened to make such a radical move legitimate?

The Prophesied Community

Paul alludes to the great shift that had resulted in his astonishing approach when he describes the effects of his preaching among the Thessalonians:

> Our gospel did not come among you in word only but also in power and in the Holy Spirit and in full assurance, just as you know what manner of

life we had among you for your sake. And you became imitators of us and of the Lord, because you welcomed the word, in the midst of much suffering, with the joy of the Holy Spirit. (1 Thess 1:5-6)

With the coming of Jesus Christ, the era of the restoration of God's people by the sanctifying presence of God's Spirit had arrived. As we have already seen in chapter two, everyone who attended the synagogue in Paul's day knew that Israel's history was not marked by unswerving commitment to the way of life described by Leviticus, and the threat of punishment and exile that accompanied the laws described there and in Deuteronomy had come to fruition. As we have also seen, however, most Jews trusted that God had not abandoned his oppressed and scattered people but had promised to restore their holiness by pouring out his Spirit on them and giving them the blessing promised to those who obey God's laws.

No prophet understood better than Ezekiel the failure of God's people to follow the standards of purity found in Leviticus, and no prophet looked more hopefully to the eschatological day when God would, by a powerful movement of his Spirit, restore the purity and sanctity of his people, making their election evident to all their oppressors (36:23). Ezekiel prophesies to his people that in the day of their restoration God himself will make his people both clean and obedient:

I shall sprinkle pure water upon you, and you shall be cleansed from all your impurity *[akatharsia]* and from all your idolatry, and I will purify you. I will give to you a new heart, and place a new spirit among you. I will take away the heart of stone from your flesh, and give to you a heart of flesh. I will place my Spirit among you and will make it so that you shall live by my requirements and so that you shall do and shall keep my judgments. (36:25-27 LXX; compare 11:19; 18:31; 37:14)

Other prophets envisioned this period as equivalent to the exodus, during which Israel was first constituted as God's people (Is 4:4-5; 49:10; Jer 23:7-8; compare Jer 31:32). Just as God had entered into a covenant with his people during those days, so he would make a new covenant with Israel when he restored their fortunes (Jer 31 [LXX 38]:31-34; 32:40; 50:5; compare Is 55:3; 59:20-21; 61:8; Ezek 37:26). One feature of this covenant would be that God would place his law on the hearts of his people so that they would not need to teach it to one another (Jer 31 [LXX 38]:34).

Paul picks up the language that Ezekiel, Jeremiah and Isaiah had used to describe this era and applies it to the Thessalonians. Not only have they experienced the presence of God's sanctifying Spirit in a powerful way (1 Thess 1:5-6), but they have done what Ezekiel predicted Israel would do in the period of restoration by turning "from idols to serve the living and true God" (1 Thess 1:9; compare Ezek 11:18; 20:33-44; 37:23). And because the Thessalonians are participating in the eschatological period of the restoration of God's people, their sanctification is absolutely necessary. Their sexual ethic must not be characterized by the "uncleanness" *[akatharsia]* that characterizes Gentiles, and that, according to Ezekiel (36:25, 29 LXX), characterized God's people prior to the era of their restoration. Instead it must be marked by "sanctification" (1 Thess 4:7, *hagiasmos*). To refuse to submit to the directions Paul has given for living a sanctified life, moreover, is not to reject a human being "but God who places his Holy Spirit among you" (1 Thess 4:8). It is, in other words, to opt out of the eschatological era prophesied by Ezekiel (Ezek 36:27; compare 37:14) and now fulfilled with the coming of the Holy Spirit to the Thessalonian community.

The close parallel between Paul's language in 1 Thessalonians 4:8 and Ezekiel's language in 36:27 shows clearly that the eschatological restoration of Israel as Ezekiel describes it is the source of Paul's ethical admonitions in this passage:

> Therefore the one who rejects [this teaching] rejects not a person but the God *who places his Holy Spirit among you [ton didonta to pneuma autou to hagion eis hymas]*. (1 Thess 4:8)
>
> *I will place my Spirit among you [to pneuma mou dōsō en hymin]*, and I will make it so that you shall live by my requirements and so that you shall do and shall keep my judgments. (Ezek 36:27 LXX)

The prophetic echoes continue with Paul's statement in 1 Thessalonians 4:9 that he has no need to write to the Thessalonians on the subject of brotherly love because they are "taught by God to love one another." Paul is here alluding to the time Jeremiah describes when God's people will not need others to teach them the law but will know it innately, since God will write it on their hearts (31 [LXX 38]:33-34). He probably also has in mind Isaiah's claim that when God establishes his covenant of peace with Israel forever, he will himself teach Israel's children (54:10, 13).[19] The content of the teaching that the Thessalonians have received is significant as well. Paul says that God himself has shown them how to "love each other," echoing Leviticus 19:18, a widely known summary of the Mosaic law.[20]

The New Covenant and the Gentiles

From Paul's perspective, then, something earthshaking had occurred when the Thessalonians believed and experienced the power of the Holy Spirit in their midst (1 Thess 1:5-6). The eschatological era predicted by the prophets had come, and a new covenant had been established with God's people. In the process of so much radical change, another shocking development had taken place: Gentiles had turned from idols to the God of Israel and had joined the eschatological people of God.

Many first-century Jews would have understood this argument, but they would have found at least two elements of it troubling. First, many would have objected to the prominent place Paul gives to the Gentiles in his understanding of the restoration of God's people. In a few passages Gentiles enter the biblical picture of Israel's restoration as enemies over whom Israel will triumph (Is 54:3; 60:1-16; 61:5-6; compare Ezek 36:23; 37:28) or as eschatological converts to Judaism (Is 66:18-24), they might have said, but Paul has given to uncircumcised Gentiles the privileges that belong to the restored Israel. Furthermore, at precisely the same time that the Gentiles take over Israel's eschatological position as the people of God, Paul assumes the prophet's mantle and claims that God's wrath lies on unbelieving Israel for its rejection of the gospel (1 Thess 2:14-16).[21] In Paul's understanding of the restoration, then, the Gentiles receive the blessings reserved in the Prophets for the restored Israel, while "the Jews" continue to live under the divine "wrath" of the exile, the condition from which the prophesied period of restoration should have rescued them.

Second, most Jews of Paul's time would have immediately objected to Paul's claims that by observing the ethical admonitions that he lays down in the Thessalonian letters, the Thessalonians have achieved the level of sanctification required in the eschatological era of restoration. Jeremiah's "new covenant" and Ezekiel's "everlasting covenant" were not different covenants from the original Mosaic version, but restorations of that covenant. If Gentiles wanted to participate on an equal footing with the Jews in the period of Israel's restoration, therefore, they would have to participate in the Jewish cult, keep the Jewish festivals and observe the Jewish sabbath (Is 66:18-24).

We do not know precisely how Paul would have responded to such objections at the time he wrote the Thessalonian letters. In answer to the first, he might have recalled Jeremiah's claim that God would show mercy to Gentiles who repent as assuredly as he had shown mercy to repentant Israel (Jer 18:7-8), or Joel's prediction that in the last days God would pour out his Spirit on all flesh (Joel 2:28), or even Jonah's displeasure that God had shown the same mercy to Assyrians that he promised to show to Israelites (Jon 4:2; compare Ex 34:1-8).[22] Perhaps he would also have pointed out several texts in the Old Testament that describe the pilgrimage of Gentiles to Zion before referring to the restoration of Israel (Is

45:14-17,20-25; 59:19-20; Mic 4:1-8).[23]

More information emerges from the Thessalonian letters on how he would have answered the second objection. The echoes of the passages that refer to Israel's restoration in Jeremiah and Ezekiel show that Paul believed the era of the "new covenant" had arrived. The character of this covenant, moreover, parallels in significant ways the character of the Mosaic covenant. It defines the boundaries of the Thessalonians' sanctification, thereby marking them off as the specially chosen people of God. Furthermore, the shape of these boundaries duplicates the shape of the boundaries that the Mosaic law provided for Israel. They demanded that the Thessalonians turn from their idols and serve the God of Abraham, Isaac and Jacob (1 Thess 1:9). They required generally the same standard of sexual propriety that Leviticus laid down for Israel (1 Thess 4:3-8). They urged the Thessalonians to display the love for one another which Leviticus demanded of God's ancient people (1 Thess 4:9-10). Paul might have pointed out to his detractors, then, that a large measure of continuity existed between the new covenant that he envisioned for the Thessalonian community and the Mosaic law.

Nevertheless, the Thessalonian letters show that Paul did not believe that in the eschatological era the Mosaic covenant would be restored. The lack of specific correlation between Paul's ethical admonitions and the behavior required of a sanctified Israel in the Mosaic law shows that for him many of the Mosaic law's specific requirements have dropped from view. Although the Thessalonians have turned from idols and sexual promiscuity, they have not become Jewish proselytes.

As controversial as this would have appeared to Jews of Paul's time, the Thessalonians apparently accepted it without argument. Paul sees no need to explain in detail his position on the Mosaic law and the restoration of the people of God; instead he assumes its validity, reminds his readers of several salient points within the scheme and dwells at greater length on the eschatological matters that were the real source of trouble at Thessalonica. The convictions about the Mosaic law and the restoration of Israel which emerge from the Thessalonian letters, then, provide only broad strokes for the picture of Paul's view of the law. These strokes are fundamental, however, because Paul appears simply to assume that they are true: uncircumcised Gentiles who turn from idols to believe the gospel constitute the fulfillment of the biblical predictions of Israel's restoration, these believers are no longer Gentiles but the people of God, and as the people of God they must observe the boundaries of sanctification that the new covenant marks out for them.

CHAPTER FOUR

SANCTIFIED GENTILES IN CORINTH: The Paradox Intensifies

If Paul's references to the sanctity of the believing community in the Thessalonian letters have an unhurried, peaceful quality, in the Corinthian correspondence they take on urgency. In at least one case the Corinthian Christians had stooped to a lower moral plane than even "the Gentiles" occupied. Moreover, the Corinthians were not happy with the style of ministry exhibited and taught by Paul, their father in the faith. This spiritual turbulence led him to respond with two letters that form a rich field of exploration for the student of Paul's view of the law. The themes of election, sanctity and the relationship between the new covenant and the old appear here in abundance and add texture to the picture of Paul's view of the law which emerged from the Thessalonian letters.

The Corinthian letters provide valuable evidence for Paul's view of the law not only because of what *is* at issue, however, but also because of what *is not* at stake. Judaizers have not arrived on the scene, nor have tensions between Jews and Gentiles arisen in the Corinthian congregation. In 1 and 2 Corinthians, then, as in 1 and 2 Thessalonians, we see Paul's approach to the law when the law itself is not a topic of debate. This is a useful theological position in which to find Paul, since one side in the discussion over whether Paul's view of the law is coherent claims that he frequently shot from the hip to address polemical needs of the moment when he discussed the law in Galatians, Philippians and Romans. If it turns out that Paul's view of the law in the Corinthian correspondence, where the Mosaic law was not the issue, is consistent with his statements in the more polemical letters, then it is highly probable that wherever they occur, Paul's assumptions and statements about the law reflect a considered position and are not salvos lobbed unreflectively at his opponents in the midst of battle.

Not everyone would agree, however, that the Corinthian situation was free from the kind of trouble over the law that we find in Galatians and Romans. Some interpreters believe that the Corinthian church was predominantly Jewish, and others that it had come under the influence of Jewish teachers whose gospel emphasized the continuing validity of the Mosaic law. In this chapter, then, I first consider the character of the Corinthian community and the shape of the opposition to Paul which arose in Corinth. I then give attention to three themes that recur in the letters and that imply a certain stance toward the Mosaic law. Paul's use of those themes, however, poses certain puzzles, and the next chapter will offer some help in solving those problems by examining Paul's explicit statements about the law.

The Ethnic Composition of the Corinthian Church

Not long after leaving Thessalonica Paul traveled to Corinth, where he met Priscilla and Aquila, two Jewish believers from Rome. They plied the same trade in the city, and Paul preached the gospel among the large and active Jewish community there (Acts 18:1-5).[1] The results were not entirely satisfactory (18:6), but with perseverance the synagogue ruler himself and his entire household believed (18:8; compare 1 Cor 1:14).[2] The Corinthian community, then, clearly included some Jews.[3]

Other Jews, however, rejected Paul's message (18:6), and by the time Paul wrote 1 and 2 Corinthians, the community was primarily Gentile. Thus 1 Corinthians is addressed to readers with a pagan past, who were once "led astray by dumb idols" (12:2; compare 8:1—10:22) and who were presently in need of a reminder to avoid typically pagan sexual vices (6:9-20; compare 5:1-8).[4] This picture receives confirmation in 2 Corinthians where Paul expresses fear that when he next visits Corinth he may find some who have committed the sins of "uncleanness, sexual immorality and debauchery" and not repented of them (12:21).[5] Such offenses presuppose a church whose temptations lie in the direction of a Gentile past.[6]

It seems certain, therefore, that although the believers in Corinth included a small group of Jews, some of whom had been influential in the Corinthian Jewish community, most of the Corinthian believers were Gentiles. Paul addresses them as former idolaters, and he indicates that, for many, a pagan past was still fresh in memory. For some it appears to have been not altogether past.

No particularly Jewish concerns, then, compelled Paul to refer to the Mosaic law. The cultural context of the Corinthian letters was instead dominated by Gentiles who appear to have been uninitiated into the spirituality of Judaism.

Paul and His Opponents in Corinth

Had the law become an issue for the Gentile Corinthians, however, much in the way that it became a point of controversy between Paul and the Gentile Galatians? Many scholars believe that both 1 and 2 Corinthians contain evidence that after Paul founded the Corinthian church, Jewish Christians suspicious of his approach to the Jewish law had entered the community and persuaded many within the church that adopting Jewish customs went hand in hand with belief in Jesus as the Messiah.[7] In 1 Corinthians this group rallied around the name of Cephas (1 Cor 1:12; compare 3:22), the apostle to the circumcision (Gal 2:9) who opposed Paul on some matters related to Gentile observance of the Jewish law (Gal 2:11-14).[8] Cephas himself, or at least a group loyal to him, had visited the community (1 Cor 9:5), had questioned the propriety of Paul's refusal to accept financial support from the Corinthian community (1 Cor 9:3-18) and ultimately had impugned Paul's claim to be an apostle (1 Cor 9:2; compare 15:9-11).[9] In addition, this group insisted against Paul that believers should abstain from food offered to idols, in accord with the apostolic decree recorded in Acts 15:29 (compare 15:20 and 21:25).[10] So although most within the Corinthian community may have had little or no acquaintance with Judaism prior to their conversion, the scholars holding to this interpretation maintain that after Paul left the community, the new believers quickly became familiar with a type of Jewish Christianity that was inimical to Paul.

In 2 Corinthians the presence of Jewish Christian opponents is clearer, and, it is said, both their teaching about the law and Paul's response to it are clear as well. Paul's reference to his opponents as "Hebrews ... Israelites

... seed of Abraham" shows without doubt that they were Jewish (2 Cor 11:22), and many scholars believe that Paul's discussion of the old covenant in 2 Corinthians 2:14—4:6 demonstrates that they tried to impose observance of the Mosaic law on the apostle's Corinthian converts.[11] Precisely who these opponents were, however, is one of the most hotly debated questions of current New Testament scholarship.[12] Some believe that they resembled Paul's opponents in Galatia.[13] Others claim that they placed less emphasis than the Galatian Judaizers on the law but, under the influence of Hellenistic Judaism, insisted that they be honored together with Abraham, Moses and Jesus as "divine men."[14] Still others think that Paul's opponents were Jews who mixed their Judaism syncretistically with Gnosticism.[15]

The bewildering variety of opinions about the nature of the opposition to Paul in Corinth is due largely to the scarcity of clear evidence in 1 and 2 Corinthians about precisely what Paul's opponents believed. The hard evidence, as it turns out, is confined to 2 Corinthians, since the passing references to Cephas in 1 Corinthians mean at most that Cephas once passed through the community and that some in Corinth rallied around him just as others became attached to Apollos. Yet even Paul's direct references in 2 Corinthians are few and simple, shedding only enough light on the opponents' position to allow a broad description.[16] After claiming in 2:17 that unlike "the many," he does not peddle the Word of God for profit, Paul contrasts himself in 3:1 with "some" who need "letters of recommendation" to or from the Corinthians. It seems safe to assume, with most commentators, that these verses refer to a group that had gained entrance to the Corinthian community by means of letters of recommendation from some authoritative source.[17] Paul goes on to argue that he does not need such letters because the Corinthians themselves are his letter, Christ the authority who sent it and Paul the courier who delivered it.[18] Moreover, Paul says, this letter was not written with ink but on human hearts (3:3).

At this point, reminded of the biblical promise of a new covenant written on the hearts of God's people, Paul begins a digression that contrasts the new covenant with the old. He does not return to his original line of thought until 4:1-2, where he says that he does not "lose heart" and has renounced "the secret ways of shame" in his ministry. It is natural to ask how closely this digression is related to the teaching of those who have entered the Corinthian community with their letters of recommendation. Did Paul's opponents emphasize conformity to the Jewish law as they interpreted it? Is Paul here arguing the opposite position? Or does Paul's contrast between letter and Spirit, between new covenant and old, between Moses and himself only illustrate the contrast between his opponents' emphasis on worldly and temporal credentials with his own interest in spiritual and eschatological credentials?[19]

Some help in answering these questions comes from the next explicit reference to those who opposed Paul in Corinth. After describing the nature of his ministry in 4:1—5:11, Paul gives the purpose for his description: "We are not commending ourselves to you again, but giving you a cause for boasting on our behalf in order that you might have something to say to those who boast in appearance rather than in the heart" (5:12). This text shows that Paul's primary point of disagreement with his opponents is not their teaching about the Jewish law but the way they conduct their ministry, not their doctrine but their demeanor. Echoing God's instructions to Samuel about choosing a king for Israel, Paul says that his opponents look on the "face" rather than on the "heart" (compare 1 Sam 16:7 LXX).[20] Like Samuel, who was impressed with the appearance of David's brother Eliab and thought that he was surely the Lord's anointed, Paul's opponents are impressed with outward credentials rather than the condition of the heart.[21]

This is confirmed by the other two references in 2 Corinthians 1—9 to trouble in Corinth. Telling the Corinthians in 6:12-13 that their affection for him has become restricted, Paul urges them to "open wide" their hearts to him just as he has opened his heart to them. Similarly, in 7:2-3 he urges the Corinthians to "make room" for him since, as he has "said before" (in 3:2), the Corinthians are in his heart.[22] He wants the Corinthians to allow him to be "written" on their hearts, just as God's Spirit has "written" them on his heart (3:2). Paul's primary concern, in other words, is that his opponents, by emphasizing their outward credentials, have alienated some of the Corinthians from him. In response, Paul appeals to those who have been alienated to recognize the importance of inward rather than outward credentials and to accept him into their hearts as he has accepted them into his. The content of his opponents' teaching is not Paul's concern, but their underhanded way of wooing his own "children" (6:13) away from him.

In chapters 10—13 the references to Paul's opponents become more frequent and the shape of their opposition more clearly defined. Paul refers to them explicitly in 10:2, when he speaks of "some who suspect us of living according to the flesh." This expression is similar to the language he used in 1:17 to deny that when he changed his travel plans and decided to visit the Corinthians only once rather than twice, he acted "according to the flesh." It may mean that Paul's opponents used his change in plans to accuse the apostle of instability and weakness.[23] This seems confirmed in 10:10, where Paul tells us that one of his opponents claims, "His letters are weighty and strong, but his bodily presence is weak and his speech amounts to nothing."

Paul says two verses later that his opponents "commend themselves," "measure themselves by themselves" and "compare themselves with themselves" (10:12). Against this attitude he claims that the Lord's commendation, not one's self-commendation, results in acceptance (10:18). The word *commend (synistēmi)*, used twice in this verse, was first introduced in 3:1, where Paul began talking about not needing letters of commendation similar to the ones that had accompanied his opponents to Corinth: "Are we beginning to commend ourselves to you again?" he asks. Since he uses the word nine times in this letter, and only five times in the rest of his correspondence combined, and since the word appears with reference to his opponents not only in 3:1 and 10:18 but in 5:12 and 10:12 as well, it seems safe to assume that a major emphasis of Paul's opponents was a comparison between his credentials and theirs.[24] Up to this point, therefore, nothing in Paul's description of his opponents indicates that the *content* of their teaching was at issue. Paul's quarrel with them continues to focus on the style of their ministry.

This assessment seems at first to be contradicted by 2 Corinthians 11:3-4, which expresses Paul's fear that the Corinthians will be led astray by the preaching of "another Jesus" and "another gospel." The next two verses, however, reveal that this alternate gospel differs from the true one at the level of conduct rather than of theological substance. Paul's denunciation of his opponents in 2 Corinthians 11:13-14 as "false apostles, deceitful workers" who disguise themselves as apostles of Christ and so imitate Satan's methods seems to confirm this understanding of 11:3-6. Here Paul's anger is directed not at the content of his opponents' verbal teaching—they are, after all, well disguised as apostles of Christ and angels of light—but at their "deeds" (11:15).

Further confirmation comes from Paul's inference that his opponents are boasting "according to the flesh" (2 Cor 11:17) and his description of their behavior when among the Corinthians: "For you submit if someone enslaves you, preys upon you, takes advantage of you, puts on airs or hits you in the face" (11:19-20). Instead of quarreling with the content of his opponents' claims about themselves, moreover, Paul persistently makes the same claims for himself, ironically imitating the way his antagonists boast of their credentials. Thus Paul says that he too is a Hebrew, an Israelite, a part of Abraham's seed and a servant of Christ (11:21-23; compare 10:7; 12:11). Similarly, when he turns to the effect his opponents are having on the Corinthians, his focus is not on false beliefs into which the Corinthians have strayed but on the reprehensible behavior into which their new leaders have drawn them: "For I fear lest when I come I find you not as I wish and lest I be found by you not as you wish—lest there be quarreling, jealousy, anger, factions, slander, gossip, conceit and disorder" (12:20).

At issue here is the *behavior* of Paul's opponents and its effects on those who follow them. This behavior, not the content of his opponents' preaching, taints their proclamation of the gospel and makes it false.

Paul's Allusions to the Mosaic Law

If the scenario painted here with the broad strokes of Paul's explicit references is correct, then his evaluation of the Mosaic covenant in 2 Corinthians 3 is not prompted by the content of his opponents' message but is Paul's own construction. It provides Paul's own theological perspective on the claims of his opponents that written letters of recommendation to and from various congregations are the marks of the true apostle. This passage, then, gives an extraordinarily clear statement of the apostle's view of the law—a statement that is all the more significant because Paul himself raises the issue and so demonstrates its importance to his theology.

The Corinthian correspondence, then, provides a unique opportunity to investigate Paul's attitude toward the law. Unlike the Thessalonian letters, which never mention the law explicitly, Paul's letters to Corinth use the word *law (nomos)* and the closely related expressions *commandments of God* and *covenant* in several passages.[25] Like the Thessalonian correspondence, however, 1 and 2 Corinthians were written to a congregation composed of Gentiles who, prior to their conversion to Christianity, had worshiped idols. In these letters, then, we can expect Paul to add depth and detail to the picture of his view of the law which the Thessalonian letters supply. These added features come not least from a close look at the passages in the letters that do not refer to the Mosaic law explicitly but rely on concepts whose full significance becomes clear only against the background of the Mosaic law.

In a number of passages that do not refer to "the law" explicitly, Paul implies that the Corinthian community, although composed primarily of uncircumcised Gentiles, is the eschatologically restored people of God described by the biblical prophets. As this eschatologically restored people, the Corinthian church will, Paul assumes, resemble the portrait of God's people painted in the Mosaic law. Like the people described in the Mosaic law, Paul believes, the Corinthian church should be "holy" or separate from those outside the church.

Paul has not simply transferred the Jewish law to the church, however, for in his mind the boundaries that mark out the holiness of the restored people of God are not identical to the boundaries laid out in the Mosaic law. The continuity and discontinuity between sanctity under the Mosaic law and sanctity within the church are particularly clear in four descriptions he provides of the Corinthian community.

The People of God
Throughout the Corinthian correspondence, and especially in 1 Corinthians, Paul assumes that the Corinthian community is part of a widespread communion of believers (1 Cor 1:2) who are the chosen people of God. This is especially clear in the opening paragraphs of the first letter, where Paul stresses the unity of the church in its common calling. Paul addresses his readers as "the *church of God* in Corinth, *sanctified* in Christ Jesus and *called to be holy*" (1:2). As study of the Thessalonian letters revealed (chapter three), these expressions recall the description of Israel in the law of Moses.[26] The Corinthians, like ancient Israel, are the "assembly of the Lord"; they are set apart from the Gentiles by their conduct; and they were called into this special status by God himself (compare 1:9).

Paul explores the nature of this calling in the initial paragraphs of the body of 1 Corinthians (1:10-31), when he expresses his dismay that the Corinthians are not unified but are instead taking pride in their adherence to various leaders, whether Paul himself, Apollos, Cephas or Christ (vv. 10-17). Against this display of divisive boasting, he argues that "no flesh may boast before God" because God has chosen ways of working that exclude worldly boasting: he has worked through the foolishness of the preaching of the cross to save those who believed, Paul says, and those who believed turned out to be a ragtag collection of the foolish, the weak, the insignificant and "the nothings" of the world (vv. 18-29).

In the course of this argument Paul reveals that he considers this group, so insignificant from the world's perspective, to be parallel to the specially chosen people of God revealed in Israel's Scriptures. Thus Paul not only refers to the Corinthians as "the called" (1:24; compare 1:26 and Is 41:9; 48:12; 51:2) but uses the word *eklegomai* to say three times (1:27-28) that "God *chose*" the Corinthians. The Septuagint uses this term to describe God's choice not only of Israel to be his people but also of Jerusalem to be his city, the temple to be his place of worship and the priests to be his special servants in the temple. The word occurs here and in only one other place in Paul's letters (Eph 1:4).[27] In 1:27-28, moreover, it occurs within the context of other language that has emphasized the status of the Corinthian church as the people of God. Thus it seems reasonable to conclude that Paul has purposely selected the word at this point in his argument because of the connotations it carried in the Septuagint. The element that Israel, Jerusalem, the temple and the priests have in common is their "sanctification": each was "called" by God to be set apart either from the rest of creation or from ordinary use for God's special purposes. Here, then, Paul reminds the Corinthians that they owe their special status as those set apart to be the people of God not to their own wisdom or social standing but to God's sovereign power to nullify "the things which are" by means of "the things which are not."

It is consistent with this conviction that Paul believes that his readers are no longer Gentiles. In chapter 5 Paul expresses his alarm that the Corinthian community continues to tolerate sexual sin in its midst, and he advises the Corinthians to take steps to solve the problem. This particular sin, Paul says, is not found "even among the Gentiles" (5:1). The clear implication is that the Corinthian believers themselves are no longer Gentiles.[28] The same kind of expression occurs in 12:2, where Paul begins his discussion of Spirit-inspired speech with the statement that when the Corinthians were "Gentiles," they were led astray to "dumb idols."

The reason that Paul considers the Corinthians to be Gentiles no longer becomes clear in chapter 10. Here he assumes that they stand in continuity with ancient Israel. Israel's ancestors are the Corinthians' ancestors, Israel's history their history (10:1).[29] Because of this, Paul says, the Corinthians should not participate in meals eaten in pagan temples as part of the worship of pagan gods.[30] Instead they should learn from the experience of their ancestors that neither baptism nor nourishment from spiritual food will exempt God's people from judgment if they sin (10:2-10).

In spite of this, it would be a mistake to think that Paul believes that the uncircumcised Corinthians are Jews, as if through believing the gospel they had become proselytes. The church seems instead to be a third entity to which the descriptions "Jew" and "Greek" do not fully apply.[31] Both Jews and Greeks stumble over the offense of the cross, but God summons both to join "the people called" (*hoi klētoi*, 1:24), and Paul considers the two labels to be irrelevant to the body of believers who have been made to drink from the one Spirit of God (12:13). This concept appears most clearly at the end of Paul's teaching on eating meat that may have been offered to idols (10:23—11:1). "Give no offense," he says, "whether to Jews, or to Greeks, or to the church of God" (10:32). The newly constituted people of God is not, therefore, "Israel" in an unqualified sense. It stands in continuity with ancient Israel and can be described in terms formerly applied to Israel, but it is itself a new entity.

The Holy People of God

When Paul echoes Ezekiel's vision of a renewed Israel, he is concerned to summon the Corinthians to a life of purity that is consistent with their status as God's eschatologically restored community. The tension between Paul and the Corinthians in this letter lies in the fundamental incompatibility between the Corinthians' attempt to define the boundaries of their community on the basis of knowledge and Paul's attempt to define its boundaries on the basis of a biblically determined holiness.[32] The Corinthians take pride in their divisions, sexual immorality, participation in pagan worship and outwardly impressive spiritual gifts. But Paul asserts that such knowledge only "puffs up" (8:1) and that the quality that should set the people of God apart is a holiness that corresponds to some extent with the holiness prescribed in the Mosaic law.

The biblical shape of Paul's concept of holiness appears most clearly in chapter 5. At issue is a case of sexual immorality so heinous, Paul says, that it is not even tolerated among the Gentiles: "a certain man has the wife of his father" (*gynaika tina tou patros echein*, 5:1). Paul's understanding of this sin and his response to it derive from the treatment of the same sin in Leviticus and Deuteronomy. Leviticus 18:7-8 (LXX) describes the sin this way: "You shall not uncover the nakedness of your father or the nakedness of your mother, for she is your mother and you shall not uncover her nakedness. The nakedness of the wife of your father *[gynaikos patros sou]* you shall not uncover: it is the nakedness of your father" (compare Lev 20:11). The similarity between this and Paul's description of the sin probably indicates that Paul had the Leviticus passage in mind.[33]

The advice Paul gives for punishing this sin also comes from the Mosaic law. Leviticus commands that those who commit the sins discussed in chapter 18 be "cut off from their people" (18:29) and in chapter 20 that the man who lies with his father's wife be put to death (20:11). Paul approximates this penalty when he advises the Corinthians "to hand such a man over to Satan for the destruction of his flesh in order that his spirit should be saved in the day of the Lord" (1 Cor 5:5). Although Paul is calling for the man's excommunication rather than his execution, the phrase "destruction of his flesh" is probably based on the biblical injunction that the offender be executed.[34] In addition, at the conclusion to his argument Paul instructs the Corinthians to "expel the evil one from among you" (5:13). These words are taken from a refrain that frequently appears in Deuteronomy after the appropriate punishment for an offender, usually death, has been described (Deut 17:7; 19:19; 22:21, 24; 24:7).

Why does Paul recommend such a harsh punishment? Because, he says in 5:6-8, the Corinthians must scrupulously maintain the character of a holy people. The language he uses to illustrate this holiness comes directly from the Mosaic law.[35] Just as a little leaven works its way through an entire lump of dough and therefore all leaven must be purged from the home at Passover, so the Corinthians are to purge themselves from evil and celebrate, uncontaminated by spiritual impurity, the Passover feast at which Christ is the sacrificial lamb (5:6-8).

Paul is concerned about the sin of the man who engaged in sexual indiscretions with his stepmother, because it is forbidden in the Jewish law. His response to the offense is roughly what the Jewish law recommends. And the rationale for dealing with the offense decisively is identical to the biblical rationale: the Corinthians are the holy people of God and must demonstrate their holiness by purging the community of those who would compromise this special status.

The biblical shape of Paul's concept of holiness also emerges from 6:1-11, where the distinctive character of God's people continues to be an issue. Some within the community have apparently defrauded (*apostereō*, v. 7; compare *kleptēs* and *harpagmos*, v. 10) other believers, and this has resulted in lawsuits between members of the community before unbelieving magistrates (vv. 1-7). Paul is appalled at this behavior for two reasons. First, it compromises the holiness of the community because it asks those outside God's people to adjudicate the very ethical conduct that constitutes the boundary between God's people and those outside (vv. 1-8). Paul expresses his disgust at the Corinthians' feeble understanding of their holy status with the rhetorical question "Is there no wise man *[sophos]* among you who is able to judge between brothers *[ana meson tou adelphou autou]*?" (v. 5). His language echoes Deuteronomy 1:15-16, where Moses describes the system of adjudication that he set up within Israel:[36]

> I took from among you wise men *[andras sophous]*, both knowledgeable and discerning, and I appointed them to rule over you as rulers of thousands, and hundreds, and fifties, and tens, and [I appointed] governors for your judges. I commanded your judges at that time saying, "Listen among your brothers *[ana meson tōn adelphōn hymōn]* and judge justly

between a man and his brother or his resident alien *[ana meson andros kai ana meson adelphou kai ana meson prosēlytou autou]*." (LXX)

Paul asserts, therefore, that the Corinthian community has violated the character of the people of God as it is described in the Mosaic law by taking its cases before unbelieving magistrates.

Second, Paul also condemns the kinds of behavior that produced the civil suits in the first place as incompatible with the status of God's restored people. "But you have been washed," he tells them, "but you have been sanctified, but you have been justified in the name of the Lord Jesus Christ and in the Spirit of our God" (1 Cor 6:11). They are the people whom Ezekiel prophesied God would purify by sprinkling and so sanctify once and for all (Ezek 36:25-29), and Paul echoes Ezekiel's vision of the restored people of God as he registers his dismay at their behavior.

The level of continuity between Paul and the Mosaic law on the subject of holiness runs deep. But it would be a mistake to think that no differences exist. Paul considers the Mosaic law's demand for holiness authoritative, but he uses the law to support this idea in a different way from the typical Judaism of his day. Paul's treatment of the Passover theme within his argument that the Corinthians should not associate with evil "brothers" illustrates the point. Whereas Paul appeals to the observance of Passover as a metaphor for purifying the community from "anyone who calls himself a brother" but who is "sexually immoral, a greedy person, an idolater, a reviler, a drunkard or a thief" (1 Cor 5:11), he nowhere calls for the observance of the festival itself as a marker of the community's sanctity.[37] The Mosaic law is important to Paul, and its call for sanctity among God's people authoritative, but the boundary markers for the sanctity of God's people are not identical to those within the Mosaic law.[38]

The Temple and God's Presence in the Old Testament

It is a natural development from the idea that the community of believers is God's eschatologically restored and sanctified people to the notion that they constitute the temple of God. Leviticus claims that if God's people are obedient to his covenant, he will bless them with his continued presence in their midst (Lev 26:11), and throughout Scripture the temple, or its early counterpart the tabernacle, is understood to be the dwelling place of God's presence among his people. Both are said to be the house where God lives (2 Sam 7:6; 1 Kings 8:13; compare Ps 27:4; 68:35) or where his name resides (1 Kings 8:29, 43-44, 48-49), and the temple is frequently the site from which God's saving action on behalf of his people comes (Ps 20:2; 28:2; 63:2; 84:1-12;

Jon 2:7-9).[39] In light of this, it seems natural for Ezekiel to equate the destruction of the temple and the exile of Israel with the removal of God's presence from his temple and thus from his defiled people (Ezek 10:18-19; 11:22-23; compare 39:23-24, 29).[40]

It also seems natural that Ezekiel's vision of Israel's restoration should include God's return to dwell among his purified people in a glorious new sanctuary. In 37:20-28 the prophet predicts that when God calls his people out of exile, he will not only unify them into a single nation, place a king like David over them, cleanse them from their sin and make a covenant of peace with them but also return to his people and establish his sanctuary in their midst. This sanctuary will be, in Ezekiel's characteristic expression, God's "holy place" (*miqdoší*, MT; *ta hagia mou*, LXX): "My dwelling place shall be with them; and I will be their God, and they shall be my people. Then the nations shall know that I the LORD sanctify Israel, when my sanctuary is among them forevermore" (37:27-28).

Ezekiel 40—48 expands this notion into a detailed picture of the future sanctuary, the climax of which is, once again, the appearance of God's Spirit and the return of God's glorious presence to dwell in the sanctuary among a people newly purified from idolatry and sexual immorality:

> And there, the glory of the God of Israel was coming from the east; the sound was like the sound of mighty waters; and the earth shone with his glory. The vision I saw was like the vision that I had seen when he came to destroy the city, and like the vision that I had seen by the river Chebar; and I fell upon my face. As the glory of the LORD entered the temple by the gate facing east, the spirit lifted me up, and brought me into the inner court; and the glory of the LORD filled the temple.
>
> While the man was standing beside me, I heard someone speaking to me out of the temple. He said to me: Mortal, this is the place of my throne and the place for the soles of my feet, where I will reside among the people of Israel forever. The house of Israel shall no more defile my holy name, neither they nor their kings, by their whoring, and by the corpses of their kings at their death. (43:2-7)

The Temple and God's Presence in the Corinthian Letters

Like Ezekiel, Paul moves easily from the notion of the restored people of God to the idea that the locus of God's eschatologically given presence among this people is the temple.

The community as God's building (1 Corinthians 3:5-17). In 1 Corinthians 3:5-17 Paul is concerned with someone who entered the Corinthian community after him and began exercising some spiritual authority (v. 10) over the church Paul had established. Paul is restrained in his criticism, but he is worried about the divisiveness that this person has brought to the community (vv. 3-4). He begins to address the problem by referring to himself and Apollos, both of whom had worked with the Corinthians and both of whom had contributed to the spiritual development of the community. He chooses an agricultural metaphor to make his point: "I planted, Apollos watered, but God caused the growth. So, then, neither the one who plants is anything, nor the one who waters, but God who causes the growth" (vv. 6-7).

He continues by pointing out that the field laborers are equally valuable and will receive pay according to their labor in the Corinthian field (vv. 8-9). As he concludes this analogy, Paul abruptly switches to another: "you are God's field, God's building" (*oikodomē*, v. 9). With the change in analogies comes a change in focus from the relationship between Paul and Apollos to the relationship between Paul's foundational work among the Corinthians and the work of another, unnamed person who is building on this foundation. Although it is intriguing to speculate who this person was and in what ways he built on Paul's foundation, the most interesting aspect of the passage for the student of Paul's view of the law is that Paul views the Corinthian "building" as the temple of God.[41] Not only does Paul hint at this through his list of building materials in verse 12, but he states it directly in verses 16-17 when he issues a strong warning to those Corinthians who, perhaps at the encouragement of their unnamed leader, are dividing the Corinthian community into competing factions: "Do you not know that you are the temple [*naos*] of God and that the Spirit of God dwells among you?[42] If anyone destroys the temple of God, God will destroy him. For the temple of God is holy, which you are."

Paul's phrase "Do you not know" shows that what he says here is not merely a rhetorical flourish but an important statement that the Corinthians should understand as a matter of course, presumably because it belonged to the foundational body of the initial instruction Paul had given while he was among them.[43] As God's eschatological temple, the Corinthian community must preserve its unity, for to be torn apart into factions was equivalent within the believing community to the destruction of Solomon's temple at the hands of the Babylonians. As God's judgment on the Babylonians showed, God does not take lightly those who treat his temple with contempt.[44]

The individual as God's temple (1 Corinthians 6:19-20). In 6:19-20 Paul continues to echo Ezekiel's imagery of the eschatological temple as the dwelling place of God's restored presence. As in 5:1-13, Paul must address the problem of the Corinthians' tolerance of sexual immorality among members of the believing community. In opposition to Paul's idea of sanctity, the Corinthians are apparently saying that "all things are lawful" (6:12), since "food is meant for the stomach and the stomach for food" (6:13). If these phrases are Corinthian slogans, then the Corinthians have probably taken Paul's relaxed stance toward Jewish dietary scruples as justification to engage in illicit sexual behavior.[45] In fact, if 8:10 is an indication that some of the Corinthians saw nothing wrong with eating cultic meals in the pagan temples of the city, then visits to these same pagan shrines may have provided the occasion for their sexual immorality.[46]

Paul will address the problem of eating cultic meals in pagan temples in 8:1-13 and 10:1-22, but here he focuses on the problem of visiting prostitutes (6:15-16). The Corinthians should "flee sexual immorality" (6:18), he says, because each believer's body functions as the temple (naos) of God, the residence of the Holy Spirit, and therefore should be used to glorify God (6:19-20).[47] Paul is telling the Corinthians that they are, as individuals, the eschatological locus of God's presence, the residence of his Spirit, and that they must live in a way that is consistent with the glorious presence of God within them. The unstated assumption is that they are the eschatological fulfillment of the prophetic promise that God's glory would one day dwell within a newly restored temple located in the midst of a people purified from idolatry and sexual immorality (Ezek 43:2, 4-9; 44:4).[48]

The community as God's temple (2 Corinthians 6:14—7:1). If any doubt remains that Paul is echoing Ezekiel's prophecies of an eschatologically restored temple in the Corinthian correspondence, 2 Corinthians 6:14—7:1 should banish it.[49] The Corinthians' antagonism toward Paul had reached a climax after they received 1 Corinthians and, instead of responding to his advice, welcomed a group of itinerant Jewish teachers into their community. These teachers both called themselves apostles and were opponents of Paul (11:12-15, 22-23).[50] An unpleasant personal encounter with Paul in Corinth ensued, and he followed this difficult visit with an anguished letter (2:4; 7:8) whose tone he began to regret shortly after he sent it with Titus (7:5, 8). Perhaps because he was anxious to find out the letter's effect on the Corinthians, Paul set out to meet Titus and encountered him in Macedonia on his return journey (2:12-13; 7:5, 8).[51] In response to what he heard from Titus, he wrote 2 Corinthians.

Although Paul's primary feeling at hearing Titus's report was relief (2 Cor 7:6-16), we learn in 3:1 and 5:12 that he was still worried that at least some of the Corinthians continued to be impressed by the outward credentials of his opponents. Paul also seems to know that his opponents continued to lead some within the community astray. "We beg you," he says in 5:20, "be reconciled to God," and in 6:1 he continues, "We exhort you not to receive the grace of God in vain."[52] He then appears to take a defensive posture in 6:3, as if answering an accusation: he gives no one any reason to take offense, he says, so that his ministry might not be faulted. Paul next seems to echo his opponents' emphasis on outward commendation when he ironically commends himself to the Corinthians by listing the various hardships he has endured as he has carried out his commission to preach the gospel.[53] The section ends with a direct appeal to the Corinthians' affections: "Our mouth is open to you, Corinthians. Our heart is wide. You are not restricted by us, but you are restricted in your affections. Instead, in return (I speak as to children), widen your hearts also" (6:11-13).

At this point Paul's tone becomes harsh, and he urges the Corinthians in a series of rhetorical questions not to be "misyoked with unbelievers" (6:14-16). The unbelievers in question are probably Paul's opponents, whom he later calls "false apostles, evil workers, people disguised as apostles of Christ," Satan's servants (11:13-15).[54] In 6:14—7:1, therefore, Paul says forcefully what he has been suggesting at various points throughout the argument so far: the Corinthians should expel these people from their midst. Paul states the reason for this harsh advice in 6:16: "What agreement has the temple *[naō]* of God with idols?[55] For we are the temple *[naos]* of the living God." He then offers a paragraph of quotations from and allusions to various passages of Scripture which speak of Israel's eschatological restoration, of God's dwelling among his people during that period and of the consequent necessity for his people to be pure and holy.

The first quotation (6:16) gives the biblical support for Paul's statement that believers are "the temple of the living God." He conflates the Septuagint's rendering of Leviticus 26:11-12 and Ezekiel 37:27 in order to show that Ezekiel's expectations of a restored people whose sanctity and purity would allow God to dwell in their midst had been fulfilled in the church. Leviticus 26 is the final chapter of the "Holiness Code" (Lev 17—26), and like Deuteronomy 28—30 it promises blessing for obedience to the code and punishment for disobedience. The section devoted to disobedience and punishment culminates in warning of the exile of Israel from the land. The final note in the chapter, however, is one of hope as the Lord promises that even in their exile he will remember his people, be merciful to them and keep his covenant with them. Ezekiel, writing from within the prophesied punitive exile, echoes the language of the blessing section of Leviticus 26 when he prophesies that God will one day restore his exiled people to their land. Just as Leviticus 26:11-12 had said that if the people of Israel obeyed the law God would dwell with them, would no longer spurn them, would move among them and would be their God, so Ezek 37:24-28 prophesies that in the period of restoration Israel would follow God's laws, God would dwell among them, and God himself would sanctify them. In 37:27 the prophet closely paraphrases Leviticus 26:11-12:[56]

> And I will put my dwelling place *[miškānî]* in your midst, and I will not spurn you. And I will walk in your midst, and I will be God to you and you will be a people to me. (Lev 26:11-12 MT)
>
> And my dwelling place *[miškānî]* will be among them, and I will be God to them and they will be a people to me. (Ezek 37:27 MT)

Ezekiel, therefore, believed that the blessings Leviticus promised to God's people if they obeyed the law would come to Israel during the period of its restoration.

Paul appears to have understood Ezekiel's echo of Leviticus and conflated elements of the Septuagint's translation of both Lev 26:12 and Ezek 37:27 in order to support his contention that the believing community was the locus of the eschatologically given presence of God. Placing the passages side by side in a literal translation shows this clearly. Elements of Paul's text which are drawn from Leviticus appear in bold type, and elements taken from Ezekiel in italic type.

> **And I will set my covenant among you, and my soul will not find you offensive. And I will move among you, and I will be your God, and you yourselves will be my people.** (Lev 26:11-12 LXX)
>
> *And my dwelling place will be among them, and I will be God to them, and they themselves will be a people to me.* (Ezek 37:27 LXX)
>
> I will dwell and **I will move** among *them,* and I will be their God and *they them*selves will be **my people.** (2 Cor 6:16)

Paul, like Ezekiel, has changed the references to Israel from the second person to the third person, but like Leviticus has kept the notion of God moving among his people. The grammar of Paul's quotation, moreover, follows the Septuagint of Leviticus 26:12 rather than the Septuagint's more literal rendering of the Hebrew in Ezekiel 37:27.[57]

All of this means that when Paul wrote he was not simply thinking of the Ezekiel text, which happens to paraphrase the Leviticus text, but that he was thinking of both texts, indeed that he viewed the Leviticus text through the interpretive lens of Ezekiel. For Paul, then, the eschatological blessing of God's presence had dawned.[58] To admit a group of false teachers into the company of the restored people of God would be to turn the clock back to the era of sin and punishment (2 Cor 6:16).

Instead, Paul continues in 6:17a, the Corinthians should remove themselves from impurity. Here he echoes Isaiah 52:1-12, another prophetic passage whose subject is the eschatological restoration of God's people after their punishment in the exile.[59] "Long ago, my people went down into Egypt to reside there as aliens," the prophet says; "the Assyrian, too, has oppressed them without cause" (52:4). In the future, however, the prophet predicts that God will rescue his people from their plight in the sight of all the Gentiles:

> Depart, depart, go out from there and do not touch what is unclean! Go out from their midst! Be separate, you who bear the vessels of the Lord! For you will not go out in confusion, nor will you flee in fear, for the Lord will go before you, and the one who gathers you together is the Lord God of Israel. (Is 52:11-12 LXX)

In the Septuagint's interpretation of the prophet's vision, Israel's return from exile will be like a new exodus; yet the flight will not take place in haste and fear as it had the first time. Instead, it will provide the opportunity for a renewal of Israel's sanctity: once again the people of God will be pure and separate from the surrounding nations. Similarly, Paul wants the Corinthians, as recipients of the promised era of restoration, to separate themselves from impurity: "Therefore go out from their midst and be separate, says the Lord, and do not touch what is unclean" (2 Cor 6:17a).

In 2 Corinthians 6:17b-18 Paul returns to a discussion of why the Corinthians must remain sanctified. He echoes two texts to show that the Corinthians must maintain the boundaries of the people of God because they are the eschatological fulfillment of the prophetic expectations that God would restore his people. First, he uses a phrase from Ezekiel 20:34 (compare 20:41) to refer to God's future gathering of his people from the lands into which they have been scattered *(kai eisdexomai hymas)*. This gathering, says Ezekiel, will involve purging all the impious and rebellious from the midst of Israel (20:38). Second, Paul echoes Nathan's prophetic utterance to David in which "the Lord God Almighty says" that he will be a father to David's son (2 Sam 7:8, 14 LXX). This text was widely interpreted in the Judaism of Paul's day as a reference to God's adoption of his people Israel as his children during the period of Israel's eschatological restoration.[60]

Read within this context, 2 Corinthians 7:1 provides an appropriate conclusion to Paul's argument: "Since we possess these promises, beloved, let us cleanse ourselves from every fleshly and spiritual defilement by perfecting holiness in the fear of God."

Paul believes that the Corinthians constitute the community in which scriptural promises of the restoration of God's presence among his people have been fulfilled. As this restored community, they have the presence of God in their midst, and so they must purify themselves by removing any "taint" *(molysmos)* of compromise with evil (7:1).

The Puzzling Shape of Sanctity in the Corinthian Letters

In summary, Paul believed that the communities he established represented the fulfillment of the prophetic promises that God would reestablish his temple and place his presence among his people in the period of Israel's restoration. With language reminiscent of Leviticus, Paul says that God's people must be pure in order to constitute an appropriate dwelling place for God's presence, and like Ezekiel, Paul believed that this Levitical concept would characterize the eschatologically restored people of God. The pattern of Paul's thinking about the sanctity of God's people in the age of restoration duplicates the pattern in these two biblical books. Moreover, as he shows by his explicit citation of these portions of the Law and the Prophets, the duplication is more than a fortuitous parallel: Paul obtained the pattern from the Bible and supported its legitimacy before his Gentile readers by citing the articulation of this pattern in these biblical books as the very words of God (2 Cor 6:16).

In spite of this deep indebtedness to the Mosaic law and the prophets, however, differences between Paul and his predecessors also emerge. As with Paul's belief that the Corinthians are the people of God and God's holy elect, the measure of continuity between Paul and the Mosaic law is balanced by a puzzling amount of discontinuity. First, Ezekiel envisioned a physically restored temple, not a spiritually restored community that could be metaphorically described as God's temple.[61] Ezekiel's detailed description of the physical arrangement and dimensions of the temple puts this beyond dispute. Paul, of course, identified the temple with the community of believers (1 Cor 3:16-17; 2 Cor 6:16) or the bodies of individual believers (1 Cor 6:19) rather than with a geographically fixed building.

Second, in an attempt to safeguard a restored Israel against the idolatry to which it had succumbed in the days of the first temple, Ezekiel banished uncircumcised foreigners from it (Ezek 44:9). Paul, on the other hand, viewed circumcision (1 Cor 7:19) and national affiliation (1 Cor 1:24) as irrelevant to the boundaries of God's metaphorical temple of believers. So once again Paul has used the pattern of biblical holiness laid out in the Mosaic law, and many of the terms the Mosaic law uses to describe that pattern, but he has transformed significant details within the broad pattern.

Given his allusions to the Mosaic law in the Corinthian letters, it is clear that Paul assumes the shape of the Corinthians' faith should roughly duplicate the shape of Israelite religion as it is described in the Mosaic law: God's people should be sanctified because God's presence dwells with them. Several of the details of this sanctity duplicate the expectations of the Mosaic law. Nevertheless, Paul's significant departures from the Mosaic law demonstrate that he did not envision a renewal of the Mosaic covenant in the period of restoration. General elements of continuity merge with elements of discontinuity, but with only Paul's allusive references to the law before us, it is difficult to see how the two are related. The picture becomes clearer when we view it from the perspective of Paul's explicit references to the law.

CHAPTER FIVE

OLD COVENANT & NEW IN THE CORINTHIAN LETTERS: The Paradox Explained

The paradox of continuity and discontinuity in Paul's allusive references to the law reemerges in clearer form, and is to a large extent resolved, in Paul's explicit references to the law in the Corinthian letters. Several of these references continue to show the familiar tension between enduring elements of the Mosaic law and the belief that the Mosaic law is no longer in force, but at several points they provide hints about how Paul held these two ideas together. When we add to these hints Paul's brief reference to "the new covenant" in one passage and his extended comparison of the new covenant with the old in another, many of the puzzling features of his allusions to the Mosaic law begin to fall into place.[1]

The Law of Moses and the Commandments of God
Paul's first explicit reference to the law in 1 Corinthians is also the most puzzling. He is busy answering a written inquiry (7:1) from the Corinthians

about sexual relationships and marriage when he articulates the principle that "each must live as the Lord has allotted, each as God has called" (7:17). The circumcised and uncircumcised should remain as they are (for circumcision means nothing), slaves should not be worried by their slavery (but should obtain freedom if possible), and the unmarried would do well to remain unmarried (although marriage is no sin; 7:18-40). In the course of his admonition that no one should change his status with respect to circumcision, Paul explains that the rite is unimportant: "Neither circumcision nor uncircumcision is anything, but keeping the commandments of God [tērēsis entolōn theou]" (7:19).

The phrase "the commandments of God" is frequently used in the Jewish and Jewish Christian literature of Paul's time to refer to keeping the law of Moses. Late in the second century B.C., for example, the grandson of the Jewish scholar Ben Sira translated his grandfather's summary of the law this way: "Guard yourself in every act, for this also is the keeping of the commandments [tērēsis entolōn]" (Sirach 32:23).

Similarly, Matthew translates Jesus' reply to the rich young man's question about how to obtain eternal life as "Keep the commandments" (tēreson tas entolas), a clear reference to the law of Moses, as Jesus' list of commandments and summary of the first table of the law from Leviticus 19:18 demonstrate (Mt 19:17-19). Moreover, the Septuagint's translation of Ezra 9:4 uses the phrase "commandments of God" as a synonym for the law of Moses. The phrase Paul has chosen to refer to God's commandments, therefore, is one that in his cultural context clearly referred to the Mosaic law.

If this is so, how can Paul contrast the irrelevance of circumcision with the importance of God's commands? Circumcision, is, after all, a prominent requirement within the law of Moses (Lev 12:3; compare Gen 17:10-27).[2] Although Paul offers no explanation for his startling statement, it significantly preserves the same paradox we have seen in Paul's allusive references to the law: certain commands, such as the commands not to worship idols and to preserve sexual purity, remain unchanged, but others, often those that particularly distinguished Jew from Gentile, are no longer valid. Paul's understanding of the nature of "the commandments of God" becomes clearer in his subsequent references to the teaching of Jesus, the new covenant and the law of Christ.[3]

The Mosaic Law and the Teaching of Jesus

Paul's approach to the law comes more clearly into focus in the passage where he first uses the term *law (nomos)*. In 1 Corinthians 8:1—11:1, according to the most likely understanding of the passage, Paul addresses two problems.[4] In 8:1-13 and 10:1-22 he argues that eating meat in the cultic setting of an idol's temple is wrong because it might cause a weaker brother to stumble and because it is idolatry. In 10:23—11:1 he argues that eating meat purchased in the marketplace is not wrong, even if the meat has been used in idolatrous ceremonies.

Chapter 9 at first seems to fit into this context only awkwardly, because it never mentions meat offered to idols and seems concerned primarily with proving the legitimacy of Paul's apostleship. Closer inspection of the chapter, however, shows that it is actually a continuation of Paul's argument in chapter 8. In 8:1-13 Paul addresses a group of Corinthians whose slogan is "we all have knowledge" (8:1) and who have apparently claimed that because they know that "an idol is nothing in the world" and that "there is no God but one" (8:4), they are free to participate in cultic meals in the many idol temples in Corinth (8:10).[5] Paul will argue in 10:1-22 that such participation in cultic meals is actually idolatry (10:14) and must therefore be stopped. Here, however, he argues that even if it were the right of the knowledgeable Corinthians to eat in such temples, doing so would not be loving toward those who are offended by the practice. "Therefore," he concludes, "if food offends my brother, I will never eat meat lest I offend my brother" (8:13).

In 9:1-27 Paul illustrates this principle by discussing how he has given up one of his rights for the sake of the gospel. As a genuine apostle, he maintains, he has the same right that "the other apostles and the brothers of the Lord and Cephas" (v. 5) have to be supported by the communities in which he ministers rather than to work for income (vv. 4-6). Nevertheless, he has given up this right, he says, so that nothing he does might hinder the gospel (v. 12; compare v. 15).

To make the case that he actually possesses the right to be supported by the communities in which he ministers, Paul appeals to two types of evidence. He calls one of these "human" and therefore implies that the other is "divine" (9:8).[6] The first set accordingly appeals to his readers' knowledge of everyday life: a soldier is paid to fight, a farmer eats from his own crops, and a shepherd enjoys some of the dairy products that his flock produces. The second set appeals first to the law, second to the temple service and finally to a command of the Lord. All three elements of this second set of references are helpful for understanding Paul's approach to the law.

First Paul quotes Deuteronomy 25:4, which he designates "the law of Moses" (1 Cor 9:9; compare 9:8): "Do not muzzle an ox while it threshes the grain." Paul identifies these as the words of God, who, he says, was not concerned about oxen but spoke "on account of us" (*di hēmas*, 9:9-10). Later, in chapter 10, Paul will say similarly that the events of the exodus happened to Israel "as examples, and were written for our instruction, to whom the ends of the ages have come" (10:11). The law of Moses still contains for believers the word of God, but it is interpreted in light of the eschatologically significant events that brought the new people of God into existence.[7]

Paul next turns to the activity of priests in the temple and uses it in the same way. "Do you not know," he says, "that those who work in the temple get their food from the temple, that those who serve at the altar share in the altar?" Since the law directed those who sacrificed to reserve a portion of the sacrifice for the priests who worked in the temple (Num 18:8, 31; Deut 18:1-2), Paul seems to be saying in this passage that as an apostle at work in God's eschatological "temple," he too is entitled to some material benefit from those he serves.[8] The relationship of priest to temple resembles Paul's relationship to the Corinthian community. The principle behind the laws that govern that relationship still apply, but the meaning those laws used to have for Israel has undergone a radical change within the new context.

The final, and climactic, witness Paul produces for his right to be supported by the communities in which he works is the command of Jesus that "those who preach the gospel should get their living from the gospel" (1 Cor 9:14). Paul feels no need, as he had in the case of Deuteronomy 25:4 a few verses earlier, to reinterpret these words or to use them in anything less than their literal sense.[9] They state simply and succinctly the principle that Paul has illustrated by means of his other witnesses. They are the final authority to which the other witnesses are subservient. And therefore they provide a critical insight into Paul's approach to the law: the law is in some sense authoritative, for it contains the speech of God, but it has been overwhelmed by the authority of Jesus' words.

In light of the eschatological situation of the believing community, some of the law, such as the command to circumcise, has been annulled, and some, such as the command governing the threshing of grain and the payment of priests, has been interpreted with an unusual boldness. All of it, however, has been placed under the authority of Christ.

The Law of God and the Law of Christ

Paul's next uses of the word *law* come only a few verses later, and within the same general context as his references in 1 Corinthians 9:8-9. Paul has now made his point that although he has the right to be supported by the communities in which he ministers, he does not make use of the right.

Instead, he says, he is willing to endure anything to advance the gospel (9:12). In 9:19-23 he illustrates the depth of his concern to "win" as many as possible by referring to his ministry among several social groups, each with particular characteristics. Paul explains that he is willing to give up his freedom and adopt the peculiar characteristics of each group in order to serve them more effectively:

> Although free from all people, I have enslaved myself to all people in order that I might win more. To the Jews I became as a Jew in order that I might win Jews. To those under the law I became as under the law, although I am not myself under the law, in order that I might win those under the law. To those without the law I became as without the law, although I was not without the law of God but subject to the law of Christ, in order that I might gain those without the law. To the weak I became weak in order that I might win the weak. To all people I became all things in order that by all means I might save some. But I do all things on account of the gospel, in order that I might jointly share in it.

Two aspects of this passage help us toward understanding Paul's view of the law generally. First, Paul uses the term *law* as a boundary marker for a particular social group. Since Paul's point is that he is willing to give up his own right not to conform to the norms of any particular group, it seems safe to assume that his reference to the law immediately after referring to the Jews means that he regards the law as a distinctive institution of Judaism. When he says that he became "as under the law," therefore, he means that he adopted certain observances that distinguished him from Gentiles and marked him off as a Jew.[10] Paul is quick to prevent misunderstanding, however, for he explains that although he did this when among Jews, he was not himself obligated to observe the particular customs of the Jews.[11]

Second, Paul says that he became "without the law" to those "without the law," and he uses a term *(anomos)* that in the Jewish literature of his period frequently referred to Gentiles. When used in this way, however, it most often carried the negative connotation of "godless Gentiles," or even "apostates from Judaism" when used of ethnic Jews.[12] To correct any misunderstanding in this direction, Paul adds that he was not "without the law of God but subject to the law of Christ *[ennomos Christou]*." This correction is significant, because it reveals that Paul equated the law of God with the law of Christ and that he considered this law to be different from the Mosaic law, at least as the Mosaic law was used to distinguish Jews from Gentiles.[13] "The law of God" here, moreover, is probably identical with "the commandments of God" in 7:19.[14]

Once again, continuity exists between Paul and Judaism with regard to the law, for he is still subject to something called "the law of God." Discontinuity also emerges, however, for Paul is no longer subject to the law that distinguishes Jews from Gentiles. Some evidence for the way Paul resolved this tension in his own thinking emerges from his use of the term *covenant* in 1 Corinthians 11:25.

The New Covenant

Paul's next reference to the law hints at a possible explanation for the puzzling mixture of continuity and discontinuity that we have seen so far in his allusions to and statements about the law. In 1 Corinthians 11:17-34 Paul admonishes the Corinthians to stop acting divisively at the Lord's Supper. Although Paul's language does not make the details of the situation clear, it seems that wealthy Corinthians were going ahead with sumptuous meals (v. 21) before the poor members of the believing community had been served (v. 33), and that all of this was happening within the context of the Lord's Supper (v. 20).[15] The result was division (vv. 18-19), illness and even death (v. 30) within the community. Understandably, Paul says that he has no praise for the Corinthians in this matter and, in order to correct the situation, reminds them at length of the tradition about the Lord's Supper which he had received from the Lord and handed on to them (v. 23).

This reminder includes the longest quotation of the words of Jesus in Paul's letters, and one that has close parallels in each of the Synoptic Gospels.[16] Although some differences exist among the four accounts, and a complicated debate has raged over which of the four preserves the most exact record of Jesus' words and actions, all four accounts agree that Jesus identified broken bread with his body, a cup of wine with his blood, and this metaphorically shed blood with the establishment of a covenant.[17] His reference to covenantal blood in Matthew and Mark takes the form "this is my covenant blood" (Mt 26:28; Mk 14:24) and in Luke, "this cup is the new covenant in my blood" (Lk 22:20). Paul's version of the statement in 11:25 is so close to Luke's that the slight differences cannot be detected in translation.[18] The version in Luke and Paul make explicit what the one in Mark and Matthew imply: Jesus interpreted his death as the establishment of the new covenant predicted in Jeremiah 31:31 and understood the blood shed in his death as analogous to the blood that, according to Exodus 24:8, Moses sprinkled on the people at the establishment of the Sinaitic covenant.

Exactly what Paul made of Jesus' description of the cup as the new covenant in his blood is not clear from this brief reference, for Paul's interest at this point in the letter lies elsewhere.[19] Nevertheless, the reference shows that he was aware of the tradition that Jesus had inaugurated the new covenant predicted by Jeremiah, and that Paul taught this traditional interpretation of Jesus' death to his newly established congregations (11:23).

If we now turn back to 1 Corinthians 9:20-21, the ambiguity surrounding Paul's references to "not being under the law," "being without the law," "not being without the law of God" and "being within the law of Christ" begins to disappear. With these phrases he may be saying that although he is not obligated to observe the customs that separate Jew from Gentile under the old covenant ("not under law"), he does not stand outside the covenant people of God ("not without the law of God"). Instead he has become a member of the people marked out by the new covenant, the covenant established in the Messiah's blood ("the law of Christ"). The boundary markers for the newly constituted people are not the old symbols of circumcision and dietary observance but (as Paul says in 10:1-22) baptism and the Lord's Supper and (as he implies in 7:19) certain "commandments of God" that are reaffirmed in the new covenant. Moreover, as Paul also says in 10:1-22, participation in the body and blood of Christ demands holiness, just as membership in the old people of God demanded holiness.

The outward boundary markers have changed with the change of covenants, but the general pattern of God's dealings with his people have not: certain symbols remain important under the new covenant, and holiness is demanded from those who by their participation in those symbols claim to belong to the people of God.[20]

The Law and Sin

Paul's next reference to the Mosaic law occurs within his discussion of the resurrection of the dead in 1 Corinthians 15. Not only is this reference unexpected within the context of Paul's immediate argument, but what it says about the law seems qualitatively different from anything said or implied in the letter so far.

In chapter 15 Paul addresses the argument of some within the Corinthian community who, contrary to his foundational teaching, have begun to deny the resurrection of the dead (v. 12). "How are the dead raised," they mockingly ask, "and with what kind of body do they come?" (v. 35). In his reply Paul first argues that the purpose of Christ's resurrection was to prepare the way for the resurrection of believers. If Christ was not raised and Christians will not be raised, he concludes, then believers are still in their sins, and believers who have died are lost (vv. 17-18). But, he continues,

Christ *has* been raised, and so the curse of death that came to Adam has been reversed. Moreover, the Corinthians' rhetorical questions about the resurrected body can be answered in ways that support the resurrection of believers. The resurrected body, unlike the body that a believer presently has, will be imperishable. Because of this, Christ will have victory over death, whose sting will have been removed (vv. 42-55). This last thought is expressed in the paraphrased words of Isaiah 25:8 and Hosea 13:14 and brings Paul's argument to a triumphant climax: "Then the word that stands written will come to pass, 'Death has been swallowed up in victory. Where, O Death, is your victory? Where, O Death, is your sting?' " (vv. 54-55).

Paul's argument seems to be over at this point, but he goes on to make a statement about the law which is as anticlimactic as it is unexpected: "But the sting of death is sin, and the power of sin is the law" (v. 56). The law has played no role in the argument of chapter 15, and the term *sin (hamartia)*, where it has appeared previously (15:3, 17), has always been plural in form. Moreover, after mentioning the connection between law and sin, Paul makes no effort to explore the subject but instead shifts back immediately to the theme of victory over death which he had introduced in verses 54-55.

Equally puzzling is the negative tone of Paul's comment. Paul's previous references to the law have sometimes appeared to subordinate its authority to God's new revelation in Christ (7:19; 9:8-9) or to reformulate it in terms of the law of the Messiah (9:20-21), but 15:56 stands apart as unmistakably and unreservedly negative. Just as sin is the sting of death, says Paul, so the law is the "power" of sin. The word he uses for "power" *(dynamis)* refers to that which enables something to accomplish a particular feat—that which makes something else effective.[21] Paul implies that the law is the means by which sin effects death and that the law will, with death, be swallowed up in the eschatological victory of Jesus Christ.

Considerations such as these have sometimes led scholars to conclude that this verse is a gloss, either by Paul himself after finishing the letter or by someone else.[22] The sentiments expressed are, however, thoroughly Pauline (compare Rom 7:8-11, 25), and Paul has wandered down similarly excursive paths at three other points in chapter 15 (vv. 9-11, 23-28, 32-34). For these reasons it is better to see this verse as the overflow of his climactic statements about the defeat of death in verses 54-55.[23] Paul had already asserted that Christ's death was "for our sins" (v. 3) and that without the resurrection believers were both still "in their sins" and had no hope of overcoming death (vv. 17-18).

It is natural, then, for Paul to connect sin with death in 15:56, and although less expected, it is easy to see how, having introduced the subject of sin, he could deviate even further from his argument to say something more specific about where it gets its effectiveness. Like a runner unable to stop at the finish line, Paul goes beyond the fitting climax to his argument to reveal an important conviction about the law which has not emerged in the rest of the letter: the law has played a dark role in salvation history by making effective sin's sentence of death on Adam's race.

Because the statement is brief, excursive and unexpected, however, it leaves a number of questions unanswered. Especially pressing is the problem of how the law that God gave, and that Paul cites as an authority in 9:8-9, can stand on the side of sin and death. Equally troubling is how Paul can claim that the law supplies sin with the ability to deal out death to humanity. He answers both of these questions, and provides a means of understanding the complexities in his attitude toward the law encountered so far, in 2 Corinthians 2:14—4:6.

The Context of 2 Corinthians 2:14—4:6
For the first time in either the Thessalonian or the Corinthian correspondence, Paul explicitly addresses his approach to the law in 2 Corinthians 3:3, 6-18. The passage is unusually important for two reasons. First, it deals with the Mosaic covenant, the part of Scripture that every Jew of Paul's day would have identified as the essence of the law. Paul, like other Jews of his era, could sometimes use the term *law* as a synonym for *Scripture* (Rom 3:19; 1 Cor 14:21), but all recognized that "the law," strictly speaking, was the Sinaitic covenant. Although Paul never uses the precise word *law* (*nomos*) in the passage, the Mosaic covenant is the subject under discussion in 3:3, 6-18. He speaks of "stone tablets" (v. 3), "the letter" (v. 6), "the dispensation . . . carved in letters on stone" (v. 7), "the old covenant" (v. 14) and the reading of "Moses" (v. 15), phrases that can only refer to the recording of the law by the finger of God on stone tablets and the subsequent giving of that law to Moses and Israel at Sinai.

Second, the length of the passage is significant. In the letters we have examined so far, Paul either never mentions the law directly or, when he does, mentions it only briefly. In this passage he engages in a discussion of the law which consumes most of an entire chapter. It seems reasonable to expect that the general nature of his discussion together with its length will produce a picture of Paul's view of the law that can help make sense of his more concise and less explicit references elsewhere.

Paul's discussion occurs as part of a much larger passage (2:14—5:19) in which the apostle describes the character of his ministry and defends himself against charges that he is not competent to be a minister of the gospel.[24] The passage begins with a description of Paul's ministry but quickly becomes apologetic with the question "Who is sufficient for these things?" (2:14-16).[25] Paul's opponents seem to have thought themselves sufficient to the task of ministry but considered that Paul's lack of letters of recommendation and "weak" personal demeanor signified that he was not.[26] Against these two charges Paul describes the nature of his credentials and deportment as a minister, and his primary evidence is the eschatological reality of God's activity among the Corinthians (3:1-3) and within Paul's ministry (3:4—4:6).

The law and the law-giver Moses enter the argument in these two subsections as the primary representatives of the age that is passing away since the eschatological activity of God's Spirit has begun. After comparing the activity of the Spirit among the Corinthians and within his ministry to the old dispensation that Moses administered, Paul returns to a description of his ministry in 4:7—5:19.[27]

Stony Tablets, Fleshly Hearts

Paul's first comments on the law appear as part of his defense that he is "sufficient" or "competent" (*hikanos*, 2 Cor 2:16) to minister the gospel. He begins in 2:17 by claiming that he does not hawk the Word of God for monetary gain, "as the many" do, but instead speaks the gospel of Christ from sincere motives that can pass the scrutiny of God himself. Then, as if responding to an objection that he knows will be leveled against his claim, Paul denies that what he has said means he is commending himself or needs letters of recommendation to or from the Corinthians to give him credentials for preaching the gospel (3:1). His commendatory letter of reference, he argues, is the Corinthians themselves (3:2), who are "a letter [*epistolē*] of Christ, delivered by us, inscribed not with ink but with the Spirit of the living God, not in stone tablets but in tablets of fleshly hearts" (3:3).[28]

Paul's primary point is clear: his "letter of recommendation" is the eschatological action of the Spirit within the Corinthian community, something far better than the mere ink and paper of which commendatory letters are composed. Paul intends to say more than this, however, as his reference to "stone tablets" indicates. Rather than referring to letters of recommendation as ink and paper, he refers to them as written with ink "in stone tablets." With this strange expression Paul defines the context of his thinking.[29] "Inscribed . . . in stone tablets" can only refer to the "two tablets of witness, stone tablets written with the finger of God" on Mount Sinai and given to Moses as a record of Israel's covenant obligations (Ex 31:18; Deut 9:10-11; compare Ex 32:15 LXX).[30] Paul's words "tablets of fleshly hearts" echo Ezekiel 11:19 and 36:26, which claim that in the period of Israel's eschatological restoration God will replace his people's stony heart with a fleshly heart so that, prompted by "a new spirit," they will meet their covenant obligations.[31]

Paul, then, is claiming that the activity of the Spirit among the Corinthians at the time that their church was established demonstrates that he is a genuine minister of the in-breaking new age, in which God's promises through his prophets are being fulfilled. This evidence, Paul argues, is far better proof of his genuineness as a minister than the possession of testimonials fashioned from paper and ink.

Death-Dealing Letter, Life-Giving Spirit

Paul next refers to the law in 2 Corinthians 3:4-6, where he returns to the question posed in 2:16. There he had asked how anyone could be "sufficient" (*hikanos*) for the kind of ministry to which God had called him, for this ministry both involved suffering and effected eternal life for some but eternal death for others. Paul claims that his sufficiency comes from God (3:5), "who also has made us sufficient [*hikanōsen hēmas*] as ministers of a new covenant, not of the letter but of the Spirit, for the letter [*gramma*] kills but the Spirit gives life" (3:6).

With this statement Paul moves to Jeremiah 31 (LXX 38):31-34, another prophetic promise of the eschatological restoration of Israel. This is the only passage in the Old Testament that uses the term *new covenant*, and like the passages in Ezekiel to which Paul alluded in 3:3, this passage refers to the hearts of God's people. In Jeremiah, as in Ezekiel, the hearts of God's people will undergo a radical change that will enable them to obey God's commandments (Ezek 11:20; compare 36:27 LXX) and so remain within the new covenant that God will establish with them (Jer 38:32-33 LXX).[32]

The element of obedience to the commandments of God in the age of the new covenant is missing from Paul. Instead he contrasts the Mosaic covenant with the new covenant. The new covenant, he says, is "of the Spirit," whereas the Mosaic covenant is "of the letter."[33] "The letter kills," he adds, "but the Spirit gives life." The obscurity of these words has prompted a virtual library of scholarly comment, most of it focused on the meaning of the term *letter* and much of it interested in defining the term in light of its several occurrences in Romans.[34] The immediate context supplies enough information, however, to show the meaning of the term here. The first and most obvious hint of Paul's meaning comes in the next verse (v. 7). Here he uses the term in the plural to refer to the "letters" carved into the stone tablets of the law. Since Paul claims that the letter "kills" in verse 6 and similarly describes that which was carved by letters in stone as "the ministry of death" in verse 7, "letter" in verse 6 must simply mean "the Mosaic law." Second, in verse 6 itself Paul's phrase "new covenant" implies a contrast with another covenant, a contrast he makes explicit a few verses later (v. 14; compare Jer 31[38]:32).

It seems logical, in light of this implied contrast between the "new covenant" and the "old covenant," to take Paul's explicit contrast of letter and Spirit as references to these two covenants as well. When he speaks of the "letter," then, he is simply using a figure of speech, well known in his time, in which a writer refers to something in its entirety by mentioning only one of its parts.[35] Again the conclusion follows that "the letter" is nothing more or less than the Mosaic law.[36]

What, then, does Paul mean when he says that the Mosaic law kills? Here too we enter a hornet's nest of controversy, but again the context of Paul's phrase both within this letter and within the wider field of his allusions to Old Testament passages makes his meaning relatively clear. First, it is significant that when Paul describes the activity of the Mosaic law in 3:6-9 he uses terms linked both with death ("kills," v. 6; "the ministry of death," v. 7) and with judgment ("the ministry of condemnation," v. 9). Paul believes that the Mosaic law deals out death to those who live within its power by condemning them. The death that comes at its hands, therefore, is a judicial punishment.

Second, the offhand way in which Paul says that the law kills and is the ministry of death shows that he did not expect his readers to require much explanation of what he meant. Probably he believed that his allusions to Ezekiel 11:19, 36:26 and Jeremiah 31[38]:31-34 were strong enough to make his meaning clear.

All three biblical passages explain the eschatological change that God would work in Israel's heart as the remedy for their disobedience to the Mosaic law and subsequent exile. The exile with its attendant suffering had come in strict agreement with the curses that according to Deuteronomy 28:15-68, 29:21-28 and Leviticus 26:14-39 would befall Israel if it disobeyed God's commands. Deuteronomy refers to these curses metaphorically and collectively as "death" (30:15, 19-20), a figure of speech that Ezekiel preserves (18:1-32; 20:25; 33:10-20). Jeremiah, although he does not echo Deuteronomy's use of "death" as often as Ezekiel, also proclaims that the disasters that have befallen Israel are the effects of disobedience to the Mosaic law (11:1-13; 31:32), and those disasters certainly included widespread, literal death.[37]

When Paul refers to the law as something that "kills" and in the next breath calls it "the ministry of condemnation," all within the context of allusions to Jeremiah and Ezekiel, the conclusion seems unavoidable that he is referring to the sentence of death that the law justly pronounced over a disobedient Israel. As we have already seen, many Jews in Paul's day believed that this sentence of condemnation was still in place. Paul's remedy for this situation, like the remedies prophesied in Jeremiah and Ezekiel, was the establishment of a new covenant (Jer 31[38]:31) and the remaking of the hearts of God's people under the power of the life-giving Spirit (Ezek 11:19; 36:26; 37:1-14; Jer 31:33). This is the "new covenant" of which Paul claims to be a competent minister.[38]

The Old Glory and the New

In the next paragraph, 2 Corinthians 3:7-11, Paul continues to compare the new covenant with the Mosaic law, but he advances the argument in four ways.[39] First, he changes texts. In verses 3 and 6 his allusions were primarily to Ezekiel and Jeremiah, but in verses 7-11 he bases his comments on Exodus 34:29-30. Second, Paul brings Moses into the argument and begins to imply a contrast between himself as minister of the new covenant (v. 6) and Moses as minister of "the ministry of death" (v. 7). Finally, Paul qualifies his stark contrast between death and letter on one hand and Spirit and life on the other by conceding in verse 6 that the Mosaic law had a measure of glory, although it was surpassed by the glory of the new covenant. Finally, in verses 7-11 he explicitly states what he had only implied in verse 3: the Mosaic law and its sentence of death is "passing away" (*katargoumenon*, v. 11).[40]

The paragraph consists of three carefully constructed comparisons all beginning with the word *if* (*ei*, 3:7, 9, 11) and completed with some variation of the phrase "how much more" (*pōs . . . mallon*, 3:8; *pollō mallon*, 3:9, 11). Each comparison is designed to show both that the new era of the Spirit is more glorious than the era of the Mosaic law and that the era of the Mosaic law is passing away. Paul begins by calling his readers' attention to Exodus 34:29-30, which literally translated from the Septuagint says,

As he came down from the mountain, Moses did not know that the sight of the pigment of his face had been glorified while he was speaking to him [the Lord]. And Aaron and all the elders of Israel saw Moses, and the sight of the pigment of his face had been glorified, and they were afraid to approach him.

Paul comments that if the "ministry of death" was inaugurated with such glory that its administrator Moses had an unbearably glorious face, then the glory of "the ministry of the Spirit" must be extraordinary indeed (vv. 7-8). He also makes a significant addition to the Exodus narrative when he comments that the glory of Moses' face, although so magnificent that the Israelites could not gaze upon it, was "passing away." With this long sentence, packed with these two points, Paul has already made his case. What follows is elaboration.

Paul's next three sentences (vv. 8-10) repeat the first of the two points using different terms for the two ministries: the one administered by Moses is now the "ministry of condemnation" and the other "the ministry of righteousness." This variation is helpful because it shows the sense in which Paul believed the ministry of the Mosaic law to be connected with death: the law pronounced the sentence of death over those who disobeyed it. It is also helpful because it shows that in Paul's thinking the opposite of the law's sentence of death is "righteousness." Since its "condemnation" must be interpreted within the context of God's covenant promises, its opposite "righteousness," at least here, must be interpreted within that context also.[41] If so, then the term *righteousness* carries both the relational connotation of God's mercy to people who have disobeyed the covenant and the juridical connotation that God has acquitted people of charges whose penalty was death.[42]

Paul's final sentence (v. 11) turns to the second of the two primary points of verses 7-8 by repeating the theme of the transitory nature of the Mosaic ministry. Here Paul deepens the thought slightly by referring to "that which is passing away." The English phrase translates a participial phrase that, significantly, is in the neuter gender *(to katargoumenon)*. This means that Paul cannot be referring simply to the transitory "glory" of the Mosaic ministry, as he had done in verse 7, for the term *glory* in Greek, *doxa,* is a feminine noun and would have required a feminine participle. Paul's use of the neuter participle shows that he means that the entire Mosaic ministry—the Mosaic covenant, its sentence of condemnation and the death that it dealt to those who disobeyed it—is passing away.[43] "How much more," Paul concludes, "is that which remains glorious" (v. 11).[44]

The Timidity of the Old, the Openness of the New

It is easy when sorting out the complexities of this section to forget that Paul's primary purpose throughout has been to refute charges that he is "insufficient" to be a minister of the gospel (2:16; 3:5-6). The contrast drawn between "the ministry of condemnation" and "the ministry of righteousness" in 3:7-11, however, by itself would not accomplish this goal. Had Paul's argument ended with verse 11, his opponents might even have responded that precisely because of the overwhelming glory of the ministry of righteousness, a minister with Paul's weak demeanor was ill-suited to the gospel's proclamation. His argument, then, requires another step, one that he takes in 3:12—4:6. "Having, therefore, such a hope," he begins, "we act with much openness." He goes on to show that unlike Moses, whose timid demeanor matched the transitory glory of his ministry, Paul acts with an "openness" or "frankness" *(parrēsia)* fully consistent with the splendid glory of the new covenant.[45]

Paul makes his case by continuing to interpret the account of Moses' mediation between God and Israel in Exodus 34:27-35, but he now shifts his focus from verses 29-30 to verses 33-35 in that passage. In the Septuagint, the text Paul uses throughout, these verses read this way:

[33]And after [Moses] stopped speaking to [the people] he placed a veil upon his face. [34]And whenever Moses entered the Lord's presence to say to him, he would remove the veil until he went out. After going out, he would say to all the sons of Israel whatever the Lord commanded him. [35]And the sons of Israel saw that the face of Moses had been glorified, and Moses placed the veil upon his face until he entered to converse with him.[46]

Exactly what Moses did is not clear from these verses. In verses 34-35 Moses seems to keep the veil on his face in the interval between speaking with the people and the Lord, but verse 35, especially when connected to the note of fear in verse 30, might be understood to mean that the people could not tolerate looking at the glory of Moses' face, and so Moses veiled himself while in their presence. Probably we are to visualize Moses at first veiling himself only when not talking either with the people or with the Lord, but changing his practice and veiling himself when addressing the people because they were afraid of his shining face.

Paul states only that Moses veiled his face when with the people and that he did so "in order that the sons of Israel might not gaze on the end of that which was passing away" (v. 13).[47] This action, Paul says, contrasts with his own "openness," an openness based on the eschatological nature of his ministry (v. 12; compare v. 11). He will complete this line of argument in 4:1-6 when he says that he has renounced "the hidden things of shame," by not "engaging in craftiness" or "disguising the word of God" and when he claims that his gospel is not "veiled" except to unbelievers.

Veiled and Unveiled Hearts

Between the beginning of his primary point and its completion, however, Paul digresses to discuss another veil not explicitly mentioned in the Exodus narrative (2 Cor 3:14-18). This veil, he says, lies over the reading of the "the old covenant" in the synagogue and corresponds to the hardheartedness of Israel during the days of Moses (v. 14).

Paul then makes a statement of great significance for understanding his approach to the Mosaic law, but whose grammar is extraordinarily complex. A literal translation of the entire sentence, with the ambiguous phrase emphasized, looks like this: "For until this very day the same veil remains at the reading of the old covenant *not lifted because [or 'that'] in Christ it is passing away [mē anakalyptomenon hoti en Christō katargeitai]."*

The sentence poses three difficulties. First, the two words *not lifted (mē anakalyptomenon)* can be taken in three ways:

1. as the predicate of *remains,* resulting in the translation "remains *unlifted,* because only through Christ is it taken away" (RSV)

2. as an adverbial phrase with an unusual lexical meaning, resulting in the rendering "the same veil remaineth, *it not being revealed* to them that it is done away in Christ" (ASV)

3. as an adverbial phrase with the common meaning of the term, yielding "*and it is never lifted,* because only in Christ is it taken away" (REB)

Second, the Greek word *hoti* can be translated as either "because" (RSV and REB) or "that" (ASV). Finally, although most translations take the subject of the verb "is passing away" to be the "veil" of the previous clause, it is unexpressed in Greek and could be something else.

This final difficulty is the easiest to deal with, since Paul provides a broad hint about the subject of the verb "is passing away" by using it three other times in the immediate context. In each of these instances the verb refers to the "passing away" of either the glory on Moses' face (v. 7) or the glory of the Mosaic ministry (vv. 11, 13). It would be odd if Paul suddenly, in his final use of the term in this context, switched its subject to something entirely different.[48]

If we add to these considerations the awkwardness of saying that a veil "is passing away" rather than that it "is being lifted," the case seems closed. Paul is probably referring to the passing away not of the veil but of the era dominated by the old covenant. Depending on which of the other options we choose, therefore, we could understand Paul to be saying that the veil

1. "remains *unlifted because* the old covenant passes away only in Christ,"

2. "remains, *it not being revealed* that the old covenant passes away only in Christ," or

3. "remains, *it not being lifted because* the old covenant passes away only in Christ."

Two considerations make the last option the best. First, it is not likely that the phrase "not being lifted" *(mē anakalyptomenon)* serves as the predicate of the verb "remains." The Greek word that Paul used for "not" *(mē)* would have been different *(ouk)* if Paul had intended to use the expression in this way.[49] Second, the verb "lift" *(anakalyptō)*, which Paul uses here, cannot mean "revealed." Paul would have used a closely related but different word, *apokalyptō,* had he meant to say that something was "not revealed" to unbelieving Jews.[50]

If these considerations are valid, then Paul's meaning would be that for unbelieving Jews the veil is not lifted from the reading of the old covenant because only in Christ is the old covenant seen to be *old.* Those outside of Christ cannot perceive that the Mosaic law is passing away. For them the old covenant remains the only covenant, and they continue to stand under its condemnation. As if to drive the point home, Paul virtually repeats verse 14 in the next verse: "but until today, whenever Moses is read, a veil lies over their hearts" (v. 15).

In verse 16 Paul supplies the solution to the dull minds and veiled hearts of verses 14-15 by paraphrasing Exodus 34:34. Just as Moses removed his veil when in the presence of the Lord, Paul says, "every time" someone turns to the Lord in faith, that person sees the Lord face to face. The "veil" is removed and the dullness of unbelief disappears. How can Paul claim that believers have the same experience of seeing the Lord face to face that Moses had? Paul answers this in verses 17-18: believers see the Lord "with unveiled face" because they experience the powerful presence of God in their midst by means of the eschatologically supplied Spirit.[51]

While composing this description of believers turning to the Lord and experiencing his presence directly, Paul seems to have been reminded of his primary line of argument—that unlike Moses, who veiled his face when with the Israelites so that they might not see the demise of the old covenant, Paul speaks and acts with "openness." Thus in verse 17 Paul adds to his interpretive comment on Exodus 34:34: "and where the Spirit of the Lord is, there is freedom." The present context demands that we interpret *freedom* as an allusion to the eschatological liberty Paul possesses to speak and act with "frankness" or "openness" in his ministry (v. 12).[52] As a minister of the new

(v. 6) and permanent (v. 11) covenant, Paul can speak and act with a boldness that those still under the Mosaic ministry cannot understand, a boldness that did not characterize Moses himself (v. 13) and that reaches even to the interpretation of the Mosaic covenant (v. 14-15).

A Complex Argument

The pathway through Paul's argument from 2 Corinthians 2:14 to 4:6 has not been smooth both because he has often expressed himself elliptically and because he has frequently digressed from his primary point. The long, bumpy journey has nevertheless been worth the effort, for a relatively full statement on Paul's convictions about the Mosaic law has come to light along the way.

First, and perhaps most significant, no doubt can exist that Paul regarded the era of the Mosaic law's domination as "passing away" (3:7, 11, 13, 14).[53] The Mosaic covenant as it functioned in the time of Moses (v. 14) and as it was understood in the synagogue of Paul's day (vv. 14-15) turned out to be a "ministry of death" (v. 7; compare v. 6) and of "condemnation" (v. 9), an "old covenant" (v. 14) whose "end" had come (v. 13).

Second, this passing away of the Mosaic ministry did not mean that Scripture itself, or what we would call the Old Testament, had passed away. Paul's convictions about the nature of the Mosaic covenant and the need for a new covenant are drawn from Scripture, specifically Ezekiel and Jeremiah. Moreover, we can reasonably assume from the way Paul deals with Exodus 34:29-35 in verses 7-18 that even the Mosaic covenant could be useful within the new era, if interpreted with the "openness" and "freedom" appropriate to those who have direct access to the Lord through the eschatological Spirit (vv. 17-18).[54] The ministry of Moses continues to possess glory, although its glory is transitory and is wholly subservient to the glory of the ministry of righteousness (vv. 9-10).

Third, despite the obvious elements of discontinuity in 2:14—4:6 between what Paul says about the law and the convictions of his unbelieving Jewish contemporaries, there is also a large degree of continuity. As chapter two clarified, many Jews of Paul's period believed that they labored under the punishment of the law's curse as a result of their own disobedience and the disobedience of their ancestors to the law. Although they would not have used Paul's language or drawn Paul's conclusions, they would have understood what he meant when he characterized the Mosaic covenant as a "ministry of death." Many would also have agreed with him on the need for a "new covenant" characterized by a fresh outpouring of God's Spirit and the renewal of his people's hearts.[55] Their primary point of disagreement with Paul would have been not on these issues but on his claim that the new covenant had been inaugurated by the shed blood of Jesus of Nazareth and that the "new covenant" spelled the end of the Mosaic covenant as it was commonly understood in the synagogue.

If this represents a correct understanding of Paul's comments on the Mosaic covenant in 2 Corinthians 2:14—4:6, then the ambiguity and complexity of the attitude toward the law evident in the rest of the Corinthian correspondence become intelligible. The Mosaic law is not evil or flawed but glorious. Paul's characterization of the law as written on "stone" tablets or as the "letter" is not meant to disparage the law or to imply that his Jewish contemporaries misuse it to assert a claim on God (legalism).[56] The need for something other than the covenant recorded "in stone tablets" arose, as Jeremiah and Ezekiel say, from Israel's transgression of the law. Paul's "openness" and "freedom," then, include the liberty to retain aspects of the Mosaic law in the era of the new covenant.[57]

The pattern of sanctity in the communities of the new covenant remains similar to the pattern of sanctity in the old: believers are to remain separate from the "Gentiles" and to expel those who flagrantly violate the holiness of the community. Several of the specific characteristics of that sanctity are even identical in the two covenant communities. Idolatry and sexual immorality are tolerated in neither, and love for neighbor is enjoined in both.

Since the new covenant is not a reestablishment of the old, however, many differences exist between the two communities defined by the two covenants. If the Corinthian believers are not Gentiles, neither are they Jews but "the church of God."[58] If "keeping the commandments" remains important, the commandment for all the males among God's people to be circumcised is now irrelevant. If the "Mosaic law" can be used in settling disputes, a word of Jesus on the same point carries greater weight. If Paul can appear to potential Jewish converts to be living "under the law," he can also appear to potential Gentile converts to be "outside the law," because his authority is now "the law of Christ." The law empowered sin and resulted in the death of God's people, and so a new covenant, established by another ritual of blood—the blood of the Messiah—was required. No longer the Mosaic covenant but this new covenant—"the law of Christ"—is now "the law of God."[59]

CHAPTER SIX

THE LAW
OF MOSES &
THE LAW
OF CHRIST
IN GALATIANS

Unlike the Thessalonian and Corinthian correspondence, Paul's letter to his Galatian congregations is almost entirely about the law. In 1-2 Thessalonians and 1-2 Corinthians the student of Paul's view of the law spends much exegetical energy sifting through isolated statements and drawing conclusions from hints about Paul's perspective in passages that do not explicitly speak of the law at all. In Galatians, however, the floodgate opens, and comments on the law burst upon the reader with such force that they are almost overwhelming.

Given this sudden flood of commentary on the law, the temptation is strong to ignore the historical situation that produced the letter and to take Paul's explicit arguments about the law here as equivalent to his comprehensive view. The temptation is understandable, since access to Paul's theology comes only through reading the small supply of his correspondence that still exists, and since Galatians addresses the topic of the law directly. Why should it not be read as Paul's own statement on his view of the law?[1] Galatians provides enough straightforward information about the situation that prompted Paul to write, however, to allow one to say safely that if his comprehensive view of the law included positive elements, he would not have been likely to dwell on them here. Paul's intention is to rescue his Galatian congregations from falling from grace (5:4), a possibility that causes him deep personal anguish (3:1; 4:19; 5:12). Within this setting it would be surprising to find a cool, detached statement neatly balancing the positive and negative, the obsolete and continuing aspects of the Mosaic law. Sensitivity to the context in which Paul first formulated his argument in Galatians, then, will help the interpreter to use wisely the wealth of information provided.

Some interpreters of Galatians have gone beyond this to say that Paul's comments on the law in the letter are so conditioned by the polemical situation in which he wrote that they cannot fit into a comprehensive description of his view of the law. They are rhetorical devices pulled from the arsenal to meet the moment's crisis, not part of a well-considered position; they are arguments, not reasons, for Paul's belief that his Galatian converts should not accept the yoke of the law.[2] Similar to this position is the claim that his statements about the law did not spring from theological convictions at all but were socially motivated. Paul wanted to preserve the sectarian nature of his congregations, according to this theory, rather than see them swallowed by Judaism, and so he invented arguments against the law to accomplish this goal.[3]

If these positions have merit, not only is it futile to take Galatians as Paul's unmediated statement on the law, but it is also futile to attempt a formulation about Paul's view of the law on the basis of Galatians at all. On such views, Paul's arguments about the law in Galatians tell us not about his view of the law but about his psychological makeup or social vision. It almost goes without saying that Galatians, on this model, offers little or nothing of theological value for the church.[4]

But a careful reading of Paul's statements about the law within the broad historical context of first-century Judaism and in light of the particular circumstances that prompted Paul to write the letter yields a different conclusion. It shows that whereas Paul's accent in Galatians is on a negative evaluation of the law, he incorporates into his argument positive references to the Mosaic law, allusions to the wider biblical tradition about the restoration of Israel, and references to another law. All of these elements are compatible with his assumptions about the law in the Thessalonian correspondence (chapter three) and closely match the more detailed and explicit references to the law in the Corinthian letters (chapters four and five).

Galatians in Context

Although the details of the situation that prompted Paul to write to his churches in Galatia teem with scholarly controversy, much about the letter's original context is clear.[5] Galatians tells us that Paul had founded these churches by preaching the gospel of Christ crucified (3:1; compare 1:8-9) amid some personal distress (4:13).[6] The Galatians, who were Gentiles (4:8), had welcomed Paul and his gospel with open arms during this initial visit (4:14-15; compare 1:6) but had all too soon turned away to a kind of antigospel (1:6-9) preached by certain "agitators" (1:7; compare 5:10) or "troublemakers" (5:12) who had arrived in Galatia from elsewhere.[7]

The differences between the two gospels are also reasonably clear. The primary feature of the agitators' gospel, at least from Paul's perspective, was its claim that circumcision was necessary for full acceptance into the people of God. Paul says that the agitators, who were themselves circumcised (6:13), were trying to compel the Galatians to accept circumcision (6:12). Since Paul hints that in addition to circumcision the agitators were attempting to enforce the observance of the Jewish holy days (4:10) and dietary restrictions (2:11-14) among the Gentile Galatians, it seems reasonable to view them as Jewish Christians who were trying to impose the entire Jewish law upon Paul's Gentile converts and whose particular interest was conformity to the three requirements of the law that both Jews and Gentiles recognized as distinctively Jewish: circumcision, observance of the Jewish calendar and keeping the law's dietary restrictions.[8] In other words, the agitators were Jewish Christians who were attempting to compel the Galatians to become Jewish proselytes.[9]

Paul says that a desire to avoid persecution for the cross of Christ motivated the agitators (6:12). It seems reasonable to assume that in addition the agitators were concerned that Paul's gospel had left the Galatians with a false impression. Paul had considered the Galatians to be members of the people of God, people who awaited the hope of righteousness (5:5) on the basis of faith alone apart from observing the Mosaic law. The agitators, however, believed that obeying the law's command to be circumcised and following the Mosaic law's diet and calendar were essential requirements for membership in Abraham's family. Their goal was to correct Paul's abbreviated—and opportunistic (1:10)—gospel with their more complete version (3:3).[10]

This motivation, and the outline of the argument that accompanied it, emerges from a careful consideration of the central portion of Paul's argument against them (3:6—5:12). Here his burden is to show that believing Gentiles, both because they imitate Abraham's faith and because they are "in Christ," are Abraham's heirs, the children of promise. His argument, moreover, appeals to Genesis 15, 16 and 21 but remains silent on Genesis 17:1-14, one of the most lucid statements in Genesis on God's covenant with Abraham.[11]

The content of Genesis 17:1-14 reveals why Paul avoided it. Here God repeats his promise from Genesis 15:7-21 to make Abraham a great nation but speaks of his covenant with Abraham as a covenant of circumcision (vv. 10, 13). In addition, God commands that this fleshly covenant be performed on all the offspring who come to Abraham as a result of God's promise (vv. 7, 10, 12-13), that the covenant be everlasting (vv. 7, 9, 12-13) and that those who do not observe it be cut off from God's people (v. 14). Taken in isolation, the case from Genesis 17 for the circumcision of the Gentile Galatians, inheritors of God's promise to Abraham, could hardly be stronger. Paul's silence on Genesis 17:1-14, despite his close attention to the chapters surrounding it, suggests that the text was used by his opponents to argue that the Galatian believers must accept circumcision in order to become part of the people of God.[12]

Some interpreters of Galatians have objected to this portrait of the agitators on the basis of 6:12-13. In verse 12 Paul says that the agitators "want to make a good showing in the flesh . . . only so that they might not be persecuted for the cross of Christ," and in verse 13 that they do not themselves "keep the law." These statements have sometimes been taken to mean that Paul's opponents were Judaizing Gentile Christians who, after responding to the gospel, became fascinated with the Jewish matrix that gave it birth.[13] They have also been understood to mean that Paul's opponents were Judean Jews attempting to avoid persecution at the hands of fiercely nationalistic countrymen.[14] Occasionally Paul's opponents are viewed as Gnostics who shunned the law generally but found circumcision to be a way of making their religion look legitimate and so of avoiding persecution.[15]

A more straightforward explanation for 6:12-13 surfaces, however, if we remember that for Paul, Christ's crucifixion meant death to the Mosaic law (2:19), death to the world of Judaism as Paul knew it prior to his conversion (6:14) and redemption from the law's curse on those who transgress it (3:13). It signified, in other words, that the Mosaic law was no longer in effect for either Jew or Gentile and that continued efforts to live by the law were futile: the law could not be kept, and had in any case been superseded.

This belief probably led to Paul's own flogging on five occasions at the hands of Jews (2 Cor 11:24), and this is probably the kind of persecution to which he refers in 4:29: "just as then [in the days of Ishmael and Isaac] the boy born according to the flesh [Ishmael] used to persecute the boy born according to the Spirit [Isaac], so also now." Thus when Paul says that the agitators are attempting to escape persecution by altering the gospel and that they do not themselves keep the law, he probably means that their refusal to face up to the incompatibility between the Mosaic law and Christ's crucifixion—between the law that cannot be kept and the eschatological solution to that problem—allows them to escape the persecution that he has been enduring at the hands of his fellow Jews.[16]

The agitators, then, appear to have been Jewish Christians who traveled to Paul's churches in order to convince them that faith in Jesus Christ was only a first step. The faith of the Galatians needed to be completed (3:3) by acceptance of the Mosaic law and full conversion to Judaism, including circumcision. The agitators were not content, however, to let matters rest in the realm of theological ideas. Instead, they accompanied the positive proclamation of their own gospel with an attempt to discredit Paul himself (4:12-20; compare 1:10; 5:11) and a policy of excluding from fellowship any Galatian believers who did not conform to their requirements (4:17; compare 2:11-14).[17] The tactic of social exclusion would have been especially painful for members of the congregation who were already considered outcasts by friends and family because of their abandonment of the traditional religions (4:8).[18]

Facing difficult questions about Paul and his gospel while suffering still more social ostracism was more than many Galatians could withstand. Thus the situation was bleak when Paul dictated his letter. He addresses the Galatians as people who had been progressing well (5:7) but are now turning away from the gospel (1:6) and are "completing" their requirements for membership in the people of God (3:3) by embracing the Jewish calendar (4:10), circumcision (5:3) and indeed the whole Mosaic law (4:21).

Exit the Law of Moses

Paul's response to this crisis is a sustained discussion of the necessary requirements for inclusion within the covenant people of God and acquittal before God on the last day. Paul's shorthand for this double-sided concept is *justification*.[19] Since his opponents have been convincing the Galatians that acceptance of the full yoke of the Mosaic law is necessary for justification, the goal of his argument is to show that the law cannot justify. Paul's task is particularly difficult because he believes that the law continues to function as authoritative Scripture (3:22) and so continues to speak (4:21). So not only must Paul show that the law cannot justify, but in the process he must also address why, if the law cannot justify, God gave it at all.[20]

Galatians is not only an argument that faith rather than the Mosaic law justifies but also an argument that justification by faith has ethical consequences. The stage is set for this discussion already in 2:11-18, where Paul tells the story and describes the logic of his disagreement with Peter at Antioch. Here Paul argues that the men from James, Peter, Barnabas and the Antiochene Jewish Christians deviated from the truth of the gospel by withdrawing from table fellowship with Gentile believers. He argues not only that this reintroduction of the Mosaic law was incompatible with the conviction that the law cannot justify (2:15-16) but also that it was a transgression because it erected barriers between believers (2:18).[21] The first readers of the letter may well have asked when reading 2:18, "A transgression of what?" If the barrier between Jews and Gentiles which the Mosaic law had erected had now been torn down, what basis for ethics was left? Paul turns to this problem in 5:13—6:10, where he argues that although the law of Moses has left the stage of God's activity, the law of Christ has entered the scene.[22]

Paul's attempt to persuade the Galatians not to accept the yoke of the Mosaic law is multifaceted:

☐ he pronounces a curse on those who follow this "other gospel which is not another" (1:8-9; compare 5:4)

☐ he urges the Galatians to remember that God had confirmed the sufficiency of Paul's gospel with the presence of the Spirit and the working of miracles (3:2, 5)

☐ he makes a moving appeal to his former friendly relations with the Galatians (4:12-20)

☐ he demonstrates that the life of the believer outside the Mosaic law is as morally upright as the life of those under the Mosaic law (5:13—6:10)

☐ he questions the motives of those who preach submission to the law (6:12-13)

Most of Paul's energy, however, is devoted to the argument that the law does not justify. To reach this conclusion he follows two paths: he argues both that the law cannot be kept and that it is now part of a bygone era.

The Law Cannot Be Kept (2:15-16)

Paul argues clearly in 2:15-16 and 3:10-14 that no one can keep the law and seems to assume that position in more concise and obscure statements in

2:19, 5:3 and 6:13. An examination of the two primary passages, and of the more obscure ones in light of them, reveals that the unfulfillability of the law was for Paul a deeply held conviction.

Paul begins his argument that the law cannot justify by giving the substance of his response to Peter during the infamous "incident at Antioch." In Antioch Peter had "lived like a Gentile" (2:12, 14) among Gentile believers until "certain men from James" (v. 12) arrived in Antioch. After their arrival, Peter withdrew from fellowship with the Gentile believers (v. 12). Paul interpreted this withdrawal as an attempt to force the Gentile believers in Antioch to conform to the dietary regulations of the Mosaic law (v. 14). In response to this deviation from the gospel (v. 14), Paul reminded Peter that even those who "are by nature Jews and not Gentile sinners" (v. 15) understand that "a human being is not justified by works of the law but through faith in Jesus Christ" (v. 16). Paul then explains why even Jews recognize that works of the law do not justify: "Even we have believed in Christ Jesus in order that we might be justified by faith in Christ and not by works of the law, because by works of the law shall no flesh be justified" (v. 16).

At first this statement looks like a bland assertion—unsupported by proof—that works of the law do not justify Jews because works of the law do not justify anyone. That Paul is saying much more than this, however, becomes clear when we recognize that his statement echoes Psalm 143:2 (LXX 142:2): "Do not enter into judgment with your servant, because nothing living shall be justified before you."

Paul has replaced the term *living* with *flesh* and inserted a reference to "works of the law"—probably because both at Antioch and at Galatia the rite of cutting the "flesh" had become the work of the law that had tragically separated believing Gentile from believing Jew.[23] Nevertheless, the term *flesh* in Galatians, as elsewhere in Paul's letters, often suggests human frailty, and particularly human sinfulness.[24] Paul, then, has skillfully altered Psalm 143:2 to make its meaning relevant to the situation at Antioch and Galatia. The psalm is a confession that no one can claim perfect innocence before the all-knowing gaze of God and a plea for God's mercy in spite of this. Paul uses the psalm's language to say that no flesh, not even circumcised flesh, can claim to be innocent of all wrongdoing. Even those who are Jews and not Gentile "sinners" know that no one can claim to have kept the law well enough to be justified by it before God.[25]

The Law's Curse (3:10-14)

The second place in Galatians where Paul clearly argues that the law cannot be kept is 3:10-14. In the argument to which these verses contribute (3:1—4:7), he claims that Gentile believers have no need of the law because they are already Abraham's children and heirs of his blessing in virtue of their relationship to Christ. Much of Paul's energy is devoted to arguing the positive point that Gentile believers are inheritors of the blessing promised to Abraham. In 3:10-13, however, he also makes the negative argument that "those who rely on the law are under a curse."

Paul appeals to four passages of Scripture, the broader contexts of which he could assume that his Galatian readers would know.[26] His argument proceeds by three steps: first, all are under the law's curse because no one has kept the law; second, in light of this, justification comes only by faith in God's eschatological provision for the redemption of his people in the gospel; and third, God has provided this eschatological redemption through Christ's death on the cross.

Argument from Deuteronomy 27:26. Paul first claims that because Scripture pronounces a curse on everyone who does not do what the law says, those who rely on the works of the law are under a curse: "For those who rely on works of the law are under a curse, because it is written, 'Cursed be everyone who does not remain in all the things written in the book of the law to do them' " (v. 10).

The logic of Paul's argument probably did not register with those unfamiliar with the literary context of Deuteronomy 27:26. Without that context, it is tempting to think that Paul meant to say either that those who rely on works of the law are under a curse because their attempt to do the law itself is evil or that Paul should have said that those who rely on the law are *not* under a curse, because Scripture curses only those who do not do the law. Paul's comment makes sense only if we take it to mean that even those who rely on the works of the law have not kept the law and therefore fall under the curse that the law pronounces on those who fail to keep it.[27]

This, as it turns out, is what Paul's quotation means within its own context. Deuteronomy 27:26 summarizes a prominent theme throughout Deuteronomy and, as we have already seen, in the Bible generally: Israel stands cursed by the law if it disobeys the law, and Israel will not obey it (or has not obeyed it). As early as Deuteronomy 4, Moses tells the people of God that they should "be careful not to forget the covenant" the Lord has made with them, but then predicts that they *will* forget and, as a result, will "utterly perish from the land" that the Lord is allowing them to conquer (vv. 23-26). The theme recurs in Deuteronomy 8:19-20 and 11:8-32 and comes to a climax in chapters 27—32. Deuteronomy 27:26 itself summarizes a long list of specific violations of the law and is followed in chapter 28 by a short list of blessings for obedience and a detailed list of curses for disobedience. The most significant difference between these two lists is that whereas the blessings are broad generalizations about "abundance and prosperity," the curses are specifically tied to the future history of Israel. They have a tone less of threat than of prophetic prediction. Everything from the establishment of a monarchy to the dispersion is foretold, and the message is clear: the curse of the law rather than its blessing will come upon Israel, because Israel will not obey the law in years to come.[28]

As we have already seen, moreover, this understanding of Israel's condition received repeated emphasis in the prophetic literature of the Old Testament, in literature written between the fourth and the first centuries and in writings from Paul's own time, as Josephus especially testifies. So when Paul says that those who rely on works of the law are under a curse, he is not saying anything particularly controversial for a Jew.[29] He is instead reminding the Galatians and his Judaizing opponents that membership in the people of God, as it is defined by the Mosaic covenant, is membership in a people with a plight—they are cursed by the very law that defines them as God's people, because they, as a people and as individuals, have not kept the law.[30]

The second step in Paul's argument is more closely tied to this first step than translations of Galatians 3:11 commonly recognize. Virtually all translations render this verse, with slight differences, this way:

But it is obvious that [hoti] no one is justified before God by the law, because [hoti] "the just shall live by faith."

This translation makes Paul's argument look disjointed, since there is no clear connection between this sentence and the immediately preceding statement that those who rely on the works of the law are cursed. Paul seems to be starting fresh and to be saying that works of the law cannot justify not only because no one can keep the law but also because justification comes through faith in any case. A better translation of Paul's Greek, however, renders the sentence as follows:

But because [hoti] no one is justified before God by the law, it is obvious that [hoti] "The just shall live by faith."[31]

The difference between the two translations lies in the placement of the word *obvious*, which translates *delon*, and the rendering of the term *hoti*, which means either "that" or "because." In the Greek text, *delon* occurs midway through the sentence (*hoti de en nomo oudeis dikaioutai para to theo delon hoti ho dikaios ek pisteos zesetai*). Virtually all translations, however, position the word at the beginning of the sentence, link it with the first occurrence of the

Greek word *hoti* and translate this first *hoti* as "that." Although either rendering is grammatically possible, the phrase *dēlon hoti*, with *hoti* immediately following *dēlon*, is a common idiom for "it is obvious that." There is no need, then, to connect *dēlon* with the *hoti* at the beginning of the sentence, when taking it with the *hoti* that it immediately precedes makes good sense in grammatical terms and better sense in the context.

The point is subtle, but it is important, because it shows that Paul considers what he says in verse 11 to be the solution to the plight he has described in verse 10. The first clause in verse 11 sums up what he has said in verse 10 and connects it with the new proposition he is about to make in the second clause of verse 11. In this translation, then, verses 10-11 read this way:

> Those who rely on works of the law are under a curse, for it is written, "Cursed is everyone who does not remain in all the things written in the book of the law in order to do them." But because no one is justified before God by the law, it is obvious that "the just shall live by faith."

In other words, Paul's solution to the plight of living under the curse that the law pronounces on the disobedient is to "live by faith."

Argument from Habakkuk 2:4. Paul proves this point by quoting again from Scripture, this time Habakkuk 2:4. Once again, both Paul and his audience probably knew the broader context of the passage from which he quotes. The short book of Habakkuk focuses on the theme of God's covenant faithfulness to his people despite the clearly visible signs of Israel's oppression at the hands of its enemies. Habakkuk 1:1—2:5 complains that although Israel has been sinful, God has punished it by a nation (Babylon) that is even more wicked. Will these wicked opponents of God's people, the prophet asks, continue their oppression of Israel unchecked? The answer to this question comes in the section of the book from which Paul quotes (2:2-4):

> And the Lord answered me and said, "Write the visions, and write them clearly on a wooden tablet so that the one who reads them may run, because there is still a vision for the right time, and it will reach its appointed goal and not be in vain. If he lingers, wait for him, because he shall come and not delay. If he draws back, my soul will not be pleased with him. But my righteous one shall live by faith."[32] (LXX)

The Lord tells the prophet to be patient, that rescue from the oppression of the wicked Babylonian, although it may take time, will eventually come to the one who has faith that God will deliver his people. Paul too intends his readers to understand that rescue from the plight of sin against God's law comes to those who have "faith" in God's provision for deliverance.

The difference between Paul and Habakkuk, of course, is that what for

Habakkuk was a general trust in God for deliverance during difficult times has become for Paul a trust specifically in deliverance from the curse of the law through the death of Christ. Thus, for Paul, *faith* in Galatians 3:11 probably has the same meaning that it had in verses 2 and 5, where he referred to the gospel message of Christ crucified (v. 1) as "the preaching that demanded faith."[33] Paul, then, has preserved Habakkuk's emphasis on faith in God's eventual response to the plight of his people, but by tying the term *faith* specifically to the gospel he has given Habakkuk's phrase a specificity that it did not have in its original context. Since the people of Israel have not kept the law and thus live under its curse, Paul says that they, and the Gentiles who want to be included among them, must rely on God's eschatological provision for the deliverance of his people in the gospel of Christ crucified.[34]

Argument from Leviticus 18:5. As if to drive this point home, Paul again contrasts living by the law with faith in the gospel by claiming that "the law is not based on faith; instead, 'the one who does these things shall live by them'" (v. 12). This quotation is from Leviticus 18:5 and again echoes the Deuteronomic theme that obedience to the law results in life, whereas disobedience brings the law's curse of death and destruction. Paul implies that the law gives life only to those who do it, that Israel has not done it and that faith in the gospel of God's provision in Christ is therefore the only course open to those who seek justification.[35]

Argument from Deuteronomy 21:23. Paul's third step, taken in verses 13-14, demonstrates why this is so. "Christ," he says, "redeemed us from the curse of the law by becoming a curse for us." He then quotes Deuteronomy 21:23, which says that one hung on a tree is cursed by God, presumably because of the dreadful nature of the person's crime.[36] In Christ's crucifixion, then, the curse that the law pronounced on Israel was focused on Christ, whose death atoned for Israel's covenant violations.[37] With this action, Paul says in verse 14, the eschatological period of God's redemption began, and the most notable evidences of its presence are the inclusion of the Gentiles in the people of God and the outpouring of God's Spirit. In a manner reminiscent of Isaiah 40—66, Jeremiah and Ezekiel, Paul claims that the remedy for Israel's disobedience is restoration, a restoration inclusive of the Gentiles and effected by God's Spirit.[38]

Death to the Law and Keeping the Law (Galatians 2:19, 5:3, 6:13)

If the above represents a correct understanding of 2:15-16 and 3:10-14, then three other brief references to the law in Galatians probably also express

Paul's conviction that the Mosaic law cannot be kept. In 2:19 Paul claims to have died to the law through the law and to have been crucified with Christ—a reference that taken on its own seems mystical and puzzling. In the light of 2:15-16 and 3:10-14, however, the meaning of the phrase takes shape: Paul died to the law because he, like all humanity, had disobeyed the law and suffered its curse of death.[39]

In 5:3 Paul claims that the Galatians who undergo circumcision are obligated to carry out the whole law. Probably he is warning his readers that their acceptance of the necessity of circumcision for membership in the people of God implies their willingness to undertake an impossible task, the keeping of the Mosaic law, and their rejection of God's gracious offer of redemption from disobedience to the law (5:4).[40]

In 6:13 Paul turns this conviction against his opponents by claiming that although they are enthusiastic about circumcision, they do not themselves keep the law. His point is probably that even his opponents, although zealots for the law, are caught in the same trap of disobedience to the law that entangles all humanity (compare 2:15-16).[41]

Transgression of the Law in Paul's Argument

If this reading of Galatians 2:15-16, 3:10-14, 2:19, 5:3 and 6:13 is correct, then at least in these passages Paul has said little that is revolutionary from a Jewish perspective. His language of having died to the law through the law certainly goes beyond anything in first-century Judaism, but the principle behind that statement and the other passages remains thoroughly Jewish: the law curses those who do not obey it; Israel has not obeyed the law; Israel continues to live under the law's curse. This is why Paul can assume that even those who are by nature Jews know that one is not justified by works of the law (2:15-16). On this point, he believes, he and other Jews are in agreement.

But here his agreement with Judaism ends. It is not immediately obvious from the Jewish perspective why the remedy to violation of the Mosaic law is to dispense with the law. Why would the solution not be—as Paul's opponents probably claimed it was—to devote oneself all the more strictly to observing the law?[42] Israel's violation of the law and subsequent curse have indeed been addressed in the atoning death of Jesus on the cross, but why should the law be excluded? Perhaps Paul's opponents claimed that Ezra and Nehemiah showed the correct attitude toward the law in periods of restoration: repentance and determination to keep the Mosaic covenant strictly. What better way to do this, Paul's opponents might have thought, than to follow the example of Ezra and Nehemiah in circumscribing association with Gentiles, whose beguiling idolatry had led Israel into sin in the first place?[43]

Abraham, Believers and the End of the Law (3:6-29)

Paul implies an answer to this logic in his second reason for claiming that the law cannot justify. Throughout Galatians, Abraham and his children dominate much of Paul's argument. In 3:6-29 Paul makes a complex case that Gentile believers are related to Abraham because they are "of Christ" and therefore Abraham's seed, and in 4:21-31 he exegetes the narrative of Isaac's birth typologically to show that believers are spiritual descendants of Abraham through Isaac rather than through Ishmael. Although 4:21-31 alludes to the Sinaitic covenant (4:25), 3:6-29 is the most extensive discussion of the law in the letter, and here Paul implies that because Gentiles are initiated into Abraham's family by faith, no role is left for the law as a means of initiation.[44] He bolsters this negative argument with the claim that the law was in effect for only a limited time and for a purpose quite different from initiating those under it into the people of God.

Paul's discussion of the relationship of Gentile believers to Abraham in 3:6-29 uses two distinct lines of reasoning. First, Paul claims that the faith of Gentile believers is analogous to (*kathōs*) the faith of Abraham (v. 6) and therefore (*ara*, v. 7) makes them "children of Abraham." Because their faith in Christ has the same quality as Abraham's faith, they represent the fulfillment of God's promise to bless the Gentiles *through Abraham* (vv. 8-9, 14).[45] As we have already seen, part of this argument is devoted to a contrast between the blessing that rests on those related to Abraham by faith and the curse that falls on those who continue to rely on the law (vv. 10-13).

Second, Paul argues that believing Gentiles are themselves Abraham's heirs and therefore the recipients of God's promises to bless both Abraham and his children. Paul makes this second argument for the relationship between Gentile believers and Abraham by noting that God made the promises to Abraham and to his "seed." Since the term *seed* is singular in Scripture, he observes, it must refer to an individual, and that individual must be Christ (v. 16). And if this is so, then Gentiles who believe in Christ Jesus must, by virtue of their identification with Christ, be Abraham's "heirs according to the promise" (v. 29; compare vv. 14, 26).[46]

As part of this second way of describing the relationship between Abraham and believing Gentiles, Paul claims that the Mosaic law was in effect only temporarily, for a specific purpose, and that in the eschatological age of God's fulfillment of his promises to Abraham, the law no longer plays a role. With an eye on his opponents' claims that membership in the family of

Abraham requires observance of the Jewish law, Paul argues that since the Sinaitic covenant came long after God's promise to Abraham, it could not nullify that promise (v. 17).[47]

Paul recognizes that his argument raises the natural question, "Why, then, the law?" (v. 19). He answers by implying both that the Mosaic covenant was given in order to reveal sin and so prepare for the gospel, and that it was temporary.

He articulates the purpose of the law with an ambiguous statement and two figures of speech that help to clarify it. He begins by asserting that the law "was added on account of transgressions" (v. 19), a sentence that by itself indicates only some general connection between the law and sin. The statement is so broad that it could be taken to mean that the law came to place limits on sin, to reveal sin, to punish sin or even, if read in the light of a similar but more specific comment in Romans 5:20, to increase sin.[48]

The choice becomes more limited, however, if the statement is understood in light of two metaphors that Paul uses to describe the purpose of the law a few verses later. First, he says, Scripture "enclosed all things under sin" (v. 22), and closely following this, "we were guarded by the law, being enclosed," presumably under sin (v. 23). Paul's reference to Scripture's enclosing "all things" under sin in verse 22 echoes his scriptural quotation in verse 10 to say that "all" who do not keep the law are under a curse. His repetition of the verb *enclose (synkleiō)* in 3:23 shows that in this verse he restates the same thought. Taken together, the two statements seem to use *enclose* metaphorically to mean that no escape was possible from the condemnation that the law pronounced on those who sinned.[49]

Second, he says that the law "was our pedagogue unto Christ" (vv. 24-25). The pedagogue in ancient Greco-Roman society was a slave charged with guarding the children of the wealthy between the time they left the arms of their mother or nurse until late adolescence.[50] His primary roles were to guard, discipline and, to a limited extent, teach the child during a specific period of time. Students of Galatians have at various times argued that each one of these roles is Paul's primary point of comparison between the law and the pedagogue.[51] The context of the metaphor, however, clearly points to the disciplinarian role as Paul's crucial point of comparison between the law and the pedagogue. If verses 22-23 refer to the law's enclosure of all things under sin, then the "so that" in verse 24 shows that the pedagogue's infamous role of checking the waywardness of his charges with a cuff or a blow from his staff stands behind Paul's use of the image. Just as Israel had sinned and so stood under the law's curse, so the unruly child fell under the disciplining rod of the pedagogue.[52]

Like all metaphors, however, Paul's pedagogue imagery generates more than one point of comparison. Whatever the other nuances of the image were for him, he intended for it to convey, in addition, the law's temporal nature. In verse 19 Paul had made the claim that the law was temporary.[53] The law, he had said, "was added on account of transgressions *until the seed should come* to whom the promise was made."

He goes on, in a notoriously difficult set of sentences, to claim that the law "was ordered through angels by the hand of a mediator" and that "the mediator is not of one, but God is one" (vv. 19-20). Whatever else these statements mean, they are intended to bolster his claim that the law was an impermanent measure, put in place only until "the seed should come."[54] Similarly, in verse 23 Paul says that we were enclosed under the law only until "the revelation of the coming faith," and when he introduces the imagery of the pedagogue in verse 24, he reiterates this point by claiming that the law, our pedagogue, lasted only "until Christ."[55] Since the pedagogue's responsibilities for children in his charge ended when they became adults, this household slave served as an appropriate illustration both of the purpose of the law to condemn sin and of the law's temporal nature.

Believers as Eschatological Heirs (3:26—4:11)

Apparently to make the law's temporal nature as clear as possible, Paul argues for it again in 3:26—4:11.[56] In 3:26-29 he reminds the Galatians that they are "of Christ" (v. 29) and "in Christ Jesus" (v. 28) because they "have faith in Christ Jesus" (v. 26), "have been baptized into Christ" and "have put on Christ" (v. 27). If they are this closely related to Christ, says Paul, and if Christ is Abraham's seed, then they too are Abraham's seed and so "heirs according to the promise" (v. 29).

As usual, however, Paul is not willing simply to make the positive case. To do so would leave him defenseless against those trying to persuade the Galatians to accept the Mosaic law. After all, they could easily argue that as heirs by faith of God's promise to Abraham, the Gentile Galatians should follow Abraham's example of accepting circumcision after believing.

In order to refute this claim, Paul, in 4:1-11, compares the Galatians to inheritors of an estate who during their childhood were subject to the watchful authority of "guardians and managers" until the father's appointed time for them to receive their inheritance. The position of such children, he says, is hardly better than that of slaves (vv. 1-2).[57] "We" were like them, he argues, but in the fullness of time God sent his Son to redeem those under the law and to make them heirs (vv. 3-7).

Paul clinches this analogy in verses 8-11 by recording his amazement that the Galatians would want to step back into the bygone era of the law, the era of their childhood, and submit again to slavery. In saying this, Paul makes a startling assumption: the Gentile Galatians, by their submission to the Mosaic law as a necessary condition for inclusion among the people of God, were in essence resubmitting to the idolatry in which they had previously lived (vv. 8-10). To submit to the yoke of the law as a requirement for justification, Paul says, is to "return again to the weak and poverty-stricken elements" that the Galatians served when they worshiped idols (v. 9; compare v. 3).

This statement is unambiguous evidence that Paul considered the Mosaic law obsolete. Since its appointed purpose of condemning sin had been accomplished and God's redemptive purposes had advanced beyond the law to faith in Jesus Christ, service to the stipulations of the Mosaic covenant was idolatrous, an implicit claim that the Mosaic covenant itself had greater significance than God. For the Galatians to turn to the Mosaic law for justification therefore was equivalent to returning to their idolatrous past. It was to render to the law a devotion that belongs to God alone, just as in their past idolatry they had placed God's creatures above the Creator and ascribed to them the glory that belongs only to God.[58]

Beneath much of Paul's discussion of the law in Galatians lies the conviction that the Mosaic covenant has accomplished its purpose of identifying sin and, by condemning it, prepared the way for the coming of Christ. Its purpose now accomplished, Paul argues, the law is obsolete. Under these changed circumstances, to make observance of the law a requirement for membership in the people of God is to commit idolatry, to commit the classic sin of apostasy, to be cut off from God's eschatological provision in Christ and therefore to fall away from grace (5:4). It is to exit the stage of God's work among his people along with the law itself.

Enter the Law of Christ

In light of Paul's energetic argument that the law cannot be kept and is obsolete, it might at first appear that Paul has turned his back on Jewish tradition. Given the significance of the Mosaic covenant in Jewish life (see chapter two), and given that Paul now considers that covenant obsolete, isn't the theology of Galatians built entirely on new foundations? Was the early heretic Marcion right to appeal to Galatians as proof that the gospel and the Jewish Scriptures are fundamentally incompatible?

Although Paul's approach to the law in Galatians is primarily negative, a close reading of the letter shows that these conclusions are not correct. As in the Thessalonian and Corinthian letters, Paul's gospel is not entirely new but duplicates at many points the pattern revealed in the Mosaic covenant of God's dealings with his people. As in those letters, Paul views the Galatian believers as the eschatologically restored people of God about whom the prophets spoke, and he constructs a picture of life in the eschatological era which borrows key features from the Mosaic covenant.

The Galatians as the Restored Israel

Despite occasional scholarly claims to the contrary, Paul's argument in Galatians depends heavily on the notion that members of the believing community, whether Jew or Greek, slave or free, male or female, constitute the eschatologically restored people of God.[59] This is already evident from Paul's description of the Galatians as those whom God has "called" (1:6; 5:8, 13)—a description that in this letter, as much as in the Thessalonian and Corinthian correspondence, echoes prophetic references to God's eschatological call of his people at the time of their restoration from exile (Is 41:9; 42:6; 48:15; 51:2). But it is even more evident in Paul's references to the presence of the Spirit among the Galatians and in his echoes, following prophetic precedent, of the biblical exodus narrative.

The promised Spirit. First, although references to the Spirit abound in Galatians, in two places Paul's language implies that he understood the activity of the Spirit among the Galatians to be the fulfillment of prophetic promises that God's eschatological restoration of his people would take place under the Spirit's power. In 3:13-14 Paul says that Christ redeemed believers from the curse of the law so that the Gentiles might receive the blessing promised to Abraham and so that "we might receive the promise of the Spirit through the faith." Since the Spirit was never promised to Abraham, Paul's reference must be to promises of the Spirit in such passages as Ezekiel 11:19, 36:26-27 and 37:1-14.[60]

Similarly, Paul's reference in 4:6 to the Spirit that God sent into the hearts of believers couples the divine Spirit with the human heart in a way that clearly echoes Ezekiel's references to Israel's need for a "new heart and a new spirit" (18:31) and God's promise to give both to his eschatologically purified people (11:19; 36:26-27).[61]

The new exodus. Second, throughout the letter Paul applies the language of Israel's redemption from Egypt to the Galatians. This same theme appears frequently in Hosea, Isaiah and Jeremiah. Hosea looks back on the wilderness wanderings as an idyllic period in Israel's history and claims that when

God renews his covenant with Israel,
  she shall respond as in the days of her youth,
    as at the time when she came out of the land of Egypt. (Hos 2:15)
Isaiah claims that when God reassembles his people from exile in Assyria, his miraculous power will be no less evident than it was "when they came up from the land of Egypt" (Is 11:16). Deliverance from Babylon, says Jeremiah, will be even a greater miracle than deliverance from Egypt, so great that Israel will look to this second exodus rather than to the first as God's greatest act of redemption (16:14-15; 23:7-8; compare 31:32).[62]

In echoing this motif throughout Galatians, Paul reveals his belief that the Galatians are participants in this second exodus. Thus he expresses his shock at the Galatians' near lapse into apostasy with words reminiscent of the biblical account of Israel's apostasy at Mount Sinai. In Exodus 32 God informs Moses that while he and Moses have been together on the mountain, the Israelites have turned to idols. "Go down from here in haste," he says, "for your people whom you led out of Egypt have acted lawlessly. They have hastily departed [parebēsan tachy] from the way that I have commanded them" (32:7-8 LXX; compare Judg 2:17). Similarly, Paul marvels that the Galatians are "so hastily turning aside" (tacheōs metatithesthe) from their calling (1:6).[63] Since the Galatians have been rescued in the long-awaited "new exodus," Paul is astounded that they would imitate the error of ancient Israel and turn aside from God's redemption.[64]

God's adoption of his people. Similarly, in 4:4-5 Paul echoes the biblical motif of the exodus when he describes the effect of Christ's redeeming work as "the adoption" of sons. Although the word *adoption* never appears in the Hebrew Scriptures, the concept surfaces in the exodus narrative, when God instructs Moses to tell Pharaoh that Israel is his "firstborn son" and that Pharaoh must therefore release the Hebrews from bondage or face the death of his own firstborn (Ex 4:4). The idea of Israel's adoption reemerges in Hosea 11:1-11, where the prophet describes Israel as God's son who has been tenderly taught and nurtured but also disciplined by exile, just as Israel of old suffered under Egyptian oppression. From this latter-day exile, Hosea says, God will rescue his people, bringing them out of "Egypt" (Assyria) and returning them to their homes.

Although Paul uses the term *adoption* in Galatians only in 4:5, he precedes it with the definite article to indicate that he speaks of a particular, presumably well-known adoption. Since the only other occurrence of the term with the definite article in early Christian literature is in Romans 9:4, where Paul speaks specifically of Israel's adoption as one of the Jews' privileges, it seems reasonable to assume that here in Galatians 4:5 the adoption of the new people of God at the time of the second exodus is in view.[65] If this is the correct background for Paul's use of the term in Galatians 4:5, then Paul is not thinking of Greco-Roman customs of adoption, as so many scholars have believed, but of God's second, eschatological act of redemption by which his people are restored to their full status as his adopted children.[66]

No longer slaves. Paul's conviction that the Gentile Galatians were part of the eschatologically restored people of God is probably also reflected in his use of images of slavery and freedom in the letter. Postexilic literature and writings from the Second Temple Period sometimes referred to the foreign domination of God's people as "slavery." Thus Ezra observes that the Jews who have returned to their ancestral lands are "slaves," but that God has not forsaken them in their "slavery" (Ezra 9:9); and Nehemiah, in his prayer of confession, comments that the returned Jews are "slaves to this day—slaves in the land" that God gave to their ancestors to enjoy (Neh 9:36).[67] This metaphorical use of the concept of slavery to describe the domination of the Jewish people by foreign powers probably echoes the prediction in Deuteronomy 28:48, 68 that if God's people disobeyed the law, he would again enslave them to foreign powers just as they had once been enslaved to Egypt. It is probably also related to the prophets' equation of the experience of slavery in Egypt with exile under the Assyrians (Hos 11:11; Is 52:3-4).

Paul's contrast between the enslaved and the free children of Abraham in Galatians 4:21-31 may also echo these themes. The passage is notoriously difficult, but on the most likely reading Paul is providing a counterinterpretation of the biblical account of Isaac's birth—a passage his opponents had used to argue that the Galatians must accept circumcision.[68] The Genesis narrative of the births of Isaac and Ishmael, he says, illustrates the conflict between his own missionary efforts, which "beget" true descendants of Abraham, comparable to Isaac, and the missionary efforts of his opponents, which beget slaves, just as Ishmael was the son of the slave woman Hagar.[69] These two ministries, he says, represent two covenants. One of these is the Sinaitic covenant and begets children into slavery. Paul is not specific about what the other covenant is, but it probably corresponds to the covenant that God made with Abraham and that Paul mentions in 3:17. This covenant is fulfilled in Christ, Abraham's seed, and all those who are "in Christ Jesus" by their Abraham-like faith.[70]

In 4:21-31, then, Paul is saying that his opponents are bearing children into slavery because they demand submission to an outmoded covenant whose just sentence of slavery the "present Jerusalem . . . with her children" (4:25) continues to experience. Paul's own ministry, however, begets children who are experiencing the eschatological redemption from bondage—the "freedom"—that the prophets predicted would come to God's people in the period of Israel's restoration.[71]

The Israel of God. If all of this indicates that Paul believed the Galatians to be part of the eschatologically restored Israel of prophetic prediction, then a statement near the end of the letter which has often puzzled commentators comes into sharp focus. Paul closes his letter with an unambiguous warning against his opponents in Galatia. Making a clear distinction between the convictions of the opponents and his own, Paul says that his opponents are compelling the Galatians to be circumcised only to avoid persecution for the cross of Christ (6:12) and to boast in the Galatians' "flesh" (6:13). As for himself, Paul says, his only boast is in the cross of Christ, through which the world has been crucified to him and he to the world (6:14).

Why does Paul say this? He tells his readers in 6:15: "For neither circumcision nor uncircumcision is anything, but a new creation." The crucifixion of Christ has placed Paul in opposition to the sinfulness of God's fallen creation ("the world"), a world in which he was once mired, and placed him on the side of God's new creation.[72] In the process, Paul has assumed a different attitude toward circumcision than he possessed when aligned with the sinful world. Because his world has been redefined, the significance of circumcision has been redefined: it is nothing. What counts now is the newly (eschatologically) created people of God.

Paul concludes this analysis of the difference between himself and his opponents with a benediction on all who see both the world and the new creation as he sees them: "And as many as walk by this rule, peace and mercy be upon them, even upon the Israel of God" (6:16).

Controversy swirls around this verse because the word translated "even" above *(kai)* could also be translated "and," and because "Israel of God" could refer to ethnic Israelites or to believers, whether Jewish or Gentile, who now constitute the people of God.[73] Paul's assumption throughout the letter that the Galatians are part of this eschatologically restored, prophetically predicted community lends considerable weight to this second explanation.[74] He is claiming, in other words, that the Galatian believers, although Gentiles, have joined believing Jews to constitute the eschatologically restored Israel. The "new creation" is a newly defined Israel—the Israel of God.

The Law's Role in the Restored Israel

Jeremiah and Ezekiel picture a restored Israel that experiences not only the presence of God's Spirit and the reshaping of human hearts but also a renewed ability and desire to keep the law of God. Strange as it may seem within a letter devoted to the notion that the Mosaic law is obsolete, Paul echoes this element of the prophets' eschatological vision for Israel. In what is commonly considered the beginning of his ethical exhortation to the Galatian community, Paul urges his readers to avoid making their freedom from the yoke of the Mosaic law an occasion for the flesh (5:13). Instead, he says, they should serve one another through love, "because the whole law is fulfilled in one word, 'You shall love your neighbor as yourself' " (5:14). This summary of the law is drawn word for word from Leviticus 19:18 (LXX) and was commonly cited in Paul's day as a recapitulation of the law's requirements concerning human relationships. Thus when Jesus used the summary, those around him appear to have accepted it as commonplace. Philo says that Jewish synagogue sermons "in every city" gave special attention to two subjects: "duty to God as shewn by piety and holiness" and "duty to men as shewn by humanity and justice."[75] All of this makes Paul's reference to it here, almost immediately after pleading with the Galatians not to submit again to the bondage of the Mosaic law (5:1), startling.

Three explanations of 5:13 are popular. Some have said that the statement simply stands in unreconcilable tension with Paul's argument on the law in the rest of Galatians.[76] Others believe that in the letter Paul has waged war not on the Mosaic law itself but on a misuse of that law for nationalistic or legalistic purposes. This verse, then, shows Paul's view of the Mosaic law when it is interpreted properly.[77] Neither of these views, however, accounts for all the evidence. The first view cannot explain why, if Paul's statements about the law are careless, contradictory missiles fired in the heat of controversy, the pattern of positive and negative comments about the law characterizes many Pauline letters—even those, like 1 Corinthians, in which the law itself is not at issue.[78] The second view cannot explain why throughout the letter it is the Mosaic law itself, not its misuse, to which Paul denies justifying power.[79]

The third explanation is the most common and is susceptible to neither of these criticisms. It claims that by carefully choosing the term *is fulfilled* (*peplērōtai*) to describe the believer's ethical relationship to the Mosaic law, Paul is showing that the law's obligations actually have no place in the present era of freedom. Paul carefully distinguishes between "doing" and "fulfilling" the law throughout his letters, it is said, and applies the idea of the law's fulfillment only to believers. Believers fulfill the law not because they continue to be obligated to it but because, by the power of the Spirit in their lives, their conduct coincidentally displays the behavior that the Mosaic law prescribes. In this verse, then, Paul is claiming that believers have no need of the Mosaic law because by their Spirit-inspired conduct they already fulfill its requirements.[80]

This explanation encounters problems, however, at both the lexical and the contextual levels. From a lexical perspective, it is difficult to see how Paul could have expected the Galatians to understand a subtle distinction between "doing" and "fulfilling" the law, since the word occurs within a context where ethical obligations are the issue. Paul probably assumed, then, that for the Galatians the word would bear the common meaning of "completing" obligations.[81] This does not mean that the term had no special connotations for Paul.[82] Paul has already used a cognate of the term in 4:4-5 to make the eschatologically potent statement that God sent his Son in "the fullness of time" to redeem those under the law. Probably his claim that the love command "has fulfilled" the law has an eschatological nuance.[83] The distinctiveness of Paul's usage, however, lies not in the way he conceives obedience but in the eschatological claims that stand behind the term: to obey the law as it is summarized in the love command is to complete the requirements of the law in some ultimate and eschatological sense.

From the contextual perspective, 5:14 gives the reason that the Galatians should serve one another in love (v. 13) and avoid biting and devouring one another (v. 15).[84] The reason Paul provides is that such loving behavior fulfills the law's own summary of its various obligations. Paul does not simply say that when the Galatians serve one another in love they fulfill the Mosaic law, but that they fulfill a specific precept of the Mosaic law (Lev 19:18), which in turn summarizes all that the law requires. Their fulfillment of the law, therefore, is accomplished through obedience to a command of the law.

This would be a strange way of putting things if Paul were trying to show that the Galatians' Spirit-inspired conduct rendered the Mosaic law unnecessary. So claiming that "fulfilling" the law is different from "doing" the law does not ease the tension between Paul's appeal here to the Mosaic law and his claim elsewhere that the Mosaic law is obsolete.

The tension does begin to ease, however, when we consider Paul's reference three paragraphs later to "the law of Christ" (6:2). The context in which this phrase occurs is similar to the context of 5:14. As in 5:14, Paul is admonishing the Galatians to work for the good of all, especially those within faith's household (6:10). In 6:1-5 he encourages the Galatians to have the proper attitude both toward members of the community who sin and toward themselves. Those who sin, he says, should be put right with gentleness, and those who put them right should realize their own vulnerability to sin (6:1, 3-5). Paul summarizes this obligation with the statement "Bear one another's burdens, and in this manner you will fulfill the law of Christ" (6:2).[85] Since Matthew, Mark and Luke all claim that Jesus summarized the law in a variety of settings by quoting Leviticus 19:18, and since Paul has also summarized the law in this way a few paragraphs earlier, it seems reasonable to conclude that his reference here to the law of Christ is primarily a reference to Christ's summary of the Mosaic law.[86]

The reference is more than a simple shorthand for "Jesus' summary of the Mosaic law," however, as two considerations show. First, Paul's phrase in 6:2 *(ton nomon tou Christou)* bears a close similarity to the phrase "in the law of Christ" *(ennomos Christou)* in 1 Corinthians 9:21. In the context of 1 Corinthians 9:19-23, the latter phrase both distinguishes the law of Moses from the law of Christ and equates the law of Christ with the law of God. In 1 Corinthians 9:21, then, the law of Christ has become God's law in place of the law of Moses.[87] When Paul speaks of "the law of Christ" in Galatians 6:2, it is likely that he assumes the same distinction between the law of Christ and the law of Moses. In Galatians, as in 1 Corinthians, the law of Christ is something new.

Second, in Galatians 2:17-21 Paul shows that his definition of sin differs fundamentally from the definition provided by the law of Moses, and the language he uses implies that another law governs his behavior.[88] In this passage the dispute between Peter and Paul over eating with Gentiles (2:11-14) continues to run beneath the surface, as Paul explains why the actions of Peter, Barnabas and the rest of the Jews in Antioch deviated from the truth of the gospel. Paul says that withdrawing from fellowship with believing Gentiles implies a distinction between "Gentile sinners" and Jews, and justification by faith in Christ, with its implication that both Jews and Gentiles are sinners, has shown this distinction to be false (vv. 15-16). "But if while seeking to be justified in Christ," Paul continues in verse 17, "we ourselves are also found to be sinners, is Christ therefore a servant of sin? Certainly not!" The implication of this statement is that by eating with "Gentile sinners" Paul does not become a sinner, although the Mosaic law might define his action as sinful.

Against this Paul says in 2:18, "For if I build again that which I have torn down, I show myself to be a transgressor." The word *transgressor (parabatēs)* is used only four other times in the New Testament, twice by Paul in Romans and twice in James. In each of these instances, it refers to transgression of a particular law, not to sin or wickedness in general (Rom 2:25, 27; Jas 2:9, 11). *Transgression (parabasis)* is used five times in the New Testament, three times by Paul and twice in Hebrews, and it too always refers to transgression of a law or a command (Rom 2:23; 4:15; Gal 3:19; Heb 2:2; 9:15).[89] It seems likely, then, that when Paul says in Galatians 2:18 that if he were to withdraw from table fellowship with believing Gentiles as Peter had done, he would prove himself to be a transgressor, he means that he would be a transgressor of some law. This cannot, however, be the law of Moses, since that law builds a boundary between Jews and Gentiles, the crossing of which is sin (2:17; compare 2:15). The law that Paul would transgress if he did not associate with believing Gentiles, then, is another law, and the "law of Christ" of 6:2, a law that incorporates the Mosaic injunction to love one's neighbor, seems the most likely candidate.[90] It was precisely this law of love for neighbor that the men from James, Peter, Barnabas and the rest of the Jews had violated in Antioch, and it is this law that Paul would transgress if he were to build again the wall that had once divided Jew from Gentile (2:18).[91]

For Paul, then, as for the prophets, in the era of the eschatologically restored Israel, "the law" continues to exist. The eschatological Israel has been rescued from bondage to sin and has embarked on the eschatological exodus, just as the prophets had predicted it would. The eschatologically provided Spirit, moreover, enables the people of God to fulfill the law. To this extent the pattern of Paul's stance toward the law reflects what we would expect from a devout Jew who believed that he lived in the era of Israel's restoration.

The differences between Paul and such a Jew, however, are as striking as the similarities, for the law of the eschatological era turns out in Paul's understanding to be different from the law of Moses. Aspects of Moses' law such as the famous summary in Leviticus 19:18 are absorbed into this new law, but the covenant that God made with Moses at Mount Sinai is considered obsolete, and in its place Paul has substituted "the law of Christ." This new law contains none of the parts of the Mosaic law that both Jews and Gentiles of Paul's time considered most distinctively Jewish, and its contents are articulated only in the broad language of love and burden-bearing. And the thrust of Paul's letter to the Galatians is that any attempt to observe the Mosaic law as if it somehow still constituted the covenant between God and his people is a step backward, out of the era of Israel's restoration and into the era of Israel's condemnation (4:21—5:12).

The Law in the Galatian, Thessalonian and Corinthian Correspondence
The theological emergency that produced Galatians differs widely from the situations that prompted Paul to write to the Thessalonians and Corinthians. Contention over the Mosaic law played no role in the production of either the Thessalonian correspondence or 1 Corinthians. Although many have claimed that a debate over the law is implied in 2 Corinthians, this may not reflect a correct understanding of the letter, and in any case no evidence exists that the opponents Paul addresses in that letter tried to use the law to force his Gentile converts to become Jewish proselytes. The Thessalonian letters seek to nurture a church composed of recent converts, whose moorings to traditional culture have been severed and who need Paul's parental advice as they face persecution from those who see them as a threat to the social order. The Corinthian correspondence addresses a cantankerous community who believe that their own spiritual attainments have excelled Paul's and who need to be called back to the traditions they first received. In Galatians, however, for the first time Paul faces a group of Gentile churches who have been persuaded that they must become Jewish proselytes in order to belong to the people of God. Here, then, Paul must articulate his stance on the Mosaic law in the face of opposition to that stance.

As we have seen, Paul's statement of his position is shaped by the type and intensity of the problem he faces. He emphasizes the discontinuity between God's present work in Christ and the Mosaic law, and avoids conceding anything to his opponents. His opponents' activity implies that the Mosaic law can justify, whereas even Jews know that because it cannot be kept, it cannot give life (Gal 2:15-16; 3:10-13). His opponents' activity also implies that the Mosaic law still demarcates the boundary of the people of God, but Paul explains that the Mosaic law, necessary in its day, is now obsolete (3:21-25).

Remarkably, even though his task would have been made easier if he had rejected the Mosaic law and the Jewish tradition altogether, Paul refuses to take this path.[92] His persistent echo of the prophetic traditions about Israel's restoration and his willingness to incorporate Jesus' summary of the Mosaic law into his newly conceived "law of Christ," while they make his view of the law in Galatians extraordinarily complex, also make it fully compatible with the view articulated under different circumstances in the Thessalonian and Corinthian correspondence.

In 1 Corinthians 15:56, 2 Corinthians 3:6-7 and Galatians 3:10-13 Paul claims that the Mosaic law led to the death of those under its authority. Yet in all five letters Paul applies the biblical language of Israel's election to the church, and in 1 Thessalonians, 1 Corinthians and Galatians he describes the conduct of the people of God in language borrowed from God's covenant with ancient Israel. In the Corinthian correspondence he refers to a "new covenant" (1 Cor 11:25; 2 Cor 3:6) that has replaced the old (2 Cor 3:14), and to living in the law of Christ (1 Cor 9:21). Similarly, in Galatians the law of Christ continues to serve as an ethical guide for the believing community (6:2).

The tension between continuity and discontinuity, between using the Mosaic law to settle community problems and considering it obsolete, may be more pronounced in Galatians, but it reflects a pattern that is present as early as 1 Thessalonians and as late as 1 Corinthians. Whatever else we might say of this approach to the law, the consistency with which it is maintained in various letters addressed to widely divergent situations demonstrates that it does not represent merely a hastily formulated broadside, more rhetorically than logically successful. The evidence indicates that this approach originated in a careful consideration of the relationship between Jewish tradition and God's action in the Messiah Jesus. Galatians is the fruit of Paul's efforts to make this carefully considered position as rhetorically persuasive as possible in light of the sudden and dismaying defection of some Galatian believers from the truth of the gospel.

CHAPTER SEVEN

RUBBISH & RESOURCE: The Law of Moses in Philippians

Like the Thessalonian letters, Philippians receives scant attention from students of Paul's view of the law. Those who deal with the letter at all go directly to Philippians 3:2-10, where Paul mentions the Mosaic law explicitly three times (vv. 5, 6, 9) and reflects autobiographically on the role the law played in his pre-Christian existence.[1] Any investigation of Paul's view of the law which did not take advantage of this rare moment of reflection on the role of the law in Paul's own life would, of course, be remiss, but this passage is not the only part of the letter relevant to formulating an understanding of Paul's view of the law.

Although Paul does not use the term *law* elsewhere, he uses the language of the Mosaic law in his allusive comparison of the Philippians with the Israelites in the wilderness (2:14-18) and in the cultic expressions with which he describes his own efforts and those of the Philippians on behalf of the gospel (2:17, 25, 30; 4:18). These passages too are relevant to the discussion of the place that the law held in Paul's theology. The letter as a whole, then, needs to be examined for its contribution to the debate over Paul's view of the law, and the examination should begin by placing Philippians within the context of Paul's career.

Philippians in Context

The basic outline of the situation that prompted Paul to write Philippians is mercifully clear. Paul was in prison (1:13-14; compare 1:30; 4:14) and had received monetary gifts from the Philippians, conveyed by their messenger Epaphroditus (2:25-30; 4:18) to help alleviate his suffering (4:14). One of Paul's objectives in the letter, then, is simply to thank the Philippians for their gifts. Paul hints at his appreciation for their efforts in his opening thanksgiving prayer when he mentions the Philippians' "fellowship in the gospel from the first day until now" and expresses his confidence, in light of this fellowship, that God will complete the good work that he has begun in them (1:5-7).[2] He does not actually thank the Philippians for the gifts, however, until the end of the letter (4:10-20), and this is evidence enough that he intended the letter to be much more than an expression of gratitude.[3] Although it would go too far to say that his gratitude for the Philippians' gifts only provided an excuse for the letter, the amount of space Paul devotes to the subject and his delayed discussion of it in explicit terms show that this was not his primary concern.

Paul spends considerably more energy discussing the Philippians' attitudes toward one another. Thus he pleads with them to "stand firm in one spirit, struggling together with one soul for the faith of the gospel" (1:27) and urges them to have the same attitude (2:2). In addition, he admonishes them not to watch out only for themselves but also to care for others (2:4), to adopt the humble attitude of Christ (2:5-11), and to do everything without arguing (2:14). In 4:2 he exhorts Euodia and Syntyche "to have the same attitude in the Lord" and begs an unknown member of the congregation to "help them" in this effort.

Paul buttresses these exhortations with references to his own conduct and to the conduct of his coworkers, in the hope that the Philippians will follow their example. Thus he informs them that in spite of personal opposition from fellow believers who preach Christ from impure motives, he continues to rejoice, for at least Christ is preached (1:15-18). He mentions that unlike others who do not pursue "the things of Christ," Timothy has been unselfishly concerned to aid him in the advancement of the gospel (2:19-22) Paul's hope that the Philippians will drop their quarrels and work among themselves for the advancement of the gospel (compare 1:27) is subtly conveyed through these narratives of his day-to-day existence.

Paul recognizes, however, that the Philippians' efforts to do this may be complicated by various kinds of opposition. In 1:27-30 he exhorts them not to be "frightened in any way by those who oppose" them (1:28), and in 3:2—4:1 he warns them both against "evil workers" who promote circumcision (3:2-3) and against "enemies of the cross of Christ" whose minds are set on earthly rather than heavenly things (3:18-20). Here too Paul's personal example provides an important basis for his exhortation. He compares the Philippians' struggle against those who oppose them with his own suffering both when he was in Philippi and in his present imprisonment (1:30; compare Acts 16:16-40) and says that in their case, as in his, suffering for Christ is a gift (1:29; compare 1:12).

Paul also follows his warning against those who promote circumcision in 3:2 with an example of how he turned from opposition to the gospel and confidence in the flesh to the righteousness that comes from God by faith in Christ (3:4-11). The warning against the enemies of Christ's cross similarly begins with the statement "Be imitators of me, brothers and sisters, and observe those who walk in the same way, just as you have an example in us" (3:17). Again, Paul hopes to persuade the Philippians to follow his example in standing firm against various kinds of opposition to the gospel.

This much is relatively clear and uncontroversial. Complications quickly arise, however, when we try to become more specific, particularly about the groups Paul opposes in 3:2—4:1. Does his admonition in this section presuppose two distinct groups or only one? Were the theological disturbances to which this passage refers present in Philippi, or was Paul only warning the Philippians against the possibility that such problems might arise? And, most important of all, what is the specific nature of the theological errors that Paul describes in 3:2—4:1? The answers to these questions hinge on the understanding of Paul's thrice-repeated command to "beware" of "evil workers" in 3:2, the identity of these "evil workers" and the nature of their relationship, if any, to the "enemies of the cross of Christ" mentioned in 3:18.

"Beware . . ."

Paul begins a new section of his letter abruptly in 3:2 with the exhortation "Beware the dogs! Beware the evil workers! Beware the mutilation!" The term *beware* is a present-tense imperative of *blepō*, a verb whose most frequent meaning is simply "I see" but which can also mean "I consider, note or mark" something, and occasionally, in its imperatival forms, "watch," "look to" or "beware of."[4] In 3:2 the term has sometimes been translated "consider" or "take proper notice of" on the grounds that if it meant "beware of" it should have been followed by a prepositional phrase (*apo* . . .) or a negated verbal clause (*mē* . . .) rather than by simple objects such as "dogs," "evil workers" and "mutilation."[5] Paul then would simply be holding up a group of people as a negative example for the Philippians' consideration, not warning the Philippians against a danger present among them.

The unusual grammar of Paul's sentence, however, should not obscure its urgency. The rhetoric of Paul's language is impressive: Paul repeats *blepete* three times in rapid succession, and for each of the three he supplies grammatical objects that begin with a *k* sound *(kynas, kakous ergatas, katatomēn)*. "Beware the curs! Beware the criminals! Beware the cutters!" approaches the rhetoric of the Greek sentence. This does not sound as if Paul is asking the Philippians merely to "consider" the character of those who promote circumcision.[6]

Primarily for this reason, most interpreters believe that Paul's sentence warns against a potential threat: Paul believes that the evil workers could influence the Philippians to deviate from the gospel, and so he urges them to beware of their influence. Among these interpreters, some believe the urgency of Paul's language to be so great that the threat to the Philippians must be present among them—outsiders have entered the congregation to lead it astray.[7] Others point out, however, that nothing in Paul's language requires the presence of outsiders within the Philippian church; they think Paul was probably simply warning the Philippians that troublemakers were at large and might at some future point enter their community.[8] This minimalist approach to the situation seems to be the best way to view Paul's statement; since Paul mentions these outsiders only in 3:2, they do not appear to have posed an active threat to the community.

"The Evil Workers"

Who are the outsiders? Paul's description of them in 3:2 and his reaction to them in 3:3-11 has stirred up a dust storm of controversy. Some have argued, on the assumption that *blepete* means "consider" or "take proper notice of," that Paul refers to unbelieving Jews. On this reading, the passage presents the Jews as a negative example to avoid—part of Paul's admonition to the Philippians not to exalt themselves over others or give in to a self-centered perfectionism. Thus Paul describes his own life as an unbelieving Jew as typical of Jewish existence. Just as they place confidence in the flesh, so did he; just as they take pride in their accomplishments, he did too. These interpreters emphasize the irony of Paul's language in 3:2. The Jews may believe that Gentiles are "dogs" because, like the dog on the street, they eat anything, but the Jew himself is a "dog." Jews may take pride in good works, but they are actually "evil workers." Jews boast in their circumcision, but that surgery is really nothing more than mutilation of the flesh.[9]

But several problems attend this understanding of Paul's polemic. First, such hostility is not typical of Paul's attitude toward Judaism and Jewish institutions elsewhere in his letters. He can certainly speak harshly of unbelieving Jews who hinder the proclamation of the gospel (1 Thess 2:15-17), and he is capable of extraordinarily strong language about the work of Jewish Christians who compel Gentiles to be circumcised (Gal 5:12), but his attitude toward unbelieving Jews and Jewish institutions in general is far more positive.[10] Circumcision has value when it is accompanied by obedience (Rom 2:25), and it served in Abraham's case as a "sign" and "seal" of his justification by faith (Rom 4:11). Israel's adoption, glory, covenants, law and temple service are positive blessings that turn the nation's rejection of the Messiah into a poignant tragedy (Rom 9:1-5). There is no animus against Judaism as a religion here, and therefore to find it in Philippians 3:2-11 would be surprising.

It is more likely that the group to whom Paul refers in this passage are Judaizing believers, similar to or identical with the group that created such turmoil among the Galatians. The term *workers* that Paul uses to describe this group is generally used in the New Testament to refer to Christian "workers" who go out to preach the gospel or who are otherwise engaged in the work of the church.[11] This is the only sense in which Paul uses the term, and in 2 Corinthians 11:13 he uses it to refer to "false apostles, deceitful workers who masquerade as apostles of Christ."[12] In Philippians 3:2, then, Paul probably uses the word in a similar way to refer to itinerant preachers who proclaim a deviant form of the gospel.

As with Paul's opponents in Galatia, the gospel that these missionaries proclaim focuses on circumcision.[13] Thus Paul ironically calls them "the mutilation" (*hē katatomē*) and styles believers, in contrast, "the circumcision" (*hē peritomē*) whose religious service (*latreuontes*) is in the Spirit of God, whose boast is in Christ and who take no confidence in the flesh (3:3). This sounds like Paul's polemic against the Galatian Judaizers, whose circumcising activity he compares with mutilation (Gal 5:12), whose motives for circumcising he attributes to the desire to boast in the Galatians' flesh (Gal 6:13) and whose emphasis on the flesh stands in contrast to his concern with the Spirit (Gal 4:29). It seems unnecessary, then, to look beyond Galatians to locate the identity of the opponents whom Paul attacks in 3:2-3.[14]

"The Enemies of the Cross of Christ"

Some scholars argue, however, that Paul's opponents in Philippi were not simply conservative Jewish Christians who continued to cling to circumcision as the identity marker of the people of God. They point out that Paul makes no clear distinction between the evil workers of 3:2 and "the enemies of the cross of Christ" *(tous echthrous tou staurou tou Christou)* in 3:18-19 who, Paul says, consider their belly to be their God and their shame to be their glory.[15] This phrase seems to describe people who make a virtue of violating moral norms. Since antinomianism was certainly not among the faults of common Jews, the argument goes, Paul must be attacking another kind of deviation from his gospel, and the group most likely to have combined an interest in the rite of circumcision with a freewheeling morality are Jewish Christian Gnostics. Gnosticism, according to this thesis, flourished in Jewish form in the early history of the church and was characterized not only by recognition of the Jewish Scriptures, albeit under an esoteric interpretation, and continued observance of circumcision but also by the notion that the adherent had achieved spiritual perfection and was free from bondage to moral taboos. The result was a mixture of appreciation for some Jewish customs with a more typically Gnostic emphasis on perfection (compare 3:12-16), denial of the importance of Christ's crucifixion (compare 3:18), rejection of the bodily resurrection (compare 3:10-11), belief in the right to indulge physical urges (compare 3:19) and appeal to esoteric revelation (compare 3:15). Thus Paul attacks the Jewish side of this movement in 3:1-11, it is said, and the Gnostic side in 3:12-19.[16]

This thesis, however, faces several fatal difficulties. First, Paul says that the primary concern of the group against whom he warns the Philippians is "circumcision" (3:2-3). Even if some Gnostic groups continued to practice circumcision, it is difficult to argue that any made it a central tenet of their religion.[17] The most likely explanation for the interest in circumcision of the group presupposed in 3:2, then, remains that they were Judaizing Christians.[18] Second, Paul's autobiographical argument against this group in 3:4-11 assumes that its confidence lies in observing the law. Thus Paul's point is that although his opponents think they have reason for confidence in fleshly qualifications—qualifications that Paul summarizes in terms of keeping the law (3:6, 9)—he has more. If the opponents were Gnostic, Paul could not have characterized them as placing confidence in the flesh, and certainly he could not have compared their devotion to the law with his own prior to conversion. For the Gnostic, even for this theory's hypothetical Jewish Christian Gnostic, knowledge and the Spirit were the center of religious devotion, not the law.[19]

Despite these problems, the Gnostic theory has the advantage of offering a single explanation for Paul's opposition both to false teaching with a Jewish character and to false teaching that because of its antinomian qualities sounds distinctly un-Jewish.[20] If Philippians was written in Ephesus in close proximity to Galatians and 1 Corinthians, however, the two-sided nature of Paul's argument in this chapter may be explainable without speculation about the existence of a single group with both sets of characteristics.[21] Paul may have wanted to warn the Philippians both of the Judaizing error he had encountered in Galatia and of the mixture of popular Platonism, sophistry and the gospel which had created such turmoil in Corinth. This may be why in 3:10-11 and 3:21 he stresses the importance of Christ's resurrection, just as he had countered objections to the resurrection in Corinth (1 Cor 15:12, 35), and why in 3:12 and 3:15 he carefully qualifies the notion that believers have entered a state of perfection in words reminiscent of 1 Corinthians 4:8 (compare 1 Cor 2:6; 3:1-2; 4:18). Similarly, in 3:19 he warns the Philippians against those who, like the Corinthians (1 Cor 1:17-18, 23; 2:2), are unimpressed with the preaching of "the cross of Christ" and who, also in a way reminiscent of the Corinthians, think the gospel liberates the believer to indulge selfish urges in matters of eating and sex (compare 1 Cor 5:1-2; 6:12-20; 8:1-13; 10:1—11:1).[22]

In Philippians, then, Paul combines an expression of gratitude and an exhortation to unity with a warning against two theological errors that have posed especially dangerous threats to his other congregations. The church has not yet fallen into doctrinal error or come into contact with Paul's opponents, and the Philippians' generous gifts to Paul imply that they are united in their support of him and his gospel (4:10, 15-16; compare 2:25).[23] Paul's intention, accordingly, is to encourage the congregation to avoid the troubles that have plagued other Pauline churches and to "stand fast in one spirit, in one soul, striving together for the faith of the gospel" (1:27). Paul's comments on and allusions to the Mosaic law form an important component of this exhortation.

The Basis of Confidence

Paul's explicit references to "the law" appear in the course of his argument against his Judaizing opponents in 3:2-11. Just as Paul provides an example for the Philippians to follow at other points in his exhortation (1:15-18, 30;

3:17; 4:9), so here he speaks autobiographically. Should the Judaizers arrive in Philippi, he hopes the Philippians will regard their message just as Paul views his former life as a law-observant persecutor of the church—as "loss" and "refuse" (3:7-8).[24] The chief point of comparison between Paul as law-observant persecutor and the Judaizing missionaries lies in the object of each party's "confidence." Rather than understanding the nature of true circumcision, serving in the Spirit of God and boasting in Christ, the Judaizers do what Paul did—they place their confidence in "the flesh" (vv. 3-4).

The term *flesh* in this context has both literal and metaphorical meanings. Since circumcision was literally an operation on the flesh, the term indicates that the Judaizers are placing their confidence in a fleshly rite.[25] As we have already seen in Galatians, however, the term refers to far more than the physical rite of circumcision; it also stands for all that is unspiritual, outward and subject to human frailty. It refers to human inability and stands in contrast to divine strength. The Judaizers' confidence in the physical operation of circumcision is wrong-headed because it implies a confidence in weak and fallen humanity rather than in God.

This is the sense in which Paul too once placed confidence in the flesh. During the time of his rejection of the gospel and zealous opposition to the church, Paul's trust was in his circumcision, family lineage, Hebraic upbringing and zealous devotion to the Mosaic law—all physical, human credentials. When Paul believed the gospel, however, the object of his confidence shifted to Christ, and all of these credentials, indeed "all things" without remainder, became "loss" and "refuse" (v. 8). Paul knows from personal experience that what the Judaizers consider central is actually inconsequential in light of the gospel. By listing his own reasons for "confidence in the flesh" and then explaining why he now considers them loss, he hopes to ensure that the Philippians will follow his lead should the Judaizers ever appear among them.

Paul uses the term *law* three times in this passage, and each instance shows that he considered the Mosaic law part of a past era, among the "all things" that he considered loss in order that he might gain Christ. In verse 5 he lists his interpretation and observance of the law after the manner of the Pharisees as one of his reasons for confidence in the flesh (compare v. 4); in verse 6 he summarizes his accomplishments as a Jew with the claim that with respect to the righteousness that comes by the law he was "blameless"; and in verse 9 he expresses the desire to be found on the final day clinging not to his own righteousness "based on the law" but to "the righteousness that comes from God through faith" in Christ. All of these "gains," however, Paul considers useless for attaining the resurrection of the dead in the final day (vv. 9-11; compare vv. 7-8).[26]

The Role of Human Effort

Paul's argument and the history of its interpretation raise three questions about his stance toward the Mosaic law in this passage. First, does his argument assume that Judaism generally held that righteousness before God and acquittal on the final day could be achieved by human effort? Second, does his claim to have been blameless with respect to the law imply that he believed the law could be fully obeyed? And third, does his assumption that the law is obsolete mean that he believed the Mosaic law held no significance for the believer?

Many interpreters of the passage have answered the first question with a hearty yes. The passage is often taken as evidence that the typical Jew in Paul's time not only kept the law as a means to salvation but did so with a haughty spirit. Thus Paul's reference to "evil workers" in verse 2 is said to be a parody of the Jews' notion that their good works make them better than others.[27] Paul's comment about boasting in Christ is supposedly a polemical thrust at Jewish self-glorification.[28] And Paul's references to the Mosaic law are believed to imply that typical Jews self-righteously imagined that their blameless observance of the law would merit salvation.[29]

The passage leaves little doubt that the pre-Christian Paul and the Judaizers believed that their obedience cooperated with God's grace to effect acquittal on the final day.[30] Thus Paul summarizes the convictions of the Judaizers and his own pre-Christian convictions three times as placing "confidence in the flesh" (vv. 3-4), and he says the privileges into which he was born and the accomplishments he achieved had seemed "gains" to him (v. 7).[31] The problem with his pre-Christian theology and with the Judaizers' version of the gospel, then, was not simply that both he and they embraced the law when they should have embraced Christ, but that he and they also placed an unwarranted confidence in the law which led them to reject the gospel of "the righteousness that comes from God through faith."[32]

This understanding of the passage does not imply, however, that every non-Christian Jew of Paul's time viewed the law in this way. Paul was an exceptional Jew who at the time of his conversion "was advancing in Judaism beyond many" of his contemporaries, who "was extremely zealous for the traditions" of his ancestors and whose "zeal" led him to persecute the church (Gal 1:13-14; Phil 3:4, 6). The Judaizers similarly were zealous in their efforts to complete the faith of Gentile adherents to Paul's gospel, as their journeys to Paul's churches and struggle to win them over demonstrate (Gal 4:17; compare Phil 3:2). From Paul's perspective, his own pre-Christian zeal to oppose the gospel and the Judaizers' zeal to interfere with his churches were the fruits of their confidence in the Jewish law, and such zeal was unusual.

Paul's Righteousness Under the Law

A second aspect of the passage that has vexed interpreters is Paul's claim that prior to his conversion he "was blameless with respect to the righteousness that comes by the law" (3:6). Some have claimed that the statement applies only to the righteousness acquired by observance of external commandments and that it leaves room for Paul to have been at fault in the more important matters of the heart.[33] Others have linked verse 6 with verse 9 and claimed that Paul considered his blamelessness his "own" and believed that in the final day he could present his faultless obedience before God and demand that God acquit him.[34] Still others have argued that the passage reveals a conviction that the law could be satisfactorily kept and a righteousness could be obtained by observing it. Paul, it is said, does not criticize this righteousness as either boastful or merit-seeking. His only quarrel with it is that it is the wrong righteousness: it is gained by means of Torah observance rather than by faith in Christ.[35]

None of these interpretations of Paul's statement is adequate. The first does not appreciate the force of Paul's language. Paul nowhere indicates that his blamelessness was limited to externals but says simply and straightforwardly that he was blameless. The second interpretation has more merit since, as we have seen, Paul claims to have placed confidence in his achievements and considered them personal gains (*en moi kerdē*, v. 7). Nevertheless, he claims neither to have boasted in his gains before God nor to have thought he could place God in his debt by observing the law. Moreover, his "blamelessness" with respect to the law is a summary term that probably encompasses the God-given privileges into which he was born as well as his personal achievements. This passage gives no evidence that Paul refused to thank God for these gracious gifts at the same time that he believed his own works would play some role in his final vindication.[36] The third interpretation fails to appreciate the evidence from the Judaism of the period that being blameless with respect to the law did not exclude a consciousness of sin and a hope for God's final eschatological redemption. Even among those who understood that blameless observance of the law involved using the means of atonement for sin, the hope often flourished that

God would redeem his people from the plight of sin.[37]

When Paul says that he was blameless with respect to the law, therefore, he probably means that he observed the commandments as conscientiously as possible and that when he transgressed them he used the means prescribed in the law itself to atone for his sin. His own righteousness—in which, according to verse 9, he does not want to be found on the final day—is not a self-righteous attitude but his inadequate righteousness. It is the flawed righteousness of which Deuteronomy speaks when it solemnly declares three times in succession that Israel will not inherit the land of promise because of its own righteousness but because of the wickedness of the nations that live there and because of God's faithfulness to the covenant made with Abraham, Isaac and Jacob (Deut 9:4-6 LXX).[38] It is the righteousness that Isaiah laments when he says of the sins of his people, "All our righteousness *[hē dikaiosynē hēmōn]* is as an unclean rag" (Is 64:5[6] LXX).[39] And it is the inadequate righteousness that God replaces for believers, through Christ's atoning sacrifice, with his own righteousness (Phil 3:9; compare Rom 3:21-26; 2 Cor 5:21).[40]

The Law's Place in the Believer's Life

If the provisional and ultimately inadequate righteousness that was available on the basis of the Mosaic law has been replaced by "the righteousness that comes from God by faith," then does Philippians 3:2-11 imply that the law has no significance for the believer? The passage itself provides a hint that Paul did not hold this view. In opposition to the Judaizers, Paul claims that believers are the "circumcision" and that they "serve" in the Spirit of God (v. 3). Since the Mosaic law considers circumcision one of the most important distinguishing marks of membership in the people of God, Paul's claim that "we are the circumcision," although not a reference to the physical rite, is a claim to be the true people of God—probably with an intentional echo of the biblical hope that Israel's heart would one day be circumcised (Deut 10:16; Jer 4:4; compare Lev 26:41).

Similarly, Paul's claim that believers "serve" *(latreuontes)* in the Spirit of God, although it has nothing to do with literal service in the temple, adopts the language the Septuagint uses for Israel's service to God as his chosen people (Ex 3:12; Deut 10:12).[41] Service "in the Spirit of God," moreover, recalls the prophetic description of the restored Israel as a place where God's Spirit would dwell (Ezek 11:19; 36:27; 37:1-14). Even within a passage that claims that the Mosaic law is "loss" and "rubbish," then, the law continues to provide the pattern for the boundaries that demarcate the people of God.

New People, New Ritual

If believers were spoken of as the new people of God who serve in a new way only in Philippians 3:2-11, we might conclude that Paul's assertions were polemically motivated—that in the heat of his argument he attempted to define his opponents' traditions so as to show that his churches were their real owners. But Paul makes the same assumptions in other passages where the Judaizers are not in view. In 1:27—2:30, for example, Paul is concerned not with Judaizing opponents but with the unity of the Philippian congregation. He urges them to "stand firm in one spirit and in one soul" as they contend for the faith of the gospel amid persecution (1:27-28); he instructs them to have the same attitude and love, to be one in soul, not to think in ways that promote selfish ambitions, and to follow the example of Christ's unselfish service (2:1-11); and he holds up Timothy and Epaphroditus as additional examples of this kind of service (2:19-30).

As a critical step in this series of exhortations, Paul pleads with the Philippians in 2:12-18 to emulate the obedience of Christ, which he has just described (v. 8), and their own previous obedience in their efforts to work out their salvation with fear and trembling (v. 12).[42] Specifically, they are to avoid murmurings and arguments (v. 14) in order to provide an example of purity within a perverse generation (v. 15). The result of their obedience in this matter will be that Paul's labor for the advancement of the gospel will not have been in vain (v. 16), their faith will be an offering to God, and Paul will rejoice with them (vv. 17-18).

For the student of Paul's view of the law, the passage is especially significant because Paul makes his argument with the help of numerous allusions to both the narrative and the legal portions of the Mosaic covenant. In verses 14-15 Paul tells the Philippians, "Do all things without murmurings and arguments in order that you might be blameless and pure, unblemished children of God in the midst of a crooked and perverse generation, in which you shine like stars in the world." Echoes of the biblical record of Israel's wilderness wandering resound clearly in this passage. They are loudest in verse 15, where Paul's language is heavily indebted to the Song of Moses. The Song of Moses stands near the conclusion of Deuteronomy (31:30—32:47) and summarizes the story of Israel's unfaithfulness to God despite God's faithfulness to Israel. After a preface calls the assembled congregation of Israel to attention, the song begins with a paragraph that states its primary theme:

> God, his works are truth, and all his ways are right. He is a faithful God, and he is not unjust. Just and pure is the Lord. They sinned, they who

were not his children, blemished *[ouk autō tekna, mōmēta]*, a crooked and perverse generation *[genea skolia kai diestrammenē]*. (Deut 32:4-5 LXX)

The theme of the song, then, is that despite God's faithfulness, Israel severed its filial ties with him through its disobedience and became a blemished, crooked and perverse generation. In contrast, Paul describes the Philippians as "children unblemished" *(tekna amōma)* who live "in the midst of a crooked and perverse generation" *(meson geneas skolias kai diestrammenēs)*. Paul's language seems intentionally formulated to signal the Philippians' status as the newly constituted people of God who, unlike Israel of old, are "unblemished" and who, rather than constituting "a crooked and perverse generation," stand in contrast to it.[43]

Paul then says that as this newly constituted and unblemished people, the Philippians "shine as stars in the world," a phrase that echoes the descriptions of Israel's vocation in Isaiah 42:6-7 and 49:6 as a "light to the Gentiles."[44] With this comment Paul implies that the Philippians not only have taken over biblical Israel's role as the unblemished people of God but have been assigned Israel's vocation as "light to the Gentiles" as well.[45]

Paul's purpose, however, is not to congratulate the Philippians but to exhort them to be unified and to fulfill the vocation of God's chosen people. Thus his exhortation begins in 2:14 with what must be, in light of the clear allusion to the Song of Moses in 2:15, an echo of the complaining of the Israelites in the wilderness. When Paul says that the Philippians must do all things without "murmurings," he uses a word *(gongysmos)* that is rare in the New Testament and early Christian literature generally and appears only here in the Pauline literature.[46] Yet it occurs frequently throughout the Septuagint's narratives of Israel's wilderness wanderings to refer to the "murmuring" of the Israelites against Moses (Ex 16:2-9; 17:3; Num 11:1; compare 14:2)—complaining that, as Moses reminds them (Ex 16:8), is actually against God.

Nothing in Paul's letter indicates that the Philippians were complaining against their leadership, whether Paul or the "overseers and deacons" he mentions in 1:1, or even directly against God as the Israelites did.[47] Their "murmuring" is instead occurring among themselves. Nevertheless, Paul's use of this distinctive term within a context that clearly echoes the biblical story of Israel's wilderness wandering shows that he intended to hold the Israelites' experience in the wilderness before the Philippians as a negative example. If they were to remain "unblemished" and complete their vocation as God's people, they needed to avoid the distracting social discord that characterized God's ancient and disobedient people and to "work out" their salvation "with fear and trembling" (2:12).[48]

Paul's belief that the Philippians are the new people of God who stand in Israel's place also emerges in the cultic language he uses to describe their status before God and their efforts to work out their commitment to the faith. First, Paul brackets the letter with references to the Philippians both corporately and individually as "holy people" (*hagioi*, 1:1; *hagios*, 4:21). The Philippians, like the Thessalonians and the Corinthians, were probably almost entirely Gentile; yet here, as in those letters, Paul describes them with a term distinctive of Israel's status as the people of God (Ex 19:6).

Second, Paul uses cultic language in a way that betrays an assumption that like Israel of old, the Philippians offer sacrifices to God. Paul describes the Philippians' monetary gifts to him through Epaphroditus as "a fragrant aroma *[osmēn euōdias]*, an acceptable sacrifice *[thysian dektēn]*, pleasing to God" (4:18). This language comes from the Septuagint, which frequently describes Israel's sacrifices as "a fragrant aroma" and "acceptable" to God.[49] The Philippians' gifts to Paul, then, serve as pleasing sacrifices to God much in the way that biblical Israel's sacrificial ritual, according to the law, was to be acceptable and pleasing to God.

Paul's description of the Philippians' faith in terms of sacrificial ritual is not confined to this verse, however. In 2:17 he speaks of the possibility of his own death and says that if he should die, his death will be a drink offering poured out "in addition to the sacrificial service" of the Philippians' faith.[50] The addition of drink offerings to various kinds of sacrifice was not unique to the Jewish sacrificial system, and some scholars have argued that in view of the predominantly Gentile composition of the Philippian church, Paul probably has pagan sacrificial custom in mind here.[51] But since 4:18 indisputably refers to the Jewish system as described in the Bible, it is better to understand Paul's language in 2:17 as an echo of the biblical system also.[52] Paul's meaning, then, would be that if he should die, his death would be added to the Philippians' efforts to "hold fast to the word of life" (2:16) in the same way that a biblical drink offering was added to the sacrifice.[53] The implication is that Paul and the Philippians are together members of a newly constituted Israel whose ritual of sacrifice includes the Philippians' material support of Paul's work (4:18) and their unified effort to maintain the faith amid difficult circumstances (2:17).[54]

The Law in Philippians: A Comparative Summary

Paul's use of the Mosaic law in Philippians is unique. Unlike Galatians, the letter offers neither an explanation of the law's purpose (Gal 3:19—4:17) nor a description of the law's connection with sin (Gal 3:19; compare 1 Cor 15:56). Unlike the Corinthian letters (1 Cor 11:25; 2 Cor 3:6, 14), Philippians does not use the term *covenant*. Unlike 1 Thessalonians, the letter contains no allusions to the ethical admonitions of Leviticus (1 Thess 4:1-12). Furthermore, in Philippians 3:2-11 Paul states more clearly than in these letters that requiring obedience to the Mosaic covenant is wrong not only because it turns the clock back to the time of sin and punishment but also because it implies a confidence in human accomplishment that effectively denies the gracious nature of God's redeeming work.

Nevertheless, the view of the law reflected in Philippians follows in significant ways the pattern that has emerged from the Thessalonian, Corinthian and Galatian correspondence. Paul argues more succinctly but no less clearly than in Galatians and 2 Corinthians that the traditional relationship between the Mosaic law and the people of God has ended and that the stubborn refusal to recognize this amounts to an ill-advised confidence in the flesh. To reintroduce the Mosaic legislation as necessary for demarcating the boundaries of the people of God is to make a travesty of the spiritual significance of circumcision and the service of God.

But the obsolescence of the Mosaic covenant does not mean in Philippians, any more than it had signified in these other letters, that the biblical pattern of sanctity has become obsolete. The Philippians, like the Thessalonians, Corinthians and Galatians, are the restored and newly constituted people of God, "saints" who must learn from the example of the biblical people of God (1 Cor 10:1-13) to avoid violating their sanctity and to complete their calling to be a light to the Gentiles. Their sanctification and salvation are a result of God's gracious work within them (Phil 2:13; 3:9) but nevertheless must be worked out with fear and trembling (2:12; compare 1:6).[55]

The most remarkable aspect of all this for the student of Paul's view of the law is, once again, its consistency over the course of many years and within letters addressed to widely different situations. Although a formal tension exists between Paul's claim that the law is "refuse" and his use of the law in his exhortations to the Philippians, the consistency with which this two-sided approach to the law is maintained in different contexts indicates that carefully considered theological convictions underlie it. What might seem contradictory to a reader of Philippians alone appears instead to be only a partial articulation of a more complex, and ultimately coherent, position when it is placed alongside Paul's other letters.

CHAPTER EIGHT

THE LAW OF MOSES, THE HUMAN PLIGHT & THE LAW OF FAITH IN ROMANS 1–4

Controversy plagues the discussion of Paul's understanding of the Mosaic law in part because interpreters must tease his view out of letters written to meet the pastoral needs of churches. In the letters examined so far in this book, Paul comes closest to abstract reflection on the relationship between the Mosaic law and the gospel in 2 Corinthians 3:1-18. That passage is so brief and leaves so many questions unanswered, however, that it can provide only tantalizing hints about Paul's broader convictions. Galatians looks promising at first, but as we have seen, the boundaries of the discussion of law and gospel in that epistle were set largely by Paul's opponents, and the pastoral situation that produced Paul's argument did not lend itself to a reflective meditation on the subject.

But what about Romans? If, as many interpreters believe, Romans 1:16-17 is the thesis statement of the letter, then Romans is about the gospel: 1:16-17 explains the gospel in summary form, and 1:18—11:36 provides a detailed explanation of this summary.[1] This letter is also about the law. The term appears seventy-two times in Romans—representing over 60 percent of its appearances in the Pauline letters—and all but two of these appearances occur in the section of the letter in which Paul explains the gospel. Moreover, since Paul did not establish Christianity in Rome and had never visited the churches there (1:13; 15:20-22), the interpreter might conclude that the letter is only loosely tied to the circumstances of the Roman Christians. Thus many have found in Romans an outline of the *ordo salutis*, a summary of the central points of Christian doctrine, or at least an abstract treatment of the great questions that vexed Paul toward the end of his missionary endeavors.[2] Does Paul in Romans, then, provide a complete explanation of his view of the law, undisturbed by the commotion of local trouble and misunderstanding?

Evidence from Romans

At least three characteristics of Romans show that a hasty and excited yes to this question would be incautious. First, 16:3-16 greets twenty-six people, more than Paul greets in any other letter.[3] If this group had become acquainted with Paul during his ministry in the east and then moved to Rome, as seems likely, then Paul's ties with the churches in Rome are closer than we might imagine on the basis of his statements that he had never visited the Roman Christians. These twenty-six men and women supplied a personal link between Paul and the Roman churches through which information about the situation in Rome may have reached him.[4]

Second, Paul's awareness of a controversy between "the weak" and "the strong" among the Roman Christians (15:1; see also 14:1-2) shows that he understood something about the situation there. The weak avoided meat and wine (14:2, 21; compare 14:17), a dietary strategy that ancient Jews sometimes adopted when properly slaughtered meat and untainted wine were not available. Since this group also observed certain days as special (14:5-6), they were probably Jews or Gentiles who had adopted Jewish customs.[5] The strong ate "anything" (14:2), considered "every day alike" (14:5) and were probably Gentiles or Jews who, like Paul (14:14; 15:1), no longer consistently observed these aspects of the Mosaic law. Paul admonishes these groups to avoid "quarrels" over such disputable matters (14:1) and to accept one another (15:7). Given the specificity with which Paul addresses this problem, it seems that Paul must have known of a dispute between a minority of Roman Christians who were attached to the Jewish law and a majority who considered themselves free from its constraints.[6]

Third, at least one section of the letter regularly described as the "doctrinal" section (1:16—11:36) contains comments suggesting that Paul is aware of conditions in the Roman church.[7] In 11:13-32 he turns directly to the Gentiles in Rome (v. 13) and admonishes them not to boast over Jews who have been cut off from God's people because of their unbelief (v. 18). Gentiles can always be cut off, he says, if they do not continue in God's kindness (v. 22), and Jews can always be grafted back into God's people if they do not persist in unbelief (v. 23). The language seems to spring from Paul's knowledge of an unseemly ethnic pride among Gentile Christians in Rome which has led them to regard God's dealings with unbelieving Jews as finished and to gloat over their majority status in the people of God.[8]

Evidence from Rome

To this evidence from the text of Romans itself we can add several pieces of information from ancient historians and first-century inscriptions. Inscriptional evidence demonstrates that the large Jewish community was only loosely organized. Authority within the Jewish community was not centralized in an "ethnarch," as in Alexandria, but seems to have been located solely in the "assemblies of elders" and the officers of individual congregations. Probably, then, Christianity spread more rapidly among the Jewish community in Rome than in cities where a centralized authority could proscribe it.[9] Indeed, the earliest form of Christianity in Rome appears to have had a decidedly Jewish bent.

This notion receives confirmation from the first description of the Roman church's origins. An anonymous commentary on the Old Latin text of Paul's letters says that

> there were Jews living in Rome in the times of the apostles, and that those Jews who had believed [in Christ] passed on to the Romans the tradition that they ought to profess Christ but keep the law. . . . One ought not to condemn the Romans, but to praise their faith; because without seeing any signs or miracles and without seeing any of the apostles, they nevertheless accepted faith in Christ, although according to a Jewish rite.[10]

From the first, then, Christianity in Rome had strong ties with the large, established Jewish community.

Relations between non-Christian Jews and their Christian counterparts, however, were not always friendly. The Roman historian Suetonius, writing in the early second century of events that occurred in A.D. 49, says that "since the Jews constantly made disturbances at the instigation of Chrestus," the emperor Claudius "expelled them from Rome" (*Claud.* 25.4).[11] Although

Chrestus was a common name among slaves in Rome, Suetonius has probably confused the name with Christus. If so, the disturbances were probably created by the preaching of the gospel within Rome's various synagogues, and Suetonius's term *constantly* probably means that they had been taking place for a lengthy period prior to the expulsion.[12]

The expulsion meant a mass exodus of both Christian and non-Christian Jews from the city, and among them were a husband and wife named Aquila and Priscilla (Acts 18:2). The couple settled in Corinth, where they met Paul and joined him in their common trade of tentmaking (Acts 18:3). By the time Nero became emperor five years later (A.D. 54), the edict against the Jews had been repealed, and presumably some Jews returned home. Paul's greetings to Prisca and Aquila in Romans 16:3-4 reveal that these close friends of his had also returned to Rome by the time of the letter's composition.[13] Perhaps Andronicus, Junia and Herodion, all of whom Paul calls his "fellow countrymen" (*syngenēs*, 16:3, 11) were also Jewish exiles who had met Paul during his work in the east but had now returned home.[14]

This understanding of external historical sources meshes well with the evidence of the letter itself. The letter's references to Gentile boasting over the Jewish rejection of the gospel (11:13-24) and to "the weak" who persist in observing Jewish customs (14:1—15:6) imply that Jewish Christians (or Gentile Christians who adopted Jewish customs) were in the minority among the Roman churches at the time the letter was written. Thus although Paul urges both parties in the dispute over dietary and calendar observance to accept one another (15:7; compare 14:3, 10), the burden of his admonition falls on those who do not have scruples about food or days (14:1, 13-23; 15:1-3).[15]

The churches in Rome, then, had probably started with a Jewish majority but after the expulsion had become predominantly Gentile. With the return of some Jews to their home congregations, the Jews would have remained in the minority and would have found themselves within communities far less oriented toward Judaism than when they had left.[16] Perhaps these predominantly Gentile communities had, in the absence of their Jewish fellow believers, succumbed to the anti-Semitic feelings that seem to run like a current within Roman culture during this period.[17] It is easy to imagine at least how the return of Jewish Christians to their homes after a five-year absence could create tensions within the church.[18] Perhaps friends like Priscilla and Aquila had alerted Paul to inappropriate attitudes toward Jews in general and to ethnic tensions within the Roman churches, and perhaps the letter is, in part, intended to address this situation.

That this was not Paul's only intention in writing Romans, however, becomes clear from the passages in which he speaks explicitly of his relationship with the Roman believers. These passages occur at the beginning and near the end of the letter, in chapters 1 and 15 (1:1-15; 15:14-33). Unique to chapter 15 is Paul's tactful request that the Romans support his future missionary efforts. He explains to them that he has finished his work in the east and now hopes to preach the gospel in Spain. He hopes further that the Romans will provide a refreshing stop on the way and will help him on his journey to that final destination (15:24; compare 15:28). He also explains that prior to turning west he must fulfill his commission to bring an offering from his predominantly Gentile churches to the needy Jewish believers in Jerusalem (15:25-26). Since he is not certain that unbelieving Jews in that city will leave him in peace, or even that believing Jews will receive him gladly, he urges the Romans to pray for the safety and success of his mission (15:30-31). It seems reasonable to conclude, therefore, that Paul wrote to the Romans in part to ask for their support of his future work both in Jerusalem and in Spain and, in light of this request, to describe the gospel whose propagation, by their support, they would sponsor.[19]

Alongside Paul's tactful request for the Romans' support of his gospel and mission in chapter 15, however, stand his carefully worded claims in both chapters 1 and 15 to spiritual authority over the Roman Christians. In chapter 1, Paul's constant prayer that he might be able to visit the Romans (v. 10) becomes a prayer that he might impart to them some spiritual gift (v. 11), bear some fruit among them just as he has among the other Gentiles (v. 13) and preach the gospel to them (v. 14). This is the gospel that he then summarizes in the letter's thesis statement (vv. 16-17). In chapter 15, similarly, he says that he has written to the Romans boldly on some points because of the grace given to him to be "a priest of Christ Jesus to the Gentiles" so that "the offering of the Gentiles might be acceptable, sanctified by the Holy Spirit" (vv. 15-16). In both chapters these claims are seasoned with tactful words about mutual spiritual support (1:12) and the spiritual competence of the Romans (15:14), but their chief point is clear: since Roman Christianity is primarily Gentile, and since Paul is the apostle to the Gentiles, he hopes that the Romans will recognize his spiritual authority over them.[20] For this to happen, Paul must preach the gospel in their midst, and his letter to them serves this role in his absence.[21]

Paul wrote Romans, then, for a variety of reasons. He hoped that the Romans would support his efforts in Jerusalem and in Spain; he felt a pastoral responsibility for them; and he was distressed to hear both of an unbefitting haughtiness toward non-Christian Jews and of a selfish intolerance for Christian Jews in Rome.[22] Romans responds to these concerns with a summary of what Paul calls in 2:16 "my gospel." Such a summary not only would describe for the Romans the message they would be advancing when they supported Paul's missionary work but also, because it engaged in vigorous dialogue with the Jewish tradition, would provide the necessary foundation for the pastoral oversight Paul would exercise in Rome not only when he arrived among them but also in the closing chapters of the letter itself.[23]

If this perspective on the situation that produced Romans is correct, then the letter is not an outline of the *ordo salutis*, a compendium of Christian doctrine, or an abstract treatment of the great questions that vexed Paul toward the end of his missionary endeavors. It is as tied to a particular situation as any of Paul's other letters. Nevertheless, those who see Romans as more systematic and abstract than Paul's other letters are not entirely mistaken, for the Roman situation called for something that the other letters could presuppose: a presentation of Paul's gospel. He certainly shaped his presentation in 1:16—11:36 to make it fit the situation in Rome, as his direct address to the Gentiles in 11:13 shows, but his running dialogue with unbelieving Judaism shows equally clearly that the extent of that shaping influence was not great. Romans, then, does not provide an abstract treatise on the relationship between the law and the gospel, but it nevertheless provides a less circumstantial and more foundational statement of that relationship than any of Paul's other letters.

The Law in Romans: A Complex Element of a Complex Argument

Paul's use of the term *law* in the argument of Romans is perhaps the most perplexing element in a notoriously complex letter. Those who claim that Paul is an inconsistent thinker, shooting from the hip according to the confrontation of the moment, point to his comments on the law in Romans as frequently as those who contend that Paul is a profound thinker whose argument in the letter repays careful scrutiny with the deepest theological insights.[24]

What makes Paul's statements about the law so complicated that highly trained specialists can, after reading them, come to these opposing conclusions? Two aspects of Paul's method appear to be the origin of this complexity. First, Paul uses *law* in several different ways in the letter, often with slightly different meanings within the same section of his argument, sometimes even using the word with several different nuances within the same sentence. He can use the word figuratively, as in 7:21—"I have discovered the law that when I want to do good, evil lies close to me"—and in 7:23, when he speaks of "another law" which he calls "the law of sin" and which wars against "the law of God" in his mind (compare 7:25). Paul can also use the word to refer to Scripture generally, as in 3:19, where he describes a string of quotations from Psalms and Isaiah (Rom 3:10-18) with the term *law*, and in 3:21 when he speaks of "the law and the prophets." Without doubt the most frequent use of the term in Romans, however, is to designate the covenant that God mediated through Moses and made with Israel at Sinai, the covenant that set apart the Jewish people as a distinct group, chosen of God and separate from Gentiles. This law, Paul says in 2:18-20, gives Jews the knowledge of God, instructs them in how to choose what is most excellent and gives them the outline of knowledge and truth necessary for leading the blind, lighting the way for those in darkness, instructing the foolish and teaching the immature. Paul can, therefore, refer to circumcised Jews in 4:14 and 4:16 as "people of the law" (compare 4:12), in 9:4 to the gift of the law as one of Israel's privileges and in 9:31 to the pursuit of the law as one of Israel's trademarks.

Closely related to this understanding of the law as "the Jewish law" are Paul's references to a law that the Gentiles possess. From one perspective the Gentiles are *anomos*, "outside the law" (2:12), but from another perspective "Gentiles who do not have the law" can do "the things of the law by nature" and so "are a law to themselves" (2:14). When they do this, he continues, "they show the work of the law written in their hearts" (2:15). The law that these Gentiles keep, however, is not merely a collection of their own ethnically specific moral standards and social customs but a rudimentary form of the Jewish law. Paul could hardly mean anything else when he speaks of Gentiles who do not themselves have "the law" but nevertheless do "the things of the law." From Paul's perspective, then, the Gentiles possess a law, but insofar as it can be called "law" at all, it is a rudimentary form of the law revealed to Moses at Sinai and given to the Jews.

Paul, then, uses the single term *nomos* in Romans in four ways:

1. as a figure of speech
2. to refer to the Hebrew Scriptures
3. as a reference to the Mosaic covenant
4. to describe the natural understanding among some Gentiles of the Mosaic covenant's basic principles[25]

This varied usage would in itself be enough to make Paul's understanding of the law difficult to decipher, but it is compounded by a second complication. Nearly half of Paul's uses of the term *law* in Romans occur in chapters

1—4, where his primary point is that all humanity, Jewish as well as Gentile, has violated the law and therefore stands under God's just sentence of condemnation (3:19). *Law* in these chapters, therefore, refers primarily to the Jewish law and the Gentile approximation of that law, and the emphasis lies on the failure of both Gentile and Jew to comply with the measure of God's law which each knows. Another equally important point of these chapters, however, is that the Jew can claim no superiority over the Gentile.[26] Thus Paul can argue so vigorously against Jewish privilege over the Gentile in chapter 2 that he anticipates the objection in 3:1, "What advantage, then, does the Jew have, or of what benefit is circumcision?" And in 4:10-18 he takes pains to show that Abraham is the father of both Gentiles and Jews who believe. Paul connects and weaves these two purposes together at surprising points in his argument and in ways that are difficult to follow, and when his fourfold use of the term *law* becomes a key element in the way he connects his purposes, the results are often extraordinarily difficult to understand.[27]

The different nuances Paul gives to the word *law*, then, and the two distinct purposes for which he employs the term in his argument place a heavy burden on the reader, especially the modern reader who, unlike the Roman Christians of the mid-first century, cannot ask Phoebe (16:1-2) or Prisca and Aquila (16:3) for clarification. For this reason it would be unwise to try to interpret Paul's statements about the law in Romans in isolation from the argument of the letter as a whole. In this investigation of the law in Romans, therefore, I will examine Paul's argument section by section in order to determine how his references to the law function within each section. This chapter looks at the role of the law in Paul's descriptions of the human plight and God's solution to that plight, and the next chapter investigates the role of the law in Paul's discussion of the new life of the believer and the election of Israel.

A Summary of Paul's Argument in Romans 1—4

In Romans 1:16-17 Paul begins his explanation of the gospel with a thesis statement: the gospel, he says, is the means of saving all who believe, both Jew and Greek, because in it a righteousness of God is revealed, a righteousness that comes by faith from first to last.[28] In 1:18—4:25 he unfolds this statement in three parts. In 1:18—3:20 he explains why the wrath of God has been revealed upon all human wickedness, whether Jewish or Gentile, and why both Jew and Gentile therefore stand in need of the gospel's saving power. In 3:21-26 he explains how the righteousness of God has effected the justification of sinful people, whether Jewish or Gentile. In 3:27-31 he explains two results of the revelation of God's righteousness, and in 4:1-25 he provides evidence that God's method of justifying the wicked by faith in the gospel has biblical precedent.

Summarized this way, Paul's argument seems smooth, logical and uncontroversial. This summary, however, would not command universal consent, and in addition, some interpreters have asked two critical questions about this section. First, does Paul's argument in 1:18—3:20 actually lead to his conclusion? Since he seems to entertain the possibility that some will be saved by their works (2:6-7, 10, 13, 26-27), how can he claim at the end of the section that no one will be justified before God by works of the law? Second, does Paul's argument rest on a false presupposition that Judaism adhered to salvation by works? If Judaism was a religion of grace, as so many voices seem to claim, why does Paul say that justification does not come by works (3:20) and uphold Abraham as an example of the justification of the impious (4:5)? Only a careful exegesis of the section can show the coherence of his argument and provide an answer to these questions.

Transgression and Privilege (Romans 1:18—3:20)

In Romans 1:18—3:20 Paul argues that the Jew, no less than the Gentile, is subject to God's wrath against human wickedness on the final day of judgment. In 1:18-32 he describes Gentile sin in a way that will encourage an imaginary Jewish reader, introduced for the first time in 2:1, to agree with his claim that the Gentile deserves God's wrath. In 2:1, however, he examines his Jewish dialogue partner's standing before God on the final day and argues that it is equal to the position of the Gentile. After countering three possible objections to his argument in 3:1-8, Paul summarizes his case in 3:9-20 with an appeal to Scripture and the claim that no one, including the Jew, will survive the final day of judgment if his or her own works form the basis for acquittal.

Sinful Gentiles (Romans 1:18-32). Paul takes the first step in the explanation of his gospel in 1:18-32. He begins by claiming in a general way that God's wrath is being revealed from heaven against all the impiety and wickedness of humanity (v. 18). He mentions no ethnic group specifically in this initial indictment, so the Jewish reader might at this point feel the rub of Paul's statement.[29] When Paul becomes more specific in verses 19-23, however, his Jewish reader would undoubtedly understand Paul's comments to be directed primarily to the Gentile.[30] Here Paul speaks of people who should have known God's attributes through the creation around them. Because of this knowledge, he says, they should have worshiped the Creator, but instead they fashioned and worshiped images of God's creatures. The conviction that Paul was indicting Gentiles would only have increased as Paul describes in verses 24-27 how God, in punishment for their idolatry, gave these people over to the classic Gentile sin of homosexuality, and eventually to a long list of perversions that the Jew would associate primarily with the godless Gentile.

Interpreters of Paul's understanding of the law typically pass over this passage, since it seems to describe Gentiles primarily and since it contains no explicit reference to "the law." Yet it is important both for understanding Paul's concept of the Jewish law and for grasping his argument in chapter 2 to recognize that in 1:32, when Paul says that those he has just described know "the requirement of God," he is claiming that the Gentiles know something of the Jewish law. This is clear from two considerations. First, the term *dikaiōma*, when it occurs elsewhere in the New Testament to mean "regulation," "requirement" or "commandment," as it does here, always refers to the Mosaic law (Lk 1:6; Rom 2:26; 8:4; Heb 9:1, 10).[31] Second, Paul describes this requirement as the penalty of death for those who commit the sins that he has just named. Since idolatry, homosexuality and most of the sins listed in 1:28-31 did not carry the death penalty in any Gentile legal code, Paul is probably echoing the language of the Mosaic code, which calls the choice between obedience and disobedience to the commandments a choice between "life" and "death" (Deut 30:19).[32] In 1:32, then, Paul refers to an innate apprehension among Gentiles of the ultimate penalty for disobedience to God as described in the Mosaic law. Although Gentiles possess no written or complete record of God's will, they share with Jews at least an understanding of God's basic requirements. Paul uses this claim to bolster his argument that the Gentile world deserves the condemnation that God's just requirement pronounces on those who sin: Gentiles are ignorant neither of God's requirements nor of the penalty for transgressing those requirements. The Gentile world, then, is without excuse.

Unexcused Jews (Romans 2:1-29). But, Paul continues, the Jewish world is also without excuse. Paul's description of Gentile vices in 1:18-32 would have been uncontroversial for many Jews.[33] Indeed, his characterization of Gentile idolatry seems to echo the portrayal in Wisdom of Solomon 11:1—16:1 of those who should have come to a knowledge of God through the visible excellence of God's creation (13:1; compare 12:1) but who instead fell into worship of the creation itself (13:2-7), are therefore without excuse (13:8-9) and will be punished by the very wickedness that they do (11:15-16; 12:23-27; 15:18—16:1).[34]

Wisdom follows its description of Gentile error with the claim that idolatrous foolishness has not led Israel astray and that even if the people of Israel should sin, they still belong to God (15:1-5; compare 11:10; 12:22). The sequel to Paul's description of Gentile idolatry, however, takes a decidedly different path. Having invited the Jew to join him in a familiar denunciation of Gentile sin, in 2:1 he turns on his Jewish reader to say, "You therefore, O one who judges, are without excuse, for by that which you condemn the other you condemn yourself, since you who judge practice the same things." Like the Gentile who sins despite a knowledge of God (1:19) and an understanding of God's requirement (1:32), Paul's imaginary Jewish reader is "without excuse." As a result, Paul says, the Jew will also experience the judgment of God (2:2).

Paul maintains the focus of these first two verses in the discussion that follows in 2:3-29. This entire portion of the argument is devoted to showing that contrary to the expectations of some Jews, Israel cannot rely on its national status as God's chosen people—a status symbolized by the Jewish law—to save it from condemnation for transgression in the final day. The Jew, then, can appeal to no special privilege over the Gentile for salvation at the day of judgment. Only obedience will save either Jew or Gentile on that day. The argument is divided into three paragraphs (vv. 3-11, 12-16 and 17-29), each of which makes this point, but with increasing levels of specificity. Thus all three paragraphs are intended to show that, in the words of 2:11, "There is no partiality with God," but the first paragraph does this by showing that God will judge both Jew and Gentile according to their "works" (v. 6), the second by showing that he will judge both according to their conformity with the "law" (v. 12) and the third that he will judge both by the criterion of inward circumcision (vv. 26-27).[35]

The first section (vv. 3-11) begins with an echo of a familiar theme from the prophets.[36] Jews who believe that they will escape God's judgment of Gentile sin but who do the same things that the Gentiles do, Paul says, have failed to recognize that God's kindness, forbearance and patience toward Israel were intended to lead God's people to repentance (vv. 3-4). As long as such hardhearted presumption continues, Israel amasses a treasury of wrath which they will receive on the day of God's righteous judgment. The reason they will receive judgment for their sins, rather than exemption because of their election, is that God is impartial. He "will render to each person according to his works" (v. 6). To those who are patient in their efforts to do what is good, God will grant eternal life, glory, honor and peace (vv. 7, 10), and to those who serve selfish ambition by disobedience to the truth, are wicked and do evil, he will give wrath, fury, tribulation and suffering (vv. 8-9). The result of this unrelenting impartiality is that both Jew and Greek are subject to the same standard of judgment (vv. 9-10), for, Paul concludes, "there is no partiality with God" (v. 11).

In the second paragraph (vv. 12-16) Paul's argument narrows its focus to deny that possession of the law—the primary symbol of Israel's election—places the Jew at an advantage over the Gentile on the final day. The Gentile, he says, is outside the law and the Jew within it, but Jewish possession of the law does not qualify the Jew for exemption from God's condemnation on the final day (v. 12). Paul explains this claim by reminding his imaginary Jewish reader of what he said in 1:19 and 1:32: the Gentile possesses some knowledge of God and understands God's "just requirement." In those verses, of course, Paul's emphasis was on Gentile violation of God's requirements, but here, in order to demonstrate God's impartial condemnation even of the Jew who sins, the emphasis is on Gentile compliance with the law:

> For when Gentiles who do not have the [Jewish] law do by nature the things of the law, they, although they do not have the law, are a law to themselves. They, by their very nature [hoitines], show the work of the law written in their hearts, their conscience bearing witness, and among each other, their thoughts condemning or providing defense in the day when God judges the hidden things of humanity according to my gospel through Christ Jesus.[37]

Here Paul echoes a phrase from Jer 31[LXX 38]:33 to show that Gentiles, although technically outside the law, have the rudiments of the Jewish law implanted in their hearts, that this knowledge informs their consciences and that it will either accuse them or defend them in the day of judgment. Paul's point is clear: both Jew and Gentile have enough of the law that by keeping what they have they could be justified, or by failing to keep it they would stand condemned. As a result, on the final day of judgment, mere possession of the law will be of no advantage to the Jew.

In the third section of the passage (2:17-29) Paul's point remains the same, but the focus of the argument narrows still more to describe how possession of the law and observance of its ethnically distinctive command of circumcision is related to being a Jew. First, he reminds the Jew that although possession of the law provides rich advantages for the intellectual grasp of truth (vv. 17-20), the Jew has responded to these advantages with disobedience (vv. 21-24). Thus Paul's quotation of Isaiah 52:5 in verse 24 reminds his imaginary Jewish reader that Israel's transgression of the law led the nation into exile and brought dishonor on God's name.[38] Jewish transgression of the law, he concludes in verse 25, renders Jewish circumcision useless and places the Jew, for purposes of God's judgment, in the same situation as the Gentile: "For circumcision is beneficial if you practice the law, but if you are a transgressor of the law, your circumcision has become uncircumcision."

Second, Paul draws the logical conclusion from this argument that an uncircumcised Gentile who keeps "the just requirements of the law" is a true Jew and will, on the last day, judge the circumcised transgressor of the law (verse 27). Again, Paul's primary point in this third paragraph is clear: Jewish election, most clearly symbolized in possession of the law and particularly in circumcision, places the Jew at no advantage over the Gentile in matters of divine judgment. Both Jew and Gentile understand enough of God's will either to do it and survive his wrath on that day or to disobey it and receive his just sentence of death.

So far, however, this explanation of chapter 2 has passed over the passage's most difficult problem. In the course of showing that the Jew cannot claim a special exemption from judgment in the final day, Paul has portrayed at least some Gentiles as capable of keeping the law.[39] In verse 14 he mentions Gentiles who instinctively do what the law requires, and in verse 27 he speaks of the physically uncircumcised who nevertheless keep the law's requirements. What has happened to the picture of the Gentile as senseless, faithless, heartless and ruthless (1:31), the Gentile before whom the knowledge of God is clearly displayed (1:19) and who knows God's just requirement (1:32) but sins anyway?[40] And how can Paul conclude that he has shown in 2:1-29 that both Jews and Greeks are under sin (3:9) when, in the process of indicting the Jew, he has portrayed the uncircumcised Gentile as one who keeps the law?[41]

An answer to this question emerges from a reading of Paul's argument which keeps in mind his twofold purpose of showing that no one can keep the law and that the sinful Jew is not exempt from judgment: Paul's references to Gentiles who are justified by doing the law are only hypothetical.[42]

In 2:5-16 Paul argues only for the *possibility* that keeping the law could lead to eternal life, glory, honor and peace (vv. 7, 10), not that anyone actually achieves these ends by doing so. His claim that God will render to each person according to his or her works in verse 6, likewise, is only the final clause of his claim in verse 5 that his imaginary Jewish reader, as a result of a hard and impenitent heart, is storing up wrath for the day of judgment. Paul's claim that God will judge according to works in this context therefore is a claim that God will condemn the unrepentant.

When Paul goes on to say in verse 7 that God will grant eternal life to those who seek glory, honor and immortality by their patience in doing the good (*hypomonēn ergou agathou*) and in verse 10 that glory, honor and peace belong to everyone who does what is good (*panti tō ergazomenō to agathon*), he is saying nothing other than what Deuteronomy says when it claims that God will grant life to his people if they obey the law (Deut 28:1-14) but then goes on to predict that Israel will instead disobey and receive the covenant's curses (28:15-68; 30:22-29). The possibility of life is extended to the people of Israel if they should keep the law, but, Deuteronomy affirms, they will disobey the law and choose death rather than life (30:15-20).

In Romans 2:14-16 Paul certainly mentions Gentiles who "do the things of the law," but this passage must not be read in isolation from verses 12-13. There Paul provides a preface to verses 14-16 in which he explicitly states what he is trying to prove: God's impartiality (v. 11) is apparent in his willingness to condemn both those outside the law and those inside the law for their sin (v. 12): "for the hearers of the law are not righteous before God, but the doers of the law shall be justified" (v. 13). The emphasis, as verse 12 shows, is on the condemnation of sinners, particularly Jewish sinners who have not correctly understood God's impartiality and think that although they sin, possessing the law and hearing it read every sabbath in the synagogue will exempt them from judgment.

In verses 14-16 Paul refutes this claim by showing that God has given even to Gentiles a rudimentary form of the Jewish law. This law is apprehended in the conscience, and Gentiles are actually led by their conscience on occasion to do what the law requires.[43] That these imaginary Gentiles do not always do good, however, is clear from two considerations. First, Paul's use of the indefinite relative pronoun *whenever (hotan)* in verse 14 implies that whereas Gentiles sometimes perform the law's requirements, sometimes they do not.[44] Second, Paul mentions in verse 15 that on occasion the Gentile conscience accuses its subject of violating the law.[45] This passage does not, therefore, claim that some Gentiles will keep the law well enough to be saved, but only that Jewish possession of the law does not exempt the Jew from judgment any more than the Gentile apprehension of the rudiments of the Jewish law exempts the Gentile from judgment. As verse 12 shows, both can expect only condemnation on that day for what they have done.

In verses 26-29 Paul carries his argument that the Jew has no special advantage on the day of judgment a step further and mentions uncircumcised Gentiles who keep "the just requirements of the law." Such Gentiles, Paul says, would judge the circumcised Jewish transgressor (v. 27), since they would be inward Jews who fulfill the hope of Deuteronomy and Jeremiah for a people whose hearts were circumcised (2:28-29; compare Deut 10:16; 30:6; Jer 4:4; 9:25-26). Two aspects of this paragraph must be highlighted if it is to be properly understood.

First, Paul lays the foundation for this scenario with a conditional sentence: "If therefore the uncircumcised person should keep the just requirements of the law, his uncircumcision will be reckoned as circumcision, will it not?" (v. 26). Paul is not saying that such a Gentile exists, but he calls on his reader to imagine a world in which he does exist.[46]

Second, Paul describes this Gentile in language that, as we have seen in other places, he uses for Gentile believers who now form part of the eschatologically restored people of God. Like them, this Gentile has a circumcised heart (compare Phil 3:3), circumcised in the Spirit rather than in the letter (compare 2 Cor 3:3, 6). It is tempting to say therefore that Paul is depicting a real situation here and is contrasting the unrepentant Jew with the Gentile believer. Perhaps Paul does have this contrast somewhere in the back of his mind, but his argument has not yet reached the point at which it is appropriate to speak of the certain existence of Gentile believers. His argument so far has focused on God's impartial condemnation of all who transgress the law's just requirement, even of the Jew who might think that possession of God's complete revelation would provide an excuse on the day of judgment. This passage contributes to that argument by posing for consideration the possibility of uncircumcised Gentiles who, although they do not possess and therefore cannot keep the letter of the law as it is articulated in the Mosaic covenant (compare 2 Cor 3:6-7), are, by the power of God's indwelling Spirit, more faithful to matters of central importance to Judaism than some Jews.

In chapter 2, then, Paul does not contradict his primary point that both Greek and Jew stand under God's condemnation for their transgression of the law. Instead he has forestalled the Jewish objection that possession of the law exempts Jews from condemnation. First, he has reminded his imaginary Jewish reader of the biblical principle that those who obey the law will receive life and those who do not obey it will be condemned. He has then extended that principle to include the Gentile (vv. 6-10). Second, Paul has claimed that even the Gentile possesses a rudimentary form of the law (vv. 11-16). Third, he has posed the possibility of Gentiles who, although uncircumcised, keep the law and so stand in judgment over the Jewish transgressor (vv. 25-29).

Three qualifications (Romans 3:1-8). By the end of chapter 2, Paul feels that he has so thoroughly refuted the notion of Jewish privilege at the day of judgment that he must guard himself against three misunderstandings:

☐ the idea that God's election of the Jews gives them no advantage over the Gentile (3:1-2)

☐ the notion that Jewish unfaithfulness to the covenant implies unfaithfulness on God's part (3:3-4)

☐ the claim that his gospel regards evil as good (3:5-8)[47]

He refutes these notions with a series of questions and answers, the first of which he puts in the mouth of his hypothetical Jewish reader: "What is the advantage, then, of the Jew, or what is the benefit of circumcision?" (3:1). If possession of the law gives the Jew no advantage over the Gentile on the day of judgment, as Paul has argued in chapter 2, then what is the value of the Jews' supposed election? Paul replies that the benefit of being a Jew is great, despite what he has said previously. The reason for this is that the Jews have been entrusted with "the oracles of God." They possess, in other words, "the form of knowledge and of the truth in the law" (2:20) and therefore, as 2:17-20 says, have an advantage over Gentiles in knowing God's will. Gentiles may possess some intuition of God's requirements and so have an elementary understanding of the law in themselves, but the Jews' possession of the law is so great an advantage that they can instruct the Gentiles in the knowledge of God.

The second misunderstanding is stated as a rhetorical question that Paul himself asks: "What then? If some were unfaithful, their unfaithfulness does not nullify the faithfulness of God, does it?" (3:3). The objection behind this question seems to originate in Paul's argument in chapter 2 that Jewish transgression of the law has nullified any advantage of the Jew over the Gentile at the day of judgment.[48] If this is so, the objector seems to ask, what becomes of God's promises to be faithful to his people Israel? In chapters 9—11 Paul will expand the brief response that he gives in 3:4, but for now he simply says that God's judgment on Israel is just, for God cannot lie.

The third and final misunderstanding Paul again formulates as a series of questions. The first three of these (3:5-6) appear to come from Paul, the fourth (3:7) from his imaginary Jewish reader and the fifth again from Paul (3:8):[49]

Q. 1 (Paul): But if our wickedness establishes God's righteousness, what shall we say?

Q. 2 (Paul): The God who inflicts wrathful punishment is not wicked, is he? I speak in a human way. Certainly not, since

Q. 3 (Jewish reader): how, then, would God judge the world?

Q. 4 (Paul): But if the truth of God abounds to his glory by means of my falsehood, why am I still judged as a sinner?

Q. 5 (Paul): It is not the case, is it, that we should do evil things in order that good things might result, as we are slandered and as some say that we say? Their condemnation is just.

These questions rise out of the possibility that Paul's quotation of Psalm 51:4 (50:6 LXX) could be misunderstood as an excuse to sin. The first half of that verse reads, "I have sinned against you alone, and I have done evil before you" (LXX). Thus Paul's quotation of the second half of the verse— "with the result that you might be justified in your words and prevail in your judging"—might be understood to mean that sin enhances God's righteousness and is therefore, under a perverse form of logic, good.[50] Thus some interpreters have viewed this part of Paul's argument as a digression from, although perhaps related to, his argument in 1:18—3:20 that humanity, especially Jewish humanity, is sinful.[51]

But the question of 3:5 may also address a further Jewish objection to Paul's argument against Jewish exemption from judgment in chapter 2.[52] There Paul had said that Jewish transgression of the law gives God the opportunity to show his impartiality by condemning the Jew just as he does the Gentile. If the disobedience of Israel provides God with the opportunity to display his impartiality and thus his righteousness, why should sinful Jews be condemned (3:5-7)? Should they not sin all the more, that good may come (3:8)? The brevity with which Paul answers these questions shows that he considers them absurd. His claim in verse 8 that some have slandered him by claiming that he is an advocate of sin probably reveals why Paul thought it necessary to raise this last series of questions at all: experience had shown that his proclamation of the gospel could be perverted in an antinomian direction.

Works of the law do not justify (Romans 3:9-20). Having answered these objections, Paul brings the first section of his argument to a close in Romans 3:9-20 with a clear statement of its primary purposes. Jews are at no advantage over Greeks on the day of judgment; rather, as he has just shown, both Jews and Greeks are under sin (v. 9). Paul then summarizes his argument with a series of biblical quotations from Psalms and from Isaiah which stress that sin infects every person (vv. 10-12), infects them deeply (vv. 13-14) and produces dire consequences (vv. 15-18).[53] Referring to these quotations as "the law," although none of them comes from the books of Moses, Paul concludes that what they say applies especially to those "within the law," with the result that "every mouth might be stopped and the whole world become answerable to God" (v. 19). The implication of this statement is that if the Jew—who relies on the law, boasts in God and knows God's will (vv. 17-18)—stands under God's judgment, surely the Gentile stands condemned as well. The reason for this, says Paul, is that "by works of the law shall no flesh be justified before him, for through the law comes the knowledge of sin" (v. 20).

The way Paul phrases this conclusion has spawned considerable discussion. Much traditional Pauline scholarship claims that this statement is an argumentative denial of a standard Jewish doctrine: people are justified before God by their works. Advocates of this understanding of verse 20 often couple Paul's statement with his indictment in chapter 2 of the Jew who relies on and boasts in the law (2:17, 23). In 3:20, it is thought, Paul clarifies his reason for mentioning reliance on the law and boasting in chapter 2: the Jew believed that since the law could be kept and justification could be obtained by lawkeeping, doing the law formed a basis for boasting before God in one's achievements. Doing the law, in other words, provided a way of placing God in one's debt. This is what Paul denies in verse 20. No one can keep the law, he says, and therefore no one can be justified by the law. As a result, to anticipate Paul's statement in verse 27, boasting is excluded.[54]

As we have already seen, the view of Judaism upon which this understanding of verse 20 is based has suffered severe criticism in recent years. The Judaism of Paul's time, it is said, was virtually free of the attitude toward the law and God which this position assumes. In light of this new understanding of first-century Judaism, two alternatives to the traditional interpretation of verse 20 have become popular.

Some have explained the statement as a reference to a nationalistic attitude toward the law prevalent among the Jews.[55] Virtually all Jews believed that their obedience to the Mosaic law distinguished them from the Gentiles, marked them off as holy and therefore served as the sign of their election. Some Jews appear to have rallied around the law—particularly those parts of it which were distinctively Jewish—as a kind of national symbol and to have emphasized the exclusion of the Gentiles from God's people. Paul, it is sometimes said, is attacking this attitude toward the law in Romans 1:18—3:20, and the claim that no one is justified by "works of the law" is therefore an assertion that a certain national or ethnic affiliation cannot save.

Others have claimed that Paul implies in 3:19-20 that Judaism held to a soteriology of salvation by works, but that this implication is a misrepresentation of Judaism and therefore Paul's counterarguments are directed at a straw man.[56]

Neither of these alternatives to the traditional understanding of Paul's statement in 3:20 is wholly satisfactory. First, it is unlikely that the phrase "works of the law" only refers to the "social function of the law." Although the phrase itself does not appear prior to verse 20, Paul refers to "works" in 2:6, to "good work" in 2:7 and to "the work of the law" in 2:15. In each of these references the emphasis is not on the Jewish law as a nationalistic badge or ethnic identity marker but simply on the deeds that the law prescribes— deeds that, as the context of all three references makes clear, Gentiles can do or neglect as well as Jews.[57]

It is true that the primary concern of 1:18—3:20 is to show that Jewish possession of the law does not imply that God will judge the Jew less severely than the Gentile on the day of judgment.[58] Nevertheless, in the course of Paul's argument for this position, he indicts all humanity with failure to produce the works required for justification on the final day. When Paul says that "no flesh" will be justified by works of the law in 3:20, therefore, he certainly intends to emphasize that the Jew is not exempt from judgment, but he also includes in this indictment the Gentile who knows God's just requirement (1:32) and intuitively understands the law's precepts (2:15). The phrase "works of the law" in 3:20, then, refers not to the law as conceived from a narrow ethnic perspective but to the works that the law demands of everyone and that neither Jew nor Gentile has produced.[59]

Second, it also seems implausible that Paul would misrepresent Judaism on so crucial a point as the means by which one may stand acquitted before God on the final day to a readership that included Jews, even if the Jewish Christians in Rome constituted a minority. If the argument of Romans 1:16—11:36 represents an explanation of the gospel as Paul often preached it, and if, as Acts says, Paul frequently began his preaching in the synagogue, it seems doubly improbable that he would distort Jewish teaching on the role of works in justification. How could he hope to persuade his audience of his position if he began by misrepresenting theirs? Romans indicates instead that Paul's preaching attempted to engage Judaism in serious dialogue and that where he perceived that Jewish readers might object to his argument, he attempted to anticipate those objections and answer them. It is significant, then, that no rhetorical question follows 3:19-20. Apparently Paul felt that he and his Jewish partner in dialogue, at least on this point, stood on common ground.[60]

Does this bring us back to the idea that Paul attributes to Judaism generally the belief that salvation comes by human effort? Although not as exegetically irresponsible as advocates of the "new perspective" believe, this interpretation errs at two points. First, it is true that Paul's own pre-Christian convictions about the law appear to have allowed human effort at least some role in justification (Phil 3:4-6). It is also true that such convictions led some Jews to trust in themselves (Lk 18:9), take an odious pride in their conformity with at least part of the law (Mt 6:1-6, 16-18; 23:5; Mk 12:40; Lk 18:12; 20:47), fail to see their need of repentance (Mt 9:13; Mk 2:17; Lk 5:32; 7:47; 15:7) and reject Jesus because of his willingness to associate with those who did repent (Mt 9:11; Mk 2:16; Lk 5:30; 7:39; 15:2). Paul, as we shall see, refutes such notions in 3:27-28.

Nevertheless, many Jews did not view their relationship to the law and to God in this way. The law itself describes obedience as a response to God's gracious acts of redemption, and the evidence is clear that many first-century Jews understood the relationship between God's grace and human obedience in precisely the way it was articulated in their Scriptures. Many of these Jews would have agreed with Paul's contention that works of the law do not justify and would have acknowledged that Scripture itself bears witness to this. Whatever Romans 3:20 means, then, it is inappropriate to suggest on the basis of this verse alone that Judaism *generally* was a self-reliant religion devoid of an understanding of human sinfulness and God's grace.

Second, at this point in the argument Paul is primarily interested in showing that because God is impartial, possession of the law does not exempt the Jew from judgment on the final day. In 2:17 and 2:23 Paul criticizes the Jew who relies on and boasts in the law, but the reliance and boast of which he speaks are in the *possession* of the law, not in its observance. Similarly, in 3:1, 3:9 and 3:19 Paul reveals that his primary purpose in 1:18—3:20 is not to argue against a Jewish boast in the performance of the law but against any special Jewish privilege over the Gentiles because of possession of the law.[61] Paul accomplishes this goal by pointing out again and again that both Gentile and Jew are transgressors of the law. The statement that no one will be justified before God by observance of the law in 3:20, then, means that all have transgressed the law and because of this, Jewish possession of the Sinai covenant will provide no advantage on the final day of judgment.

Summary of Paul's view of the law in Romans 1:18—3:20. Paul's comments in this section of Romans have produced a wealth of information about his view of the law. Three aspects of his view emerge as particularly important. First, Paul believed that everyone, both Gentile and Jew, apprehended enough of the Jewish law to be saved by doing it or to be condemned by transgressing it. The Gentile understood God's attributes well enough to know that God should be honored and thanked (1:21; compare 1:19) and comprehended God's requirement that evil actions are worthy of death

(1:32). Thus conscience could lead the Gentile to do "the things of the law" occasionally (2:14-15) and so could provide a basis for judgment on the final day (2:6-10, 15-16).

Second, Paul believed that no one had kept enough of the law to be justified by such works on the day of judgment. Thus, although 1:18-32 primarily describes the Gentile from the Jewish point of view, there Paul does not refer to the wicked people he describes specifically as Gentiles but instead uses the all-encompassing term *human beings* (v. 18). Paul's statement in 3:9, the collection of biblical quotations in 3:10-18 and his conclusion to the whole section in 3:19-20, moreover, could hardly be more explicit on this point. Yet Paul made this point not to refute a Jewish soteriology of works but to remind his Jewish dialogue partner of something that every Jew should know: no one can be justified before God by works of the law.

Third, Paul is especially concerned throughout the section to demonstrate that Jewish possession of the law does not exempt the Jew from judgment for sin on the final day. Thus in 2:4 Paul also reminds his imaginary Jewish reader that God's kindness was intended to lead his people to repentance, in 2:13 that the doer of the law, not the one who merely hears it, will be justified on the final day, in 2:17-24 that an intellectual knowledge of God's will as revealed in the law is of no benefit to the transgressor of the law, in 2:25 that physical circumcision counts for nothing if obedience does not accompany it, and in 3:19 that the biblical claim that all are transgressors applies to the Jew, who possesses the Scriptures, as well as to the Gentile.

In the last phrase of the section, in a way characteristic of his style, Paul introduces a new aspect of his understanding of the law which he will explore more fully later. Works of the law will justify no one before God, he says, "because *[gar]* through the law comes the knowledge of sin" (3:20). Paul's conclusions about the relationship between the law and humanity in 1:18—3:20 have been entirely negative, as the summary statement in 3:20 shows. The question why God gave the law at all, then, naturally arises. Here Paul briefly indicates the answer: the law was given to bring sin to light. Leaving the details of this thought for later, however, he immediately moves to the next step in his argument.

Christ's Sacrifice and Its Effects (Romans 3:21—4:25)

In 3:21 Paul begins to describe God's solution to the plight that 1:18—3:20 portrayed so vividly. This portion of his argument advances in three stages: in 3:21-26 he describes God's gracious solution to the human plight of sin, in 3:27-31 he explains two consequences of this solution, and in 4:1-25 he demonstrates that this solution and its consequences have scriptural support.

Grace and covenant (Romans 3:21-26). Echoing the thesis statement of the letter in 1:16-17, Paul claims that God's solution to the human plight comes through a righteousness of God, appropriated by faith in Christ Jesus. Then, recalling the argument against Jewish privilege in 1:18—3:20, Paul states that just as there is no difference between Jews and Gentiles in their sin and lack of God's glory, so there is no difference between the two groups in the distribution of God's redeeming work (3:23-24).

Two aspects of Paul's discussion are particularly helpful in clarifying his view of the law. First, in 3:21-26 he highlights for the first time since chapter 1 the term *grace* (v. 24) and places special emphasis on the term *faith* (vv. 22, 25-26).[62] Within this paragraph these terms emphasize the undeserved character of God's work of redemption through Christ Jesus and the inability of human beings, given their sinful plight (v. 23), to do anything but trust that what God had done in Christ will be effective.

Second, Paul describes the faith by which both Jews and Gentiles are justified in language that recalls biblical references to both the ritual on the Day of Atonement and the public display of blood at the ceremony ratifying God's covenant with Israel. In verse 25 Paul says that in order to redeem those who have faith, God "presented" Christ Jesus "as a means of atonement [*hilastērion*] . . . by his blood." The phrase clearly echoes the language of Leviticus 16, in which Aaron is instructed to atone for his own sins and for the sins of the people by sprinkling blood both on and before the atonement cover (LXX *hilastērion*) of the ark of the covenant (Lev 16:14-16). Christ's death, then, was the ultimate Day of Atonement sacrifice, the offering by which God atoned for all sin previously left uncondemned (Rom 3:25; compare 2:4). Paul's use of the term *presented* in connection with the shedding of Christ's blood is also reminiscent of the public display of sacrificial blood at the institution of the Mosaic covenant in Exodus 24:5-8.[63] In that ceremony Moses sacrificed oxen, poured half their blood against the altar and sprinkled half on the assembled people. He concluded the ceremony with the words, "See the blood of the covenant that the LORD has made with you in accordance with all these words" (Ex 24:8). By echoing these passages, Paul seems to be saying that Christ's blood is not only the ultimate Day of Atonement sacrifice but also the beginning of a new covenant.

The law of faith excludes boasting (Romans 3:27-31). With these two aspects of Romans 3:21-26 in mind, we are now in a better position to understand Paul's complex references to the law in 3:27-31. The rhetorical questions in the paragraph reveal its primary purpose. It resumes the dialogue style dropped briefly in verses 10-26 and states two consequences of the atoning death of Christ: boasting is excluded (v. 27) and God is revealed to be the God of Gentiles as well as of Jews (v. 29).[64] At first this seems to be a simple restatement of Paul's argument in 2:17—3:20 that possession of the law gives the Jew no ultimate advantage over the Gentile, but Paul has introduced two new elements into this paragraph which merit close attention.

First, the term *boasting* now refers not merely to confidence in possession of the law as it did in 2:23 (compare 2:17) but to confidence in observing the requirements of the law.[65] Thus Paul asks rhetorically whether boasting has been excluded through "[the law] of works" (3:27). The simplest way to understand this phrase is as a reference to the character of the Mosaic law—it is a law that requires obedience.[66] Since Paul answers his question by denying that the law that demands works has excluded boasting, it seems reasonable to conclude that he believed obedience to the Mosaic law was for some Jews a source of boasting.

Paul's next statement confirms this understanding of the phrase. He contrasts "[the law] of works" with what he calls "the law of faith." The "law of faith," he says, excludes boasting because "a person is justified by faith apart from works of the law" (v. 28). If "works of the law" in verse 20 meant, as I argued above, "works that people do in conformity with the law," then Paul's contrast in this verse is clearly between faith and human effort, not primarily between two different eras in salvation history, one characterized by the Mosaic law and the other characterized by faith in Christ, or between two attitudes toward the law, an emphasis on national privilege versus an acceptance of the broadened boundaries provided in the gospel.[67] The contrast, as the old Protestant consensus insisted, is between salvation wholly from God and therefore by his grace and salvation in which human effort plays some part.[68]

Why would Paul suddenly speak of "boasting" in doing the law in verses 27-31 when throughout the argument of 1:18—3:20 the notion of boasting refers to a misplaced Jewish confidence in the possession of the law? The reason for the shift lies in the way Paul has described the revelation of God's righteousness in the previous paragraph. There, for the first time in the body of the letter, he has stressed the gracious character of God's work of redemption and the human appropriation of this work solely by faith. This new emphasis, then, drives him to speak in 3:27-28 not only of the exclusion of boasting in the possession of the law but of the exclusion of boasting in doing the law as well. "The law of faith" has excluded boasting of both types because of its overwhelmingly gracious character.

If this is a correct understanding of 3:27-28, though, has Paul finally attributed to the Jewish religion a legalistic approach to God? Does his denial that the gracious character of redemption leaves any place for boasting in works mean that Jews generally boasted before God in their works?[69] Paul was probably familiar with Jews who, like himself before his conversion (Phil 3:4-6), believed that their acquittal before God's tribunal on the final day would come not only through their membership in God's elect people but also through their own obedience to the law, and this passage appears to be directed against such convictions. If so, however, Paul's argument is not directed against Judaism generally but against a type of Judaism that placed less stress on the indelible, insidious character of human sin and less emphasis, therefore, on the need for God's gracious and re-creative work in the human heart. Paul's intention is to urge his Jewish debating partner, to whom he now attributes this belief, to consider the scriptural evidence that human sin runs too deep to allow human effort any role in God's saving purposes for his people. He also urges him to consider the evidence of the gospel that God has graciously responded to this plight in the atoning death of "Messiah Jesus" (v. 24).

The second new aspect of Paul's argument which is significant for understanding his approach to the law is his reference to "the law of faith" (v. 27). After aligning the term *law* with the plight of human disobedience in 1:18—3:26, why does he suddenly bring the term over to the other side of the ledger and couple it with faith? Again Paul's meaning becomes clear if we remember that in 3:27-31 he is building upon what he has just said about God's redemptive work in verses 21-26. There Paul said that God effected his gracious act of redemption through "faith" in the blood of Christ, and he described Christ's death in language that echoed biblical descriptions of the Day of Atonement ritual and the ratification of God's covenant with Israel.[70] "The law of faith," then, probably refers to the *new* covenant that God would establish with his people according to Jeremiah, and by which he would "forgive their iniquity, and remember their sin no more" (Jer 31:34). In Paul's hands this eschatological covenant, put into effect by the atoning blood of Christ, has become God's means of justifying all, whether Jew or Gentile, who believe.

The "law of works" and the "law of faith," then, are two different laws.[71] The law of works is the covenant given to Moses on Sinai which recorded God's will and cursed all who did not obey it—a covenant revealed to some extent to the Gentiles but in its complete form revealed only to the Jews. The law of faith, however, is a new law, the new covenant in Christ's blood. Only the law of faith excludes boasting, because whereas the Jew's possession of the complete "oracles of God" (v. 2) led to the erroneous notion that the Jew had an advantage over the Gentile at the day of judgement and, among some at least, that human effort played a role in acquittal on the final day, the law of faith as Paul has defined it erases any soteriological distinction between Jew and Gentile and opposes any notion that justification is deserved: "For there is no difference. For all have sinned and come short of the glory of God and are freely justified by his grace through the redemption that comes in Christ Jesus" (vv. 22-24). The law of faith offers justification to all at the same time and apart from any success at obedience to the law.

But if Paul is right, his imaginary Jewish reader asks (v. 31), has Paul not nullified the law? The law, after all, upholds both the election and the sanctity of Israel; it makes a distinction between circumcised and uncircumcised. No, Paul responds; instead of nullifying the law he upholds it. In 4:1-25 he attempts to prove his point.

Grace, Faith, Inclusiveness and the Law (Romans 4:1-25)

To do this he turns not to the Sinaitic code with its demand for works but to a narrative portion of the law, the story of Abraham. The purpose of Romans 4:1-25 is to argue once again the primary points of 1:18—3:31: that all humanity is sinful, that the Jew can claim no exemption from judgment and that all humanity, without distinction, stands in need of God's grace.[72] This new section, however, argues these points in a different way. Thus in 4:1-8 Paul bases his case not on observations about the depth of human sin, nor on the judgment of the prophets and the writings on the ability of humanity to do good, but on "the law" itself. Furthermore, in this passage Paul seeks to prove his point about human sinfulness and the need for God's grace from the life of Abraham, who in the eyes of many of Paul's fellow Jews was Israel's greatest and most righteous patriarch.[73] If any Jew could claim exemption from Paul's indictment of humanity, surely Abraham could. Finally, in verses 9-25 Paul transforms his argument that the Jew can claim no special soteriological advantage over the Gentile on the basis of the possession or performance of the law into an argument first that circumcision provides the Jew with no special access to God's grace (vv. 9-12; compare 2:25-29; 3:30), and second that if the Jew could claim some advantage over the Gentile, God's covenant with Abraham would go unfulfilled (vv. 13-25).

The story of Abraham excludes boasting (Romans 4:1-8). Paul begins his scriptural proof in Romans 4:1-8 by arguing as he had in 3:21-28 that the universality of sin and the gracious character of God's redeeming work nullify the possibility of acquittal before God on the basis of "works." Here, however, instead of making a case in general terms, he focuses on one Jew, the one most likely to be exempt from Paul's general indictment in 2:1—3:20. Abraham was Judaism's greatest patriarch (compare 4:1, 12) and was sometimes said to be without sin.[74] In verses 1-8, however, Paul encourages a sober reckoning of Abraham's status before God. His focus, as in 3:27-28, is on whether Abraham's "works" were sufficient to result in his justification and so to form a legitimate ground for boasting (kauchēma). Thus Paul raises the possibility that Abraham was justified by his works; if so, he says, Abraham would have some ground for boasting of what he had done. Abraham was not completely obedient, however, and so no boast was possible "before God" (v. 2).[75] Instead he was justified in the same way that "all flesh" must be justified before God—by faith (v. 3; compare 3:20).

Paul then illustrates his meaning with a commercial metaphor and a quotation from Scripture (vv. 4-8). This part of his argument resounds with echoes from 3:21-28. The wage earner, Paul says, is paid according to work accomplished, not "according to grace" (v. 4; compare 3:24), but the person who does not work must trust in God, who reckons righteousness to the "ungodly" (v. 5; compare 3:23; 1:18). Similarly, David pronounces a blessing on the one to whom God reckons righteousness "without works" (3:21, 27, 28). The assumptions that lie beneath this paragraph are that everyone, even Abraham, is "ungodly" and no one therefore can claim to deserve acquittal on the final day as a result of obedience to the law.

The story of Abraham includes Gentiles (Romans 4:9-25). Paul's argument cannot end here, however. His imaginary Jewish reader could easily respond that Paul had provided an excellent illustration of how the descendant of Abraham *who is circumcised* in accord with the covenant made with Abraham in Genesis 17:1-14 could be justified by faith. Perhaps Paul's imaginary Jewish reader was now ready even to concede that such faith had to be in God's eschatological provision of Christ's atoning death. But, he might continue, nothing is said in the Abraham narrative about the justification of the ungodly Gentile. Must not the Gentile who wants to follow in the footsteps of Abraham's justification by faith first accept circumcision and so be numbered among Abraham's descendants?[76]

Paul responds to this objection in two ways. First, he observes that Abraham was justified while still uncircumcised (vv. 9-10). According to the order of events in the Genesis narrative, his circumcision (Gen 17:24) came only after God had reckoned him to be righteous on the basis of his faith (Gen 15:6). Paul interprets this ordering of events to mean that Abraham's circumcision came only as a "confirmation" *(sphragida)* of the justification he had already received by faith (Rom 4:11). The consequence of this, Paul says, is that Abraham is the father of all who believe, whether they are uncircumcised or circumcised (v. 12).[77]

Paul's second response focuses on God's promise to give Abraham many descendants (Gen 15:5), a promise that he interprets in light of God's commitment to make Abraham the father of many nations (Gen 17:5). Paul now brings the term *law* back into the discussion for the first time since 3:31. There, however, Paul used it as shorthand for a portion of Scripture, the five books of Moses. Here he uses it in a slightly different way to refer to the covenant that God had made through Moses with his people and that distinguished them from other nations. His thesis in verses 13-25 is that the Jewish people, distinguished by their possession of the Mosaic law, are not Abraham's sole heirs but that Gentiles are included among Abraham's heirs as well.

He brings forward three arguments to support his case. First, in verse 13 he says that "the promise to Abraham, or to his seed, that he would be the inheritor of the world came not through the law but through righteousness by faith." This statement probably means that God's promise to give Abraham numerous heirs was made at the time that God reckoned him righteous through faith and therefore prior to God's covenant with Israel.[78] Paul's reference to the law here intends to recall the giving of the law at Sinai, and therefore he is probably making the simple observation that the identity of Abraham's descendants was decided prior to that time.

Second, Paul claims that if the people of the law *(hoi ek nomou)* alone were Abraham's heirs, faith would be empty and the promise void (v. 14), "because the law effects wrath, and where there is no law there is no transgression" (v. 15). The meaning of this verse becomes clear when we remember that Paul's references to wrath prior to 4:15 have always had to do with the visitation of God's wrath upon the wicked (1:18; 2:5, 8; 3:5). When Paul says that the law produces wrath, then, he probably means that disobedience to the law results in God's just punishment, in accord with the law's own stipulations (Lev 26:14-39; Deut 28:15-68; 29:19-29; 30:15-20). Furthermore, Paul has already argued at length that Israel has not kept the law and stands under the law's just sentence of condemnation (see especially 2:24 and 3:19). Thus if the people defined by the Mosaic covenant are Abraham's inheritors, Abraham has no inheritance: the people of God defined in this way have broken the law and have therefore fallen under the law's condemnation.[79]

If this understanding of the first part of verse 15 is correct, then when

Paul says that "where there is no law there is no transgression," he is probably referring to the effect of the Mosaic law on Israel. Sin was certainly in the world prior to the coming of the law (5:13), and God revealed his wrath against such sin in various ways, especially death, during that time (5:14; compare 1:32). But the Mosaic law represented the full revelation of God's will—"the oracles of God," as Paul describes it in 3:2—and when it came it brought a more complete "knowledge of sin" (3:20).[80] The law therefore transformed disobedience to a general revelation of God's will into rebellion against directly revealed, specifically articulated commands. Paul calls this rebellion "transgression," and Israel's scriptural history is a story both of transgression against the law of Moses and of the wrath that God revealed against Israel for that transgression. According to Romans 4:15, then, the people of the law cannot be the heirs of God's promise to Abraham, because where the law is present, transgression is present, and transgression of the law brings the wrath of which Paul has spoken in 1:18—3:20.

Paul's third argument that the Gentiles are among Abraham's heirs begins with an inference drawn from the second. In 4:16 Paul says that since the people of the law have been the recipients of the law's wrath, justification must come by faith and grace, with the result that God's promise to Abraham is confirmed not only by means of the Jew *(tō ek tou nomou)* but also by means of the Gentile *(tō ek pisteōs Abraam)*. Paul explains this point more fully in verses 17-18, where he observes that the promise to Abraham was that he would become the father of many nations (Gen 17:5; compare 18:18; 22:17). Paul implies, then, that if the Gentiles are not included among Abraham's heirs, the promise remains unfulfilled.

Summary of Paul's view of the law in Romans 3:21—4:25. Paul's comments on the law in this complex section of the letter have reflected the positions he took in 1:18—3:20, but with two significant differences. In the earlier section Paul's purpose was to show that everyone, Jew or Gentile, has sinned, and therefore Jewish possession of the law provides the Jew with no advantage over the Gentile on the day of judgment. What counted, Paul had said, was not possession but obedience. Although the Jew does have an advantage of access to the complete "oracles of God," Gentiles know enough of the law to obey it occasionally, while Jews do not obey the full account of it which they possess.

In 3:21—4:25 Paul adds to this argument first the notion that God's response to the human plight is consistent with the language of atonement and covenant making within the law itself. Through the death of Christ, God has established a new covenant, "the law of faith." Paul adds, second, the concept that the graciousness of God's response to the human plight excludes any confidence that human efforts to obey the law can play a part in justification. Everyone from uncircumcised Gentile to revered patriarch, Paul argues, is "ungodly," and thus justification can come only as a gift and only by faith.

This does not mean that Paul assigned to Judaism generally a doctrine of salvation by works. Instead, he was probably aware of some who believed that their obedience to the law cooperated with God's electing grace to produce acquittal on the final day. His intention was to persuade any who held this position to reckon soberly with the human condition as the Bible describes it, to remember the biblical promise of a new covenant and to recognize that God has fulfilled that promise by establishing what Paul calls "the law of faith."

"The law of faith," moreover, marks out a new people of God, whose distinguishing feature is not circumcision but faith in Jesus Christ, and which can therefore include Gentiles as well as Jews. As a result, God's promise to make Abraham the father of many nations has been fulfilled, for Abraham serves as the father not only of Jewish believers but also of Gentile believers who, like Abraham prior to his circumcision, believe in God and are justified.

In Rom 1:18—4:25, then, Paul has taken the position of a prophet and reminded his Jewish debating partner of two fundamentally biblical convictions: before God's tribunal no one can claim to be righteous on the basis of doing good, and God is an impartial judge who will not acquit Jews merely because they possess the law. Paul has also argued, however, that through the sacrificial blood of Christ, God has dealt with the sins that he mercifully overlooked in previous times in order to lead his people to repentance. And just as God's condemnation included the Jew as well as the Gentile, so God's redemption now includes the Gentile as well as the Jew.

All of this leaves two critical questions unanswered. First, if the law brings wrath upon God's elect people, then is the law an ally more of sin than of God? Second, if Jews cannot appeal to their possession of the law and their election as reasons for exemption from judgment, then what becomes of God's biblical promises to the people of Israel? In the rest of Romans these questions will first intensify and then be resolved.

CHAPTER NINE

OLD COVENANT SIN & NEW COVENANT SANCTITY IN ROMANS 5–15

With the Mosaic law firmly on the side of the human plight, Paul now turns in Romans 5—8 to a description of the life that characterizes those who have peace with God. We might expect him to leave the law behind in this section, but instead it reemerges bearing all of the paradoxical features that have characterized his approach to it in other letters. Somehow the law simply refuses to stay within the era of sin and curse that is now disappearing. Thus despite a view of the law so negative that Paul must engage in an excursus to defend its holiness, the law's concerns with the election of God's people and their sanctity are applied to believers in Romans 5—8 and 12—15. This application is so thoroughgoing that in Romans 9—11 Paul must safeguard himself against another misunderstanding—that God's promises to historical Israel have not been kept. Throughout this complicated process of statement and qualification, many of the basic features of Paul's view of the law come into sharp focus.

The Law Increases Transgression (Romans 5:1-21)

In chapter 5 Paul's primary goal is to summarize what he has said about the human plight and God's solution to it in a way that carries the discussion forward into a description of the believer's present existence and future hope.[1] Thus in verses 1-11 he describes again the death of Christ, but now it serves as a demonstration of God's love (vv. 5, 8). The greatness of God's love serves as a basis for the believer's hope that God has reconciled himself to believers and will therefore save them from the eschatological wrath that will be poured out on the final day (vv. 5, 9). This hope, furthermore, receives confirmation from the presence of the Holy Spirit in the believer's heart and from the new, eschatological perspective the believer gains on suffering (v. 5).

In verses 12-21 Paul continues to describe the magnitude of Christ's accomplishment and the assurance it gives to believers about their future. In this section, however, he accomplishes this through a comparison of the effects of Adam's disobedience with the effects of Christ's obedience. Just as Adam's sin brought death to many, he says, so Christ's righteous act of obedience will bring life and righteousness to many (vv. 12, 18-19). Paul carefully qualifies this comparison to show that the righteous act of Jesus Christ was far more powerful in its effects than the disobedience of Adam (vv. 13-17).

The law plays a subsidiary role in the argument of the chapter. It is not mentioned at all in verses 1-11, and within verses 12-21 it appears only in a parenthetical comment (vv. 13-14) and a more substantive, but brief, remark (vv. 20-21). Despite their subsidiary nature, however, both comments confirm important aspects of Paul's view of the law already revealed in 1:18—4:25, and the comment in 5:20-21 begins a discussion that will culminate in his detailed treatment of the law in chapter 7.

Sin, transgression and law (Romans 5:13-14). Paul begins his comparison of the effects of Adam's disobedience and of Christ's obedience in Romans 5:12 with a description of how death entered the world through Adam's sin. Before he refers to the second half of the comparison, however, his argument digresses in two directions. The second and longer of these (vv. 15-17) seeks to show that the effects of Christ's obedience are analogous to the effects of Adam's disobedience only in the sense that both had an impact on many people. Paul seems to say that the comparison is inept because the effects of Christ's obedience are so much greater than the effects of Adam's disobedience.

The first, and shorter, digression (vv. 13-14) centers on the Mosaic law.

Having just said that Adam's sin brought death into the world and that death then passed to all people because all sinned (v. 12), Paul clarifies how sin could be present and death reign even in the period between Adam and Moses, when no concrete expression of God's will existed. Adam had violated a command that God had directly revealed to him. Israel violated commands that God had directly communicated to Moses and Moses had in turn mediated to them. But in what sense had those who lived between Adam and Moses sinned?

Paul does not answer the question in detail but only recognizes it and affirms that even in the interim period people sinned. As a result of their sin, death continued the reign that Adam's sin initiated. Nevertheless, Paul recognizes a difference between the sin of Adam and Israel on one hand and the sin of those who lived after Adam but prior to the coming of the law on the other. In the intermediate period, since no "law" existed in the sense of a direct revelation of God's will, sin was not "reckoned" (v. 13). Those who lived in this period, although they sinned, can be distinguished from Adam because they did not commit "transgression" against a precept directly revealed to them from God (v. 14). To put the matter succinctly, in these verses Paul distinguishes between "sin" and "transgression." Transgression is the form that sin takes when one disobeys a direct revelation of God's will. Both the command given to Adam and the law given through Moses qualify as direct revelations of God's will, and therefore sin against either qualifies as transgression.[2]

The passage, then, is consistent with what Paul has said about the law in the first major section of the letter. In 2:14-16 Paul mentioned Gentiles who were capable of doing good works, had the law written on their hearts and were therefore a law unto themselves. These Gentiles apprehended the law so well that their knowledge of it could be used as a basis for judgment on the final day. Nevertheless, Paul implies that these Gentiles did not have access to "the oracles of God" (3:2)—the direct revelation of God's will to the Jews. That, by definition, was a Jewish advantage, and therefore the sin of these Gentiles does not qualify as "transgression"—rebellion in its fullest sense. This does not mean that God took no notice of their sin—Paul's statement in 1:32 shows that their sin offended God, and that they both understood this and knew the penalty for the offense. Nevertheless, Adam's sin against God's specific command and Israel's sin against the Mosaic law were rebellions of a different and more serious kind; and so by comparison with them, Paul could say that "sin is not reckoned when there is no law" (5:13).[3]

The purpose of Israel's transgression (Romans 5:20-21). Paul's comparison between Adam and Christ concludes in Romans 5:18-19 with a complete statement of Paul's basic argument. Just as transgression and condemnation came to all people through Adam's transgression, Paul says, so "the righteousness of life" has come to all people through Christ's act of righteousness (v. 18), and just as the disobedience of Adam made many sinners, so the obedience of Christ made many righteous (v. 19). Paul seems to recognize, however, that this historical summary is incomplete, since it does not mention the role of the law and of Israel. He corrects this omission in verses 20-21: "But the law slipped in so that the transgression should increase. But where [hou] sin increased, grace abounded that much more, so that just as sin reigned by death, so also grace should reign through righteousness unto eternal life through Jesus Christ our Lord."

Paul's claim that the law "slipped in" so that "the transgression might increase" probably means that God's purpose in giving the law was to identify sin as the violation of his directly revealed will. Transgression increased because with the coming of the law Adam's transgression against a single commandment became Israel's transgression of a whole range of commandments. Thus Paul's reference to the increase of "the transgression" in verse 20 is not a sudden blurring of the distinction between sin and transgression so carefully preserved to this point in the argument, but a reference to *the* transgression of Adam taken to new depths in the transgression of Israel.[4]

The *where (hou)* that begins the second half of verse 20, then, is not simply a rhetorical device but a reference to Israel as the place where Adam's sin increased.[5] Israel's disobedience to the law, prophesied in Deuteronomy and Leviticus and recounted in the historical books of Israel's Scriptures, provides the background for this statement. Adam's sin reached national proportions in Israel, and so Paul says that when God established his covenant with Israel through Moses, sin actually increased. He goes on to say, however, that in the very place where sin increased—Israel—grace abounded that much more. Here he probably refers to Israel's Messiah—Christ Jesus—through whose redeeming death God has demonstrated his grace (3:24).[6]

With this concluding paragraph Paul has stepped beyond the bounds of common ground with Judaism, for no Jew would feel comfortable with the idea that the law "slipped in" or with the claim that the law's effect was to increase sin. Paul has prepared his imaginary Jewish reader for this step, however, with his frequent claim in the previous section that Israel had violated the law. Every Jew who knew the Scriptures could agree with this, and Paul has used this common ground as a bridge to the more controversial notion that if the law has been disobeyed, God's intention must lie behind this disobedience.

Sin, Sanctity and the Law

Paul's next comment reveals that he understands the radical nature of what he has just said about the law. Posing as his Jewish debating partner, he asks, "What then shall we say? Should we remain in sin that grace may increase?" (6:1).[7] If Israel's history has shown that the intention of the law was to increase sin so that grace might abound all the more, then perhaps transgression of the law was and is a virtue. Paul responds to this idea with his characteristic "Certainly not!" followed by a rhetorical question of his own, "How shall we who died to sin live in it still?" (v. 2).

Thus Paul carries the reader from his summary of the benefits of Christ's work into a discussion of the basis for the believer's behavior. In this discussion the Mosaic law plays an entirely negative role—so negative in fact that in the next section of his argument Paul will qualify what he has said. There he will show that he did not intend to equate the law with sin or to lay the responsibility for death at the feet of the law. Paul divides his discussion of the basis for the believer's behavior into two parts, as the rhetorical questions of verses 1-3 and verses 15-16 show.

Freedom from the Law and Identity with Christ (Romans 6:1-14)

The first part (6:1-14) argues that the believer's life should not be characterized by sinful behavior but should instead be identified with Christ's death and resurrection. Just as Christ died, so the believer should be dead with respect to sin, and just as Christ was resurrected, so the believer should live in a way that anticipates the resurrection (vv. 3-11). Because of this *(oun)* the believer should put himself not at the disposal of sin (v. 12) and wickedness (v. 13) but at the disposal of righteousness. Paul concludes this part of the discussion with this sentence: "For sin shall not be master over *[kyrieusei]* you; for you are not under law but under grace" (v. 14).

Since the law has played no role in the discussion of verses 1-13, its appearance here at first comes as a surprise. Once the reader remembers that 5:20-21 generated the discussion in 6:1-14, however, the reference seems more natural. In 5:20-21 Paul had said that the law's entrance into Israel's history caused sin to increase. Here he applies that conviction to the individual: the person "under law" will discover that sin becomes master. Thus the increase of sin under the law in Israel's history is matched by the exercise of sin's power in the life of the individual who lives under law.

Freedom from the Law and Service to Sanctity (Romans 6:15-23)

Since Paul's statement in 6:14 is so similar to his controversial statement in 5:20-21, he follows it, as he had followed 5:20-21, with a rhetorical question about the statement's implications. Does it mean that the believer should sin? The way Paul supports his resounding no to this conclusion in verses 16-23 differs from the way he supported it in verses 3-14. In verse 17 he thanks God that although his believing readers were once slaves of sin, they have now become obedient. He describes their obedience as both "from the heart *[kardias]*" and "to the pattern of teaching *[didachēs]*" to which they were handed over.[8]

Here Paul's language echoes the Jeremiah and Ezekiel passages that predict that after God's people have been punished for their disobedience by defeat and exile, God will restore them by giving them a new heart (Jer 24:7; Ezek 36:26; compare Ezek 18:31) or by putting his will into their hearts (Jer 31:33; 32:40-41 LXX; Ezek 11:19). In Jeremiah 31:34 (38:34 LXX) the prophet says that in those days the will of God will be so firmly planted in the hearts of God's people that "each person will not teach *[didaxōsin]* his fellow citizen and his brother saying, 'Know the Lord,' because they shall all, from the least to the greatest, know [God]" (LXX). If Paul's claim that his readers have become obedient to a pattern of teaching that they have received was intended to resonate with these passages from the prophets, then he is claiming that believers, whether Jewish or Gentile, constitute the fulfillment of the prophetic prediction that God would restore his people.

This notion is strengthened by Paul's contrast of the believer's former life of "uncleanness" *(akatharsia)* and "lawlessness" *(anomia;* v. 19) with the "sanctification" *(hagiasmos,* vv. 19, 22) that should characterize their present existence. Paul's terms for "uncleanness" and "lawlessness" recall Ezekiel's descriptions of the wickedness that caused God to punish the people of Israel with defeat and exile (Ezek 9:4, 9; 22:2, 5, 15; 36:17, 19, 25, 29 LXX). Paul's term for "sanctification," although itself rare in the Septuagint, is semantically related to the term *holy (hagios),* which is the Septuagint's adjective of choice for describing the distinctiveness of God's people.

In Romans 6:15-23, then, Paul is probably claiming that the era of the restoration of God's people—the period of the new covenant—had begun with the death and resurrection of Jesus. This new era is evident, he implies, in the appearance of a community united by their belief in the effectiveness of this event and their experience of its transforming effects.

Is the Mosaic Law Sin?

Much of Paul's argument so far has been made on common Jewish presuppositions. Paul has maintained that

1. the Mosaic law reveals God's will

2. Gentiles can understand enough of the law to be condemned by it

3. Jews dare not suppose that their violation of the law will go unpunished simply because they possess the law

4. justification on the basis of doing the law's commands is not possible

5. the law brings sin to light

6. the law justly pronounces the sentence of God's wrath upon the disobedient

Paul considers each of these conclusions to be biblically founded and therefore to constitute common ground between himself and his imaginary Jewish reader.

In 5:20, however, Paul made a comment about the law that most Jews would have resisted strongly: the law was given so that sin, in the form of trespass against God's clearly revealed will, might increase. A Jewish reader would have responded that the law was given to the people of Israel so that they might know God's will and live by it, not so that sin might increase. If the law was given so that sin might increase, then people should sin so that they might live in accord with God's purposes in giving the law!

Paul recognized the radical nature of his position, and in chapter 6, rather than defend the notion itself, he attempted to put to rest the false inference that his view of the law encouraged sin. In chapter 7 he attempts to explain what he means by the idea that the law causes sin to increase (5:20-21) and that those under law have sin as their master (6:14). He begins in verses 1-6 with a full statement of his position and continues in verses 7-25 with an attempt to qualify his position in a way that exculpates the law itself from blame for sin and death.

The Mosaic Law Brings Sin and Death (Romans 7:1-6)

Paul begins the new section, as he had both 6:1-14 and 6:15-23, with a rhetorical question. Unlike the questions in the previous sections, however, this question does not originate with his imaginary Jewish reader but with Paul himself. He uses it not so much to forestall false inferences about the law from his statements in 5:20-21 and 6:14-15 as to introduce his own further explanation of what those statements mean: "Or do you not know, brothers, for I speak to those who know the law, that the law is master over *[kyrieuei]* a person as long as he lives?" (7:1).

Two aspects of this question are critical for a proper understanding of the notoriously difficult passage that follows. First, the question is principally a statement about the temporal character of the law and the means by which the law's power ceases. The law, Paul says, has power for only a limited period of time, and the law's power comes to an end through death. Second, and more subtle, the question is a statement about the connection between the law, sin and death. When Paul speaks of the law being "master over a person," he uses a term that he has used only twice before in this letter, once in 6:9 to say that Christ's resurrection broke the grip of death over Christ forever and that therefore "death is no longer master over him," and once in 6:14 to say that because believers are no longer under law but under grace, sin should "no longer be master over" them. Now, in 7:1, we learn that the law's mastery over the believer has also come to an end. In the paragraph that follows Paul will explain in greater detail the relationship between the law, sin and death and the mastery that they once had over all people.

Paul first pursues the relationship between the law, the believer and Christ's death and resurrection with a complex illustration from the law of marriage:

> For the married woman is bound to her husband by law as long as he lives. But if her husband dies, she is freed from the law of her husband. Therefore if she should become another man's while her husband is alive, she will be called an adulteress. But if her husband dies, she is free from the law, so that she is not an adulteress if she becomes another man's. So, my brothers, you also have been put to death with respect to the law through the body of Christ in order that you might belong to another, to the one who was raised from the dead in order that we might bear fruit for God. (vv. 2-4)

The illustration is confusing because the rhetorical question in verse 1 which prompts it and the focus on the wife encourage the reader to identify with the wife. When Paul applies the illustration in verse 4, however, the believer becomes analogous not only to the wife who is released from the law of her husband through his death but also to the husband who died. Has Paul written nonsense?[9]

The illustration is undoubtedly difficult, but the difficulty arises from the complexity of the subject rather than from some deficiency in Paul's communication skills. Throughout chapter 6 Paul has argued that the believer, like Christ, has both died and continues to live. The believer's death has been a death to sin, and the believer's new life, he has said, should be a life of obedience and righteousness. Now, in 7:1-6, Paul hopes to show where the law fits into this scheme, and he argues that it belongs on the side of the believer's existence prior to belief. This existence, and the role of the law within it, has died, and the believer continues to live, now under the power of the risen Christ.

Although Paul's application of the illustration in verse 4 only mentions the analogy between the believer and the wife, the believer is both the husband and the wife, the husband prior to faith and the wife afterward.[10] Like the husband, the believer was aligned with the law ("the law of the husband") and underwent a "death" by identification with Christ. Like the wife, however, the believer continues to live, now freed from the law, through identification with "the one who was raised." The illustration, then, is an attempt to explain how the law fits into the death and resurrection scheme of chapter 6, and its primary purpose is to say that the law's power over the believer has come to an end.[11]

Paul must still explain, however, why it was necessary for the law's power over the believer to cease. Why must the law be affiliated with death and sin and so come to an end in the age of God's eschatological deliverance? Paul addresses this question in verses 5-6 and here finally explains both what he meant when he said that the law had caused the trespass to increase (5:20) and why he had connected the law with sin's mastery over people (6:14): "For when we were in the flesh, sinful passions brought about through the law [ta pathēmata tōn hamartiōn ta dia tou nomou] were at work in our members to bear fruit for death" (v. 5).

The law did not prevent sin but instead became the stimulus to sinful desires. The sinful acts that resulted were then punished with death, in accord with the law's own stipulations. In verse 6, then, Paul's claim that the law "used to hold us prisoner" means that prior to faith the law held the believer captive both to sin and to the curse of death that the law pronounces on those who sin. The believer, Paul says in summary, has been set free from this law.

The final part of verse 6 indicates the result of having been set free from the law: "we serve in the newness of the Spirit, not in the oldness of the letter." Since the Mosaic law has been the subject of verses 1-6, and since Paul uses the term *letter* in 2 Corinthians 3:6-7 to refer to the Mosaic covenant, "the letter" here must refer to the Mosaic law as well—the law written in letters on tablets of stone on Mount Sinai. Mention of the letter-Spirit contrast recalls Paul's definition of the true Jew in 2:25-29 as one who places no

confidence in physical circumcision but who instead keeps "the just require
ments of the law" and whose heart is therefore circumcised "in the Spirit,
not in the letter."

Although in 7:6 Paul does not refer to the believer as a "true Jew" or make
an already complex argument more confusing by claiming that the believer
fulfills the just requirements of the law, the reappearance of the Spirit-letter
contrast at this point in the argument shows that in Paul's thinking believers
now fill to some extent the place of those who in 2:26-29 were simply a
hypothesis for the sake of argument. The "oldness of the letter" (*grammatos*)
then, refers to the old covenant, the Mosaic law that was "engraved with
letters *[grammasin]* on stone" (2 Cor 3:7), and the "newness of the Spirit" to
the arrival of the eschatological era predicted by the prophets in which God
would restore his people by placing his Spirit among them.[12] Believers, as
members of the eschatologically restored people of God, serve in the
"newness of the Spirit." Paul will explain how they do this more fully in 8:1-11.
At present, however, he must address another false inference from his
comments on the law.

The Mosaic Law Is Neither Sin Nor Death (Romans 7:7-25)

The interpretive difficulties that attend Romans 7:7-25 make it one of the
most complex sections of the letter and one of the most hotly debated
passages in New Testament scholarship.[13] Its importance for determining
Paul's approach to the law is obvious, since he uses the term *law* more
frequently here than in any other passage of equivalent length in his letters.
A careful reading of the passage within its context brings clarity at least to
the passage's overarching purpose and basic structure.

The key to the purpose of the passage within Paul's argument and the
structure of the passage itself lies in the rhetorical questions in verses 7 and
13. From 6:1 onward Paul has indicated the primary divisions in his argument with rhetorical questions, and except for the question that begins 7:1-6,
these questions have articulated the objections of his imaginary Jewish
reader to Paul's view of the law and set in motion the discussion that follows
them. In verses 7 and 13 he provides the same clues to the structure and
purpose of his argument. Paul has used the same word (*kyrieuō*) to describe
the law's power over people in verse 1 that he had used in 6:9 to describe the
power of death and in 6:14 to describe the power of sin.[14] In 7:1-6 he has
articulated a clear connection between the law, the sinful passions it produces and the death that comes as a result. Now he attempts to answer the
natural question, in light of his discussion, whether the law is to be identified

with sin (v. 7) and death (v. 13). Paul's now familiar "Certainly not!" to both questions reveals his basic stance, but as in 6:1-2 and 6:15, he follows this strong denial with a supportive argument.

The Mosaic law is not sin (Romans 7:7-12). Paul's argument that the law is not to be identified with sin proceeds through two basic steps. First, Paul recalls and explains his brief comment in 3:20 that the law brings knowledge of sin. In 7:7 he says that he could know precisely what sin was only through the definition of sin that the law provides.[15] Paul argues that he would not have known what coveting was had the Mosaic law not said, "You shall not covet" (compare Ex 20:17; Deut 5:21).[16] Far from being sin, then, the law provides a clear definition of sin.[17]

Second, Paul argues that the law was sin's innocent tool in deception and death (vv. 8-12). Outside the law sin lay dead, but when the commandment came, sin was able to use it as an entry point for attack and, by means of deception, as an instrument to kill those within its power (vv. 8, 11). The fault belongs entirely to sin; the commandment, whose purpose was to give life (v. 10), remains "holy and righteous and good" (v. 12).

The basic point of the passage, then, is clear: the law is not sin, nor ultimately at fault, in the situation that Paul describes in 5:20-21, 6:14-15 and 7:1-6; instead sin used the law as a tool for accomplishing its own purpose of death.[18]

The Mosaic law has not become death (Romans 7:13-25). Paul's comments on the law's entanglement with death lead naturally to a discussion of the second false inference from his stance on the law: "Did what is good then become death for me?" Paul follows this question with "Certainly not!" and then gives a short statement on the correct understanding of the relationship between sin, the law, death and self (v. 13). He finally engages in a long explanation of this short statement's meaning (vv. 14-25).[19]

Sin, Paul says in the brief statement that begins the section, used the good law to bring death "so that sin might be revealed as sin" and "so that through the commandment sin might become sinful to an extraordinary degree" (v. 13). Just as Paul had said in 5:20-21 that the effect of the law's coming in Israel was the increase of sin, so here he says that behind sin's use of the law to create death lay the divine intention to reveal sin as utterly sinful.[20]

Paul's next step explores in detail how this happens.[21] Sin, he says, takes advantage of the self's fleshly nature to keep the self from obeying the law.[22] Thus the self, or at least its fleshly nature, is "sold under sin" (v. 14; compare v. 18) and so is not able to do the law, although it agrees that the law is good (vv. 16-20). Paul summarizes this observation in verse 21: "So I discover this law: when I want to do what is good, that which is evil lies close at hand."

His use of the term *law* at this point has produced a flurry of comment from interpreters of the passage, but the best explanation seems to be that he uses the term to mean not the Mosaic law, which has been the subject of the section so far, but something like "the axiom" or "the principle" that sin so controls the self that the self cannot obey the law that it knows to be good.[23] This axiom, then, is probably identical with "the other law," "the law of sin" and "the law of sin in the flesh" to which Paul refers in verses 23 and 25.[24] Those expressions, if this reading is correct, do not refer to the Mosaic law, which remains in his thinking "the law of God," the law with which his mind agrees (vv. 22-23, 25). Instead they refer to the principle that the whole section is attempting to prove, that sin controls the self and prevents it from obeying the law.[25]

In 7:7-25, then, Paul has argued that the law is not sin and is not responsible for the death that sin's use of the law brings to the individual. He has done this first by showing that sin has used the holy, righteous, good law to take control of the self and lead it to do precisely what the law forbids. Next he has focused on how sin has used the flesh to control the self and keep the self from obeying the law that it knows to be good. The result of sin's use both of the law and of the self to create disobedience to the law has been death. This does not mean that the law itself is evil. Instead, Paul maintains, sin has used a law that is holy, righteous, good (v. 12), spiritual (v. 14) and from God (vv. 22, 25) to create sin and death in the fleshly self.

Two Laws or One? (Romans 8:1-17)

Having explained and defended his radical statements about the law, Paul now returns to the principal argument of chapters 5 and 6. In those chapters he had described the character of the believer's new life. In chapter 5 he had discussed the end of hostility between God and humanity as a result of Christ's death and resurrection, and in chapter 6 he had explained the transforming implications of Christ's death and resurrection for the believer's life. Now in chapter 8 he turns to the role of the Holy Spirit in the transformation of the believer's conduct (vv. 1-17) and the hope that characterizes the life transformed in this way (vv. 18-39).[26]

In verses 1-17 Paul contrasts life in the Spirit with life in the flesh. Christ's atoning death (v. 3), he says, has delivered the believer from a just sentence of condemnation (v. 1), from sin's grip on the believer's flesh (v. 3) and from the death that results (vv. 2-3).[27] The Spirit of Christ, who indwells the believer (vv. 9-10), is the means through which the believer has been rescued from "the mind of the flesh" and has been given "the mind of the Spirit" (vv. 5-6). Because of the transforming work of this indwelling Spirit, Paul says, enmity with God has ceased (v. 7), life and peace have come (v. 6), and the believer is able to please God (v. 8). Those whom God's Spirit leads, moreover, are adopted into the family of God's children (v. 14) and so become both God's heirs and fellow heirs with Christ himself (v. 17).

References to "the law" play an important part in this discussion. The term appears five times, twice in verse 2 and once each in verses 3, 4 and 7. Paul's first two uses of the term are among his most controversial references to the law in Romans. They appear in a sentence that gives the reason for his opening statement that there is now no condemnation for those who are in Christ Jesus (v. 1). The reason for this *(gar)*, Paul says, is that "the law of the Spirit of life in Christ Jesus has set you free from the law of sin and death" (v. 2). Although it is possible that this statement refers to the same law viewed from two different perspectives, the sentence's most obvious meaning is that there are two laws, one characterized by "the Spirit of life in Christ Jesus," the other by "sin and death," and that the first law has freed the believer from the second.[28]

This apparent meaning becomes a virtual certainty when we consider the verse within its context. First, Paul's use of the verb *set free (eleutheroō)* looks back to his use of the adjective *free (eleutheros)* in the illustration from marriage (7:1-6). There it described the believer's freedom from the law (7:3) through identification with Christ's death (7:2, 6). In that passage, this freedom placed the believer on a new course of identification with Christ's resurrection (7:4). If the language of 8:2 echoes that passage, then "the law of the Spirit of life in Christ Jesus" is probably a reference to the work of Christ—his death and resurrection—which has freed the believer from the Mosaic law's power to stimulate sinful passions (compare 7:5).[29]

Second, Paul's statement in verse 2 prepares the reader for his claim in verse 3 that "what was impossible for the law, because it was weak through the flesh, God did by sending his own Son in the likeness of sinful flesh and as a sin offering, thus condemning sin in the flesh." Here instead of "the law of the Spirit of life in Christ Jesus" setting the believer free from entanglement with sin, it is Christ's sacrifice for sin that accomplishes this task. For Paul's purposes in verse 3, then, Christ's atoning work and "the law of the Spirit of life in Christ Jesus" are synonymous.

All of this is confirmed when we look back to Paul's use of the phrase "the law of faith" in 3:27. Within its own context the phrase referred back to the believer's trust that in the shedding of Christ's blood God provided the ultimate atonement for sin and established the new covenant of prophetic expectation. Paul's reference now to "the law of the Spirit of life in Christ Jesus" places the emphasis on the eschatological signs that mark the arrival of the new age (the Spirit and life; compare Ezek 37:3-14), but his allusion to Christ's death for sin in verse 3 shows that this law is identical with the new covenant established in Christ's death and described in 3:25, 27. The "law of the Spirit of life in Christ Jesus," then, is a different law from the "law of sin and death." It is "the law of faith," the new covenant established by the sacrifice of Christ.

The "law of sin and death," on the other hand, is the Mosaic law.[30] Indeed, the phrase is a brief summary of chapter 7, which first described the relationship between the Mosaic law and sin (7:1-12; compare 7:7 with Ex 20:17; Deut 5:21) and then the relationship between the law and death (7:13-25; compare 7:10 with Lev 18:5; Deut 4:1; 30:15, 19-20; 32:47; Ezek 18:9; 20:11).[31] The clarification of the Mosaic law's relationship with sin and death in chapter 7 allows Paul to speak of "the law of sin and death" here without fear of being misunderstood to mean that the law *is* sin or *is responsible* for death. Instead, with the clarifications of chapter 7 behind him, Paul can use the phrase as a concise term for sin's use of the law.[32] The "law of sin and death," then, must be the Mosaic law as it is described in chapter 7: an instrument that, although holy, righteous, good, spiritual and of God, had been used by sin as a means of multiplying transgression and bringing death. From this law, Paul says in 8:2, the death of Christ, by which the new covenant was established, has set the believer free.

Paul uses the term *law* three more times in chapter 8. In verse 3 he speaks of "the inability of the law" to condemn sin in the flesh. In verse 4 he says that "the just requirement of the law" is fulfilled in those who walk according to the Spirit. And in verse 7 he says that the mind of the flesh "does not submit to the law of God, for it is not able to do so." *Law* in verses 3 and 7 seems to refer to the Mosaic law, since this is the law that Paul faults people for not keeping throughout the letter and that he depicts as the weak tool of sin in chapter 7.

The most natural understanding of the term in 8:4, then, is also as a reference to the law of Moses: Paul gives no indication that he has suddenly used the word to refer to an entirely different entity.[33] If this is true, however, Paul's meaning is difficult to grasp. How can he speak of the law as if believers have been released from it by the death of Christ, only to affirm immediately a continuing role for it in the life of the believer?[34]

The tension can be relieved slightly when we recall that the purpose of

7:7-25 was to exonerate the law from blame for sin and death. Sin emerged from that chapter as the culprit ultimately responsible for death, and the law emerged as sin's innocent tool. Since Paul claims in 8:3 that the death of Christ has dealt with sin by condemning it in the flesh, the conclusion seems reasonable that he viewed the eschatological age as a period in which the Mosaic law could assume a role consistent with its holy, righteous, good and spiritual nature.

This explanation does not relieve the tension in Paul's remarks entirely, however, for it still leaves unexplained the uncompromising nature of Paul's statement that "now we have been set free from the law, having died to that by which we were held prisoner" (7:6), a judgment with which 8:2 appears to agree. In addition, he seems to have redefined the law of Moses in terms that focus on such commands as "You shall not covet" but specifically exclude the command that every Israelite male should be circumcised (2:26; 7:7; compare 13:8-10).[35] To add even further to the confusion, if the understanding of 3:27 and 8:2 articulated above is correct, then Paul believes that a new covenant has replaced the old.

All of this forces the interpreter to ask whether the Mosaic law was still valid for Paul, and if so, how Paul could exclude certain commandments from it. It also poses the problem of describing the relationship between the Mosaic law and both the "the law of faith" (3:27) and "the law of the Spirit of life in Christ Jesus" (8:2). Help with these problems comes in Paul's next explicit discussion of the law.

The Mosaic Law and God's Promises to Israel

A troubling question has run beneath the current of Paul's argument in 1:16—8:39. It bubbled to the surface briefly in 3:1-8, where his Jewish interlocutor responded to the claims of chapter 2 with the query "What advantage, then, has the Jew?" Behind this question stood the objection that if, as Paul had argued, the Jew had no advantage over the Gentile on the final day, it was difficult to see in what sense God could be considered faithful to his covenant with Israel. Paul's answer in 3:1-8 was brief—Israel, not God, had been unfaithful, and therefore God's righteousness stood intact. Paul did not lay out his position fully in those verses, however, and the troubling undercurrent continued unabated into his subsequent argument.

In 3:9—8:39 it only gathered force. Thus in 4:9-25 Paul brought believing Gentiles into the family of Abraham together with believing Jews, but implied that unbelieving Jews did not belong. In chapters 5—8 he described this newly defined family as the recipients of the biblical promises that God would one day rescue his people from the plight of disobedience (6:17), put his Spirit in their midst (5:5; 7:6; 8:1-30) and make a new covenant with them (8:2). In chapter 8 the problem became acute when Paul attributed to the believing community Israel's status as God's adopted children (vv. 14-17; compare Hos 11:1) and asked, speaking of the relationship with God that Christ has established for the believer, "Who will bring charges against the elect of God?" (v. 33).[36]

All of this raises the question, then, how a righteous God (see 3:5, 25-26) could transfer Israel's status as "the elect of God" and the fulfillment of the prophetic promises of Israel's restoration to a group dominated by Gentiles.[37] If the explanation of Paul's gospel in 1:16—8:39 is true, then are God's promises to Israel untrue?

Unbelieving Jews who asked this question might reject the gospel, and believing Gentiles who asked it might be tempted to claim that the gospel implied the rejection of the Jews and their traditions. The turn Paul's argument takes in 11:11-24 shows that some believing Gentiles in Rome had already drawn anti-Jewish conclusions from the gospel. For reasons both intrinsic to the argument of Romans 1—8 and integral to circumstances within the Roman church, then, Paul addresses this question in chapters 9—11.

He states the problem sharply in 9:1-6, concluding his introductory paragraph with the thesis that his response will explore: "But it is not as though the word of God has failed" (v. 6). His response then proceeds in three stages. The first stage attempts to prove from Scripture that God alone—and no human qualities, whether ethnic or moral—decides who will receive his mercy (9:6-29; compare 11:5-6). His second step argues that at the present time many within Israel, although they have heard the gospel, have rejected it and so have not become part of God's people (9:30—10:21). The third and final step in Paul's argument claims that despite the rejection of the gospel in the present by the majority of Israel, God has not rejected his people. Even now, Paul says, God is constituting a remnant of Israel; and at the end, when God's mysterious purposes are finished, many within Israel will join Paul among the remnant who will be saved (11:1-36).[38]

The Mosaic law features prominently in the second stage of the argument as part of Paul's discussion of Israel's failure to submit to the preaching of the gospel (9:30—10:21). This section can be divided into two parts.[39] In the first Paul discusses the role the law has played in Israel's rejection of the gospel (9:30—10:13), and in the second he shows that Israel cannot claim not to have heard the gospel as an excuse for not submitting to it (10:14-21).

The first part, of primary concern here, can be further divided in two. First Paul states his thesis about Israel's failure to submit to the gospel (9:30—10:4), then he proves his thesis from Scripture (10:5-13).[40]

The Law's Role in Israel's Stumbling (Romans 9:30—10:4)

Paul begins the passage in Romans 9:30-31 with a summary of the anomaly that 9:6-29 has posed. That passage argued that God has surprisingly included Gentiles among his people at the same time that Israel, at least for the present, has been largely unresponsive to the gospel. It is as surprising that this should happen, Paul has argued, as that God should choose Isaac to carry out his purposes rather than Ishmael and Jacob rather than Esau, although both Ishmael and Esau deserved the honor by right of primogeniture (vv. 6-13).[41] What one deserves, however, has nothing to do with whether one will receive God's mercy (vv. 12, 16), and so, against all expectations, Gentiles outnumber Jews in the newly constituted people of God. In 9:30—10:33 Paul explains why this has happened: "What, then, shall we say? That Gentiles, who have not pursued righteousness, have attained [katelaben] righteousness, but righteousness by faith. But Israel, although pursuing a law of righteousness, has not reached [ephthasen] law" (9:30-31).

Paul is using the imagery of a race. Thus he speaks of pursuit, of attaining a goal and of falling short of a goal.[42] Since he focuses on two parties, the Gentiles and the Jews, it would be easy at first to view them as competitors in the same race, the Gentiles ironically winning although they did not even compete, and Israel losing although they ran like the wind. A closer look at Paul's language reveals, however, that at least at the level of Paul's imagery the two goals are distinct. The Gentiles reach the goal of "righteousness by faith," and the Jews fail to reach the goal of the "law." Thus two races are at issue—one that Paul describes succinctly in 9:30 and one that he recounts at greater length in 9:31—10:4.

In the first description Paul says that Gentiles have won a race that they failed even to enter: although not pursuing righteousness, they attained it in the form of the righteousness that comes through faith. By this Paul probably means that the Gentiles have entered a covenant relationship with God although, like Jacob (9:10-13) and the Israelites themselves (9:15-16), they did nothing good to deserve it.[43] Against all expectations, then, and apart from any human will or effort (9:16), the Gentiles have become part of the eschatologically constituted people of God. This has happened, Paul says, "by faith"—through their trust in the gospel.

In the second race, Israel pursues a "law of righteousness" but has not attained "law" (9:31). The sentence is confusing because we expect Paul to say that although the people of Israel pursue a law of righteousness, they have not attained righteousness.[44] If we remember that Paul is using the imagery of a race, however, and look ahead to 10:4—where he uses a common word for the goalpost in a footrace to say that "Christ is the goal [telos] of the law"—his meaning becomes clear. Although the Jews pursue a righteous law, they have not responded to the preaching of Christ with faith and so have not reached the goal toward which the law should have led them.[45] Unlike the Gentiles, Israel possessed all the advantages listed in 3:2 and 9:4-5 but has failed to reach the goal toward which these benefits pointed.

Why this failure? Paul responds to this question in 9:32-33: "Because [they do] not [pursue the law] by faith but as [if it were] by works. They stumbled over the stumbling stone, just as it is written, 'Behold, I lay in Zion a stone of stumbling and a rock of offense, and the one who believes in him shall not be ashamed.' "

Israel has failed to attain the goal toward which the law was pointing, Paul says, because they pursue the law "by works" rather than "by faith."[46] His meaning seems to be that if Israel had viewed the law from the standpoint of faith in Christ, they would see that the gospel is the goal toward which the law led. Instead, Israel pursued the law "by works."

These verses have often been understood to mean that the Jews have for many years striven to do enough of the law's requirements to merit salvation, and that their attempt to use the law in this way is the source of their failure in God's eyes.[47] A close look at the broader context of the phrase, however, shows that Paul's statement is not a critique of the Jewish religion generally but indicates why many Jews who had heard the gospel during the short period of its proclamation had rejected it. Thus Paul explains his statement that Israel pursues the law "by works" with a reference to Israel's rejection of Christ, the stumbling stone (9:32-33). Instead of realizing that Christ marked the end of the race and the goal toward which "the law of righteousness" was leading, the Jews saw Christ as only an obstacle in the path toward another, improper goal, which Paul will describe in 10:3.

Moreover, the larger context of 9:30—10:4 shows that Paul's concern is with Jews who have heard the gospel, not with Israel's religion for centuries past. Thus in 10:14-21 Paul argues that *in recent times* preachers have been sent to Israel (v. 15) who have preached the gospel (v. 14), and that *in recent times* Israel has heard (v. 14; compare v. 18), but that not all within Israel have believed (v. 14; compare v. 16) and called on the name of the Lord (v. 14).[48]

Paul's statement about Israel's pursuit of the law "by works," then, is probably not a claim that Israel's historic religion or the religion of all Jews in Paul's time was a self-oriented affair based on the assumption that salvation was earned by accruing merit.[49]

Instead, when Paul says that Israel has pursued the law "by works," he means that they have heard the gospel of redemption from the curses of the law but have rejected it, insisting on continuing the race after God brought it to an end.[50] Their rejection of the gospel implies a rejection of God's eschatological provision for their salvation, and all that remains is their own ethnic and moral qualifications, their own "works," which—as Paul has just argued in the case of the Gentiles (9:12, 16), and as he believes every Jew should know on the basis of their Scriptures (3:10-20)—do not form the criteria for membership in the newly constituted people of God.

Paul pursues this theme in 10:1-4. After repeating in a way reminiscent of 9:1-3 his concern for the salvation of Israel (v. 1), he acknowledges the Jews' "zeal" for God but says that it is not enlightened (v. 2). The reason for this (gar), he says, is that "being ignorant of the righteousness of God, and seeking to establish their own righteousness, they have not submitted to the righteousness of God" (v. 3). Having stumbled over the gospel ("the righteousness of God"; compare 1:16-17), Israel continues the race, but it is a race in their own righteousness, a righteousness that Deuteronomy itself says can accomplish nothing (Deut 9:4, 6; compare 7:8; 8:11-18).[51] Prior to hearing the gospel, then, many in Israel had properly pursued a law of righteousness and were on the way toward that law's goal. When the gospel came, however, Israel, against all expectations, rejected it. They continued the race beyond the finish and therefore in their own strength.[52]

Paul brings his description of Israel's failure, and his allusions to the racecourse, to a close in 10:4. "For the goal of the law," he says, "is Christ, so that righteousness might come to all who believe." If the understanding of 9:30—10:3 presented above is correct, then, the meaning of this much-contested passage is clear. It gives the reason why (gar) Paul believes that his assessment of Israel's failure in verse 3 is correct. Thus, although the word goal can mean "end" or "termination," its well-attested use to refer to the goal or winning-post in a race matches the racing imagery of the rest of the passage so well that this is probably the best choice.[53] So in verse 4 Paul reaches back to the imagery of 9:31, which pictured Israel pursuing "a law of righteousness" but not reaching it, and of 9:32-33, which says that they did not reach it because they stumbled over Christ. Paul now summarizes this imagery and brings the first part of his discussion of Israel's failure to a close by saying that the goal toward which the law pointed ("the goal of the law") was Christ.

To summarize, in 9:30—10:4 Paul has attempted to explain why believing Gentiles, once "no people" (9:25-26), now predominate among God's people, while Israel's representation has been reduced to a remnant. His explanation pictures two races, one in which Gentiles win the prize of "righteousness by faith" and one in which Israel fails to reach the goal of the law. Paul briefly describes the Gentiles' success in 9:30 and then discusses Israel's failure at length in 9:31—10:4. Israel's race involved the proper pursuit of the law, but Israel did not attain the "law" because it stumbled over the gospel and therefore over the winning-post of the race, the prize toward which the law pointed. Instead of recognizing the end of the race as God had designed it, Israel continued to run along its own course, in its own works and by its own righteousness.

The Law Preaches the Gospel (Romans 10:5-13)

In the second part of his description of Israel's failure, Paul attempts to show from the law itself that Christ is the goal toward which the law pointed—that although "the righteousness that comes by faith" has brought the Mosaic law to its divinely appointed end, the resulting situation nevertheless stands in continuity with the Mosaic covenant. Paul accomplishes this by contrasting Moses' description of "the righteousness that comes by the law" with the words of a personification of "the righteousness that comes by faith." Surprisingly, the words that "the righteousness that comes by faith" speaks are heavily dependent on the Mosaic law.

In Romans 10:5 "the righteousness from the law" uses the words of "Moses" to say that "the person who does these things shall live by them." The sentence is a paraphrase of Leviticus 18:5 and echoes Paul's claim in 7:10 that the intention of the law was to give life. But as Leviticus 26:14-39 shows, and as all who knew the biblical account of Israel's history understood, Israel had not kept the law and had not received the life that the law promised.

Thus in verses 6-13 "the righteousness that comes through faith" speaks. The message of this righteousness is that salvation (vv. 9-13) lies close at hand (vv. 6-7) and is available to anyone who believes "the word of faith" that Paul and others preach (v. 8). The Mosaic law had promised life to those who observed its precepts but nearly in the same breath had predicted Israel's failure to observe them. "The righteousness that comes through faith," however, has made salvation as near as "the word of faith" that Paul and others preach. The law, in other words, pointed the way to life but has shown, negatively, that Israel will not obtain life by keeping the commandments of the covenant. The gospel has shown, however, that salvation from this situation comes through God's gracious work of redemption in the resurrected Lord Jesus.[54]

The most puzzling aspect of the passage, in light of the contrast Paul has just posed between the Mosaic law and faith, is that his description of the nearness of salvation in the gospel paraphrases the language of the law itself. Moreover, the passage to which it alludes, Deuteronomy 30:11-14 (LXX), emphasizes how easily the law can be obeyed:

This commandment, which I am commanding you today, is neither immensely great nor far from you. It is not in heaven above, so that you might say, "Who will go up into heaven for us and get it for us? Then, having heard it, we will do it." Nor is it across the sea so that you might say, "Who will cross to the other side of the sea for us and get it for us? Then it will be audible to us, and we will do it." The word is very near you, in your mouth and in your heart and in your hands so that you might do it.

Although Paul does not specifically say that he is quoting Scripture, and although his quotations are not direct, his language is so close to this passage that his echoes of it must be intentional:

But the righteousness that comes by faith speaks this way, "Do not say in your heart, 'Who will go up into heaven?' " (that is, to bring Christ down), "or 'Who will go down into the abyss?' " (that is, to bring Christ up from the dead). But what does it say? "The word is near you, in your mouth and in your heart" (that is, the word of faith that we preach).[55] (10:6-8)

What can Paul mean by drawing a contrast between the law and the gospel but then making the gospel speak the language of the law? The answer to this question is found within the wider context of the passage on which his paraphrase is based. The passage is the final scene in Moses' account of Israel's history in Deuteronomy 29:2—30:20. It begins as a straightforward warning not to disobey the covenant that Moses has mediated between God and Israel. If Israel disobeys, Moses says, "all the curses written in this book will descend on them" (29:20; see also 29:27). As the warning progresses, however, it changes from an admonition not to abandon the Mosaic covenant into an account of Israel's historical disobedience and subsequent punishment. At its conclusion, the passage becomes pure prophecy, and Moses begins the final scene with the words "When all these things have happened to you" (30:1).

That final scene describes Israel's eschatological hope. In their exile, says Moses, Israel will come back to the Lord and obey his commands. God will circumcise their hearts so that they will love him with their whole heart and soul, and live (30:2-10). At this point Moses speaks the words that Paul echoes in Romans 10:6-8. The language shifts from prophecy back to the present and lays on Israel full responsibility for keeping the commandments of the covenant, since, as Moses says, they are not too hard for Israel to keep (v. 11) nor too difficult for Israel to understand (vv. 12-14). Although the focus in this passage is back on the present, the preceding paragraphs have shown that the obedience Moses urges on Israel will happen only after Israel's failure to keep the covenant and God's gracious intervention to circumcise their hearts (v. 6).

Because Paul believes that this eschatological era has dawned with the coming of the gospel, he is able to make "the righteousness that comes by faith" speak the language of this passage. The Mosaic law has been transformed into the gospel, and in this form Deuteronomy 30:11-14 has become a reality for believers in a way that it never was for Israel.

For Paul, the Mosaic law was disobeyed in Israel's history, had accomplished its purpose and had come to its divinely appointed end with the death and resurrection of Christ Jesus. Because the new order of faith retained some continuity with the Mosaic covenant, however, it could occasionally speak the language of that covenant. Even as it brought the Mosaic law to an end (Rom 10:5), the new order of righteousness by faith could speak the language of the Mosaic law (vv. 6-13).

This method of interpreting Scripture supplies the key to understanding the tension that exists between Romans 7:6 and 8:2 on one hand and 8:4 and 8:7 on the other. The believer has been released from the law of Moses, for that law died in God's economy when Christ died on the cross, and it also died existentially for each believer at baptism (7:4). Nevertheless, aspects of that law, such as the principle of the sanctity of God's people (6:19, 22) and the command not to covet (7:7), maintain a place within the new order because they represent God's eternally valid will. Thus the believer fulfills the law of Moses and submits to it insofar as it is incorporated in "the law of faith" and "the law of the Spirit of life in Christ Jesus."

The New Shape of Old Covenant Sanctity (Romans 12:1—15:6)
The practical outworking of the relationship between the new order and the old as it is expressed in the contrast between the Mosaic law and the new law in Romans 3:27, 8:2 and 10:5-13 is visible in Paul's ethical exhortation in

12:1—16:27. Thus despite his sensitivity to the concerns of the Jewish minority in 14:1—15:13, in 14:14 Paul agrees with the position of "the strong" in the Roman community that "nothing is impure in itself," and in 15:1 he leaves no doubt that the scruples of those who persist in observing the dietary laws and calendar of the Mosaic covenant are "frailties" *(asthenēmata)* that "we who are strong" ought to tolerate. These aspects of the Mosaic covenant, like circumcision in 2:25-29, have no continuing validity for Paul. Instead, violating them defiles a brother or sister only if that person is convinced that they are still valid (14:14). In Paul's view, then, the commandments within the Mosaic law that distinguished Jew from Gentile are no longer binding.[56]

Despite all this, Paul continues to use the Mosaic law in his ethical admonitions. He advises his readers to repay no one evil for evil, to live at peace with all people and, echoing the first half of Leviticus 19:18, not to avenge themselves (12:17-19). A few sentences later, in 13:8-10, he quotes the second half of Leviticus 19:18 as a summary of the sixth, seventh, eighth and tenth of the Ten Commandments:[57]

> Owe no one anything except the debt of love. For the one who loves the other fulfills the law. The commandments "You shall not commit adultery; you shall not murder; you shall not steal; you shall not covet," and any other commandment, are all summarized in this phrase: "You shall love your neighbor as yourself." Love does no harm to its neighbor; therefore love is the fulfillment of the law.[58]

In some sense, therefore, the Mosaic law continues to function for the believer as the boundary marker between conduct that pleases God (compare 8:7-8) and sin (compare 3:20; 7:7). It contains God's will, the believer should fulfill it (compare 8:4), and therefore it cannot simply be discarded.

In 12:1—15:6, then, the boundaries of holiness by which the Sinaitic covenant defined God's people have been erased. Dietary restrictions and sabbath observance have become irrelevant to the sanctity of God's people. Their importance has passed away with the Sinaitic covenant itself. Nevertheless, the principle of establishing clear boundaries between the people of God and those outside continues to be important, and Paul sometimes uses the language of the Sinaitic covenant to describe these boundaries. The era of the new covenant has replaced the old, but the new structure has absorbed elements of the old and is not therefore entirely new.[59]

The Law in Romans: A Summary
This study of the law in Romans has wended along the difficult path of Paul's argument, but impressive vistas on his understanding of the law have opened

up along the way. At the end of such a trek, it makes sense to review our discoveries.

Although Romans is not an abstract theological treatise on the relationship between the gospel and the law, because of its peculiar character it provides a more comprehensive statement about that relationship than Paul's previous letters. Unlike Galatians, the letter responds to no threat from Jewish believers who insist that Gentiles couple their faith in Christ with observance of the law, and unlike all of Paul's other letters it presupposes no knowledge of his gospel among its recipients. Paul has never preached in Rome. Instead Romans represents his response to a unique combination of concerns about his future missionary endeavors and about the Roman church. Paul wants the support of the Romans for his preaching of the gospel but also believes that they need to hear his gospel and benefit from his pastoral oversight. In order to fill these diverse needs, he provides an explanation of the gospel that he has preached in synagogues scattered across the eastern Mediterranean basin.

This gospel interacts deeply with the Jewish tradition from which it emerged. It seeks to find common ground with Judaism, to take its objections seriously and yet to persuade its adherents of the truth of the gospel. As part of this effort, Paul frequently brings the Mosaic law, the sign of Israel's election, into the discussion. His purpose for doing this is twofold: he wants to demonstrate first that everyone, whether Gentile or Jew, has violated the law, and second that because of this Jews can neither claim an advantage over Gentiles on the final day of judgment nor have any legitimate confidence that works done in obedience to the law will help them on that day.

Paul begins his argument by undermining any Jewish claim to special exemption from judgment. He does this in two ways. First, he shows that even the Gentile innately understands enough of the Jewish law to be saved by doing it or to be condemned for violating it (1:32; 2:6-16, 26-29). Second, he observes that God's impartiality requires that God treat Jewish transgression and Gentile disobedience with equal severity (2:9-12). All have sinned, Paul concludes, and no one can claim exemption from judgment on the basis of possession of the law (3:9, 19-20) or boast in works done in obedience to it (3:27—4:8). Far from rescuing those who possess it or partially comply with it from judgment, Paul maintains, the law is connected with sin and wrath. Although holy, righteous, good (7:12), spiritual (7:14) and from God (7:22, 25), the law brings sin to light (3:20) and increases sin in those who live within its authority (5:20; 6:14) by providing the sinful self with a pointed means of rebelling against God (7:1-25).

God has responded to this situation with the atoning death of Christ Jesus, an event whose justifying benefits belong to all who have faith in them. Paul uses the language of the Day of Atonement ritual and of the covenant ratification ceremony at Sinai to describe Christ's death. For Paul, then, Christ's death appears to have signified an ultimate atoning sacrifice that instituted a new covenant. He refers to this redemptive action of God as "the law of faith" (3:27) and "the law of the Spirit of life in Christ Jesus" (8:2). Unbelieving Judaism, he maintains, has missed this divinely appointed means of rescue from the penalty of death, the penalty that the law itself pronounces on all who transgress it (9:30-33). The Jews' rejection of the gospel and continued pursuit of the Mosaic law after it came to its divinely appointed end imply a vote of confidence in their own righteousness—a righteousness that the Mosaic law itself claims is not adequate to merit God's blessing (10:1-4).

The era of the Mosaic law, then, has come to an end. With its end has come the end of sin's domination over the believer's life. Gone too are circumcision, sabbath observance and dietary regulations as boundary markers for the people of the covenant. This law and these boundary markers have been replaced with the "law of faith" and a sanctity defined by "the pattern of teaching" handed down to believers in the gospel. This new order has absorbed elements of the Mosaic law and so has some continuity with it, but the Sinaitic covenant as the sign of the election of God's people and as the definitive guide to their sanctity has come to an end.

CHAPTER TEN

OLD CONVICTIONS IN NEW SETTINGS: The Law of Moses in Paul's Later Letters

After Paul wrote Romans, he pursued his plans to take an offering from his predominantly Gentile churches to the Jewish Christians in Jerusalem, but in Jerusalem his ambition to travel to Spain was thwarted by arrest and long imprisonments in Caesarea and Rome (Acts 20:3—28:31). Although the historical sources for Paul's life after his Roman imprisonment are sketchy, he seems to have been acquitted and resumed his missionary labors, not in Spain as he had originally planned, but once again in the eastern provinces of the Roman Empire.[1]

During this period Paul produced a series of letters that, with the exception of Philemon, have such a different literary style and theological tone from his earlier correspondence that a number of scholars believe Paul could not have written them. These documents are probably not forgeries, however, but letters composed for purposes widely different from those of the earlier group, perhaps with the help of different secretaries who were more active in shaping their idiom.[2]

All of these letters are closely connected with the Roman province of Asia, a region in which Paul ministered for over two years (Acts 19:10; 20:31) and where the gospel received vigorous challenges from an early time.[3] Thus the letters to the seven churches of Asia in Revelation express concern about deviant forms of Christianity, particularly those that promote immorality (Rev 2:14-15, 20-21). Ignatius's letters to various churches in Asia, written early in the second century, show a deep concern that Christians in the area not fall under the spell of a docetic form of Christian teaching (*Letter to the Ephesians* 7; *Letter to the Trallians* 9—10; *Letter to the Smyrneans* 3) and contain occasional hints that some Christians have twisted the gospel into a license for ethical laziness (*Trallians* 6.2; *Letter to the Philadelphians* 2.2; *Smyrneans* 6.2). Both Revelation and Ignatius's letters, moreover, imply that around the turn of the century Christians in Asia were being attracted to the synagogue or to a heavily Jewish form of Christianity (Rev 2:9; 3:9; Ignatius *Letter to the Magnesians* 8—10; *Philadelphians* 6.1; 8-9; compare *Smyrneans* 5.1).

It is possible that these defections and near defections from the faith were the result of a spiritual malaise that began to fall over the Pauline churches of western Asia Minor during the waning years of the apostle's career and in the decades after his death. The connection of some of these churches with Paul had been weak from the first, since they were founded through his coworkers and did not know Paul himself (Eph 3:2; Col 2:1), and some Christians within them apparently found the apostle's long periods of imprisonment during this time discouraging (Eph 3:13). This disillusionment seems to have led some to stray from the faith into deviant forms of Christianity, whether docetic, Jewish, antinomian or a combination of these tendencies. It may have also led some to abandon the faith altogether for the ancient and widely respected religion of the synagogue.[4]

But Paul considered himself to be the apostle of these churches, part of the foundation on which their faith was built (Eph 2:20; 3:1; Col 2:1-4). Their discouragement was his concern, their temptation to stray from healthy teaching his problem. To meet these changed conditions, Paul reshaped the way he expressed his convictions about the Mosaic law. Some elements of his view of the law which were important in earlier years are missing entirely from these letters, and others reappear to be used for new purposes.

The Mosaic Law and Angelic Visions at Colossae

Although the references to Epaphras in Colossians and the connection between Colossians and Philemon have provided the foundation for a series of intriguing portraits of the Colossian church, the most important aspect of Colossian Christianity for the student of Paul's view of the law is that the Colossians were Gentiles.[5] Thus Paul says that they have been circumcised, but not with a circumcision accomplished through human hands. They have instead received a "Christian circumcision" (2:11).[6] In addition, Paul regards them as representatives of the Gentiles in whom Christ dwells and who therefore have "the hope of glory" (1:27; compare 1:21).

Their inclusion among God's people came through the efforts of Paul's coworker Epaphras, who was himself a Colossian and may have met Paul during the apostle's long stay in Ephesus (Acts 19:10). He may have been the means through which people not only in his own town but also in Laodicea (Col 2:1; 4:13, 15) and Hierapolis (4:13) heard the gospel. Since that time the church's faith had prospered (1:4-6), and when Paul wrote the letter, the church's "order and firmness" were cause for rejoicing (2:5).[7] Despite this, a troublesome teaching had recently gained enough of a hearing in the church to prompt Epaphras to go to his imprisoned father in the faith and seek his advice.[8] The letter to the Colossians is the result.

Epaphras brought word of false teachers who were advancing convincing arguments for a "philosophy" (2:8) that some Colossians believed to be compatible with faith in Christ but that Epaphras knew to be at odds with the Pauline gospel.[9] The clearest references to this false teaching appear in chapter 2. In 2:1-3 Paul tells the Colossians that although he does not know them personally, he has frequently struggled for them and other believers in the Lycus Valley so that their "hearts might be encouraged and united in love, so that they might have all the wealth of full understanding and therefore know the mystery of God, that is Christ, in whom all the treasures of wisdom and knowledge are hidden."

Paul follows this full statement of the purpose for his concern with another purpose statement: "I say this in order that no one might deceive you with fine-sounding arguments" (v. 4). If Paul says that in Christ "all the treasures of wisdom and knowledge are hidden" to prevent the Colossians' deception by specious arguments, then it seems reasonable to say that the specious arguments themselves gave to something else the superiority that belongs to Christ alone.[10]

This understanding of 2:1-4 is confirmed in 2:8-9, where the next explicit reference to the problem at Colossae appears. In verse 8 Paul warns the Colossians against one who might take them captive "through philosophy and empty deception, according to human tradition, according to the elements of the world and not according to Christ." He then gives the reason why this philosophy is only "empty deception" and "human tradition": "because in [Christ] dwells all the fullness of the Godhead bodily, and you have been given fullness in him, who is the head of every ruler and authority" (vv. 9-10).[11] It seems clear, then, that the false teaching at Colossae was subordinating Christ, at least as he was preached among the Colossians at the beginning (v. 6), to another religious system.

A few of the specific tenets of that system are mentioned in 2:16-19. Here Paul tells the Colossians not to let anyone condemn them "in matters of food and drink, or with regard to a festival, new moon, or sabbath" (v. 16), nor to let anyone "disqualify" them "who delights in humiliation and in the worship of angels, entering into that which he has seen, puffed up by the mind of his flesh and not holding fast to the head" (vv. 18-19). He then asks the Colossians rhetorically why they should subject themselves to such worldly rules as "do not handle, do not taste, do not touch" (vv. 20-21)—rules, he says, that have no value for controlling fleshly indulgence (v. 23).

The false teaching at Colossae, then, subordinated Christ to a religious system that promoted conformity to certain rules about diet and observance of special days, and those who urged these rules on the community placed a heavy emphasis on visions in which angels played some role. Paul's statement that such rules have no value for controlling fleshly indulgence, moreover, seems to be a counterattack on a claim of the false teachers that without their regulations the Colossians would have no sure ethical guidance.

But can we be more specific? The lack of detail in Paul's own account of the false teaching has provided fertile ground for speculation about its origins, and the variety of attempts to identify the error more specifically is bewildering.[12] Yet two aspects of the error are clear. First, it was Jewish. Paul's warning to the Colossians not to allow the false teachers to judge them "with regard to a festival, new moon or sabbath" (2:16) recalls the language the Septuagint uses to summarize observance of the Jewish calendar, and his claim that the Colossians have received a Christian rather than a physical circumcision is probably a response to the false teachers' requirement that the Colossians accept physical circumcision.[13] Second, those promoting the error have placed a particular emphasis on visions in which the worship of angels plays some role. Thus Paul describes a typical false teacher as one "who delights in self-abasement and the worship of angels, entering into that which he has seen" (2:18).

The religious milieu that can best accommodate both elements is the world of Jewish apocalyptic literature. The apocalyptic writings extant during the first century frequently feature seers whose conformity to the law is exemplary and whose visions include judgment scenes where a verdict is rendered on the basis of a record, kept by an accusing angel, of one's good and evil deeds.[14] Angels figure prominently in these apocalypses. An angel interpreter often guides the seer on a heavenly tour that includes scenes of angels worshiping God, and frequently the angelic guide is so dazzling that at the first sight of him the seer falls to the ground under the mistaken impression that he is God.[15]

The false teachers in Colossae may have linked these visions with their teaching on the Mosaic law in several ways. They probably used their visions as proof of their right to exercise spiritual authority over the Colossians, and this may account for Paul's reference to their boastful attitude in 2:19. In addition, they may have urged the Colossians to accept the Mosaic law as a first step toward experiencing such visions themselves. Almost certainly, however, they claimed that the Mosaic law would provide the Colossians with the moral guidance they would need to live a life worthy of a favorable verdict at the time of judgment.

In light of the importance the false teachers attached to observance of the law and to their own heavenly visions, it is not surprising that Christ's work of forgiveness and reconciliation played at best a secondary role in their scheme. Thus Paul charges them with not "holding fast" to Christ and, through their inattention to him, of endangering the whole body of believers in Colossae (2:19).[16]

The Role of the Law in Paul's Response

Although Paul never uses the word *law* in Colossians, the Mosaic covenant nevertheless has a significant place in his response to the trouble at Colossae. First, throughout the letter Paul reminds the Colossians that they are already part of the people of God and implies that because they have received Christ Jesus as Lord, they do not need to conform to the Mosaic law. Second, he emphasizes the sufficiency of Christ's death for dealing with transgression against the Mosaic law and implies that the Colossians need have no fear that any failure to comply with the law's demands will result in condemnation before God's tribunal.[17]

Colossian Gentiles as the people of God. Paul begins his letter by referring to the Colossians as "the holy *[hagiois]* and faithful brothers in Christ at Colossae" (1:2) and so applies to them the language that the Mosaic covenant uses to describe Israel. Just as Israel in the Old Testament is God's "treasured possession out of all the peoples . . . a priestly kingdom and a holy nation"

(Ex 19:5-6; compare Lev 11:44-45), so the Colossian believers are set apart from others.

This theme receives repeated emphasis throughout the letter. Thus in 1:12 Paul recalls the biblical description of the "portion" *(klēros)* that God gave to the Israelites in the land of Canaan (as in Ex 6:8; Josh 17:4) when he describes the Colossians as those who have received a "share of the portion *[klērou]* of the saints *[hagiōn]* in light," and in 1:13-15 his claim that God "has rescued" and has provided "redemption" for believers from the rule of darkness recalls God's rescue of Israel from bondage in Egypt (Ex 6:6 LXX).[18] This redemption, he says, involved "the forgiveness of sins" (1:14), a statement that echoes prophetic descriptions of the time when God would establish a new covenant with his people and forgive their iniquity (Jer 31:34).[19] Similarly, in 1:21-22 he reminds the Colossians that although they were once estranged and hostile to God, now, because of Christ's death, they are "holy," and when he says in 2:11-14 that the formerly disobedient Colossians have been circumcised with the circumcision of Christ, he alludes to the biblical promise that God would one day circumcise the wayward hearts of his people (Deut 30:6). It comes as no surprise, then, that in 3:12 Paul transfers three classic designations of Israel's special status to the Gentile Colossians: they are the "elect of God, holy and beloved."[20]

Paul probably used this language to counteract the claims of the false teachers that the Colossians must accept circumcision, observe the dietary restrictions and keep the calendar of the Mosaic law in order to belong to the people of God. Far from needing to perform such duties, Paul says, the Colossian Gentiles have inherited all the promises given to Israel. Although their baptism has not made them Jews (3:11), and Jews remain in some sense "the circumcision" (4:11), the Gentile Colossians are none the worse for this. They stand in continuity with the people of God throughout the ages, and along with Jews who claim Christ Jesus as Lord (2:6), they are recipients of the privileges of God's ancient people.

Colossian transgressors as the forgiven people of God. The false teachers in Colossae had probably tried to convince the Colossians that the traditions they had received about Jesus Christ did not provide them with sufficient ethical guidelines (2:23) and that this deficiency would place them in a particularly precarious position at the day of judgment (2:13-15). The Mosaic law, they probably claimed, could remedy this problem. The commandment to accept circumcision (2:11) and the laws of purity (2:16, 21) were sometimes interpreted in the Judaism of Paul's era as symbols of ethical purity, and the false teachers at Colossae may have emphasized their value, in a similar way, not only for bringing the Colossian Gentiles into the people of God as the Mosaic law defined it but also for reminding them of the life of moral purity they needed to live if they hoped to receive a favorable verdict at the time of judgment.[21]

Paul's attack against these notions takes two forms. First, he claims that the use to which the false teachers put the law is equivalent to Gentile idolatry. They have turned the dietary commands and the calendar of the Mosaic covenant into nothing more than "human tradition" and made them equivalent to the former rudimentary religious practices, or "elements of the world," which had dominated the Colossians' lives before they received Christ Jesus as Lord (2:8, 16).[22] Similarly, Paul claims that if they are going to observe the purity laws within the Mosaic covenant as if they could curb indulgence of the flesh, they might as well return to their former life as Gentiles (2:20), for these laws address the use of things that are destined to perish, not eternal matters (2:22).[23] The false teachers' insistence that the laws be observed if one is to receive a favorable verdict on the final day has transformed these laws into mere "human regulations and teachings" (2:22). The problem lies not with the Mosaic law itself but with the false teachers' failure to recognize the limits of its purposes: its regulation of diet and calendar was a shadow of things to come, and Christ is the reality for which the shadow provided a mere outline (2:17).

Second, Paul reminds the Colossians that Christ's death on the cross "blotted out the handwriting [to . . . cheirographon] that was against us and opposed to us with respect to the decrees [tois dogmasin]" (2:14). Although it is difficult to know exactly what Paul means by "the handwriting that was against us" and "the decrees," these phrases probably refer to a heavenly court scene in which the records of an accusing angel are produced and people are either allowed to enter heaven or banished from it on the basis of their recorded deeds.[24] The false teachers in Colossae apparently defined good and evil deeds strictly according to the Mosaic law, and therefore "the decrees" are probably the Mosaic law's sanctions against the disobedient.[25] Against the false teachers' claim that the Colossians will be judged before a heavenly tribunal on the basis of their conformity with the Mosaic law, Paul's point is simply that Christ has forgiven the Colossians' transgressions and nailed the charges that might be brought against them to the cross (2:13-14; compare 1:14, 20, 22).

Paul puts all of this in the past tense in order to emphasize that the Colossians need have no fear that a lack of conformity to the Mosaic law will lead to an unfavorable verdict on the final day. They have already been rescued from the authority of darkness and transferred into the kingdom of God's beloved Son (1:13). They already have the redemption, the forgiveness of sins (1:14), have already been reconciled to God (1:22) and have already died and been raised with Christ (2:12-13). Christ has already forgiven their transgressions and nailed the law's charges against them to the cross (2:14). In the process he has already triumphed over all accusing forces and divested them of their power and authority (2:15).

To the claims of the false teachers that the Colossians must conform to the law or face condemnation at the time of judgment, therefore, Paul responds that because the Colossians have received Christ Jesus as Lord (2:6), they have received forgiveness, have been raised with Christ and live with him in heavenly regions and at God's right hand (3:1). They need seek no further access to the heavenly world, and they need fear no future judgment against them. Their judgment has, to put it in Johannine terms, already taken place, and they have passed from death to life.

The Shape of Paul's View of the Law in Colossians

In Colossians several of Paul's most deeply held convictions about the Mosaic law reappear. All Christians, whether circumcised or uncircumcised, belong to a newly constituted people of God that has inherited the promises given to ancient Israel (3:11). The boundaries of this people, however, are not defined by the Mosaic law. Those boundaries are instead drawn by the implications of receiving "Christ Jesus as Lord" (2:6), being buried with him in baptism and being raised with him through faith (2:12) to dwell with him spiritually at God's right hand (3:1-4). The Mosaic law, moreover, is obsolete in the new age, having fulfilled its purpose of pointing toward Christ (2:17), and therefore reversion to it as if it still held pride of place in God's redemptive purposes is such a serious misuse of the law that Paul can compare it with the idolatry that Gentile believers practiced prior to coming to faith (2:8, 20). Finally, the Mosaic law justly pronounced a curse on all for their disobedience, but Christ's death has removed that curse (2:14; compare 1:20).

These familiar elements of Paul's view of the law are matched by important differences. Colossians contains less of an emphasis than do Paul's other letters on the place of the law in salvation history and a stronger emphasis on the complete victory of Christ over all forces, including the sanctions of the Mosaic law, which threaten the Christian's reconciliation with God. Thus although a hint of Paul's perspective on salvation history appears when he says the Mosaic law provided a shadow of *things to come* (2:17), the relationship of the Mosaic covenant to the promises to Abraham is not discussed (compare Rom 4:1-15; Gal 3:15-23), the age of the law is not contrasted with the age of the Spirit (compare Rom 8:2; Gal 3:13-14; Phil 3:3), no need arises for a discussion of God's purpose in giving the law (compare Rom 5:20; Gal 3:19-20), there is no comparison of the new covenant with the old (compare 2 Cor 3:6,14), and the language of justification, with its covenantal overtones, is absent (compare Rom 3:21-26; Gal 2:15-16).

Instead, Paul's focus is the contrast between two understandings of the heavenly world. In the false teachers' understanding of that world, an accusing angel awaits those who want to enter heaven, and only those whose deeds pass the inspection of his unerring eye will enter into fellowship with God. Against this notion Paul assures the Colossian Christians that spiritual reality reflects what they experienced in baptism: they were buried with Christ and have been raised with him. Far from having to fear an unfavorable verdict in some future judgment according to works, they are already seated with Christ at God's right hand in the heavens (3:1). Because of this their behavior should not be motivated by fear that God will not accept them if they transgress an obsolete law, but by the knowledge that their lives are united with that of the living and victorious Christ (3:1-4).

Philemon and Knowledge of the Good
Paul's "beloved brother" Tychicus carried Colossians to its destination (Col 4:7), and with him went Onesimus, another "faithful and beloved brother" (Col 4:9). Onesimus was a slave who had run away from his master Philemon (Philem 17) and had probably stolen some money when he left (vv. 18-19).[26] We do not know how Onesimus came into contact with Paul, but through his relationship with the apostle, he became a Christian (vv. 10, 16) and such a good friend that Paul wanted to keep him at his side to help him in his imprisonment (vv. 12-13). His owner Philemon, however, was also a friend and coworker of Paul (v. 1), and Paul felt that to detain Onesimus without Philemon's consent would be unwise: it would impose on his generosity (v. 14) and might interfere with God's intention to bring slave and master together as beloved brothers in the Lord (vv. 15-16).[27] Paul therefore sent Onesimus back to Philemon, with Tychicus, and with them went a second letter whose purpose is as straightforward as its text is brief: Paul wants Philemon to pardon Onesimus (v. 17).[28]

The letter says nothing explicit about the law of Moses, but for two reasons it is not irrelevant to the study of Paul's view of the law. First, the law did touch on the subject of runaway slaves (Deut 23:15-16), and Jews in antiquity debated exactly what it required them to do, but Paul takes no account of the relevant passage and shows no inclination to enter the debate.[29] Although Paul and Philemon are members of the sanctified people of God (vv. 5, 7), the Mosaic law's perspective on the issue between them does not appear to have been important.[30]

Paul's appeal instead seems to stand on the two-layered foundation of his own authority as an apostle and his trust that Philemon will do what is good freely, without the compulsion of Paul's authority. First, Paul tells Philemon plainly that he has the authority to command him to do what is right. "I have much boldness *[parrēsian]* in Christ to order you *[epitassein]* to do what is proper," Paul says (v. 8). As the combination of the two words *parrēsia* ("boldness") and *epitassō* ("command") shows, this is unusually strong language.[31] It seems clear, then, that although Paul does not intend to use the authority he possesses, he wants to remind Philemon that he has this authority (compare 1 Cor 9:1-15). It seems reasonable to conclude from this that for Paul, the place the Mosaic law once played in ethical guidance has been filled by the authoritative teaching that, as an apostle, he hands on to others.[32]

Second, and paradoxically, Paul states three times in the letter that he believes Philemon will do what is right freely and without the compulsion of a direct, authoritative command. In verses 8-9 he says that he will not order Philemon to do what is proper but will instead exhort him to do it on the basis of love, in verse 14 he says that he did not want to keep Onesimus with him without Philemon's knowledge so that Philemon might not do his "good deed" from compulsion but "freely," and in verse 21 Paul expresses his confidence that Philemon will do what he asks and even more.

In verse 6 Paul provides a hint of the reason he is so confident: he prays that Philemon might have the "knowledge of everything good in us in Christ." Although the Greek of this statement is notoriously ambiguous, the most likely understanding of it is that Paul wants Philemon to act in a way that is consistent with his knowledge of God's will.[33] In light of what we have seen elsewhere of Paul's understanding of the law, the knowledge that Paul claims for Philemon in verse 6 is probably the innate knowledge of God's will that Jeremiah predicted would come in the time of Israel's restoration. At that time God would establish a new covenant with his people and they would all "know the LORD" (Jer 31:34).[34] Paul's confidence in Philemon stems at least in part from his assurance that his friend has experienced the eschatological blessing of a renewed heart that perceives innately what God's will is in specific situations.[35]

In Philemon, therefore, Paul applies the ethics of the new covenant to a relational breach between believers. Although he has all the authority of Moses, and even more (2 Cor 3:12), to order Philemon to do what love demands, he refrains from using his authority because he knows that Philemon has the insight into God's will that characterizes those who have entered into the new covenant with God. He is confident that apart from any authoritative command, Philemon will do the loving and good thing.[36]

The Riddle of Ephesians

When Tychicus and Onesimus left Paul to travel to the Lycus River valley, they took with them not only letters to the Colossian church and to Paul's fellow worker Philemon but two other letters as well: one to the church in Laodicea, which has since disappeared, and a letter whose title in modern versions of the Bible says that it was sent "to the Ephesians."[37] The character of Ephesians, however, is strikingly different not only from its two companion letters but from Paul's earlier correspondence as well, and its approach to the Mosaic law forms an important part of this distinctiveness.

In many ways Ephesians is not the kind of letter that, on the basis of his other correspondence, we would expect Paul to write. It contains no clear reference to the problems that prompted him to write it and offers no greetings at its conclusion. Moreover, although its first recipients were later thought to have been the Ephesians, the oldest and most reliable manuscripts of the letter show that Paul addressed it neither to the church in any particular city nor to any particular person. It is simply a letter to "the saints who are also faithful in Christ Jesus" (Eph 1:1).[38] What might have led Paul to write such a letter?

The close relationship of Ephesians to Colossians and Philemon and its eventual association with the church at Ephesus make it likely that Paul intended the letter for churches in the Roman province of Asia, perhaps those founded by his coworkers during his long stay at Ephesus (Acts 19:10). If the addressees of the letter represent the ethnic composition of these churches, they must have been predominantly Gentile (Eph 2:11-13; 3:1; 4:17).[39]

Although the letter itself gives no specific information about the problems facing these Gentile believers, and although Paul seems generally pleased with their spiritual health (1:1, 16), several passages indicate that he had some concern about the state of their faith. His thanksgiving for them (1:15-16) quickly turns into a petition on their behalf that God might give them a complete understanding of the privileges they have as believers

(1:17-19), and he urges them to contrast their spiritual state prior to faith with their present position as recipients of God's mercy (2:4), love (2:4), grace (2:5, 7-8) and work of reconciliation (2:11-22). This concern reappears in 3:14-19, where Paul intercedes for his readers that they might be strengthened inwardly (3:16), that Christ might dwell in their hearts (3:17) and that they might have the ability to grasp the profundity of Christ's love (3:18-19). If these petitions were designed to address the needs of the group to whom Paul wrote, then it seems safe to say that they were Gentile believers who were discouraged (compare 3:13) and forgetful (compare 2:11) of the blessings they had as Christians.[40]

Discouragement and forgetfulness, moreover, appear to have led to undisciplined behavior. Thus after reminding his readers of the glorious nature of their calling in 1:3—3:21, Paul encourages them in 4:1—6:20 to "live lives worthy of the calling" they have received (4:1). He urges them to maintain a high ethical standard in the church (4:1—5:21), in society generally (4:17—5:21) and within their families (5:22—6:9) and appeals to them not to succumb to false teaching (4:14; 5:6).

If many Pauline Christians in Asia were beginning to rethink their commitment to the gospel of an imprisoned apostle whom they had never seen (3:2, 13), some perhaps giving up the discipline of the Christian life and others attending synagogue services, then Ephesians begins to make sense. Paul may have written the letter to several different churches in Asia to remind them of the wealth of their inheritance in Christ, to explain the relationship between Judaism and Christianity, and to encourage them to live in a way that was consistent with their calling.

Paul's Approach to the Law in Ephesians

As part of this attempt to encourage the dispirited Christians of Asia, Paul repeatedly reminds his readers that they are the people of God as the Mosaic law defines those people. Thus Paul frequently calls the Ephesians the "holy" (*hagios*) people of God (1:1, 4; 2:19; 3:18; 4:12; 5:3) and tells them, in a way reminiscent of Israel's calling at Sinai, that they should "no longer walk as the Gentiles walk in the futility of their thinking" (4:17; compare Ex 19:5-6).[41] Just as in the law holiness is a consequence of observing the difference between clean and unclean (Lev 20:24-26), so Paul tells the church to avoid "uncleanness" *(akatharsia)* and to walk in morally upright ways, "as is fitting for the holy" (5:3; compare 5:5). Men, for example, should love their wives "as Christ loved the church and gave himself for her in order that she should be sanctified *[hagiasē]*, making her clean *[katharisas]* by the washing of water

225

in the word" (5:25-26; see also 5:27).[42] This moral cleanliness, moreover, is defined in certain instances by the Mosaic covenant. Thus Paul instructs children to obey their parents in obedience to the fifth commandment (6:2-3; compare Ex 20:12; Deut 5:16).

Paul does not leave this identification of the church with Israel in the realm of allusion and hint, however, but in 2:11-13 clearly states that his readers stand in continuity with the Old Testament people of God. Although they were once Gentiles and considered by Jews to be uncircumcised, were once outside the people to whom the Messiah was promised, were aliens to the commonwealth of Israel and were strangers to the covenants of promise, now they have been included within the circle of God's people. In the words of 2:19, they are "fellow citizens with the saints and members of God's household."[43] Clearly, these physically uncircumcised Gentiles have become the people of God. How has this happened?

Paul says that the crucifixion of Christ on behalf of the church effected this dramatic change (2:13, 16; 5:25) by making peace both horizontally between Jews and Gentiles (2:15) and vertically between this reconciled group and God (2:16). Christ's death accomplished this by tearing down "the dividing wall [to mesotoichon tou phragmou] and nullifying in his flesh the hostility, the law of the commandments with its decrees [dogmasin]" (2:14). In this statement Paul has in mind two effects of the Mosaic law in the history of Israel. First, in the words of the Letter of Aristeas, the law "walled in [periephraxen]" the Jews "with unbroken palisades and iron walls [teichesin] so that" they "might in no way mingle with any of the other nations" (139; compare 142; Lev 18:2-5; 20:22-26). In other words, the Mosaic covenant clearly separated Jew from Gentile.

Second, since he says the crucifixion effected not only the reconciliation of Jew and Gentile with one another but also the reconciliation of both with God (2:16), Paul probably has in mind the role of the law in condemning transgression as well.[44] Christ's crucifixion ushered in a new era in which Jew and Gentile could live in harmony together, and both together could live in peace with God.

Paul conceives of the era of reconciliation, moreover, as the time predicted by the prophets in which God would restore his people to fellowship with himself. Thus he echoes Jeremiah's promise of a new covenant (Jer 31:34) when he describes the redemption of Christians as "the forgiveness of transgressions" (1:7) and Ezekiel's promise that God will put his Spirit among his people (Ezek 11:19; 36:26; 37:1-14; compare 18:31) when he says that the church has been sealed for the day of redemption "by the Holy Spirit of promise" (Eph 1:13; compare 4:30).[45] In addition Paul probably has Ezekiel's vision of a new, eschatological temple in mind when he describes the church as a "building joined together" which "will grow into a holy temple in the Lord" (2:21). Just as the eschatological temple in Ezekiel is the dwelling place of God's glory (Ezek 43:1-5), so in Ephesians the church is the building in which God's Spirit dwells (2:22).

Paul also recalls the language of exile and restoration in Isaiah and Zechariah to describe the church in Ephesians. When he speaks of the reconciliation of Jews to Gentiles and both to God through the gospel in 2:17, for example, he echoes two passages in Isaiah which speak of the restoration of the people of Israel after their disobedience and punishment. The image of Christ preaching the good news of peace recalls Isaiah 52:7 LXX, in which God promises that after Israel's oppression he will be present in their midst as one who preaches to them the good news of peace and of Zion's salvation.[46] Similarly, the image of Christ preaching peace to the far off as well as to the near recalls Isaiah 57:18-19, in which, after describing Israel's idolatry, the prophet promises a time of divine healing and comfort. At that time, the prophet says, God will give "peace upon peace to those who are far and near" (v. 19).[47]

In a way that is consistent with this theme, Paul urges his readers to speak the truth with one another (Eph 4:25)—a moral standard that according to Zechariah should characterize the restored community of Israel (Zech 8:16 LXX). He also warns his readers not to grieve the Holy Spirit (Eph 4:30), something that Isaiah says that Israel did during its time of rebellion (Is 63:10 LXX).[48]

Despite all this, it is clear that the Gentiles to whom Paul writes have not merely become Jewish proselytes. Although the church that has been constituted by Christ's death and that Paul's readers have entered by their baptism stands in continuity with the people of God as they are defined in the Old Testament, it is nevertheless a new entity, and the redemption it offers is as necessary for the Jew as for the Gentile. Thus although Paul is himself a Jew, he includes himself and all Jews in his description of his Gentile readers' plight prior to their conversion (Eph 2:1-3).[49] He goes on to argue that the law by which the people of God in the Old Testament were defined and which separated them from the Gentiles has been abolished; as a result, the Gentiles have become not Jews but part, together with Jews, of "one new person" (2:14-15). Both have been reconciled to God and therefore form "one body" (2:16; compare 3:6), a temple whose defining characteristic is the presence of God's Spirit (2:18, 22). Unlike the temple in Ezekiel's vision, from which uncircumcised foreigners were excluded (Ezek 44:7, 9) and in which the Mosaic law would be scrupulously kept (Ezek 44:15-27), this building consists of both Jews and Gentiles and is constructed on the foundation of Christian apostles and prophets (Eph 2:20; compare 4:11).

The Gentiles to whom Paul writes, then, were once estranged from the blessings that characterized God's people because they were, by the definition provided in the Mosaic law, excluded from Israel. Now, however, they have been united with Jews in God's people not by becoming Jewish proselytes but by their participation in the newly defined people of God. The Mosaic law's emphasis on the holiness and purity of God's people continues within this newly defined group, and some of the law's commandments continue to play a role in how holiness and purity are now defined (6:2-3), but the Mosaic law in the form it took at Sinai and in its actual effects of alienating Jew from Gentile and both from God has been abolished. Jew and Gentile have now been reconciled "in one body to God" (2:16).

Paul has accomplished his purpose in this letter by reminding his readers of the privileges they have inherited as Christians. They should not be discouraged, and any discouragement should certainly not lead them to resort to the synagogue. Instead they should dwell on the wealth to which they are heirs in the gospel (1:18) and on their participation with Jewish believers in the fulfillment of the promises contained in Israel's covenants (2:11-22).[50]

The Shape of Paul's View of the Law in Ephesians

In Ephesians familiar themes from Paul's treatment of the law in his earlier letters reemerge, but with new emphases designed to address a situation unlike anything Paul had faced before. In Romans Paul had also reminded Gentiles of their Jewish heritage, but his purpose there was to resist the notion that the Gentiles' majority position in the church gave them some ethnically based privilege over Jews (11:17-24). In Ephesians the opposite situation—one in which Gentiles feel insecure about their spiritual identity—brings a similar reminder, but now intended to show Paul's readers the great privilege of their position as Christians.

The influence of this new situation on the way Paul handles the law is particularly prominent in his use of the language of sanctity and his discussion of the law's role in salvation history. In his other letters Paul often uses sanctification language to emphasize the distinctive behavior that should characterize believers and set them apart as God's elect people (for example, Rom 1:7; 6:19; 1 Cor 1:2; 6:11; 1 Thess 4:3-4, 7), and he can certainly use sanctification language that way in Ephesians as well (see Eph 5:3, 26). But in Ephesians Paul often adds another dimension to this language when he stresses the privilege of belonging to the sanctified people of God.[51] "The saints" are God's own rich and glorious inheritance (1:18). They are the group that believers join when they become members of God's household (2:19), the company to which Paul himself belongs (3:8) and the people who grasp the width and length, height and depth of Christ's love (3:18-19). In Ephesians, then, Paul is interested not only in the ethical responsibilities that attend the believer's status as a member of God's sanctified people but in the immense privilege of this status as well.

Paul's strong interest in the privilege of the Gentile believer also influences the way he pictures the law's function in salvation history. As in Galatians, Philippians and Romans, he argues that outside the realm of faith all people—Jews as well as Gentiles—live in a state of transgression against God's will and therefore of hostility toward God, that the law plays a role in this hostility and that it is Christ's death on the cross that has brought this enmity to an end.[52] The role of the Mosaic law in forming a barrier between Jews and Gentiles and the role of Christ's death in tearing down that barrier, moreover, are as important in Galatians and Romans as in Ephesians.[53]

Nevertheless, these convictions function in a different way in Ephesians than they do in Galatians, Philippians and Romans. Paul uses the conviction that all have transgressed God's will not to combat an inappropriate sense of Jewish privilege over the Gentile, as is in Galatians and Romans, but to remind Gentiles of the bleakness of their former lives so that they may appreciate the magnificence of God's gracious work of salvation on their behalf. Thus the characteristic antithesis of "faith" to "works of the law" in Galatians and Romans becomes in Ephesians an antithesis between the overpowering greatness of God's grace and the inadequacy of human effort in general.[54]

In addition, whereas Paul customarily speaks of justification as an accomplished work with salvation lying still in the future, in Ephesians the language of justification drops out of the grace-works antithesis entirely and is replaced by an emphasis on the salvation that God has accomplished for all people who believe, whether Jewish or Gentile.[55] The reason for this transformation is that Paul is not arguing in Ephesians for the acceptance of Gentiles as Gentiles within the people of God but reminding Gentiles of the "extraordinary greatness" (1:19) of what God has done for them in order to urge them to press forward in faithfulness to the Pauline gospel.

In Ephesians, then, Paul's basic convictions about the law reappear, but in new configurations to answer new problems. The paradoxes of sanctified Gentiles and of a law that, although abolished, can be used to mark the boundaries of the new people of God both reappear. The equation of Gentile believers with the expected restoration of God's people and temple is present also, as is Paul's emphatic exclusion of human effort from any role in salvation. Paul puts these convictions to use, however, within a pastoral situation that he had not faced in the earlier phases of his ministry. A sense of despair and forgetfulness of the blessings of salvation within a group of predominantly Gentile churches has led him to use these themes as reminders of the rich heritage to which Gentile believers are heir and of the difference between what these believers once were and what they now are in Christ.

The Setting of the Pastorals

Finally acquitted of the charges that had landed him in prison in Rome (see Acts 26:32), Paul traveled with his two trusted coworkers Titus and Timothy to the island of Crete, where they established churches in several cities (Tit 1:5). He then left Titus in charge of these new churches and traveled on with Timothy to Ephesus, where he discovered that the church leadership had succumbed to a pernicious deviation from the gospel. Paul left Timothy at Ephesus to undo the damage and pressed on to Macedonia (1 Tim 1:3), where he wrote 1 Timothy and Titus. Eventually he traveled to Nicopolis (Tit 3:12), Corinth (2 Tim 4:20), Troas (2 Tim 4:12) and Miletus (2 Tim 4:20), and somewhere in the course of these travels was arrested. Second Timothy finds him in prison in Rome again (2 Tim 1:17), certain this time of his condemnation at trial and eager to have Timothy at his side (2 Tim 4:6-8, 16-18, 21).[56]

The primary purpose for 1 Timothy, and an important secondary concern of Titus and 2 Timothy, was to help Paul's coworkers combat false teaching within the churches over which he had given them authority. The letters do not describe this teaching in detail, and scholars are divided over which of the known religious movements in the first and second centuries provides the best analogy to it.[57] Nevertheless, several aspects of the false teaching seem reasonably clear from the evidence in the letters themselves. This evidence reveals several general characteristics of the false teachers' strategy and of the teaching they sought to promote.

According to the letter to Titus, Christian households have played a strategic role in the spread of the heresy. The false teachers have promoted their ideas, Paul says, by moving from household to household and convincing those within to follow them (Tit 1:11).[58] They have apparently focused their persuasive efforts on the women within these households (2 Tim 3:6), and once persuaded, these women have become especially zealous advocates of the new teaching (1 Tim 5:13; compare 2:11-15). In Ephesus the younger widows, who are supported by the church and have the leisure to spend time visiting in houses other than their own, have provided a particularly effective means of spreading the teaching (1 Tim 5:9-16).[59] The teachers and their followers, moreover, encourage debate, and this has led to some dissension among believers (1 Tim 6:4-5; 2 Tim 2:23-26; Tit 3:9-11; compare 1 Tim 1:4-7).

The teaching itself is concerned with "myths" whose content includes "genealogies" (1 Tim 1:4; compare Tit 3:9) and which Paul characterizes as "endless," "irreligious," "silly" and "Jewish" (1 Tim 1:4; 4:7; Tit 1:14). The "Jewish" character of the myths coheres well with Paul's claim that the false teachers are themselves Jewish (Tit 1:10) and imagine themselves to be teachers of the law (1 Tim 1:7; compare Tit 3:9), although their approach to the law would have appeared eccentric to most Jews.[60] They claim that the resurrection has already occurred (2 Tim 2:17-18), forbid marriage (1 Tim 4:3) and believe in abstaining from certain foods. Their motive for abstinence from these foods is probably not the preservation of their distinctiveness as God's people but the expression of their belief that aspects of God's creation are indelibly tainted with evil (1 Tim 4:3-5; compare 1 Tim 5:23; Tit 1:15). In addition to all this, the false teaching lays heavy stress on the acquisition of esoteric knowledge (1 Tim 6:20).

Although elements of this picture neatly parallel key elements of the second-century Gnostic systems, it is unlikely that Gnosticism was fully developed at the time the Pastorals were written.[61] It has greater affinity, both theologically and chronologically, with the aberrations Paul encountered in Corinth.[62] In both Ephesus and Corinth some were denying the reality of a future resurrection, a conviction that probably originated in an overrealized eschatology. This eschatology seems to have led in Corinth, as it was leading in Ephesus and on Crete, to asceticism (1 Cor 7:1-7; 1 Tim 4:3), a fascination with knowledge (1 Cor 8:1-2; 1 Tim 6:20) and a violation of commonly observed social boundaries for slaves and women (1 Cor 7:17-23; 11:2-16; 14:34; 1 Tim 2:9-15; 6:1-2). There were, of course, differences between the two situations: the Corinthians denied the resurrection altogether (1 Cor 15:12), whereas Hymenaeus and Philetus claimed that it had already occurred (2 Tim 2:17-18), and the Corinthian error does not appear to have had a Jewish element. Nevertheless, the combination of a realized eschatol-

ogy with an ascetic outlook and an emphasis on esoteric knowledge make
the Corinthian situation a relatively close parallel to the problems in Ephesus
and on Crete.[63]

When Paul wrote the Pastorals, then, he faced a new challenge, close to
but not precisely consistent with the trouble in Corinth. Jewish Christian
teachers had arrived in Ephesus and on Crete proclaiming the common
Jewish belief in the resurrection of the dead but saying that this event had
already taken place. Probably because of their conviction that the final days
had already come, they advocated a world-denying posture, saying that
Christians should avoid certain foods and shun marriage. They supported
these ideas in part through an esoteric exegesis of Scripture which they were
happy to debate with others, despite the discord it brought to the church.

The effect of this teaching within the church at Ephesus was devastating.
Social custom was so radically overturned that the church stood in danger
of making its proclamation of the gospel to the wider world ineffective and
bringing unnecessary censure on church members (1 Tim 5:7, 14; Tit 2:5,
8). As a result, the leadership of the church at Ephesus, which had succumbed to the teaching, had to be replaced (1 Tim 1:19-20; 3:1-13), the
means of distributing beneficence within the church had to be restructured
to prevent the false teachers from using the system to their own profit and
to the spiritual detriment of the church (1 Tim 5:3-16; Tit 1:7, 11), and those
most responsible for bringing social censure on the church—women and
slaves—had to be admonished to resume social positions that would not
destroy the church's witness to unbelievers (1 Tim 2:1-15; 6:1-2).

The effect of the false teaching on the churches of Crete had not been as
serious, perhaps because Titus had been there continuously since Paul left.[64]
Nevertheless, Paul does not want the fiasco at Ephesus to recur among the
young churches on Crete, and so he instructs Titus to appoint a church
leadership that is not only above social reproach but also able to refute false
teaching when it arises (1:5-9).

The Shape of Paul's View of the Law in the Pastorals

Since the false teachers at Ephesus and on Crete were apparently interested
in the Mosaic law only as a source-book for their esoteric teachings, and since
Paul had no desire for Timothy or Titus to enter into debate with them about
those matters (1 Tim 4:7; 6:20; 2 Tim 2:16, 23; 3:5; Tit 3:9), Paul's explicit
interaction with the Mosaic law in the Pastorals is minimal.[65] Nevertheless,
one explicit reference to the law and several other allusions to it show again
how Paul could shape his basic convictions to meet new problems.

Paul begins 1 Timothy with a warning to Timothy about certain people within the church at Ephesus who have deviated from the "healthy teaching" (*hygiainousa didaskalia*) of Paul's gospel, in part through "fruitless talk" (*mataiologia*) about the Mosaic law (1:6-7, 10). Paul does not feel compelled to refute their understanding of the law in any detail, but instead makes several brief assertions about it. He implies that the false teachers are using the law improperly, claims that despite this misuse the law itself is good (*kalos ho nomos*, v. 8), and states that the law was laid down not for the righteous (*dikaiō*) but for the "lawless and rebellious" (*anomois de kai anypotaktois*, v. 9).

Paul continues with a description of what he means by "lawless and rebellious," and his language recalls the prohibitions of the Decalogue. He moves from those who violate the first table of the law ("impious and sinners, wicked and irreligious," v. 9) to references to especially notorious transgressors of each commandment in the second table ("murderers of fathers and mothers," "murderers," "the sexually immoral," "male homosexuals," "slave-traders" and "perjurers," vv. 9-10).[66] He then adds to this list the summary statement that the law is also intended for "anything else that opposes the healthy teaching according to the gospel of the glory of the blessed God, with which I have been entrusted" (vv. 10-11). This summary reveals Paul's primary purpose in the passage. He is not interested in developing a theology of the Mosaic law but in associating the false teachers in Ephesus with the long list of wicked people whose evil deeds any body of law, including the Mosaic, hopes to restrain.[67] The false teachers' obsession with the Mosaic law is in one way appropriate, he intends to say, since the law was meant to deal with people like them.

When Paul says that "the law was not laid down for the righteous" (v. 9), then, he probably does not use the term *righteous* (*dikaios*) with the pregnant theological sense that it often bears in Romans. It does not refer to those who are "righteous" because they live by faith (Rom 1:17) or to the status that no one can obtain by works of the law (Rom 2:13; 3:10; compare 3:19-20) or to the character of the covenant-keeping God (Rom 3:26). Instead, the word simply means "honest" or "innocent" (compare Lk 23:47; Rom 5:7) and refers to those who still cling to the "healthy teaching" of the gospel and have not become diseased by the "fruitless talk" of the false teachers.[68]

In this passage, then, Paul refers to the Mosaic law only because the false teachers are using it as a source for their teaching. He focuses not on the role of the law in salvation history but on a feature it has in common with all law—the restraint of evil. His purpose is to point out that the false teaching that has become so popular in the church at Ephesus is fundamentally as wicked as the most notorious violations of the Mosaic covenant.[69]

Despite the false teachers' Jewish origins and their misuse of the law, Paul shows no tendency in the Pastorals to reject either his Jewish heritage or the law itself. Instead he asserts that the law is good if used "lawfully" (*nomimōs*, 1 Tim 1:8) and honors the purity of his ancestors' service to God (2 Tim 1:3).[70] Moreover, he considers Timothy's training in the "Holy Scriptures" valuable not merely from the time of Timothy's conversion but indeed from his Jewish infancy (2 Tim 3:15; compare Acts 16:1).

Nowhere is Paul's positive valuation of the Mosaic law more explicit, however, than in Titus 2:11-14. In this passage he says that God's saving grace has taught Christians to live decent lives while they await the final appearing of Jesus Christ, "who gave himself for us in order that he might redeem *[lytrōsētai]* us from all lawlessness and purify *[katharisē]* for himself a special people *[laon periousion]*, zealous for good works" (2:14). Just as according to the law God redeemed *(elytrōsato)* Israel from Egypt (Deut 7:8 LXX) and constituted them as his special possession (*laon periousion*, Deut 7:6 LXX), so Paul says that Jesus Christ has redeemed his people from lawlessness and purified them to be his treasured possession.[71]

It is consistent with this notion that at other places in the Pastorals Paul urges "holiness" upon his readers (1 Tim 2:15), refers to salvation as a "holy calling" (2 Tim 1:9) and compares the Christian who rejects wickedness to a vessel "sanctified" for noble use (2 Tim 2:21). As in Paul's other letters, the emphasis on the special relationship between God's people and God, borrowed from the Mosaic law, remains firm.

Nevertheless, two clear differences emerge between Paul's use of the Mosaic law in the Pastorals and his use of it in his earlier letters. First, the language of universal human sinfulness, of God's grace and of denial to human works of any role in salvation is as clear in the Pastorals as anywhere else in Paul's letters, but it is not connected with his understanding of the Jewish law. Since the entry of uncircumcised Gentiles into the people of God apart from any requirement to observe the Mosaic law was not an issue for the false teachers in Ephesus and on Crete, Paul did not feel compelled to link his understanding of God's grace with his understanding of the Mosaic law as he had in Galatians, Philippians and Romans. The gospel of God's gracious deliverance of a thoroughly sinful humanity is simply a fundamental element of the "healthy teaching" that Paul wants Timothy to reassert in Ephesus and Titus to emphasize on Crete in order to undermine the work of the false teachers (1 Tim 1:15; 2 Tim 1:9-10; Tit 3:3-7).

Second, although the notion of the believer's sanctity or distinctiveness from the rest of society appears in the Pastorals, as it does in the Mosaic law and in Paul's other letters, the Pastorals place greater stress than the other letters on the believer's conformity to the most noble virtues of the wider society. Thus Paul's insistence in the other letters that believers live "no longer . . . as the Gentiles" (Eph 4:17; compare 1 Cor 5:1; 1 Thess 4:5) gives way in the Pastorals to admonitions to pray for the governing authorities and "to lead a peaceful and quiet life with all piety and reverence" (1 Tim 2:1-2; compare Tit 3:1-2). Paul can even say that a primary result of salvation is that people might "live sober, righteous and pious lives in the present time" (Tit 2:12; compare 3:3-8). The conduct of the sanctified community in the Pastorals, then, is spelled out not so much in terms that distinguish the church from the wider society—terms that in the other letters were often borrowed from the Mosaic law itself—as in terms that will make the church attractive to outsiders.

The reason for this is not that the supposedly feverish expectation of the end of the world in the first generation of Christians has been replaced by the conviction that the world will go on and Christians must therefore learn to live within it.[72] Rather, Paul's purpose in adopting this strategy is that Christians should attract outsiders to the faith and give them no reason for maligning the gospel (1 Tim 4:15-16; 5:7, 14; Tit 2:5, 8, 10).[73] If the leaders of the Pauline churches in Ephesus and on Crete were teaching that the social structures of the world had already passed away, and if they were expressing this belief by overturning various social customs, then the gospel in these places may have indeed looked offensive to those on the outside.[74] To preserve the witness of the church, therefore, the shape of sanctity in the Pastorals takes a form that is more friendly to the social customs of the time than is usual in Paul's letters. While not calling for compromise with the world, Paul nevertheless emphasizes the value of making Christian witness attractive by living as responsible citizens within the world.

In summary, the false teachers whom Paul combats in the Pastorals appear to have become fascinated with bizarre "myths" and to have promoted a way of life based on the premise that the eschatological resurrection had already taken place. Their world-denying asceticism and efforts to overthrow society's customary roles for women and slaves made the church an object of scorn to outsiders. Paul opposed this teaching by attacking its obsession with its own esoteric exegesis of the Mosaic law and reemphasizing the fundamental content of the gospel. He also urged Timothy and Titus to define the church's sanctity in ways that would not offend the surrounding culture but would affirm its most noble ethical ideals.

The Implications of Paul's Later Treatment of the Law

Paul's theology, including his view of the Mosaic law, took on new forms of expression and stretched to meet unprecedented challenges under the new conditions that began to emerge toward the end of his career. In the letters studied in this chapter, former convictions about the law have been reconfigured in three ways.

First, only a few references to the place of the law in salvation history appear in these letters. Paul briefly mentions that the law was a shadow of things to come (Col 2:17) and that it has been nullified (Eph 2:15), but nowhere does he discuss the role of the law in God's redemptive purposes in the way that is so characteristic of Galatians and Romans (Gal 3:15-23; Rom 4:1-15). Second, the obedience enjoined in each of the later letters is more domestic in quality than in the earlier correspondence. The conduct of the Christian husband, wife, child and slave within the household takes on greater importance, and the impression the church leaves on outsiders receives greater emphasis (Eph 5:22—6:9; Col 3:18—4:1; 1 Tim 2:1-15; 6:1-2; Tit 2:1—3:2; Philem 8-21). And third, while Paul claims as clearly as in any part of his earlier correspondence that salvation is a gift of God's grace, a product of his mercy and not of "works" (Eph 2:8-9; 1 Tim 1:14-15; 2 Tim 1:9; Tit 3:3-7), the works of which he speaks are not specifically "works of the Mosaic law," and salvation is not usually described in terms of justification.[75]

These differences are not so pronounced, however, that they must be considered the product of an entirely different set of convictions about the law. Three pieces of evidence indicate their basic compatibility with positions that Paul has taken before.

First, the slight discussion of the law's place in salvation history is probably related to the changes in the problems Paul faced. In the earlier letters the contrast appears most clearly when he is in dialogue and debate with Jews, and those under their influence, over the continuing validity of the Mosaic law.[76] In the later letters, however, this debate has dropped almost entirely from the scene. The problem at Colossae comes closest to this earlier context, since the false teachers there were apparently trying to convince Gentile believers to accept the Mosaic law. Even in this situation, however, there was a significant difference from the earlier period. Unlike the Judaizers in Galatia, and Jews generally, the Colossian false teachers coupled their insistence on conformity with the Mosaic law to their interest in the heavenly court. Paul's response emphasizes, correspondingly, not the change of the ages, as in Galatians, but the difference between his own understanding of the heavenly world and that of the false teachers.

Second, Paul's interest in domestic concerns and the articulation of the grace-works antithesis without reference to the Mosaic law have precedent in his earlier letters. For example, he urges the Roman Christians to accept subjection to the governing authorities and the dutiful payment of taxes (Rom 13:1-7) and admonishes the Philippian Christians to embrace whatever is true, honorable, just, lovely and appealing (Phil 4:8). Similarly, in 1 Corinthians Paul denies, without reference to the law, that human social position has anything to do with redemption, claiming that God chooses whom he will so that "no flesh may boast before" him (1 Cor 1:26-31), and in several passages in Romans God's grace is contrasted with human effort generally rather than with works of the Mosaic law in particular (Rom 4:4; 11:6; compare 9:11).

Third, several major aspects of Paul's view of the law in the early letters reappear unchanged in the later correspondence. In both groups of letters Christians constitute God's chosen and holy people, and in both the predominantly Gentile people of God fulfill the prophetic promises that God will one day restore his people to fellowship with himself.[77] Both groups of letters also show evidence of the characteristically Pauline paradox that the Mosaic law has passed away but certain commandments within the law are still valid.[78]

In these epistles, then, Paul has given old convictions about the law a new shape in order to address radically different problems from those he had faced before. The characteristic interplay between continuity and discontinuity, between old covenant and new, appears in these letters in a new form. The very persistence of this paradox, however, shows that the view of the law that lies beneath them stands in continuity with the view expressed in earlier times.

CHAPTER ELEVEN

PAUL & THE LAW IN CONTEXT

We have now heard Paul's letters speak on the subject of the law, and each has been allowed, as much as possible, to speak for itself. They have sometimes spoken with a faint echo, sometimes with an angry shout and occasionally with a clear, distinct voice. From all of this several common themes have emerged. In this chapter I will first show how these themes help to answer three critical questions that arise from the debate over Paul's understanding of the law and then attempt to assess the impact of my answers to these questions on the debate as a whole.

Was Judaism a Legalistic Religion?
Paul was aware that some Jews believed in a cooperation between human effort and God's grace as the means for obtaining acquittal on the final day. He himself had once believed this, the Judaizers' failure to understand the obsolescence of the Mosaic law implied that they believed it too, and he

apparently encountered Jews in Colossae who thought that entrance into heaven depended on doing more good than evil. Paul takes such beliefs into account in Philippians 3:2-11, where he compares his own pre-Christian conviction that his personal achievements would help him to attain justification on the final day with the claims of the Judaizers that Gentiles must be circumcised. He also mentions them in Romans 3:27—4:8, where he excludes boasting on the basis of works and claims that justification must be entirely a matter of God's grace. In Colossians 2:13-14 he counters this notion with the conviction that Christ has freely forgiven the believer's transgressions by nailing the record of them to the cross.

Nevertheless, the way Paul argues about the law with Jews and those under their influence shows that he did not regard all Jews as legalists or Judaism generally as a legalistic religion. His argument in Galatians 2:15-16 that justification comes by faith and not by works of the law is based on an appeal for the Judaizing Galatians to realize what those who are "Jews by nature" understand—that no one can be justified "by works of the law." Similarly, Paul's dialogue with his imaginary Jewish debating partner in Romans 1:18—3:26 calls on the Jew to recognize that faith in Christ is the solution to a plight that every Jew familiar with Scripture should acknowledge: Israel has been unfaithful to the covenant, and God's future judgment will be impartial.

This study has argued that far from attributing to most Jews a notion of salvation by works, these passages assume that most Jews understand that works of the law do not justify. Paul hopes that once reminded of the standard Jewish position on the plight of Israel, Judaizing Christians and unbelieving Jews will realize that the period of Israel's restoration has dawned, the Mosaic covenant is obsolete and they should embrace the gospel of God's redemptive work in Christ.

Paul's argument in Romans 9:30—10:4 that Israel's failure lies in its effort to pursue the law "by works" is not an exception to this stance. Rather, as we have seen, the standard Jewish conviction that works cannot justify is the foundation on which Paul's case rests. His argument is directed against the many Jews who have heard the gospel as he has outlined it in Romans 1:18—3:26, rejected it and gone about the business of obeying the law as if nothing important had happened. Such people, Paul says, are left to their own resources on the day of judgment.

The absence from Paul's letters of the accusation that Judaism generally is legalistic should not come as a surprise. The common ground on which he argues with his Jewish compatriots and their followers is the Jewish

Scriptures themselves, and in those Scriptures obedience is not the means of earning God's favor but the proper response to God's redemptive work. Thus at the center of the Mosaic covenant, and at the beginning of a summary of its obligations, stands the reminder of God's gracious act of deliverance from Egypt: "I am the LORD your God, who brought you out of the land of Egypt, out of the house of slavery; you shall have no other gods before me" (Ex 20:2-3; compare Lev 11:45; 22:32-33).[1] Here God's grace precedes God's demand. Moreover, on the other side of the demand, after the commandments have been disobeyed, God's grace is also boldly emphasized in the means of atonement provided for sin, particularly in the Day of Atonement ritual of Leviticus 16. This ritual, like the narrative of the exodus, is part of the law itself. Obedience in the Old Testament, then, is hemmed about with expressions of God's grace.

Although some Jews had an optimistic appraisal of the human ability to avoid transgression and believed that their works would aid them in gaining salvation on the final day, many others understood the biblical witness to God's prevenient grace. Paul points both groups to the Bible's story of Israel's disobedience, its affirmation of God's impartiality and its promise that one day God would graciously intervene to restore his people to fellowship with himself.

Does the Law Contradict the Gospel?
It should also comes as no surprise, therefore, that the pattern of Christianity in Paul's letters parallels the pattern of Judaism in the Mosaic law. Just as God's gracious acts of redemption precede the divine imperative in the Mosaic covenant, so in Paul's letters the justifying grace of God leads to the destruction of the barrier between Jew and Gentile, slave and free, and therefore to love for one's neighbor (Gal 2:15-21; 3:28; Eph 2:11-22; Col 3:11; Philem 9, 16). Just as the Old Testament maintains that in the time of Israel's redemption God will circumcise his people's hearts (Deut 30:6), put his law in their minds (Jer 31:33) and cleanse them from impurity (Ezek 36:22-32), so in Paul's letters God works in believers to effect their obedience (Rom 8:1-17; Gal 5:16-26; Eph 2:10; Phil 2:13). The need for obedience is clear in both the Old Testament and Paul, but the prevenience of God's grace is also clear in both.

Moreover, the function of this obedience in the Old Testament and in Paul is identical. The Israelites' obedience to the Mosaic law marked them off from the other nations as God's "treasured possession" (Ex 19:5; Lev 18:1-5; 19:24-26) and made them an appropriate dwelling place for God's presence (Lev 15:31). Likewise, in Paul's letters the conduct of believers separates them from "the Gentiles" (1 Cor 5:1; 2 Cor 6:17; Eph 4:1; 5:3; Col 3:12; 1 Thess 4:5) and purifies their bodies and their congregations as temples for God's indwelling Spirit (1 Cor 3:16-17; 6:19; 2 Cor 6:16; Eph 2:21).

This similarity between the pattern of Christianity in Paul's letters and the pattern revealed in the Mosaic law goes deeper than simply the concept of obedience as a social boundary and act of purification. The specific commands that the members of God's people are to obey are often also similar. Proper sexual conduct separates Israel from the surrounding nations (Lev 18:1-30) just as it separates the Thessalonians and the Corinthians from their unbelieving neighbors (1 Thess 4:3-8; 1 Cor 5:1-2). The love command is a prominent feature of Pauline ethics (Rom 13:9; Gal 5:14), and Paul takes over several of the Ten Commandments wholesale (Rom 13:9; Eph 6:2-3). On one occasion Paul recalls a rule from "the law of Moses" to help settle a dispute over the rights of preachers of the gospel (1 Cor 9:9).

Paul's gospel, therefore, follows the pattern of religion revealed in the Mosaic law in critical ways. Like the Mosaic law, the gospel places God's gracious act of redemption prior to the demand for obedience. It sanctifies the people of God to separate them from others as God's chosen people and to make them a fit dwelling place for God's presence. And it supplies specific ethical direction for Paul's churches.

Why, Then, the Gospel?

If this represents a correct understanding of the religion of the Old Testament, and if most Jews of Paul's time understood these principles and kept them in balance, then what advantage did the gospel have over the Mosaic law from Paul's perspective, and why would any Jew believe the gospel?[2]

This study has answered this question by arguing that most Jews of Paul's time believed that they lived under the covenant's curses—"the evil time," as 2 Maccabees calls it (1:5), or "the present evil age," as Paul refers to it in Galatians (1:4). Israel was subject to foreign domination and scattered among the nations because they transgressed the law. This was not merely the view of a few prophetic voices, moreover, but was common conceptual currency within the Judaism of the first century, as prayers of confession from the period and Josephus's philosophy of history demonstrate. The principle that justification could not come through works of the law therefore was not only an acknowledgment that grace is antecedent to obedience but also a sober reminder that the law had not been kept and Israel had suffered God's wrath as a result (Rom 3:19-20; 4:15; 2 Cor 3:6, 9; Gal 2:15-16; 3:10-14).

It is true that the law itself provided means of atonement for sin and that Judaism affirmed the efficacy of repentance. But alongside this belief in atonement and repentance, many Jews of Paul's time looked forward to God's intervention on their behalf to re-create their hearts, restore their obedience and reestablish their nation. This eschatological redemption is Paul's focus.[3] He claims that the shedding of Christ's blood reached backward into ages past to atone for the sins that God in his forbearance had not punished (Rom 3:25-26; compare 2:4), and he views that event as the inauguration of the new covenant (Rom 3:25; 1 Cor 11:25; 2 Cor 3:6). This is why some Jews and God-fearing Gentiles, despite the law's own provisions for atonement, nevertheless believed Paul's gospel.

Many more, however, rejected the gospel, for although Paul's gospel had structural similarities to the law, it was not the Mosaic covenant revisited.[4] Paul considered the Mosaic covenant obsolete, and he regarded believers as not only free from the law's sentence of condemnation but free from the law in other ways as well (Rom 7:6; 2 Cor 3:9). The most important, and controversial, consequence of this conviction was that Gentiles could enter the people of God without passing through the barricades of circumcision, sabbath keeping and dietary observance (Rom 14:5, 14; 1 Cor 7:19; Gal 2:11-21; 5:6; 6:15).

The result of this was a new group whose character mirrored the elements of continuity and discontinuity in Paul's approach to the Mosaic law. Paul held that Jewish and Gentile believers together formed "the assembly of God" (1 Cor 1:2; 2 Cor 1:1; 1 Thess 1:1; 2 Thess 1:1) and stood in continuity with Israel of old (1 Cor 10:1; Gal 6:16; Eph 2:11-13). Even believers who had been born Gentiles were no longer Gentiles but stood apart from the nations, just as Israel had in times past (1 Cor 5:1; Eph 4:17; 1 Thess 4:5). Nevertheless, Gentile believers were not Jews, for they had not become proselytes. The people of God formed a third entity that was neither Jewish nor Gentile (1 Cor 11:32; Eph 2:15-18).

Continuity and discontinuity, then, are a hallmark of Paul's view of the law. Does this mean that his view is inconsistent, that his claim that believers have been released from the law (Rom 7:6) stands in irreconcilable tension with his statement a few paragraphs later that the law's just requirement has been fulfilled in believers (Rom 8:4)?

Two pieces of evidence that have emerged from this study count against that view. First, Paul maintains both that the believer is free from the law and that the believer fulfills the law in letters as diverse as Galatians (2:19; 5:14),

Romans (7:6; 8:4; 13:8-10) and Ephesians (2:15; 6:2-3). The consistency with which the tension is expressed in precisely these terms in various letters written over a number of years counts against the thesis that Paul's view of the law was developed ad hoc, without careful thought.

Second, the reasons for the tension appear clearly in two passages. In 2 Corinthians 3:12-18 Paul contrasts the veil that lies over the minds of those who hear Moses read in the synagogue with the "freedom" of those who stand face to face with God by means of the indwelling Spirit. This freedom allows him to act with great "boldness" in his preaching and ministry (3:12; compare 3:4), and this freedom reaches even to his interpretation of the old covenant. Led by the Spirit, he is able to understand the reading of the old covenant in a different way from those who have not turned to the Lord, and under this new reading the old covenant and the new can speak with one voice. In Romans 10:5-8 Paul demonstrates this principle in operation when, while drawing a contrast between law and gospel, he nevertheless makes the gospel speak in the language of the law. The Mosaic law continues to speak as Scripture for Paul, but it is sovereignly interpreted by the gospel. Again, it is significant that this approach to the Mosaic law appears in two letters widely separated by time and circumstance.

Paul's position on the law, therefore, is not inconsistent. It is instead a complex development of his conviction that the Mosaic law is the authoritative word of God which the Spirit has nevertheless interpreted in unforeseen ways. The Mosaic law is absorbed by the gospel, but only under the transforming influence of the eschatological Spirit.

A Return to the Debate

If this approach to Paul's view of the law is correct, then it has a bearing on the debate over Paul and the law from Aquinas onward. Luther, as it turns out, was correct to emphasize God's antecedent grace against Aquinas's view that grace cooperated with works to gain salvation for the Christian.

Some Jews, such as the pre-Christian Paul, reserved a role for works in their understanding of salvation, and others, such as Judaizing Christians and Jews who rejected the gospel, implied by their failure to bow before God's righteousness that their own righteousness was superior. Paul would have none of this, and so behind his contrast between faith and works in Galatians 2:15-16 and Romans 3:21—4:8 and 9:30—10:4 lies the conviction that all the piety of Abraham and all the privileges of Israel were but wickedness and sin for purposes of justification: justification must come at God's initiative through Christ Jesus.

The centrality of this insight to Paul's gospel is confirmed in letters that do not debate the place of the law in salvation history. In 1 Corinthians 1:26-31, Ephesians 2:8-9 and Titus 3:3-7, in contexts far removed from the conflict over the entrance of Gentiles into the covenant people, Paul affirms his belief that human social standing and effort can have no role in salvation. Salvation must instead come entirely from a gracious God. Luther, then, was right to see the importance to Paul of this conviction, and right to detect its presence in Paul's discussions of the Jewish law.

Calvin in turn provided an appropriate emphasis on the fundamentally gracious character of the Mosaic law. He understood that when Paul implied a contrast between law and gospel, he did not imply a contrast between law and grace: God's covenant with Israel was based on God's gracious act of deliverance, just as obedience in the new era for Paul was based on "the grace of our Lord Jesus Christ" (2 Cor 8:8-9). This understanding of Paul's letters was developed after Calvin in Puritan theology and, if the understanding of Paul's view of the law proposed here is correct, is a genuinely Pauline insight.

The more recent treatments of Paul's view of the law by Montefiore, Moore, Räisänen, Dunn and especially Sanders have provided a corrective to a depressing chapter in the history of biblical interpretation, and this study has tried to avoid the errors they exposed. Although some Jews, including Paul himself, recognized a role for human effort in salvation and this conviction led some to boast of their righteousness, Paul's statements about the law do not supply evidence that most Jews held these convictions. Paul cannot be used, in other words, as evidence that first-century Judaism was a degenerate religion, devoid of an understanding of God's grace.

Yet this study joins two other interpretations of Paul's approach to the law in their criticism of Sanders's portrait of Paul. First, Dunn has correctly discovered more of a dialogue between Paul's theology and Judaism than Sanders was willing to allow. Dunn believes that the dialogue centers on whether Gentiles must follow the Jewish law in order to belong to the people of God, whereas this study claims that it focuses on whether and how the gospel represents the fulfillment of Israel's eschatological hopes. Nevertheless, both Dunn's work and my proposal attempt to fill a historical gap in Sanders's understanding of Paul.

Second, this study joins Westerholm's invitation to both Sanders and Dunn to read Luther again. The contrast between "works of the law" and "faith" is, as Luther said long ago, a contrast between the inadequacy of human resources and God's grace.

Perhaps the present work, however, can stand as a modest correction to

Westerholm's fine achievement. Westerholm believed that the Mosaic law itself advocated a cooperative arrangement between God's grace and human effort in attaining life. This derived not from a "legalistic spirit" inherent in the Old Testament, he claimed, but from an optimistic view both of the human ability to obey God and of God's willingness to forgive. Jews in Paul's day understood their Scriptures well, according to Westerholm, and adopted the same stance. Paul stands apart from both the Old Testament and Judaism, he argues, in his insistence that justification comes by grace alone and not by doing God's commands.[5]

In contrast to this picture, the present study proposes that Paul, along with many Jews of his time, adopted the understanding of the relationship between grace and obedience which emerges from a careful reading of the Old Testament. In that relationship, God's grace and human effort did not cooperate to produce blessing and life. As in Paul, the people of God were constituted by God's gracious acts of redeeming them from their plight and entering into a covenant with them. The difference between Paul and common Judaism, then, was not in the way each struck the balance between God's grace and human achievement but in the position of each within salvation history. The Old Testament looked forward to the restoration of Israel and the establishment of a new covenant, Judaism carried that hope forward into the first century, and Paul proclaimed that it had been fulfilled.

The tragic rejection of God's ultimate act of redemption among many Jews led Paul, when he preached to Israel, to take the stance of a prophet. Like Jeremiah of old, he reminded his hearers of the depth of their sin and of their need for God's eschatological intervention. "Because no one is justified before God by the law," he must have often said, "it is obvious that the just shall live by faith" (Gal 3:11).

Notes

Preface

[1]Heikki Räisänen, *Beyond New Testament Theology* (London: SCM Press/Philadelphia: Trinity Press International, 1990).

[2]See, for example, Udo Schnelle, *Wandlungen im paulinischen Denken*, Stuttgart Bibelstudien 137 (Stuttgart: Katholisches Bibelwerk, 1989); Heikki Räisänen, *Paul and the Law*, Wissenschaftliche Untersuchungen zum Neuen Testament 29 (Tübingen, Germany: J. C. B. Mohr/Paul Siebeck, 1983); and E. P. Sanders, *Paul, the Law and the Jewish People* (Philadelphia: Fortress, 1983).

[3]Francis Watson, *Paul, Judaism and the Gentiles: A Sociological Approach* (Cambridge: Cambridge University Press, 1986), pp. 180-81. By way of contrast, see the relatively positive comments of Victor Paul Furnish, "Paul the Theologian," in *The Conversation Continues: Studies in Paul and John in Honor of J. Louis Martyn*, ed. Robert T. Fortna and Beverly R. Gaventa (Nashville: Abingdon, 1990), pp. 19-34.

[4]The exceptions include Douglas Moo, *Romans 1—8*, Wycliffe Exegetical Commentary (Chicago: Moody Press, 1991); Thomas R. Schreiner, *The Law and Its Fulfillment: A Pauline Theology of Law* (Grand Rapids, Mich.: Baker Book House, 1993), pp. 114-21; and Timo Laato, *Paulus und das Judentum: Anthropologische Erwägungen* (Åbo, Finland: Åbo Akademis Förlag, 1991). Compare Mark Seifrid, *Justification by Faith: The Origin and Development of a Central Pauline Theme*, Supplements to *Novum Testamentum* 68 (Leiden, Netherlands: Brill, 1992), pp. 78-135.

[5]W. D. Davies, *Paul and Rabbinic Judaism*, 4th ed. (Philadelphia: Fortress, 1980), p. 222.

[6]Heikki Räisänen, *The Torah and Christ*, Publications of the Finnish Exegetical Society 45 (Helsinki: Finnish Exegetical Society, 1986), pp. 22, 288.

[7]Watson, *Paul, Judaism and the Gentiles*, pp. 177-79.

[8]Stephen Westerholm's *Israel's Law and the Church's Faith* (Grand Rapids, Mich.: Eerdmans, 1988) is an eloquent exception.

[9]See, for example, Sanders, *Paul, the Law and the Jewish People;* Räisänen, *Paul and the Law;* Westerholm, *Israel's Law;* and Schreiner, *Law and Its Fulfillment.*

[10]I have attempted to arrange the letters chronologically, although none of my conclusions is based on this arrangement. With slight variations, I have followed the chronological scheme of A. H. McNeile, *Introduction to the New Testament*, 2nd ed. (Oxford: Oxford University Press, 1953), pp. 124-87, especially pp. 180-85.

[11]On the meaning of the term generally and in Paul's letters specifically, see especially Michael Winger, *By What Law? The Meaning of Νόμος in the Letters of Paul*, Society of Biblical Literature Dissertation Series 128 (Atlanta: Scholars Press, 1992).

Chapter 1: Paul, the Law & Judaism

[1]Those who rejected Paul include the author of the "Preaching of Peter," translated in Edgar Hennecke, *New Testament Apocrypha*, ed. Wilhelm Schneemelcher, 2 vols. (Philadelphia: Westminster Press, 1963-1964), 2.111-27, esp. 122. Marcion is the most famous example of

those who believed that Paul was the only faithful apostle. See Tertullian *Against Marcion* 1.20 and Adolf von Harnack, *Marcion: The Gospel of the Alien God* (orig. ed. 1920; Durham, N.C.: Labyrinth, 1990), pp. 25-51.

[2]Timothy George, *Theology of the Reformers* (Nashville: Broadman, 1988), points out that at the Council of Trent, a series of meetings designed by the Roman Catholic Church to respond to the issues raised by the Protestant Reformation, Thomas's *Summa Theologica* was placed on the altar next to the Bible (p. 42).

[3]See T. H. L. Parker, *Calvin's New Testament Commentaries* (Grand Rapids, Mich.: Eerdmans, 1971), pp. 49-68, 79-92, and Donald K. McKim, "Calvin's View of Scripture," in *Readings in Calvin's Theology*, ed. Donald K. McKim (Grand Rapids, Mich.: Baker Book House, 1984), pp. 48-49.

[4]For this insight, and several others in what follows, I am indebted to the lucid discussion of nature and grace in Thomas in Roger Haight, *The Experience and Language of Grace* (New York: Paulist, 1979), pp. 54-78.

[5]Haight (ibid., pp. 54-66) attributes this aspect of Thomas's thought to Aristotle and says that it marks a shift from Augustine's view of grace. Augustine pictured grace as that which was needed to overcome the effects of the Fall, whereas Thomas pictured it as that which was needed to elevate people from the natural to the supernatural realm.

[6]Denis R. Janz, *Luther on Thomas Aquinas: The Angelic Doctor in the Thought of the Reformer*, Veröffentlichungen des Instituts für Europäische Geschichte 140 (Stuttgart: Franz Steiner Verlag, 1989), pp. 56-65, points out that contrary to Luther's accusations, Thomas did not believe that justification, or the initial point at which one believes, came by works. This point, as far as it goes, seems correct.

[7]Quoted in Heinrich Bornkamm, *Luther and the Old Testament*, ed. Victor I. Gruhn (Philadelphia: Fortress, 1969), p. 137.

[8]See ibid., p. 140.

[9]This corresponds in some respects to Luther's belief that the law of Moses included many wise civil laws from which the secular civil authorities could profit. Luther made it clear, however, that using the Old Testament in this way was in no way obligatory. See *LW* 35:167.

[10]Calvin's belief that the primary function of the law was the revelation of God's will and that it functioned as an ethical guide for the Christian became an important feature in Puritan theology. See Ernest F. Kevan, *The Grace of Law: A Study in Puritan Theology* (Ligonier, Penn.: Soli Deo Gloria, 1993).

[11]Luther was probably reacting to a distortion of Thomas's teaching on merit in such passages as *Summa Theologica* 1a2ae.114.3-6.

[12]I have used the translation by T. H. L. Parker in *The Epistles of Paul the Apostle to the Galatians, Ephesians, Philippians and Colossians* (Grand Rapids, Mich.: Eerdmans, 1965).

[13]Julius Wellhausen, *Prolegomena to the History of Ancient Israel* (Cleveland, Ohio: World, 1957), pp. 402-25, esp. p. 422. The first edition of this epoch-making work was published in 1878 under the title *Geschichte Israels I*. It was revised and retitled *Prolegomena zur Geschichte Israels* in 1883. The English edition is a translation of this revision. For Wellhausen's negative assessment of the role of the law in the evolution of Judaism, see Ronald E. Clements, *One Hundred Years of Old Testament Interpretation* (Philadelphia: Westminster Press, 1976) pp. 142-43.

[14]Martin Noth, *The Laws in the Pentateuch and Other Studies* (Philadelphia: Fortress, 1967), p. 103. Noth first published the article on which this summary is based in 1940. In the English-language edition of Noth's collected essays his position is hailed as a "fundamental insight" (p. vi).

[15]Ferdinand Weber, *Jüdische Theologie auf Grund des Talmud und verwandter Schriften*, ed. Franz Delitzsch and Georg Schnedermann, 2nd ed. (Leipzig: Dörffling Franke, 1897). The book was originally published in 1880 under the title *System der altsynagogalen palästinischen Theologie oder Die Lehren des Talmud* (System of Theology of the Ancient Palestinian Synagogue, or the

Teaching of the Talmud).

[16]Weber, *Jüdische Theologie*, p. 25.

[17]Ibid., pp. 48, 279.

[18]Ibid., pp. 292, 334-36.

[19]Weber included in his analysis the targums, the midrashic writings, the Mishna, the Tosephta and the Talmuds. See ibid., pp. xv-xxxiv.

[20]William Sanday and Arthur C. Headlam, *A Critical and Exegetical Commentary on the Epistle to the Romans*, 5th ed., International Critical Commentary (Edinburgh: T & T Clark, 1902), pp. 137-38. This commentary was reprinted seventeen times from 1895 to 1952.

[21]Ibid., p. 331.

[22]Emil Schürer, *A History of the Jewish People in the Time of Jesus Christ*, 2 div., 5 vols. (New York: Scribner's, 1885-1891).

[23]Ibid., 2:2:93.

[24]Ibid., 2:2:95-96.

[25]Ibid., 2:2:120.

[26]Ibid., 2:2:91 n. 3; 2:2:115 n. 82.

[27]For Bultmann's dependence on Schürer see Rudolf Bultmann, *Primitive Christianity in Its Contemporary Setting* (New York: World, 1956), pp. 59-71 and especially p. 214 n. 10. For a complete account of the connection between Bultmann's picture of Judaism, the picture of Judaism in the works of Bultmann's teacher Wilhelm Bousset, and the work of Ferdinand Weber together with a full evaluation of the far-reaching impact of Weber's work on the Protestant understanding of Jewish religion, see E. P. Sanders, *Paul and Palestinian Judaism: A Comparison of Patterns of Religion* (Philadelphia: Fortress, 1977), pp. 1-59. See also the needed corrective to Sanders's overzealous criticism of Bultmann in Mark Seifrid, *Justification by Faith: The Origin and Development of a Central Pauline Theme*, Supplements to *Novum Testamentum* 68 (Leiden, Netherlands: Brill, 1992), pp. 31-32 n. 97.

[28]See the article on Montefiore's life and thought in the *Encyclopedia Judaica*, ed. Cecil Roth and Geoffrey Wigoder, 16 vols. (Jerusalem: Keter, 1971), 12:267-68.

[29]Claude G. Montefiore, "Rabbinic Judaism and the Epistles of St. Paul," *Jewish Quarterly Review* 13 (1900-1901): 161-217.

[30]Ibid., pp. 170-71.

[31]Ibid., p. 192.

[32]Ibid., pp. 171, 194, 196.

[33]Ibid., pp. 174-75; Claude G. Montefiore, *Judaism and St. Paul: Two Essays* (London: M. Goschen, 1914), pp. 28-33.

[34]Montefiore, "Rabbinic Judaism," p. 176; *Judaism and St. Paul*, pp. 33-37.

[35]Montefiore, "Rabbinic Judaism," p. 178; *Judaism and St. Paul*, pp. 37-44.

[36]Montefiore, "Rabbinic Judaism," pp. 193-96.

[37]Ibid., pp. 196-208. Montefiore's description of rabbinic Judaism, like his thought in general, has produced its share of controversy. The controversy, however, does not question his defense of rabbinic religion against Protestant caricatures but centers primarily on those elements of rabbinic religion that Montefiore rejected because they did not conform to his goals for liberal Judaism. See Joshua Stein, *Claude Goldsmid Montefiore on the Ancient Rabbis*, Brown Judaic Studies 4 (Missoula, Mont.: Scholars Press, 1977), and Maurice Gerald Bowler, *Claude Montefiore and Christianity*, Brown Judaic Studies 157 (Atlanta: Scholars Press, 1988), pp. 8-9.

[38]George Foot Moore, "Christian Writers on Judaism," *Harvard Theological Review* 14 (1921): 197-254. Moore appears to be writing exactly forty years after the 1880 edition of Weber's work, which would presumably mean that he was aware of Christian works on Judaism up to 1920.

[39]Ibid., pp. 231-33.

[40]Ibid., pp. 232-33; compare p. 213.

[41]Ibid., pp. 228-31.

[42]Ibid., pp. 228-29.

[43]Ibid., pp. 234-36.

[44]Ibid., pp. 237-40, 247-48.

[45]Ibid., pp. 238-40, 243-46.

[46]Among the exceptions are W. D. Davies, *Paul and Rabbinic Judaism: Some Rabbinic Elements in Pauline Theology,* 4th ed. (Philadelphia: Fortress, 1980), p. 215, and Richard N. Longenecker, *Paul, Apostle of Liberty: The Origin and Nature of Paul's Christianity* (orig. ed. 1964; Grand Rapids, Mich.: Baker Book House, 1976), pp. 65-85.

[47]See, for example, the use of Moore's *Judaism in the First Centuries of the Christian Era: The Age of the Tannaim,* 3 vols. (Cambridge, Mass.: Harvard University Press, 1927-1930) in James S. Stewart, *A Man in Christ: The Vital Elements of St. Paul's Religion* (London: Hodder & Stoughton, 1935), pp. 33-48, 83-98, and the comments on a similar use of Moore in other standard works of New Testament scholarship in Sanders, *Paul and Palestinian Judaism,* pp. 55-57. Moore often took pains within his work to oppose such interpretations of Judaism. See, for example, *Judaism in the First Centuries,* 1:116-17, 2:93-95.

[48]Donald A. Hagner is probably also correct when he claims that Sanders succeeded in gaining a hearing because his work "was the first lengthy and strongly articulated statement of the case in the post-holocaust era." See Hagner's "Paul and Judaism: The Jewish Matrix of Early Christianity—Issues in the Current Debate," *Bulletin for Biblical Research* 3 (1993): 112.

[49]Sanders, *Paul and Palestinian Judaism,* p. 17.

[50]Ibid., p. 13.

[51]Ibid., p. 19.

[52]From a methodological standpoint, however, this is not inappropriate, since in terms of length the mass of literature covered in the section on Judaism dwarfs the brief epistles of Paul.

[53]Sanders, *Paul and Palestinian Judaism,* pp. 1-59. Sanders extends Moore's review of non-Jewish New Testament scholars who have written on Judaism to include H. L. Strack and Paul Billerbeck, *Kommentar zum Neuen Testament aus Talmud und Midrasch,* 6 vols. (Munich: Beck, 1922-1961). The last two volumes were prepared by Joachim Jeremias.

[54]Sanders, *Paul and Palestinian Judaism,* p. 423.

[55]Ibid., p. 75; compare pp. 236, 422-23.

[56]Ibid., p. 422.

[57]Ibid., p. 427. Sanders expanded his argument to include literature from Judaism outside Palestine in "The Covenant as a Soteriological Category and the Nature of Salvation in Palestinian and Hellenistic Judaism," in *Jews, Greeks and Christians: Studies in Honor of W. D. Davies,* ed. R. G. Hamerton-Kelly and Robin Scroggs, Studies in Judaism in Late Antiquity 21 (Leiden, Netherlands: Brill, 1976), pp. 11-44. He expands the literary evidence still further in *Judaism: Practice and Belief 63 BCE—66 CE* (London: SCM Press/Philadelphia: Trinity Press International, 1992), pp. 262-78.

[58]In Montefiore, *Judaism and St. Paul,* pp. 1-129. See also Montefiore, "Rabbinic Judaism," pp. 161-217.

[59]Montefiore, *Judaism and St. Paul,* p. 126.

[60]Ibid., pp. 95-112.

[61]Ibid., p. 97.

[62]Ibid., pp. 113-22.

[63]Hans Joachim Schoeps, *Paul: The Theology of the Apostle in the Light of Jewish Religious History* (Philadelphia: Westminster Press, 1961), p. 26.

[64]Ibid., pp. 31-32.

[65]Samuel Sandmel, *The Genius of Paul: A Study in History* (Philadelphia: Fortress, 1979), pp. 48-53. See also Samuel Sandmel, *Judaism and Christian Beginnings* (New York: Oxford University Press, 1978), p. 336.

[66]This is my translation of the Greek text found, together with a photograph of the inscription,

in Adolf Deissmann, *Light from the Ancient East: The New Testament Illustrated by Recently Discovered Texts of the Graeco-Roman World* (Grand Rapids, Mich.: Baker Book House, 1978), p. 440.

[67]See Davies, *Paul and Rabbinic Judaism*, pp. 5-8; J. N. Sevenster, *Do You Know Greek? How Much Greek Could the First Jewish Christians Have Known?* Supplements to *Novum Testamentum* 19 (Leiden, Netherlands: Brill, 1968); Martin Hengel, *Judaism and Hellenism: Studies in Their Encounter in Palestine During the Early Hellenistic Period*, 2 vols. (Philadelphia: Fortress, 1974); and Martin Hengel, *The Hellenization of Judaea in the First Century After Christ* (London: SCM Press/Philadelphia: Trinity Press International, 1989). On the influence of Palestinian Judaism on Diaspora practice, see E. P. Sanders, *Jewish Law from Jesus to the Mishnah: Five Studies* (London: SCM Press/Philadelphia: Trinity Press International, 1990), pp. 255-308.

[68]Moore, *Judaism in the First Centuries*, 2:93-95, 94 n. 1; compare 1:282.

[69]Sanders, *Paul and Palestinian Judaism*, pp. 429-556; Sanders, *Paul, the Law and the Jewish People*; and E. P. Sanders, *Paul: Past Master* (New York: Oxford University Press, 1991). See also E. P. Sanders, "Patterns of Religion in Paul and Rabbinic Judaism: A Holistic Method of Comparison," *Harvard Theological Review* 66 (1973): 455-78, and "On the Question of Fulfilling the Law in Paul and Rabbinic Judaism," in *Donum Gentilicium: New Testament Studies in Honour of David Daube*, ed. Ernst Bammel, C. K. Barrett and W. D. Davies (Oxford: Oxford University Press, 1977), pp. 103-26.

[70]Sanders, *Paul and Palestinian Judaism*, pp. 442-46.

[71]Ibid., pp. 475-97.

[72]Sanders is more willing to speculate about the origin of Paul's view of the law in *Paul, the Law and the Jewish People* than he was in *Paul and Palestinian Judaism*. If Paul was dissatisfied with the law prior to his conversion, he says (pp. 152-53), it was probably because of the law's exclusion of Gentiles from the elect people of God.

[73]Sanders, *Paul and Palestinian Judaism*, pp. 482-84, 492-93; *Paul, the Law and the Jewish People*, pp. 17-27. Compare his *Paul: Past Master*, pp. 56-63.

[74]Sanders, *Paul and Palestinian Judaism*, pp. 484-85; *Paul, the Law and the Jewish People*, pp. 137-39.

[75]Sanders, *Paul and Palestinian Judaism*, pp. 505, 551; *Paul, the Law and the Jewish People*, pp. 43-44, 139-41. Sanders makes a similar argument about Romans 9:30—10:13 in *Paul, the Law and the Jewish Law*, pp. 36-43. See also *Paul: Past Master*, p. 122.

[76]Sanders, *Paul and Palestinian Judaism*, pp. 485-90; compare *Paul, the Law and the Jewish People*, pp. 32-36. Sanders frequently says that the interpreter must distinguish between the arguments Paul advances for his beliefs and the "real" reasons Paul held those beliefs. Paul's arguments are often secondary rationalizations of his core beliefs. See *Paul, the Law and the Jewish People*, pp. 4, 26, and *Paul: Past Master*, pp. 36-38, 52, 56-63.

[77]Sanders, *Paul and Palestinian Judaism*, pp. 509-10.

[78]Ibid., p. 516; *Paul, the Law and the Jewish People*, pp. 123-35.

[79]See the chart in Sanders, *Paul, the Law and the Jewish People*, p. 75, and *Paul: Past Master*, pp. 93-98.

[80]Sanders, *Paul and Palestinian Judaism*, pp. 511-18, 543-56.

[81]Sanders, *Paul and Palestinian Judaism*, pp. 513, 515-18; *Paul, the Law and the Jewish People*, pp. 94-96; *Paul: Past Master*, pp. 89-90, 106-15. See also Sanders, *Judaism: Practice and Belief*, pp. 241-78, where Paul's letters are cited frequently as evidence for the "common theology" of first-century Judaism.

[82]Sanders, *Paul and Palestinian Judaism*, 499-500, 513-15, 543-49.

[83]Ibid., p. 552; compare p. 491. In *Paul, the Law and the Jewish People*, pp. 45-48, Sanders clarifies this position by arguing that while Paul did not attack the nonexistent enemy of Jewish legalism, he did attack the well-known Jewish idea that the possession of the law conferred on Israel a favored status in God's eyes (in Gal 2:15-21; Rom 3—4; Rom 9—11).

[84]Montefiore believed that Paul was responding to a form of Judaism. Sanders is less comfortable than Montefiore was about speaking of Judaisms at all and is, in any case, unconvinced that

any Jewish background can explain Paul's religion. Contrast Montefiore, *Judaism and St. Paul*, p. 4, with Sanders, *Judaism: Practice and Belief*, pp. 46-49, and *Paul and Palestinian Judaism*, pp. 423, 496.

[85]Sanders, *Paul and Palestinian Judaism*, pp. 496-97; *Paul, the Law and the Jewish People*, pp. 102-3.

[86]Heikki Räisänen's principal writings on Paul's view of the law are *Paul and the Law*, Wissen schaftliche Untersuchungen zum Neuen Testament 29 (Tübingen, Germany: J. C. B. Mohr/Paul Siebeck, 1983); *The Torah and Christ: Essays in German and English on the Problem of the Law in Early Christianity*, Publications of the Finnish Exegetical Society 45 (Helsinki: Finnish Exegetical Society, 1986); and *Jesus, Paul and Torah: Collected Essays, Journal for the Study of the New Testament* Supplement Series 43 (Sheffield, U.K.: JSOT Press, 1992).

[87]Räisänen, *Paul and the Law*, 1st ed., p. v; 2nd ed, pp. xxvi-xxix; *The Torah and Christ*, p. 29.

[88]Räisänen, *Paul and the Law*, pp. 23, 108, 118-19, 154.

[89]Ibid., pp. 177-91; *The Torah and Christ*, pp. 37-38.

[90]Sanders, *Paul and Palestinian Judaism*, pp. 509-10.

[91]Räisänen, *The Torah and Christ*, p. 18.

[92]Räisänen, *Paul and the Law*, 2nd ed., pp. xvi, 266-67.

[93]Räisänen, *Jesus, Paul and Torah*, pp. 15-47. Compare Heikki Räisänen, "Paul's Conversion and the Development of His View of the Law," *New Testament Studies* 33 (1987): 404-19.

[94]J. Christiaan Beker, *Paul the Apostle: The Triumph of God in Life and Thought* (Philadelphia: Fortress, 1980).

[95]Ibid., pp. 3-41.

[96]Ibid., pp. 52-56.

[97]Ibid., pp. 56-58, 104-8.

[98]Ibid., p. 35.

[99]Ibid., p. 235.

[100]Ibid., p. 243.

[101]Ibid., pp. 182-89, 243.

[102]Ibid., p. 239.

[103]Ibid., pp. 242-43.

[104]Beker's student Mark A. Seifrid has closed this gap in Beker's analysis in *Justification by Faith*. Seifrid argues that Paul's preconversion convictions were closely akin to those articulated in the *Psalms of Solomon*, where only the pious within Israel receive mercy. For the authors of this literature, therefore, "obedience was a pre-requisite of salvation" (p. 133). After his conversion Paul argues against the cooperation between divine mercy and human obedience with his claim that justification comes by faith apart from works of the law.

[105]Much of Dunn's work on Paul and the law was once scattered throughout scholarly journals, *Festschriften* and collections of essays. Happily, many of these contributions have now been assembled in James D. G. Dunn, *Jesus, Paul and the Law: Studies in Mark and Galatians* (Louisville, Ky.: Westminster/John Knox, 1990). See also his *Romans 1-8*, Word Biblical Commentary 38A (Dallas: Word, 1988); *Romans 9-16*, Word Biblical Commentary 38B (Dallas: Word, 1988); and *The Partings of the Ways Between Christianity and Judaism and Their Significance for the Character of Christianity* (London: SCM Press/Philadelphia: Trinity Press International, 1991), pp. 117-39.

[106]Dunn, *Jesus, Paul and the Law*, pp. 158-59, 185-86, 242; *Romans 1-8*, pp. liv-lxvi; *Partings of the Ways*, pp. 13-15.

[107]Dunn, *Jesus, Paul and the Law*, pp. 186-88, 246; *Romans 1-8*, p. lxvi.

[108]Ibid., p. 216.

[109]Ibid., pp. 188-200, 216-25, 242-45; Dunn, *Romans 1-8*, pp. lxix-lxxii; *Partings of the Ways*, pp. 136-39.

[110]Dunn, *Jesus, Paul and the Law*, pp. 188-200, 242-45.

[111]Ibid., p. 231; *Romans 1-8*, p. lxxii; *Partings of the Ways*, pp. 137-38.

[112]Dunn, *Jesus, Paul and the Law,* pp. 191-95, 219-25. Dunn's first expressions of this principle appeared to limit Paul's criticism of "works of the law" to three distinctively Jewish aspects of the law—circumcision, dietary observance and sabbath keeping. In subsequent works, however, he has clarified his position by claiming that Paul resisted the effort to make the law as a whole a point of nationalistic pride and a barrier to the Gentiles. See *Jesus, Paul and the Law,* pp. 4, 175, 210, 213, 218, 223, 238; *Partings of the Ways,* p. 137; and James D. G. Dunn, "Yet Once More—'The Works of the Law': A Response," *Journal for the Study of the New Testament* 46 (1992): 100-104.

[113]Dunn, *Jesus, Paul and the Law,* p. 227.

[114]Ibid., pp. 228-29.

[115]Sanders has, however, lodged an indirect protest against Dunn's view that due to the turbulent years leading up to the Jewish revolt against Rome, Jewish nationalism and the use of the law as a nationalistic symbol had become increasingly strident. These years, he argues, were not especially turbulent; life proceeded along normal lines until the rapid succession of events leading to the revolt took everyone by surprise. See *Judaism: Practice and Belief,* pp. 35-43.

[116]Stephen Westerholm, *Israel's Law and the Chruch's Faith: Paul and His Recent Interpreters* (Grand Rapids, Mich.: Eerdmans, 1988), pp. 106-9.

[117]Ibid., pp. 111-19.

[118]Ibid., pp. 118-19.

[119]Ibid., p. 119.

[120]Ibid., p. 122.

[121]Ibid., pp. 143-44.

[122]Ibid., pp. 144-50, 169.

[123]Westerholm was neither the first nor the last scholar to make this point. See R. H. Gundry, "Grace, Works and Staying Saved in Paul," *Biblica* 66 (1985): 1-38; Thomas R. Schreiner, " 'Works of Law' in Paul," *Novum Testamentum* 33 (1991): 241-42; Thomas R. Schreiner, *The Law and Its Fulfillment: A Pauline Theology of Law* (Grand Rapids, Mich.: Baker Book House, 1993), pp. 114-21; Moisés Silva, "The Law and Christianity: Dunn's New Synthesis," *Westminster Theological Journal* 53 (1991): 347-50; Timo Laato, *Paulus und das Judentum: Anthropologische Erwägungen* (Åbo, Finland: Åbo Akademis Förlag, 1991); Douglas Moo, *Romans 1-8,* Wycliffe Exegetical Commentary (Chicago: Moody Press, 1991), pp. 216-18; Seifrid, *Justification by Faith,* pp. 78-181; Joseph A. Fitzmyer, *According to Paul: Studies in the Theology of the Apostle* (New York: Paulist, 1993), pp. 19-24; Hagner, "Paul and Judaism," pp. 116-123; and Donald A. Hagner, "Paul's Quarrel with Judaism," in *Anti-Semitism and Early Christianity: Issues of Polemic and Faith,* ed. Craig A. Evans and Donald A. Hagner (Minneapolis: Fortress, 1993), pp. 136-41.

[124]Westerholm, *Israel's Law and the Church's Faith,* pp. 151-52. Seifrid (*Justification by Faith,* pp. 71-73) is unwilling to make this concession to Sanders and criticizes Westerholm for doing so. Seifrid believes that Paul's own conversion and his emphasis on grace are a response to the kind of piety visible in *Psalms of Solomon.*

[125]Westerholm, *Israel's Law,* pp. 152-53, 172-73, 219-22.

[126]Sanders's entry "Truth, ultimate" in the index of subjects to *Paul and Palestinian Judaism* betrays the intellectual climate in which he wrote. The page numbers Sanders lists for this entry are 30, 32 and 430. Each of these pages is blank. Jacob Neusner believes that Sanders's portrait of Judaism is driven by a liberal Protestant desire to refashion Christianity on a basis that is not anti-Semitic. See his blistering critique of Sanders's *Judaism: Practice and Belief* in *Judaic Law from Jesus to the Mishnah: A Systematic Reply to Professor E. P. Sanders,* South Florida Studies in the History of Judaism 84 (Atlanta: Scholars Press, 1993), pp. 275-95.

[127]See James D. G. Dunn, "The Justice of God: A Renewed Perspective on Justification by Faith," *Journal of Theological Studies* 43 (1992): 1-22.

[128]Compare Silva, "Law and Christianity," pp. 348-49; Schreiner, " 'Works of Law,' " pp. 243-44;

Schreiner, *Law and Its Fulfillment*, pp. 120-21.

Chapter 2: Oppression, Election & Salvation

[1]Annie Jaubert (*La notion d'alliance dans le Judaïsme aux abords de l'ère Chrétienne*, Patristica Sorbonensia 6 [Paris: Éditions du Seuil, 1963], p. 44) refers to the pervasive Old Testament theme of the making and breaking of the covenant followed by the covenant's curse, Israel's repentance and God's mercy as "the rhythm of the covenant."

[2]A growing body of literature affirms this. In addition to the evidence presented below, see Odil H. Steck, *Israel und das gewaltsame Geschick der Propheten: Untersuchungen zur Überlieferung des deuteronomistischen Geschichtsbildes im Alten Testament, Spätjudentum und Urchristentum*, Wissenschaftliche Monographien zum Alten und Neuen Testament 23 (Neukirchen, Germany: Neukirchener Verlag, 1967); David P. Moessner, *Lord of the Banquet: The Literary and Theological Significance of the Lukan Travel Narrative* (Minneapolis: Fortress, 1989), pp. 82-257; Frank Thielman, *From Plight to Solution: A Jewish Framework for Understanding Paul's View of the Law in Romans and Galatians*, Supplements to *Novum Testamentum* 61 (Leiden, Netherlands: Brill, 1989), pp. 28-45; Frank Thielman, "The Story of Israel and the Theology of Romans 5-8," in *Society of Biblical Literature 1993 Seminar Papers*, ed. Eugene H. Lovering (Atlanta: Scholars Press, 1993), pp. 230-33; N. T. Wright, *The New Testament and the People of God* (Minneapolis: Fortress, 1992), pp. 268-72; James M. Scott, "Paul's Use of Deuteronomic Tradition," *Journal of Biblical Literature* 112 (1993): 645-65; and James M. Scott, "Restoration of Israel," in *Dictionary of Paul and His Letters*, ed. Gerald F. Hawthorne, Ralph P. Martin and Daniel G. Reid (Downers Grove, Ill.: InterVarsity Press, 1993), pp. 796-805.

[3]For the influence of Nehemiah 9:5-37 on the prayers of the postexilic synagogue, see Leon J. Liebreich, "The Impact of Nehemiah 9:5-37 on the Liturgy of the Synagogue," *Hebrew Union College Annual* 32 (1961): 227-37. Carey A. Moore ("Toward the Dating of the Book of Baruch," *Catholic Biblical Quarterly* 36 [1974]: 315) points out that the use of the first-person plural in Daniel 9:4-19 demonstrates that it was composed not simply with Daniel himself in mind but as a confession for God's people. The prayer in Baruch is placed in a liturgical setting and was intended as a corporate confession. See Baruch 1:10-15 and Moore, "Toward the Dating," p. 316.

[4]The concluding petition for continued mercy is missing in Ezra's prayer, but it is clearly implied both by the confessional nature of the prayer itself and by the statement of Shecaniah after the prayer that "there is hope for Israel in spite of this" (10:2).

[5]Baruch 1:15-2:19 probably has some literary relationship with Daniel 9:4-19, although the precise nature of the relationship is not clear. Compare Baruch 1:15-18 with Daniel 9:5-11; Baruch 2:1-2 with Daniel 9:11-12; and Baruch 2:8-10 with Daniel 9:13-14.

[6]Daniel and Baruch occasionally reflect even the wording of Deuteronomy. Compare Daniel 9:11-14 and Baruch 1:20 and 2:28-29, for example, with Deuteronomy 28:15-68. The prayers in 1 Kings 8:12-53 and Jeremiah 32:17-25 also reflect this perspective. Psalms 78 and 106, although not prayers in a technical sense, were probably used liturgically. They too reflect the theology of Deuteronomy.

[7]Although some scholars have attempted to date Judith in the Persian period, the book, at least in its final recension, probably comes from a period after Antiochus IV Epiphanes. See George W. E. Nickelsburg, *Jewish Literature Between the Bible and the Mishnah* (London: SCM Press, 1981), pp. 108-9.

[8]Second Maccabees was probably written between the late high-priesthood of John Hyrcanus and the Roman invasion of Judea, or between 107 and 63 B.C. This dating is derived from 2 Maccabees 12:29-31 on one hand (which may be a subtle argument against John Hyrcanus's treatment of the city of Scythopolis) and 2 Maccabees 15:37 on the other (which says that Jerusalem has been in Hebrew hands until the writer's time). See Jonathan A. Goldstein, *II Maccabees: A New Translation with Introduction and Commentary*, Anchor Bible 41A (New York:

Doubleday, 1983), pp. 71-72.

[9]On the importance of this theme in 2 Maccabees see ibid., pp. 12-13, and Goldstein's notes on the passages cited above.

[10]Josephus's *War* is usually dated between A.D. 75 and 79, and the *Antiquities* was completed sometime during the year A.D. 93-94. See the discussion of H. W. Attridge in Michael E. Stone, ed., *Jewish Writings of the Second Temple Period*, Compendia Rerum Iudaicarum ad Novum Testamentum 2 (Phildelphia: Fortress/Assen, Netherlands: Van Gorcum, 1984), 2:192, 210.

[11]Josephus has changed the shape and intensity of this theme in his writings in order to accommodate his Gentile audience, but the biblical origins of the theme are still clear. See Harold W. Attridge, *The Interpretation of Biblical History in the "Antiquitates Judaicae" of Flavius Josephus*, Harvard Dissertations in Religion 7 (Missoula, Mont.: Scholars Press, 1976), pp. 76-92, 145-51.

[12]See 4.134, 201, 258, 317, 323, 343, 348, 382-83, 386-87; 5.8, 102, 343, 411-12.

[13]In addition, Josephus may have been interested in refuting anti-Semitic notions that Jews were social misfits by showing that they held certain convictions in common with other peoples of the Greco-Roman world. One such conviction was the belief in divine retribution. See Steve Mason, *Josephus and the New Testament* (Peabody, Mass.: Hendrickson, 1992), p. 66.

[14]Compare the speech of Achior to Holofernes in Judith 5:5-21.

[15]See Baruch A. Levine, *Leviticus*, JPS Torah Commentary (Philadelphia: Jewish Publication Society, 1989), p. 248.

[16]See Paul Hanson, *The People Called: The Growth of Community in the Bible* (New York: Harper & Row, 1986), pp. 216-24.

[17]See Leviticus 20:7-8; 21:8, 15, 23; 22:9, 16, 32. The term "Holiness Code" was first used of this section by scholars in the late nineteenth century. See Levine, *Leviticus*, pp. 110-11, 207 n. 1, and Martin Noth, *Leviticus: A Commentary* (Philadelphia: Westminster Press, 1965), pp. 127-28.

[18]On the kinship between Ezekiel and Leviticus in these passages, see Walther Zimmerli, *Ezekiel 1: A Commentary on the Book of the Prophet Ezekiel, Chapters 1-24*, Hermeneia (Philadelphia: Fortress, 1979), pp. 379-85, 457-59.

[19]See the definitive discussion of these events in Otto Mørkholm, *Antiochus IV of Syria*, Classica et Mediaevalia, Dissertationes 8 (Copenhagen: Gyldendalske Boghandel, 1966).

[20]On this chapter in Jewish history, see Peter Green, *Alexander to Actium: The Historical Evolution of the Hellenistic Age* (Berkeley: University of California Press, 1990), pp. 506-8.

[21]The ancient sources for Antiochus's Egyptian campaigns, his sack of the temple and his slaughter of Jerusalem's inhabitants are confused. Here I have followed the reconstruction of events in Mørkholm, *Antiochus IV*, pp. 142-48.

[22]The evidence for Antiochus's self-deification comes from coins. See Green, *Alexander to Actium*, pp. 437-38. The reasons for Antiochus's policy toward Judea are a subject of intense scholarly debate. See the summary of the issues in Goldstein, *II Maccabees*, pp. 98-112, and Green, *Alexander to Actium*, pp. 505-6. Jonathan A. Goldstein (*I Maccabees: A New Translation with Introduction and Commentary*, Anchor bible 41A [New York: Doubleday, 1976], pp. 131-40) offers the fascinating suggestion that Antiochus was copying the Roman suppression of the Bacchanalia (rites of worship for the Greek god Dionysus) in 186 B.C. This suppression occurred during the time that Antiochus was a young hostage in Rome.

[23]The focus on sabbath, festival keeping, circumcision and food is also evident in 1 Maccabees 1:41-63. This book was probably written several decades before 2 Maccabees, but is missing much of that work's detailed information about the period. Some literature written or popularly read around the time of Antiochus's persecutions focuses on the food laws as a rallying point for those loyal to the law. See Judith 9:5; 11:12-13; 12:1-4; Daniel 1:8-16.

[24]Goldstein, *II Maccabees*, pp. 85-89.

[25]Although the author of 2 Maccabees honored the temple, he probably disagreed with the

author of 1 Maccabees that it was still the only place where legitimate sacrifice could be offered. See Goldstein, *II Maccabees*, pp. 13-17.

[26]Compare *Antiquities* 14.242, 261, 264.

[27]Mørkholm, *Antiochus IV*, p. 148.

[28]Compare Mason, *Josephus and the New Testament*, p. 61.

[29]The sabbatical year is described in Exodus 23:10-11; Leviticus 25:1-7; Deuteronomy 15:1-18; 31:10-11.

[30]See, in addition, Josephus's comments on Herod's siege of Jerusalem during a sabbatical year in *Antiquities* 14.475. Leviticus 26:34-35 prophesies that God will send Israel into exile because it has neglected to give the land its seventh-year rest. Jews who lived in Palestine during the first and second centuries B.C. may have taken the command to observe the sabbatical year so seriously because they were familiar with this passage.

[31]Similar to these accounts, but more tendentious, are Josephus's claims that when the Roman general Pompey took Jerusalem in 63 B.C., the priests continued their sacrifices as Roman artillery fired missiles around them. Many priests, he goes on to say, lost their lives while calmly fulfilling their sacred duties to carry out the prescribed sacrifices as the Roman forces surged into the temple area (*War* 1.148-50).

[32]We also know from a passing reference in the *Antiquities* that many priests, when their tithes were stolen, preferred starvation to violation of the law that instructed them to live off the tithe rather than raise crops of their own (20.181; compare 20.207).

[33]See also Sanders, *Judaism: Practice and Belief*, pp. 156, 513 n. 16.

[34]Jewish devotion to the law is not only clear from friendly sources, like Josephus, but from antagonistic ones as well. See, for example, Tacitus *Histories* 5.1-13 and Apion's position according to Josephus *Against Apion* 2.

[35]See also Hanson, *The People Called*, pp. 42-46, 170-76.

[36]Compare Deuteronomy 4:1, 40; 6:3, 24; 7:12-16; 11:13-17, 26-28; 12:28; 13:17-18; 28:1-29; 32:46-47, which if isolated from their broad theological context might be construed this way also.

[37]See Timo Laato, *Paulus und das Judentum: Anthropologische Erwägungen* (Åbo, Finland: Åbo Akademis Förlag, 1991), pp. 83-84; Mark Seifrid, *Justification by Faith: The Origin and Development of a Central Pauline Theme*, Supplements to *Novum Testamentum* 68 (Leiden, Netherlands: Brill, 1992), pp. 126-27; and Peter Stuhlmacher, *Paul's Letter to the Romans: A Commentary* (Louisville, Ky.: Westminster/John Knox, 1994), p. 155.

[38]On the date and setting of the prayer, see James H. Charlesworth, "Prayer of Manasseh," in *The Old Testament Pseudepigrapha*, ed. J. H. Charlesworth, 2 vols. (New York: Doubleday, 1983-1985), 2:627.

[39]This is Charlesworth's translation of the Syriac text (ibid., pp. 634-35), the earliest extant form of the prayer.

[40]These attributes of the prayer did not go unnoticed during the Protestant Reformation. Luther considered the Prayer of Manasseh such an appropriate expression of his own convictions about sin and grace that he quoted it often, translated it and appended the entire text to his "Discussion on How Confession Should Be Made." See *LW* 39:46-47.

[41]The words of the publican may even echo the Prayer of Manasseh. The publican's phrase "to me the sinner" (*moi tō hamartōlō*, Lk 18:13) is virtually identical to the statement in the Greek version of the Prayer of Manasseh that God "has appointed repentance for me the sinner" (8, *emoi tō hamartōlō*).

Chapter 3: Sanctified Gentiles in Thessalonica

[1]Some scholars believe that 2 Thessalonians is pseudepigraphic. But Robert Jewett (*The Thessalonian Correspondence: Pauline Rhetoric and Millenarian Piety*, Foundatoins and Facets: New Testament [Philadelphia: Fortress, 1986], pp. 1-18) and Charles Wanamaker (*The Epistles to*

the Thessalonians: A Commentary on the Greek Text, New International Greek Testament Commentary[Grand Rapids, Mich.: Eerdmans, 1990], pp. 17-28) offer sound reasons for accepting the letter as authentic.

[2]Ernest Best, *A Commentary on the First and Second Epistles to the Thessalonians*, Harper's New Testament Commentary (New York: Harper & Row, 1972), pp. 5, 82; F. F. Bruce, *1 and 2 Thessalonians*, Word Biblical Commentary 45 (Waco, Tex.: Word, 1982), pp. xxiii, 18; Wanamaker, *Thessalonians*, p. 85; Jewett, *Thessalonian Correspondence*, pp. 118-23.

[3]On the Jewish character of Paul's admonitions in this passage, see Raymond F. Collins, *Studies on the First Letter to the Thessalonians*, Bibliotheca Ephemeridum Theologicarum Lovaniensium 66 (Leuven, Belgium: Leuven University Press/Uitgeverij Peeters, 1984), pp. 328-34, and Peter J. Tomson, *Paul and the Jewish Law: Halakha in the Letters of the Apostle to the Gentiles*, Compendia Rerum Iudaicarum ad Novum Testamentum 3/1 (Minneapolis: Fortress/Assen, Netherlands: Van Gorcum, 1990), p. 91.

[4]Aristarchus, one of Paul's traveling companions from Thessalonica, bore a Jewish name and was therefore probably one of the few Jews among the Thessalonian Christians. See Acts 20:4, Colossians 4:10-11, Philemon 24 and the discussion in Jewett, *Thessalonian Correspondence*, pp. 118-19. On the workshop as the place for Paul's evangelistic activity, and the parallels to it in the activity of itinerant philosophers of Paul's era, see Abraham J. Malherbe, *Paul and the Thessalonians: The Philosophic Tradition of Pastoral Care* (Philadelphia: Fortress, 1987), pp. 17-20.

[5]Whereas Wanamaker (*Thessalonians*, pp. 53-63) and Best (*Commentary on the First and Second Epistles to the Thessalonians*, p. 15) believe that problems in the community were minimal, Jewett (*Thessalonian Correspondence*, pp. 92-109) argues that conflicts over "ecstatic manifestations," a critical attitude toward Paul's leadership, problems with "obstinate resisters of authority" and a proto-Gnostic anthropology could all lie beneath the surface of Paul's language.

[6]Wanamaker (*Thessalonians*, p. 149) generally agrees, although he believes that the stern warning in 4:8 shows that Paul had heard of some sexual deviation among the Thessalonians. There may be some connection between the behavior Paul emphasizes in the ethical admonitions of the Thessalonian letters and specific problems in the Thessalonian congregation. First Thessalonians, however, is a paraenetic letter, and like many such letters it is probably only loosely related to any problems in the situation to which it is addressed. See the comments of George Lyons, *Pauline Autobiography: Toward a New Understanding*, Society of Biblical Literature Dissertation Series 73 (Atlanta: Scholars Press, 1985), pp. 186-87, 218-19. On paraenetic letters generally see Stanley K. Stowers, *Letter Writing in Greco-Roman Antiquity*, Library of Early Christianity 5 (Philadelphia: Westminster Press, 1986), pp. 94-106, and on 1 Thessalonians as a paraenetic letter see Abraham J. Malherbe, *Paul and the Popular Philosophers* (Minneapolis: Fortress, 1989), p. 51.

[7]See Malherbe, *Paul and the Popular Philosophers*, pp. 38-39. For a humorous look at the philosophical charlatans from whom Paul sought to distinguish himself see Lucian's *The Runaways*, composed in the second century.

[8]The phrase is found in Romans 1:13; 11:25; 1 Corinthians 10:1; 12:1; 2 Corinthians 1:8; and here. In Romans 1:13 and 2 Corinthians 1:8 it is used to forestall or correct misunderstandings about Paul's travel plans. The other references, however, introduce subjects vital to the proper belief or conduct of the communities to which Paul writes.

[9]Best (*Commentary on the First and Second Epistles to the Thessalonians*, pp. 144-45), Bruce (*1 and 2 Thessalonians*, p. 69) and Wanamaker (*Thessalonians*, p. 139) make the general observation that 1 Thessalonians 3:10 prepares the reader for Paul's admonitions in chapters 4—5. In light of Paul's positive statements in 4:1, 4:9 and 5:1 about the Thessalonians' progress in the faith, however, it seems advisable to narrow the Thessalonians' "lack" to the eschatological information about which Paul does not want them to be uninformed (4:13).

[10]Bruce, *1 and 2 Thessalonians*, pp. 122-23, 205.

[11]On the idleness of some members of the Thessalonian community, see Jewett, *Thessalonian Correspondence*, pp. 161-78. Compare Best, *Commentary on the First and Second Epistles to the Thessalonians*, p. 230.

[12]Bruce (*1 and 2 Thessalonians*, p. 7) is not impressed by the parallel between Paul's use of the phrase and Deuteronomy 23; but see Collins, *Studies on the First Letter*, pp. 287-89; Traugott Holtz, *Der Erste Brief an die Thessalonicher*, Evangelisch-katholischer Kommentar zum Neuen Testament 13 (Zurich: Benziger/Neukirchener, Germany: Neukirchener, 1990), p. 38; and especially T. J. Deidun, *New Covenant Morality in Paul*, Analecta Biblica 89 (Rome: Biblical Institute Press, 1981), pp. 10-12.

[13]On *ekklēsia* see Henry George Liddell and Robert Scott, *A Greek-English Lexicon*, rev. and aug. Henry Stuart Jones, 9th ed. (Oxford: Oxford University Press, 1990), and Walter Bauer, *A Greek-English Lexicon of the New Testament and Other Early Christian Literature*, trans. and aug. William Arndt, F. Wilbur Gingrich and Frederick W. Danker, 2nd ed. (Chicago: University of Chicago Press, 1979), s.v. For the frequency of the term *kaleō* in the LXX and its various senses, see K. L. Schmidt, "καλέω," in *Theological Dictionary of the New Testament*, ed. Gerhard Kittel and Gerhard Friedrich, 10 vols. (Grand Rapids, Mich.: Eerdmans, 1965), 3:489-90.

[14]The phrase "each of you know how to control his own sexual urges" *(eidenai ekaston hymōn to heautou skeuos ktasthai)* is literally "each of you know how to take his own vessel" and may refer to taking a wife in marriage. Regarding the phrase as a reference to controlling one's own sexual drive, however, is equally possible grammatically and fits the context better: Paul is not discussing how one should marry or how one should have marital relations in this passage but sexual immorality *(porneia*, 4:3) and illicit sexual desire *(pathei epithymias*, 4:5). See Wanamaker, *Thessalonians*, p. 152.

[15]Deidun (*New Covenant Morality*, pp. 18-19) draws attention to the close relationship between Paul's phrase "who do not know God" and the description of Gentiles in Jeremiah 10:25.

[16]In addition to incest, these chapters mention homosexuality (Lev 18:22; 20:13), adultery (20:10), bestiality (18:23; 20:15-16) and sexual intercourse with a menstruant (18:19; 20:18).

[17]Paul also echoes the language that these chapters use to refer to sexual improprieties. In Leviticus 18:19 and 20:21 the LXX uses the term *uncleanness (akatharsia)* to refer to various sexual offenses. This is precisely the term Paul uses in 1 Thessalonians 4:7.

[18]See also Deidun, *New Covenant Morality*, pp. 18-28, 53-63.

[19]Ibid., p. 20; Wanamaker, *Thessalonians*, p. 160. The Thessalonians' teacher, of course, was Paul (1 Thess 4:2, 11-12; 2 Thess 2:15). At least in his letters, however, his ethical teachings do not reach the level of specificity that we find, for example, in Leviticus 18 and 20.

[20]E. P. Sanders (*Judaism: Practice and Belief 63 BCE—66 CE* [London: SCM Press/Philadelphia: Trinity Press International, 1992], pp. 257-60) cites Matthew 7:12 and Tobit 4:15, among other examples, to show how Leviticus 19:18 or a rough equivalent was commonly taken to summarize the whole law.

[21]That Paul is assuming a prophetic position in this passage and not suddenly becoming anti-Semitic (as Best believes [*Commentary on the First and Second Epistles to the Thessalonians*, p. 22]) is clear from the parallels between Paul's language and such passages as 1 Kings 19:10, 2 Chronicles 36:15-21, Nehemiah 9:30 and Daniel 9:6. Compare W. D. Davies, *Jewish and Pauline Studies* (Philadelphia: Fortress, 1984), p. 125, and James M. Scott, "Paul's Use of Deuteronomic Tradition," *Journal of Biblical Literature* 112 (1993): 651-57. In light of these parallels it is unnecessary to ferret out reasons that 1 Thessalonians 2:13-16 could be a non-Pauline interpolation in order to exonerate Paul of anti-Semitism. See, for example, Birger A. Pearson, "1 Thessalonians 2:13-16: A Deutero-Pauline Interpolation," *Harvard Theological Review* 64 (1971): 79-94.

[22]Paul Hanson, *The People Called: The Growth of Community in the Bible* (New York: Harper & Row, 1986), pp. 316-21.

[23]See Scott, "Paul's Use of Deuteronomic Tradition," pp. 664-65, especially n. 91.

Chapter 4: Sanctified Gentiles in Corinth

[1]For the archaeological evidence for Judaism in Corinth, see S. Safrai and M. Stern, *The Jewish People in the First Century: Historical Geography, Political History, Social, Cultural and Religious Life and Institutions,* Compendia Rerum Iudaicarum ad Novum Testamentum 1 (Philadelphia: Fortress/Assen, Netherlands: Van Gorcum, 1974), p. 159.

[2]If the Sosthenes who joined Paul in writing 1 Corinthians (1:1) is identical with the second Corinthian synagogue ruler mentioned in Acts (18:17), then he also became a Christian.

[3]As Wolfgang Schrage points out (*Der Erste Brief an die Korinther (1 Kor 1,1-6,11),* Evangelisch-katholischer Kommentar zum Neuen Testament 7 [Zürich: Benziger/Neukirchen, Germany: Neukirchener, 1991], p. 32), 1 Corinthians 7:18, 10:32 and 12:13 also indicate that the Corinthian community included at least some Jews. Some scholars go much further than this to contend that the community was predominantly Jewish. See, for example, Jacques Dupont, *Gnosis: La connaissance religieuse dans les épîtres de Saint Paul,* 2nd ed. (Louvain, Belgium: Nauwelaerts/Paris: Gabalda, 1960), and Richard A. Horsley, "Gnosis in Corinth: 1 Corinthians 8.1-6," *New Testament Studies* 27 (1980): 32-51.

[4]The origin of the problem behind 8:1—10:22 has sometimes been viewed as a dispute between scrupulous Jewish Christians and liberal Gentile Christians. See, for example, Dupont, *Gnosis,* pp. 283-85. The situation presupposed by 8:7 and 8:10, however, shows that Paul has in mind Gentile Christians, some of whom are being tempted *back* into idolatry by the participation of others in cultic meals. See Gordon Fee, "Εἰδωλόθυτα" Once Again: An Interpretation of 1 Corinthians 8-10," *Biblica* 61 (1980): 172-97, and Peter J. Tomson, *Paul and the Jewish Law: Halakha in the Letters of the Apostle to the Gentiles,* Compendia Rerum Iudaicarum ad Novum Testamentum 3/1 (Minneapolis: Fortress/Assen, Netherlands: Van Gorcum, 1990), pp. 188, 195.

[5]Horsley ("Gnosis in Corinth," p. 41) believes that the Corinthians represent a type of proselytizing Judaism that played down many peculiarly Jewish customs, such as circumcision, and emphasized belief in "the One true God" as the chief requirement for admission to Judaism. This might explain some of the more Hellenistic characteristics revealed in the letters. It cannot, however, explain the problems within the community over sexual matters. Even Hellenistic Jews who, for example, emphasized the spiritual value of circumcision were strict about sexual matters, often using circumcision itself as a symbol of sexual purity. See the passage that Horsley cites from Philo *Questions and Answers on Exodus* 2.2.

[6]Two other, slightly more ambiguous pieces of evidence also support the thesis that the Corinthian community was predominantly Gentile. In several places Paul quotes slogans that were being bandied about the Corinthian community: "all things are permitted," "food for the stomach and the stomach for food," "it is good for a man not to have relations with a woman" (6:12-13; 7:1; 10:23; compare 8:2, 4, 8). These slogans reflect attitudes toward food and sex which were not typical of Judaism. The thesis also receives confirmation from Romans 15:22-32, where Paul assumes that the believers in Achaia, who have contributed to his collection for needy Jewish believers in Jerusalem, are Gentiles.

[7]See, for example, C. K. Barrett, *Essays on Paul* (Philadelphia: Westminster Press, 1982), pp. 1-117, and Gerd Luedemann, *Opposition to Paul in Jewish Christianity* (Minneapolis: Fortress, 1989), pp. 65-80.

[8]Barrett, *Essays on Paul,* pp. 28-39; Luedemann, *Opposition to Paul,* p. 80.

[9]C. K. Barrett (*The First Epistle to the Corinthians,* Harper's New Testament Commentary [New York: Harper & Row, 1968], pp. 87-88, and *Essays on Paul,* pp. 32-33) follows the suggestion of T. W. Manson (*Studies in the Gospels and Epistles* [Philadelphia: Westminster Press, 1962], p. 194) that Paul's mention of another person who is building on the foundation he laid (1 Cor 3:10-15) contains a subtle reference to the meaning of Cephas's name, "rock" (compare Mt 16:18; Gal 2:9). Luedemann (*Opposition to Paul,* pp. 76-78) adopts a similar position.

[10]Barrett, *Essays on Paul,* pp. 21-22, 33-34, 53. Luedemann (*Opposition to Paul,* p. 263 n. 71)

believes that Barrett is wrong to locate the heart of the contention between Paul and his Corinthian opponents in the supposed introduction of Jewish legal observances into the Corinthian community. The primary point of disagreement, he says, was Paul's style of ministry.

[11]Already in 1915 Alfred Plummer could refer to this as "the usual view." See his *Critical and Exegetical Commentary on the Second Epistle of St. Paul to the Corinthians*, International Critical Commentary (Edinburgh: T & T Clark, 1915), p. xl.

[12]See the summaries of the scholarship on this issue in Victor Paul Furnish, *II Corinthians*, Anchor Bible 32A (New York: Doubleday, 1984), p. 49, and Jerry L. Sumney, *Identifying Paul's Opponents: The Question of Method in 2 Corinthians*, Journal for the Study of the New Testament Supplement Series 40 (Sheffield, U.K.: Sheffield Academic Press, 1990), pp. 13-73.

[13]See, for example, R. H. Strachan, *The Second Epistle of Paul to the Corinthians*, Moffatt New Testament Commentary (London: Hodder & Stoughton, 1935), pp. xxxii-xxxiii.

[14]The definitive case for this position appears in Dieter Georgi's monograph *The Opponents of Paul in Second Corinthians* (orig. ed. 1964; Philadelphia: Fortress, 1986). See especially pp. 27-82, 229-313.

[15]Rudolf Bultmann, *The Second Letter to the Corinthians* (Minneapolis: Augsburg, 1985), p. 215.

[16]For the superiority of this method of identifying Paul's opponents to more speculative approaches, see Furnish, *II Corinthians*, p. 50, and Sumney, *Identifying Paul's Opponents*, p. 127.

[17]See Plummer, *Critical and Exegetical Commentary*, pp. 77-78; Strachan, *Second Epistle of Paul to the Corinthians*, pp. 78-80; Philip Edgcumbe Hughes, *Paul's Second Epistle to the Corinthians*, New International Commentary on the New Testament (Grand Rapids, Mich.: Eerdmans, 1962), pp. 82-85; and Furnish, *II Corinthians*, p. 178.

[18]Literally, Paul says, "You are a letter of Christ, *served* by us." The term *served (diakonētheisa)* is an unusual one for the delivery of a message (although see Josephus, *Ant.* 6.298), but Paul uses it here in anticipation of his discussion of his role as "minister" (*diakonos*, 3:6) and apostle of the "ministry" (*diakonia*) of the Spirit (3:8) and of righteousness (3:9). See Richard B. Hays, *Echoes of Scripture in the Letters of Paul* (New Haven, Conn.: Yale University Press, 1989), p. 127.

[19]This is the position of Furnish (*II Corinthians*, p. 197), in contrast to most commentators. He claims, for example, that the phrase "*ministers of a new covenant* [in 3:6] . . . is apparently an ad hoc formulation to which Paul has found himself led by the momentum of his own argument in the preceding verses. It does not provide any sure evidence that Paul's rivals were Judaizers of some kind."

[20]Compare 2 Corinthians 5:12 *(tous en prosōpō kauchōmenous kai mē en kardia)* with 1 Kingdoms 16:7 *(anthrōpos opsetia eis prosōpon, ho de theos opsetai eis kardian)*.

[21]Furnish (*II Corinthians*, pp. 324-25) believes that in 5:13 Paul alludes to the ecstatic experiences that his opponents claim for themselves but deny to him (12:1). These, he says, were part of the basis for the boast of Paul's opponents and were the outward signs in which they put confidence.

[22]Hans Lietzmann (*An die Korinther I-II*, 5th ed., Handbuch zum Neuen Testament 9 [Tübingen, Germany: J. C. B. Mohr/Paul Siebeck, 1969], p. 131) suggests that Paul may also be referring to 6:11. Plummer's comment (*Critical and Exegetical Commentary*, p. 214) that Paul has said nothing like this before is puzzling, especially since he accepts the reading *hēmōn* ("our") at 3:2. Contrary to the position of many commentators, the reading *hēmōn* in that verse is probably original rather than *hymōn* ("your"), since it is both the better attested and the more difficult reading. See the definitive argument of Scott Hafemann, *Suffering and the Spirit: An Exegetical Study of II Cor. 2:14—3:3 Within the Context of the Corinthian Correspondence*, Wissenschaftliche Untersuchungen zum Neuen Testament ser. 2, no. 19 (Tübingen, Germany: J. C. B. Mohr/Paul Siebeck, 1986), pp. 186-88.

[23]See Furnish, *II Corinthians*, p. 461.

[24]On *synistēmi* see Georgi, *Opponents of Paul*, p. 243.

[25]The term *law (nomos)* appears nine times (discounting the clearly secondary reading *nomō* in 7:39), *covenant (diathēkē)* three times, and the phrase "commandments of God" *(entolai theou)* once.

[26]See T. J. Deidun, *New Covenant Morality in Paul,* Analecta Biblica 89 (Rome: Biblical Institute Press, 1981), pp. 12-14.

[27]The cognate adjective *eklektos,* however, appears in Romans 8:33; 16:13; Colossians 3:12; 1 Timothy 5:21; 2 Timothy 2:10; and Titus 1:1.

[28]See Deidun, *New Covenant Morality,* p. 28.

[29]See especially the comments of Barrett, *First Epistle to the Corinthians,* p. 220, and Gordon D. Fee, *The First Epistle to the Corinthians,* New International Commentary on the New Testament (Grand Rapids, Mich.: Eerdmans, 1987), p. 444.

[30]So Fee, "Εἰδωλόθυτα," pp. 187-95, and *Corinthians,* pp. 357-63.

[31]So also Barrett, *First Epistle to the Corinthians,* p. 279.

[32]The Corinthian concern to define the gospel in terms of "knowledge" can be seen behind Paul's comments in 1:5, 1:18—2:16, 8:1-13 and 13:2, 8. In 8:1-7 Paul counters this position with his own emphasis on love of the one God (8:4, 6), identified with the Messiah Jesus, and love of those for whom the Messiah died (8:11). In other words, as N. T. Wright has persuasively argued (*The Climax of the Covenant: Christ and the Law in Pauline Theology* [Edinburgh: T & T Clark, 1991], pp. 125-29, 132-35), Paul opposes the Corinthian emphasis on *gnōsis* ("knowledge") by referring to the great monotheistic creed of Judaism found in Deuteronomy 6:4 and its implications for life within the believing community. This confession and its ethical implications, remarks Wright, "marked the community out sociologically as well as theologically" (p. 132).

[33]See the comments of Fee, *Corinthians,* pp. 200-201.

[34]The text is notoriously difficult. Most commentators claim that Paul consigns the offender to the outer realm of evil and thus to sickness and death (compare 11:30). See, for example, James Moffatt, *The First Epistle of Paul to the Corinthians,* Moffatt New Testament Commentary (London: Hodder & Stoughton, 1938), p. 56; Lietzmann, *An die Korinther,* p. 23; Barrett, *First Epistle to the Corinthians,* p. 126; Hans Conzelmann, *1 Corinthians,* Hermeneia (Philadelphia: Fortress, 1975), pp. 97-98; Schrage, *Erste brief an die Korinther,* pp. 376-77; compare Michael Newton, *The Concept of Purity at Qumran and in Paul,* Society for New Testament Studies Monograph Series 53 (Cambridge: Cambridge University Press, 1985), p. 90. A few interpreters argue that Paul calls only for the man's excommunication. See, for example, Fee, *Corinthians,* pp. 208-12. In either case, Paul's advice is cloaked in language whose severity echoes the drastic penalties prescribed in the Mosaic law. Perhaps, as Tomson suggests (*Jewish Law,* pp. 101-3), Paul's advice is an early form of the rabbinic practice of "extirpation." Under this practice capital offenders were handed over to death "at the hands of Heaven" during periods when Jewish courts could not exercise the death penalty.

[35]See also Deidun, *New Covenant Morality,* pp. 29-30. For the cultural environment from which Paul's language emerges see Hans Windisch, "ζύμη," in *Theological Dictionary of the New Testament,* ed. Gerhard Kittel, 10 vols. (Grand Rapids, Mich.: Eerdmans, 1964), 2:902-6, and Fee, *Corinthians,* pp. 215-16. Paul's metaphorical use of Passover to teach an ethical lesson was not typical of the Judaism of his time (although Philo comes close to Paul at this point), but the use of leaven as a symbol of evil was common in both Jewish and Greco-Roman circles. Nevertheless, the lesson that Paul teaches (that God's people should be holy) and the basis for his metaphor (Ex 12:18-20; Num 28:16-17; Deut 16:3-4) show the large extent to which he was working within the pattern established by the Mosaic law.

[36]Deidun, *New Covenant Morality,* p. 30.

[37]Contrast Exodus 12:19, which penalizes those who eat leavened bread during the feast, whether alien or native-born, with expulsion from the land of Israel.

[38]Tomson (*Jewish Law,* pp. 221-81) believes that the requirements for sanctity for Gentile

believers were different from those for Jewish believers. Jewish believers were to maintain their observance of the Jewish law (pp. 274-81), while Gentile believers were to avoid idolatry, sexual immorality, and bloodshed (pp. 271-72). Although Paul felt strongly that Gentile believers and Jewish believers were to be free to associate with one another in the church (pp. 221-58), Jews remained Jews and Gentiles remained Gentiles. It is difficult to see, however, how Paul's assumptions that Gentiles were no longer Gentiles (1 Cor 5:1) and that the "church of God" was an entity distinct from either Jews or Gentiles (1 Cor 10:32) square with this thesis.

[39]See Baruch A. Levine, "On the Presence of God in Biblical Religion," in *Religions in Antiquity: Essays in Memory of Erwin Ramsdell Goodenough*, ed. Jacob Neusner, Studies in the History of Religion 14 (Leiden, Netherlands: Brill, 1968), pp. 81-85.

[40]Ezekiel believes that God graciously dwells with his exiled people to a small extent (11:16) but that he cannot tabernacle among his people fully until they are sanctified by God himself during the period of restoration (37:28). See Walther Zimmerli, *Ezekiel 1: A Commentary on the Book of the Prophet Ezekiel, Chapters 1-24*, Hermeneia (Philadelphia: Fortress, 1979), pp. 261-62.

[41]Scholarship since the nineteenth century has often identified the "other" (*allos*) of 3:10 and the "someone" (*tis*) of 3:12 with Peter, a position that receives substantial support from Paul's clear reference in 1 Corinthians 9:5, 12 to his own deviation from the method of financial support that "Cephas" practiced. For a more recent articulation of this position see Luedemann, *Opposition to Paul*, p. 78 (compare Manson, *Studies in the Gospels and Epistles*, pp. 190-208, and Barrett, *Essays on Paul*, pp. 28-39). An obvious candidate for the position is Apollos, since Paul mentions him explicitly in 3:4-6 and admonishes the Corinthians for forming a faction who follows him (Schrage, *Erste brief an die Korinther*, 1:295-96), although as Moffatt points out (*Corinthians*, p. 40), the language seems too general to refer to one whom Paul has named explicitly only a few verses earlier (compare Lietzmann, *An die Korinther*, p. 16).

[42]Paul uses two terms for "temple" in his correspondence, *naos* (1 Cor 3:16, 17; 6:19; 2 Cor 6:16; 2 Thess 2:4) and *hieron* (1 Cor 9:13). *Naos* most often refers to the believing community (2 Thess 2:4 is the exception). *Hieron* refers to the Jerusalem temple. Paul's selection of terms is significant since in the LXX *naos* is the term of choice for the most holy parts of the temple, including the Holy of Holies, the dwelling place of God's presence. *Hieron*, on the other hand, refers most often to the entire temple complex. See Newton, *Concept of Purity*, p. 54. Paul's reference to the dwelling of God's Spirit "among" the Corinthians (*en hymin*) is a clear echo of Ezekiel's promise that in the time of restoration God will put his Spirit "among" his people (*en hymin*, 36:26; compare 11:19; 39:29 LXX).

[43]Paul uses the phrase *ouk oidate* twelve times, twice in Romans (6:16; 11:2) and ten times in 1 Corinthians (3:16; 5:6; 6:2, 3, 9, 15, 16, 19; 9:13, 24). The phrase refers to information that Paul's readers should know because it is part of the common fund of proverbial wisdom (Rom 6:16; 1 Cor 5:6; 9:24), common knowledge from the Scriptures (Rom 11:2; 1 Cor 6:16; 9:13) or part of the Christian tradition he had taught them (1 Cor 6:2, 3, 9, 15). He uses it in connection with the thesis that the Corinthians are God's temple here in 3:16 and in 6:19, the only subject for which he uses it twice in widely separated passages.

[44]See, for example, Isaiah 13:1-22 and Jeremiah 50:1-46. Compare 2 Maccabees 9:5-29; *Psalms of Solomon* 2:2, 25-26. Moffatt observes that the death penalty was the common punishment in many parts of the ancient world for desecration of a temple (*Corinthians*, p. 42), but Paul's indebtedness in 3:12 to the biblical description of the temple probably means that he is thinking in specifically biblical and Jewish terms here.

[45]See Fee, *Corinthians*, p. 255.

[46]Gordon Fee observes that some of the same pagan temples at which banquets were held in Corinth also offered the services of cultic prostitutes ("II Corinthians VI.14-VII.1 and Food Offered to Idols," *New Testament Studies* 23 [1977]: 149).

[47]Thus, as commentators often observe, the temple imagery applied to the community in 3:16 is now applied to the individual believer. See, for example, Conzelmann, *1 Corinthians*, p. 112,

and Fee, *Corinthians,* p. 264.

[48]Ezekiel 11:19 says that God will give his restored people another heart, a new spirit and a heart of flesh rather than their hardened heart of stone. The purpose of these gifts, says verse 20, is that Israel might live in God's commandments and keep his righteous decrees. Similarly, Ezekiel 36:23-26 claims that God will be sanctified among his people in the sight of the Gentiles, will sprinkle them with pure water, will cleanse them from all impurities and idolatries and will give to them both a new heart and a new spirit. Paul's notion of the Corinthian's sanctity closely parallels these ideas. Thus he urges the Corinthians to avoid a sizable list of activities that are incompatible with life in the kingdom of God (6:9-10). They should avoid them, he says, because they have experienced the eschatological cleansing of God's Spirit: "You were washed, sanctified and justified in the name of the Lord Jesus Christ and by the Spirit of our God" (6:11).

[49]Some scholars believe that Paul did not write this passage or place it in its present location, others that it is a fragment of another Pauline letter to the Corinthians (perhaps the one mentioned in 1 Cor 5:9), and still others that it is a block of non-Pauline material included at this point in the argument by Paul himself. Furnish (*II Corinthians,* pp. 375-83) provides a thorough discussion of the exegetical history of the passage, and Fee ("II Corinthians VI.14-VII.1," pp. 140-61) gives sound reasons that the passage is best seen as a logical step in the development of Paul's argument.

[50]C. K. Barrett believes that Paul's opponents entered the Corinthian community either before the composition of 1 Corinthians or soon thereafter (*The Second Epistle to the Corinthians,* Harper's New Testament Commentary [New York: Harper & Row, 1973], p. 6). Here I follow Fee, who argues that Paul's only opponents in 1 Corinthians are the belligerent Corinthians themselves (*Corinthians,* p. 8). The outsiders entered later.

[51]Barrett believes (*Second Epistle to the Corinthians,* pp. 8, 206) that although Paul was concerned about the Corinthian church, he was primarily concerned both that the Corinthians treat Titus well and that Titus arrive safely with the large sum of money collected for the saints in Jerusalem (see 2 Cor 8—9). But if Paul's description of his comfort at meeting Titus in Macedonia (7:6-7) indicates the character of his anxiety prior to Titus's arrival, then his anxiety was over the church and its response to the severe letter. Compare Furnish, *II Corinthians,* p. 171.

[52]Furnish, *II Corinthians,* pp. 652-53; Ralph P. Martin, *2 Corinthians,* Word Biblical Commentary (Dallas: Word, 1986), pp. 165, 167.

[53]Barrett, *Second Epistle to the Corinthians,* p. 185; Furnish, *II Corinthians,* p. 354. Martin entertains this possibility but thinks it equally probable that Paul "cannot resist setting himself up as an example" (*2 Corinthians,* p. 172).

[54]Furnish believes that Paul cannot be referring to his opponents in this passage, because elsewhere he never calls erring Christians "unbelievers." That term, Furnish says, is always reserved for those who lay no claim to belief in Christ (*II Corinthians,* p. 382). This objection carries considerable weight, but in light of Paul's belief that his opponents are allied with Satan (2 Cor 11:15) and preach "another Jesus . . . another spirit . . . another gospel" (2 Cor 11:4), it seems likely that he would also consider them unbelievers.

[55]In light of Paul's argument against idolatry in 1 Corinthians 10:1-22 (compare 5:10-11), his warning here may refer to literal idolatry among the Corinthians, the kind of idolatry that caused Israel's downfall, as he recognizes in 1 Corinthians 10:1-11. Probably Paul's reference to idols is metaphorical, however, and is intended as a warning against worshiping "another Jesus" (compare 2 Cor 11:4; 1 John 5:21; 1QS 2.11, "Cursed be the man who enters this Covenant while walking among the idols of his heart"). For a comparison between Paul and Qumran on the metaphorical use of the term *idol* see Bertil Gärtner, *The Temple and the Community in Qumran and the New Testament: A Comparative Study in the Temple Symbolism of the Qumran Texts and the New Testament,* Society for New Testament Studies Monograph Series 1

(Cambridge: Cambridge University Press, 1965), p. 51.

[56] Walther Zimmerli, *Ezekiel 2: A Commentary on the Book of the Prophet Ezekiel, Chapters 25-48*, Hermeneia (Philadelphia: Fortress, 1983), p. 277.

[57] The Septuagint translation of Leviticus 26:11-12 renders the phrases "your God" and "my people" idiomatically by using genitive-case pronouns. In Ezekiel, however, the translation follows the Hebrew idiom for indicating possession more literally by using dative-case pronouns to render the phrases "their God" and "my people." Paul uses the idiomatic rendering of Leviticus in his use of cases but imitates Ezekiel in using a third-person rather than first-person pronoun in the phrase "their God."

[58] James M. Scott demonstrates that the "covenant formula" ("I shall be your [their] God and you [they] shall be my people"), which appears in both Leviticus 26:11-12 and Ezekiel 37:27, frequently surfaces within literature current in Paul's era as a description of the new covenant that God will make with his eschatologically restored people (*Adoption as Sons of God: An Exegetical Investigation into the Background of* ΥΙΟΘΕΣΙΑ *in the Pauline Corpus*, Wissenschaftliche Untersuchungen zum Neuen Testament ser. 2, no. 48 [Tübingen, Germany: J. C. B. Mohr/Paul Siebeck, 1992], pp. 198-201). If so, then the likelihood increases that Paul is admonishing the Corinthians to maintain the sanctity appropriate to the community of the new covenant.

[59] Barrett observes that although the statement resembles Jeremiah 51:45, Paul's language is closer to Isaiah 52:11 than to any other Old Testament text (*Second Epistle to the Corinthians*, p. 200).

[60] See Scott, *Adoption as Sons*, pp. 96-117, 209-11.

[61] A parallel to Paul's identification of the church with the temple may exist in the Qumran community, who believed that the Jerusalem temple was defiled. See Gärtner, *The Temple and the Community*, pp. 56-60, and Jacob Neusner, *The Idea of Purity in Ancient Judaism*, Studies in Judaism in Late Antiquity 1 (Leiden, Netherlands: Brill, 1973), pp. 50, 119. The Qumran community was far more interested in the literal temple than Paul was, however, and may (the point is controversial) have had hopes for an eschatological temple. See 1QTemple 29. Newton compares the Pauline idea of the community as the temple with the notion of the rabbis after A.D. 70 that Israel constituted the temple and that the purity regulations once applied to temple worship now applied to the entire community (*Concept of Purity*, pp. 7, 113).

Chapter 5: Old Covenant & New in the Corinthian Letters

[1] Although 1 Corinthians 14:21 and 34 use the term *law*, neither uses it to refer to the Mosaic law, and so neither is addressed in the discussion below. The reading *nomō* at 7:39 is clearly secondary. Aspects of the argument in this chapter repeat, in revised form, material in my article "The Coherence of Paul's View of the Law: The Evidence of First Corinthians," *New Testament Studies* 38 (1992): 235-53.

[2] Paul's statement may not have been as baffling to Hellenistic Jews of the Diaspora, especially those who were Christians. See Heikki Räisänen, *Jesus, Paul and Torah: Collected Essays, Journal for the Study of the New Testament* Supplement 43 (Sheffield, U.K.: Sheffield Academic Press, 1992), pp. 189-97, and Frank Thielman, *From Plight to Solution: A Jewish Framework for Understanding Paul's View of the Law in Romans and Galatians*, Supplements to *Novum Testamentum* 61 (Leiden, Netherlands: Brill, 1989), pp. 54-59.

[3] Peter J. Tomson believes 1 Corinthians 7:19 supplies evidence that Paul believed the Jews should keep the Mosaic law and Gentiles the Noachian code (*Paul and the Jewish Law: Halakha in the Letters of the Apostle to the Gentiles*, Compendia rerum Iudaicarum ad Novum Testamentum 3/1 [Minneapolis: Fortress/Assen, Netherlands: Van Gorcum, 1990], pp. 270-74). The only principle clearly articulated in 1 Corinthians 7:19, however, is that circumcision is ultimately irrelevant to obedience to God.

[4] The following reconstruction of Paul's argument follows Gordon D. Fee, "II Corinthians

VI.14-VII.1 and Food Offered to Idols," *New Testament Studies* 23 (1977): 148-54, and Gordon D. Fee, "Εἰδωλόθυτα Once Again: An Interpretation of 1 Corinthians 8-10," *Biblica* 61 (1980): 172-97; and Gordon D. Fee, *The First Epistle to the Corinthians*, New International Commentary on the New Testament (Grand Rapids, Mich.: Eerdmans, 1987), pp. 357-63.

[5]Tomson believes that 8:10 is only a rhetorical tactic intended to shock the "knowing" into realizing the effect on weak Gentiles of their relaxed approach to eating meat offered to idols (*Jewish Law*, p. 196). Nothing in the passage, however, indicates that the picture that 8:10 paints of attendance at cultic meals is hypothetical.

[6]Paul's contrast of human arguments and those from the divine realm is often assumed to be limited to the analogies in 9:7 and the quotation of Scripture in 9:9 (as in James Moffatt, *The First Epistle of Paul to the Corinthians*, Moffatt New Testament Commentary [London: Hodder & Stoughton, 1938], p. 116; C. K. Barrett, *The First Epistle to the Corinthians*, Harper's New Testament Commentary [New York: Harper & Row, 1968], p. 205; Fee, *Corinthians*, p. 406), but the rhetorical balance of three human analogies and three analogies that share a religious significance is probably not accidental.

[7]Controversy surrounds Paul's hermeneutical method in 9:9-10. Some scholars believe, for example, that Paul allegorizes the text in a way reminiscent of Philo (Hans Conzelmann, *1 Corinthians*, Hermeneia [Philadelphia: Fortress, 1975], pp. 154-55), and others that Paul uses the law about oxen only as an analogy because he is primarily interested in the general principle it articulates (Fee, *Corinthians*, p. 408). As Richard B. Hays observes (*Echoes of Scripture in the Letters of Paul* [New Haven, Conn.: Yale University Press, 1989], p. 166), the most distinctive aspect of Paul's hermeneutical procedure here is that he believes the Old Testament text speaks directly to his own situation.

[8]Michael Newton, *The Concept of Purity at Qumran and in Paul*, Society for New Testament Studies Monograph Series 53 (Cambridge: Cambridge University Press, 1985), p. 59. C. K. Barrett (*The Second Epistle to the Corinthians*, Harper's New Testament Commentary [New York: Harper & Row, 1973], p. 208) and Fee (*Corinthians*, p. 412) correctly point out that the custom Paul describes here was widely observed in the religions of antiquity. Nevertheless, it is likely that Paul speaks out of his own tradition.

[9]See Fee, *Corinthians*, p. 412. Conzelmann's thesis (*1 Corinthians*, p. 157) that Paul's quotation of the words of Jesus is simply part of an unsystematic assembly of evidence is therefore improbable.

[10]See also Fee, *Corinthians*, p. 428.

[11]In order to support his thesis that Paul was always an observant Jew himself but did not require observance of Gentile believers, Tomson (*Jewish Law*, pp. 276-77) follows the reading of two ninth-century Western uncials and several minuscules that omit the word *as* (*hōs*) in the phrase "to the Jews as a Jew" in 9:20. He also prefers the reading of several relatively late and primarily Western and Byzantine uncials that omit the phrase "not myself being under the law" in 9:20 to an array of earlier manuscripts of a variety of text types which include the phrase. (Compare his argument on "and not in a Jewish way" at Gal 2:14 [ibid., p. 229].) As the editors of the standard critical editions of the New Testament agree, however, the weight of the textual tradition is against both omissions.

[12]Wisdom of Solomon 17:2 and 3 Maccabees 6:9 use *anomos* negatively of Gentiles, whereas 1 Maccabees 7:5; 9:23, 58, 69; 11:25; 14:14; and possibly 3:5-6 use the term of renegade Jews. The term, then, does not simply mean "wicked" but "outside the covenant and *therefore* wicked."

[13]The unusual phrase *ennomos Christou* has produced great ferment among interpreters of 1 Corinthians and of students of Paul's view of the law. Does it mean that Paul knew of a concrete "law of Christ" similar in nature to but different in content from the Mosaic law, perhaps consisting of a selection of Jesus' ethical teachings? The classic case for this position is C. H. Dodd, "ΕΝΝΟΜΟΣ ΧΡΙΣΤΟΥ," *Studia Paulina in Honorem Johannis de Zwaan Septuagenarii*, ed. J. N. Sevenster and W. C. van Unnik (Haarlem: Erven F. Bohn, 1953), pp. 96-110.

Or does the phrase mean merely that Paul was under subjection to Christ rather than in subjection to the law? This is the interpretation of the great majority of scholars. See, for example, Otfried Hofius, "Das Gesetz des Mose und das Gesetz Christi," *Zeitschrift für Theologie und Kirche* 80 (1983): 281, and H. Balz, "ἔννομος," in *Exegetical Dictionary of the New Testament*, ed. H. Balz and G. Schneider, 3 vols. (Grand Rapids, Mich.: Eerdmans, 1990-1993), 1:456. Most scholars recognize, however, that this verse alone will not decide the question.

[14]I owe this observation to private correspondence with Douglas Moo.

[15]This is the explanation of Gerd Theissen (*The Social Setting of Pauline Christianity: Essays on Corinth* [Philadelphia: Fortress, 1982], pp. 145-74).

[16]From v. 23b to v. 25 Paul probably quotes from an established liturgical tradition which he modifies slightly to address his immediate concerns. The traditional nature of this material is indicated not only by the parallels to it in the Synoptic Gospels but also by Paul's reference in v. 23a to having handed on to the Corinthians a tradition that he received. The presence of the words *anamnēsis* ("remembrance") and *hosakis* ("as often as"), which occur nowhere else in the Pauline corpus, lend support to this notion. See Joachim Jeremias, *The Eucharistic Words of Jesus* (London: SCM Press, 1966), pp. 101-5.

[17]For a summary of the debate over which of the four accounts preserves the most primitive tradition, see I. Howard Marshall, *Last Supper and Lord's Supper* (Grand Rapids, Mich.: Eerdmans, 1980), pp. 30-56.

[18]Luke has *touto to potērion hē kainē diathēkē en tō haimati mou*, and Paul *touto to potērion hē kainē diathēkē estin en tō emō haimati*.

[19]Unique to Paul's version of Jesus' words is the repetition of the command to celebrate the meal "in remembrance of me." As Fee points out (*Corinthians*, pp. 555-56), Paul probably intended this repetition to remind the Corinthians of the supper's purpose in light of the abuses that marred their celebration of it.

[20]Paul's next two uses of *law* come in 14:21 and 14:34. In 14:21 he describes his paraphrase of Isaiah 28:11-12 as "the law," and in 14:34 he refers to an otherwise unknown rule that women should keep silent in the churches as "the law." Since neither reference is to the law of Moses, they are of limited relevance to our purposes here.

[21]Walter Bauer (*A Greek-English Lexicon of the New Testament and Other Early Christian Literature*, trans. and aug. William Arndt, F. Wilbur Gingrich and Frederick Danker, 2nd ed. [Chicago: University of Chicago Press, 1979], s.v. δύναμις 7) renders Paul's statement "what gives sin its power is the law."

[22]Moffatt couples this verse with 14:34-35 and comments that these are the two places within the letter where non-Pauline glosses have made their way into the text (*Corinthians*, pp. xxiv, 265, 268). See also Johannes Weiss, *Der erste Korintherbrief*, Meyer Kommentar, 10th ed. (Göttingen, Germany: Vandenhoeck & Ruprecht, 1925), p. 380.

[23]Barrett, *First Epistle to the Corinthians*, p. 383; Conzelmann, *1 Corinthians*, p. 293.

[24]This follows the division of the letter in Victor Paul Furnish, *II Corinthians: A New Translation with Introduction and Commentary*, Anchor Bible 32A (New York: Doubleday, 1984), p. 348.

[25]Whereas some commentators have interpreted this question solely as Paul's response to the overwhelming responsibility of preaching a gospel with eternal consequences for its hearers, most recent scholars believe that the question is also related to questions about Paul's sufficiency in Corinth, or at least to claims from his opponents that they are sufficient. For the first position, see R. H. Strachan, *The Second Epistle of Paul to the Corinthians*, Moffatt New Testament Commentary (London: Hodder & Stoughton, 1935), p. 78; R. V. G. Tasker, *The Second Epistle of Paul to the Corinthians* (Grand Rapids, Mich.: Eerdmans, 1958), p. 58; Philip Edgcumbe Hughes, *Paul's Second Epistle to the Corinthians*, New International Commentary on the New Testament (Grand Rapids, Mich.: Eerdmans), p. 82; and Thomas E. Provence, " 'Who Is Sufficient for These Things?' An Exegesis of 2 Corinthians ii 15—iii 18," *Novum Testamentum* 24 (1982): 54-57. For the second position see Rudolf Bultmann, *The Second Letter to the*

Corinthians (from lecture notes penned between 1940 and 1952; Minneapolis: Augsburg, 1985), p. 69; Barrett, *Second Epistle to the Corinthians*, pp. 102-3; Furnish, *II Corinthians*, p. 191; Ralph P. Martin, *2 Corinthians*, Word Biblical Commentary 40 (Waco, Tex.: Word, 1986), p. 49; and Jerome Murphy-O'Connor, *The Theology of the Second Letter to the Corinthians* (Cambridge: Cambridge University Press, 1991), p. 31. Scott Hafemann believes that Paul's reference to his own sufficiency begins the contrast with the sufficiency of Moses which Paul will continue in 3:4—4:6 (*Suffering and the Spirit: An Exegetical Study of II Cor. 2:14—3:3 Within the Context of the Corinthian Correspondence*, Wissenschaftliche Untersuchungen zum Neuen Testament ser. 2, no. 19 [Tübingen, Germany: J. C. B. Mohr/Paul Siebeck, 1986], pp. 98-101).

[26]The opponents' charge that Paul did not possess the correct apostolic credentials lies behind his rhetorical question, "Or do we need, *as some do,* letters of recommendation to you or from you?" (3:1). The issue of Paul's weakness and competence appears to have been present in Corinth even before these opponents arrived on the scene, as 1 Corinthians 2:1-5 and 13 demonstrate. The opponents evidently seized the opportunity that Paul's self-confessed "weakness" and unpersuasive preaching (1 Cor 2:3-4) gave them (2 Cor 10:10; 11:6), added the charge that his vacillating travel plans showed his cowardly nature (2 Cor 1:15—2:2; compare 10:1-2, 10) and concluded that his deportment was not consistent with his claim to be an apostle (compare 2 Cor 11:20-21; 12:11-12). They may also have used against Paul his refusal to accept monetary support from the Corinthians while he ministered among them (2 Cor 11:7-8; 12:13; compare 1 Cor 9:1-18).

[27]Even in 4:7—5:19, however, apologetic concerns are not far from the surface, as 5:11-13 demonstrates.

[28]The expression "tablets of fleshly hearts" is an attempt to render the difficult Greek phrase *plaxin kardiais sarkinais,* smoothed out in some manuscripts to read *plaxin kardias sarkinais.*

[29]Some have claimed that Paul's harsh image of letters written with ink on tablets of stone reflects his desire to introduce polemic against the Mosaic law in light of a supposed tendency among his opponents to impose the Mosaic law on the Corinthians. See Strachan, *Second Epistle of Paul to the Corinthians,* p. 80; Murphy-O'Connor, *Theology of the Second Letter,* p. 32; and Jerome Murphy-O'Connor, "*Pneumatikoi* and Judaizers in 2 Cor 2:14-4:6," *Australian Biblical Review* 34 (1986): 42. Postulating a hypothetical background in Corinth, however, is not necessary to explain the harshness of the metaphor. Paul's metaphors frequently take surprising turns in order to provide greater theological precision. See, for example, Romans 7:1-6, Romans 11:16-24 and 1 Corinthians 5:6-8.

[30]Lloyd Gaston argues that Paul did not take the imagery of stone tablets from the narrative of the giving of the law but from his opponents' supposed claim that they had received visions of stone tablets (*Paul and the Torah* [Vancouver: University of British Columbia Press, 1987], p. 155). Paul's allusions to and quotations from Exodus 34 in 3:7-18 point to the source of his imagery, however, and make such speculative theories unnecessary.

[31]Paul's previous references to God's Spirit and to the tablets of the Mosaic covenant make it unlikely that in the phrase "tablets of fleshly hearts" he is merely using the language of Proverbs 7:2-3 LXX ("Keep my commandments and my words as the pupil of your eye, and you shall live. Put them around your fingers, and write them upon the tablet of your heart"). In the Ezekiel passages, as in Paul, both the Spirit and the commandments form an integral part of the argument. Moreover, in both Ezekiel (11:19-20; 36:26-27) and Paul, the Spirit, the commandments and the heart are all mentioned within an eschatological context foreign to Proverbs 7:2-3. Paul's reference to "tablets," moreover, is probably derived from the expression "tablets of stone" rather than from the singular term *tablet* in Proverbs 7:3.

[32]Heikki Räisänen is skeptical of the idea that Jeremiah 31(38):31-34 influenced Paul's thinking about the law (*Paul and the Law,* Wissenschaftliche Untersuchungen zum Neuen Testament 29 [Tübingen, Germany: J. B. C. Mohr/Paul Siebeck, 1983], pp. 240-45). He believes that 2 Corinthians 3:3 and 3:6 can be plausibly understood without reference to Jeremiah 31, and

that even if Paul does refer to it, his reference forms "at best . . . a marginal theme which is not developed" (p. 245). Similarly, Christian Wolff argues flatly that no allusion to Jeremiah exists in this passage because, unlike Paul, Jeremiah mentions neither the Spirit nor its life-giving function in connection with the new covenant (*Jeremia im Frühjudentum und Urchristentum*, Texte und Untersuchungen 118 [Berlin: Akademie Verlag, 1976], p. 136). But this position is too cautious for two reasons. First, it is difficult to believe that in an argument where Paul mentions writing on the heart (3:3; compare Jer 31[38]:33) in such close proximity to the distinctive phrase "new covenant" (3:6; compare Jer 31[38]:31) he did not have the Jeremiah passage in mind. Second, in the contexts in which Paul and Jeremiah use the phrase, they share the conviction that Israel's breaking of the covenant brought death and that God will intervene eschatologically to remedy this situation. See Hays, *Echoes of Scripture*, p. 128, and N. T. Wright, *The Climax of the Covenant: Christ and the Law in Pauline Theology* (Edinburgh: T & T Clark, 1991), p. 176 n. 7.

[33]Murphy-O'Connor believes that "not of the letter but of the Spirit" qualifies the phrase "new covenant" and implies that Paul's opponents were claiming to be ministers of the new covenant as well (*Theology of the Second Letter,* p. 33). By using these qualifying terms, Paul would then be saying that his opponents are ministers of a new covenant of the letter but he of a new covenant of the Spirit. Since the evidence that Paul is attacking Judaizers in this passage is not conclusive, however, and since in the next verse he will refer to the written nature of the Mosaic law, it seems best to take his statement here as a contrast between the new covenant and the old.

[34]Romans 2:27, 29; 7:6. Paul also uses the term in its plural form in Galatians 6:11 to refer to the letters of the alphabet. A survey of both ancient and modern interpretations of the term appears in Bernardin Schneider, "The Meaning of St. Paul's Antithesis 'The Letter and the Spirit,' " *Catholic Biblical Quarterly* 15 (1953): 163-207. For the interpretation of the contrast in 2 Corinthians 3:6 in light of Romans see Alfred Plummer, *Critical and Exegetical Commentary on the Second Epistle of St. Paul to the Corinthians*, International Critical Commentary (Edinburgh: T & T Clark, 1915), p. 88; Gottlob Schrenk, "γράμμα," in *Theological Dictionary of the New Testament*, ed. Gerhard Kittel, 10 vols. (Grand Rapids, Mich.: Eerdmans), 1:767; Strachan, *Second Epistle of Paul to the Corinthians*, p. 81; Bultmann, *Second Letter to the Corinthians*, p. 78; Schneider, "Meaning of St. Paul's Antithesis," p. 204; Hughes, *Paul's Second Epistle to the Corinthians*, pp. 96-102; Barrett, *Second Epistle to the Corinthians*, p. 113; Furnish, *II Corinthians*, pp. 200-210; and Martin, *2 Corinthians*, p. 54.

[35]The figure is called "synecdoche" and was well known to Paul's contemporaries. See the discussions in the *Ad Herennium* 4.33.44-45 and Quintilian's *Institutio Oratio* 8.6.19-22.

[36]If this is so, then the term *letter* is not intended to disparage a supposed Jewish misuse of the law, as so many lexicographers, commentators and theologians have thought. See, for instance, Joseph Henry Thayer's *Greek-English Lexicon of the New Testament*, s.v. *gramma*, 2c; Schrenk, "γράμμα," pp. 766-68; and especially the influential article by Ernst Käsemann, "The Spirit and the Letter," in *Perspectives on Paul* (Philadelphia: Fortress, 1971), pp. 148-55. In response to this interpretive tradition see Stephen Westerholm, "Letter and Spirit: The Foundation of Pauline Ethics," *New Testament Studies* 30 (1984): 229-48. On the other hand, the context shows that *gramma*, although unusual, does refer to the Mosaic law and not, as Gaston contends (*Paul and the Torah*, pp. 156-57), to "the ministry of the rival missionaries."

[37]Jeremiah 21:8 alludes to the death-life language of Deuteronomy, but only with reference to Israel's obedience or disobedience to Jeremiah's advice, not with reference specifically to the Mosaic covenant. Nevertheless, Jeremiah frequently refers to Israel's suffering as "sword, famine and pestilence" (14:12; 21:7, 9; 24:10; 27:8, 13; 29:17, 18; 32:24; 34:17; 38:2; 42:17, 22; 44:13), terms that recall the curses for violating the covenant in Leviticus 26:25, 33, 36-37 and Deuteronomy 28:21, 53-57; 32:35. See J. A. Thompson, *The Book of Jeremiah*, New International Commentary on the Old Testament (Grand Rapids, Mich.: Eerdmans, 1980), p. 637.

[38]The contrast between "the letter" and "the Spirit" in this passage, then, is not a contrast

between two ways of interpreting Scripture (P. Richardson, "Spirit and Letter: A Foundation for Hermeneutics," *Evangelical Quarterly* 45 [1973]: 208-18), between the Jewish misuse of the law and the proper Christian understanding of it (Provence, " 'Who Is Sufficient,' " pp. 62-81), between an erroneous hermeneutic that misinterprets the law legalistically and a correct one that sees it as promise (Käsemann, "Spirit and the Letter," pp. 148-55) or between two ways of ethical service (Westerholm, "Letter and Spirit," p. 240) but between two eras, the first dominated by the law and its condemnation and the second dominated by the Spirit and righteousness. Compare J. D. G. Dunn, "2 Corinthians III.17—'The Lord Is the Spirit,' " *Journal of Theological Studies* n.s. 21 (1970): 311 n. 6.

[39] Some scholars have claimed that in this passage Paul is presenting his own, corrected edition of his opponents' written exegesis of Exodus 34:29-35. The theory is elaborately explained in S. Schulze, "Die Decke des Moses, Untersuchungen zu einer vorpaulinischen Überlieferung in 2 Cor. iii 7-18," *Zeitschrift für die neutestamentliche Wissenschaft* 49 (1958): 1-30, and Georgi, *Opponents of Paul*, pp. 246-71. The theory attempts to account for what Georgi (*Opponents of Paul*, p. 248) calls "Paul's 'jerky' argumentation" but has not met with wide acceptance. Many interpreters agree with W. C. van Unnik's judgment in " 'With Unveiled Face': An Exegesis of 2 Corinthians iii 12-18," in *Sparsa Collecta: The Collected Essays of W. C. van Unnik*, 3 parts, Supplements to *Novum Testamentum* 29-31 (Leiden, Netherlands: Brill, 1973-1983), 1:197, that the theory "solves no riddles, but only creates new ones."

[40] The verb *katargeō* appears in 3:7, 11, 13, and 14 and is the hinge on which hangs a proper understanding of Paul's argument throughout the section. Paul uses it many times elsewhere to mean "abolish" (as in 1 Cor 2:6) "set aside" (as in 1 Cor 13:11) or "nullify" (Rom 4:14), and there is no indication that the term means anything else here. See Hays, *Echoes of Scripture*, pp. 133-35.

[41] So also Wright, *Climax*, p. 178 n. 13.

[42] Both the juridical and the relational senses, however, are associated with the idea of God's covenant with his people. See W. C. van Unnik, "La conception paulinienne de la Nouvelle Alliance," in *Sparsa Collecta: The Collected Essays of W. C. van Unnik*, 3 parts, Supplements to *Novum Testamentum* 29-31 (Leiden, Netherlands: Brill, 1973-1983), 1:186.

[43] This is the position of Furnish (*II Corinthians*, p. 205) and poses a grave difficulty for the view of Provence that this passage contrasts two *ministries* rather than two *covenants* (" 'Who Is Sufficient,' " pp. 67-68 n. 36).

[44] The Greek phrase is *pollō mallon to menon en doxē*. For the use of *en* in a descriptive sense see C. F. D. Moule, *An Idiom-Book of New Testament Greek*, 2nd ed. (Cambridge: Cambridge University Press, 1959), p. 79.

[45] In the realm of ancient Greek politics, *parrēsia* was the freedom of public discourse that was necessary for truth to emerge within a democracy. In the realm of ancient Greek philosophy, it was the candid explanation of the truth to a friend or follower who needed to hear it (compare 2 Cor 7:4). According to Philo (*Who Is the Heir?* 14-21), Moses' *parrēsia* when speaking with God was a measure of his greatness and proof that he was God's friend. See Heinrich Schlier, "παρρησία," in *Theological Dictionary of the New Testament*, ed. Gerhard Kittel and Gerhard Friedrich, 10 vols. (Grand Rapids, Mich.: Eerdmans, 1967), 5:871-86; Walter Bauer, *A Greek-English Lexicon of the New Testament and Other Early Christian Literature*, trans. and aug. William Arndt, F. Wilbur Gingrich and Frederick Danker, 2nd ed. (Chicago: University of Chicago Press, 1979), s.v.; H. Balz, "παρρησιάζομαι," in *Exegetical Dictionary of the New Testament*, ed. H. Balz and G. Schneider, 3 vols. (Grand Rapids, Mich.: Eerdmans, 1990-1993), 3:45-47; and Abraham J. Malherbe, *Paul and the Thessalonians: The Philosophic Tradition of Pastoral Care* (Philadelphia: Fortress, 1987), pp. 35-48. In the context of a letter to Corinth, these Greco-Roman uses of the word probably have a greater bearing on Paul's meaning than the Syriac idiom discussed by van Unnik in " 'With Unveiled Face,' " pp. 200-210, and "The Semitic Background of παρρησία in the New Testament," in *Sparsa Collecta: The Collected Essays of W.*

C. van Unnik, 3 parts, Supplements to *Novum Testamentum* 29-31 (Leiden, Netherlands: Brill, 1973-1983), 2:290-306.

[46]Paul's reliance on the Septuagint rather than on his own reading of the Hebrew is clear from the near word-for-word agreement in places between Paul and the Septuagint. In 3:13, for example, Paul says, *Mōÿsēs etithei kalymma epi to prosōpon autou.* The Septuagint has *epethēken epi to prosōpon autou kalymma* (Ex 34:33). Similarly, in 3:15-16 Paul uses the unusual expressions *hēnika an* and *hēnika ean* to mean "whenever" and "every time that" (Walter Bauer, *A Greek-English Lexicon of the New Testament and Other Early Christian Literature*, trans. and aug. William Arndt, F. Wilbur Gingrich and Frederick Danker, 2nd ed. [Chicago: University of Chicago Press, 1979], s.v. *hēnika*), respectively. These expressions occur nowhere else in the New Testament, but in Exodus 34:34 the Septuagint uses the expression *hēnika . . . an* to describe Moses' removal of the veil "whenever" he entered the Lord's presence.

[47]Although according to its form, the participle *katargoumenou* ("that which is passing away") could be either masculine or neuter, its gender probably matches the neuter *katargoumenon* in 3:11. *Katargoumenou*, however, cannot refer merely to the "glory" (feminine) of the Mosaic ministry. "That which is passing away," then, is once again the entire era of the Mosaic ministry. See Furnish, *II Corinthians*, p. 207, and Hays, *Echoes of Scripture*, p. 138.

[48]So also Dunn, "2 Corinthians III.17," p. 311 n. 7.

[49]See Bultmann, *Second Letter to the Corinthians*, pp. 86-87, and Furnish, *II Corinthians*, p. 209.

[50]See Furnish, *II Corinthians*, p. 209; and Martin, *2 Corinthians*, p. 69.

[51]In 3:17 Paul probably gives his own interpretive gloss on his paraphrase of Exodus 34:34 in the previous verse. We might paraphrase Paul's thought this way: " 'Every time someone turns to the Lord, the veil is lifted.' Now 'the Lord' in this sentence for us means the Spirit." In other words, by the presence of the Spirit in the midst of the believing community and within each believer, believers' access to the Lord is as direct as that of Moses. See Barrett, *Second Epistle to the Corinthians*, pp. 122-23; Furnish, *II Corinthians*, p. 212; and especially Martin, *2 Corinthians*, pp. 73-74.

[52]Furnish, *II Corinthians*, pp. 237-38. It is true, as most commentators point out, that included within this "freedom" is freedom from the old covenant, but nothing within the text justifies Barrett's claim that Paul is speaking of freedom from "legalistically conceived religion" (*Second Epistle to the Corinthians*, p. 124). Paul's argument is not that the Mosaic administration was "legalistic" in Barrett's sense, nor that the law had been misused "legalistically" by Jews of Paul's time. It is rather that the law justly cursed those who transgressed its provisions, a point with which Jeremiah, Ezekiel and many subsequent Jews would have agreed.

[53]So, correctly, Räisänen, *Paul and the Law*, pp. 44-45, 56-57.

[54]Although it might at first glance seem that Paul says this explicitly in 3:14-16, in those verses he is not referring to the veiling of the proper interpretation of Scripture in general, but to the veiling of the insight that the Mosaic covenant is passing away. A denial that 2 Corinthians 3:6-18 contains an explicitly articulated hermeneutical theory, however, does not exclude the possibility that it implies a certain hermeneutical approach to the Old Testament. Hays develops this idea with two important differences (*Echoes of Scripture*, pp. 125, 146-51). First, he unpacks more hermeneutical freight from the "letter" side of the letter-Spirit antithesis than the above exegesis allows (*gramma* means the Mosaic covenant's impotence "to effect the obedience that it demands" [p. 131]), and second, he believes that the interpretive freedom that Paul applies to the Old Testament has implications for the way the church understands any scriptural text (compare Richardson, "Spirit and Letter," pp. 215-18.) Nevertheless, if Hays's general approach and the one articulated here are correct, then Paul's interpretation of Scripture and of the law in particular is considerably more thoughtful than E. P. Sanders (*Paul, the Law and the Jewish People* [Philadelphia: Fortress, 1983], pp. 160-62) and Räisänen (*Paul and the Law*, pp. 82-83) believe.

[55]On this, in addition to chapter two above, see van Unnik, "La nouvelle alliance," pp. 179-83.

Sanders (*Paul, the Law and the Jewish People,* pp. 138-39) believes that 2 Corinthians 3:10-18 reveals the chief problem that "plagues" Paul's statements about the Jewish law: that the law both kills and is glorious, that it is both abolished and continues to bear witness to Christ. Sanders believes that this confusion results from Paul's unsystematic approach to the law. Paul thought backwards from the gloriousness of Christ to the inferiority of the law but was left with the problem that God gave the law and it must therefore have been glorious. But if Jews of Paul's day acknowledged that the law justly measured out death to those who deserved it and that a new covenant would remedy this situation, then the pattern (if not the language) of Paul's thinking is similar to the Jewish pattern. Compare Thielman, *From Plight to Solution,* pp. 28-45.

[56]At least with respect to the stone imagery, Hafemann has shown this conclusively (*Suffering and the Spirit,* pp. 208-13).

[57]Morna Hooker argues that 2 Corinthians 3—4 illustrates "Paul's ambivalent attitude toward the law" ("Beyond the Things That Are Written? St. Paul's Use of Scripture," *New Testament Studies* 27 [1981]: 303-4, 306). The Mosaic covenant is abolished, but Scripture remains valid insofar as it points to Christ. Paul's positive stance toward the law, however, extends not simply to its role as a witness to Christ but to many of its particular commands as well.

[58]This is another point on which many Jews would have taken issue with Paul. See van Unnik, "La nouvelle alliance," pp. 189-91.

[59]The new covenant, to which Paul is probably referring when he uses the phrase *ennomos Christou* in 1 Corinthians 9:21, is in this sense a "new law." Sanders argues against such an interpretation on the basis that Paul offers no theoretical distinction between the law of Moses and some other law (*Paul, the Law and the Jewish People,* p. 102; compare pp. 103, 104-5, 113). Sanders believes instead that Paul possessed fundamentally Jewish convictions about moral, and occasionally cultic (as with idolatry), issues, and when called upon to adjudicate behavior, which occurred often in his correspondence with the Corinthians, he fell back on the Mosaic law itself and a Jewish system of repentance, reward and punishment (ibid., pp. 93-114). Nevertheless, in an unsystematic and ad hoc manner, Paul excised from the law any requirement that seemed to exclude the membership of Gentiles as Gentiles in the people of God. This approach does not take into account, however, the possibility that Paul's reference to "the law of Christ" in 9:21, the "new covenant" in 11:25, and the contrast of new covenant with old demonstrate a considered approach to the Mosaic law and to Scripture generally.

Chapter 6: The Law of Moses & the Law of Christ in Galatians

[1]Compare J. Christiaan Beker, *Paul the Apostle: The Triumph of God in Life and Thought* (Philadelphia: Fortress, 1980), p. 37.

[2]See E. P. Sanders, *Paul, the Law and the Jewish People* (Philadelphia: Fortress, 1983), pp. 3-4, 143-48; Heikki Räisänen, *Paul and the Law,* Wissenschaftliche Untersuchungen zum Neuen Testament 29 (Tübingen, Germany: J. C. B. Mohr/Paul Siebeck, 1983), pp. 256-63, 267; and Heikki Räisänen, *Jesus, Paul and Torah: Collected Essays, Journal for the Study of the New Testament* Supplement 43 (Sheffield, U.K.: Sheffield Academic Press, 1992), pp. 188-89. These statements summarize the positions of both scholars on Paul's view of the law in general, but Paul's statements on the law in Galatians have provided much of the evidence for their conclusions.

[3]Francis Watson, *Paul, Judaism and the Gentiles: A Sociological Approach* (Cambridge: Cambridge University Press, 1986), pp. 61-72, 177-78.

[4]See the statements of Sanders, *Paul, the Law and the Jewish People,* p. 148; Räisänen, *Paul and the Law,* pp. 266-69; and Watson, *Paul, Judaism and the Gentiles,* pp. 180-81. Again, these summary statements are based in large measure on each scholar's reading of Galatians.

[5]On using the text of Galatians itself to reconstruct the situation to which the letter was addressed, see John M. G. Barclay, "Mirror-Reading a Polemical Letter: Galatians as a Test Case," *Journal for the Study of the New Testament* 31 (1987): 73-93, and John M. G. Barclay, *Obeying*

the Truth: A Study of Paul's Ethics in Galatians (Edinburgh: T & T Clark, 1988), pp. 37-41. Barclay is more optimistic than George Lyons (*Pauline Autobiography: Toward a New Understanding*, Society of Biblical Literature Dissertation Series 73 [Atlanta: Scholars Press, 1985], p. 96) about mining information on Paul's opposition from the letter, but is aware of the problems that can arise from the circular reasoning that "mirror-reading" inevitably involves.

[6]"Weakness of the flesh" (compare "your trial in my flesh" in 4:14) probably refers to an illness or other physical disability. See Richard N. Longenecker, *Galatians*, Word Biblical Commentary 41 (Dallas: Word, 1990), pp. 190-91.

[7]Although the contrast between Paul's references to the agitators in the third person and his references to the Galatians in the second person indicates that the agitators came from outside, nothing indicates their place of origin. The vagueness of Paul's language in 1:7, 3:1, 5:7 and 5:10 may mean that he was uninformed on this point. See Barclay, *Obeying the Truth*, pp. 43-44, especially n. 18, and Christopher D. Stanley, " 'Under a Curse': A Fresh Reading of Galatians 3.10-14," *New Testament Studies* 36 (1990): 489.

[8]It is sometimes said that since Paul argues primarily against the Galatians' acceptance of circumcision (5:3) and the Jewish calendar (4:10), and because 5:3 and 6:13 seem to accuse the Galatians and Paul's opponents of being unwilling to observe the whole law, the opponents were not trying to compel complete conformity to the Jewish law. For a survey of the scholarship on this issue together with convincing reasons for the understanding of the situation adopted here, see Barclay, *Obeying the Truth*, pp. 60-65, and "Mirror-Reading," p. 86.

[9]On the important role that circumcision played in the conversion of Jewish proselytes, see Paula Fredriksen, "Judaism, the Circumcision of Gentiles and Apocalyptic Hope: Another Look at Galatians 1 and 2," *Journal of Theological Studies* n.s. 42 (1991): 532-64, especially 536 n. 11.

[10]See the reconstructions of the agitator's position in Beker, *Paul the Apostle*, pp. 43-44; Barclay, "Mirror-Reading," pp. 86-90; and Longenecker, *Galatians*, p. xcvii.

[11]It is true, as Hans Dieter Betz says (*Galatians: A Commentary on Paul's Letter to the Churches in Galatia*, Hermeneia [Philadelphia: Fortress, 1979], p. 156), that in 3:16-17 the terms *covenant* and *seed* are coordinated in a way reminiscent of Genesis 17:1-11, but the same coordination appears in Genesis 15:18.

[12]Compare Barclay, *Obeying the Truth*, pp. 53-55; Longenecker, *Galatians*, p. xcvii; and Frank J. Matera, *Galatians*, Sacra Pagina 9 (Collegeville, Minn.: Liturgical Press, 1992), p. 9.

[13]See Johannes Munck, *Paul and the Salvation of Mankind* (Atlanta: John Knox, 1959), pp. 87-89, 130-34. Munck focuses on the middle voice of *peritemnomenoi* in 6:13.

[14]See Robert Jewett, *Paul's Anthropological Terms: A Study of Their Use in Conflict Settings*, Arbeiten zur Geschichte des Antiken Judentums und des Urchristentums 10 (Leiden, Netherlands: Brill, 1971), pp. 19-20, and "The Agitators and the Galatian Congregation," *New Testament Studies* 17 (1971): 198-212, especially pp. 204-6. Jewett focuses on Paul's statement in 6:12 that the agitators seek to avoid persecution.

[15]Walter Schmithals (*Paul and the Gnostics* [Nashville: Abingdon, 1972], pp. 32-43) focuses on both Paul's claim in 6:12 that the agitators seek to avoid persecution and his claim in 6:13 that they do not themselves keep the law.

[16]That Paul endured the punishment at all, however, shows that he did not believe the gospel and the religion of the synagogue to be discontinuous. "Punishment," as Sanders says, "implies inclusion" (*Paul, the Law and the Jewish People*, p. 192). Fredriksen argues that Jewish persecution of Christianity was motivated by the Jewish Christian proclamation of the soon-coming kingdom to Gentiles who might, through this politically volatile message, destroy the positive but delicate relationship between Judaism and Rome ("Judaism, the Circumcision of Gentiles," pp. 548-58). Little explicit evidence exists, however, that the early Christian message was as consumed with the immediate establishment of the kingdom as Fredriksen thinks. If Paul, for example, was so eschatologically oriented that he sought (in a way reminiscent of Albert

Schweitzer's Jesus) "to inaugurate the Endtime" by bringing a Gentile into the temple (p. 564), then why, just prior to this event, did he plan a leisurely trip to Spain (Rom 16:28)? It is more likely that Paul received synagogue discipline because his position on the Mosaic law implied the inclusion of uncircumcised but believing Gentiles and the exclusion of unbelieving but circumcised Jews. Synagogues that did not follow the kind of logic present in Galatians would surely find such a view sectarian and socially disruptive. The result would be persecution. See Martin Hengel, *The Pre-Christian Paul* (London: SCM Press/Philadelphia: Trinity Press International, 1991), p. 80.

[17]Perhaps Paul's opponents took advantage of his policy of becoming like one who lives under the law to those under the law (1 Cor 9:20) and of his conviction that circumcision in itself was not evil (1 Cor 7:18-19; Gal 5:6; 6:15) to claim that Paul preached circumcision when it was convenient to do so but not when it did not suit his purposes. So Betz, *Galatians,* pp. 268-69 (with hesitance); M.-J. Lagrange, *Saint Paul Épître aux Galates* (Paris: Librairie Lecoffre, 1950), 141; F. F. Bruce, *The Epistle to the Galatians: A Commentary on the Greek Text,* New International Greek Testament Commentary (Grand Rapids, Mich.: Eerdmans, 1982), pp. 236-37; Ronald Y. K. Fung, *The Epistle to the Galatians,* New International Commentary on the New Testament (Grand Rapids, Mich.: Eerdmans, 1988), p. 240; Longenecker, *Galatians,* pp. 232-33; Matera, *Galatians,* p. 191. Herman N. Ridderbos (*The Epistle of Paul to the Churches of Galatia,* New International Commentary on the New Testament [Grand Rapids, Mich.: Eerdmans, 1953], pp. 193-94) believes that Paul is speaking hypothetically.

[18]See Barclay, *Obeying the Truth,* pp. 58-59. Many commentators, however, take 4:17 to refer to the agitators' exclusion of the Galatians from the gospel of God's grace. See J. B. Lightfoot, *Saint Paul's Epistle to the Galatians,* 10th ed. (London: Macmillan, 1890), p. 177, and Ernest de Witt Burton, *A Critical and Exegetical Commentary on the Epistle to the Galatians,* International Critical Commentary (Edinburgh: T & T Clark, 1921), p. 246. Others believe that the verse refers to exclusion from fellowship with Paul and those who follow his gospel. See Lagrange, *Saint Paul Épître,* p. 116; Bruce, *Epistle to the Galatians,* p. 211; Fung, *Epistle to the Galatians,* p. 200; Longenecker, *Galatians,* pp. 193-94; Matera, *Galatians,* pp. 165-66.

[19]The terms *justification* and its cognates *justify* and *just* have prompted enormous controversy. Do they refer to an imputed status (the classic Protestant position), an imparted ability to act morally (the classic Roman Catholic position) or both equally (the position, for example, of Karl Kertelge, "δικαιοσύνη," in *Exegetical Dictionary of the New Testament,* ed. H. Balz and G. Schneider, 3 vols. [Grand Rapids, Mich.: Eerdmans, 1990-1993], 1:326-30)? Do they refer primarily to legal innocence (the classic Protestant position) or a covenantal relationship (the position, for example, of N. T. Wright, *The New Testament and the People of God* [Minneapolis: Fortress, 1992], pp. 271-72)? James D. G. Dunn believes that Luther and many of his Protestant followers focused too narrowly on the justification of the individual and thereby impoverished the church of the doctrine's social implications ("The Justice of God: A Renewed Perspective on Justification by Faith," *Journal of Theological Studies* 43 [1992]: 1-22). Compare Krister Stendahl, *Paul Among Jews and Gentiles* (Philadelpia: Fortress, 1976), pp. 23-40. Galatians certainly provides evidence for the social dimensions of Paul's understanding of justification: the subject of the letter is, after all, the inclusion of uncircumcised Gentiles within the people of God. Nevertheless, as Paul argues this point he often applies justification language to the individual believer (2:16, 21; 3:6, 11), and by associating righteousness with grace and eschatological judgment in Galatians (2:21; 5:4-5) he implies, as the Reformers argued, that justification provides believers with an alien righteousness necessary for acquittal on the last day (5:5).

[20]Betz believes that in 3:22 Paul distinguishes between Scripture and law because he cannot assign to the law a positive role in salvation (*Galatians,* p. 175). Matera claims that "Scripture" in this verse is synonymous with "God" (*Galatians,* p. 175). But when Paul uses the term *scripture* with the definite article, as he does in 3:22, he customarily has in mind a certain passage of

Scripture. Here he probably looks back to his quotation of the law (Deut 27:26) in Galatians 3:10 in order to show that all have sinned and are therefore under the law's curse. See Lightfoot, *Saint Paul's Epistle to the Galatians*, pp. 147-48; Bruce, *Epistle to the Galatians*, p. 180; and Longenecker, *Galatians*, p. 144.

[21]It is not correct, then, to say with Albert Schweitzer (*The Mysticism of Paul the Apostle* [New York: Seabury, 1931], p. 295; followed with some reservations by E. P. Sanders, *Paul and Palestinian Judaism: A Comparison of Patterns of Religion* [Philadelphia: Fortress, 1977], pp. 438-40) that Paul derives his ethical teaching not from his convictions about justification by faith but from his understanding of participation in Christ. Galatians 2:11-21 is clear evidence that for Paul justification implied showing love for one's neighbor and so fulfilling the law of Christ. Compare Barclay, *Obeying the Truth*, pp. 223-25.

[22]Compare Barclay, *Obeying the Truth*, pp. 76-83, 108, 118.

[23]A whirlwind of controversy swirls around the phrase "works of the law." Some believe that it refers to the Jewish misuse of the Mosaic law. Some believe that it refers to the attempt to achieve salvation by keeping the law regardless of whether the law can be kept (for example, Rudolf Bultmann, *Theology of the New Testament*, 2 vols. [New York: Scribner's, 1951-1955], 1:263-64). Still others believe that it denotes a nationalistic misuse of the law to exclude Gentiles from the people of God (for example, James D. G. Dunn, *Jesus, Paul and the Law: Studies in Mark and Galatians* [Louisville, Ky.: Westminster/John Knox, 1990], pp. 4, 191-94, 219-25). Occasionally scholars argue that the phrase refers to the law's disastrous effects (for example, Lloyd Gaston, *Paul and the Torah* [Vancouver: University of British Columbia Press, 1987], pp. 100-106). Paul's claim in 2:16 that no "flesh" can be justified by works of the law, however, and his argument in 3:10 that a curse falls on those who fail to comply with all the law's stipulations show that the phrase simply means "the works that the law requires." His claim that justification could not come through doing the works that the law requires, moreover, was an uncomplicated claim that no flesh, whether Israelite or Gentile, had obeyed the law. See Frank Thielman, *From Plight to Solution: A Jewish Framework for Understanding Paul's View of the Law in Romans and Galatians*, Supplements to *Novum Testamentum* 61 (Leiden, Netherlands: Brill, 1989), pp. 60-65; Stephen Westerholm, *Israel's Law and the Church's Faith* (Grand Rapids, Mich.: Eerdmans, 1988), pp. 109-21; and Thomas R. Schreiner, *The Law and Its Fulfillment: A Pauline Theology of Law* (Grand Rapids, Mich.: Baker Book House, 1993), pp. 58-59.

[24]The term *flesh* appears already in descriptions of circumcision in Genesis 17:11-14, Leviticus 12:3 and Ezekiel 44:7, 9. Robert Jewett (*Paul's Anthropological Terms: A Study of Their Use in Conflict Settings*, Arbeiten zur Geschichte des antiken Judentums und des Urchristentums 10 [Leiden, Netherlands: Brill, 1971], pp. 95-98) is probably right, therefore, to see in Paul's use of the term in Galatians a polemic against his opponents' interest in circumcising the flesh (see especially 6:12-13). Paul can, moreover, use the term to refer simply to "humanity in contrast to God" (Gal 1:16) and "human life" (2:20). In other places, however, *flesh* clearly connotes human frailty (4:13-14) in a way reminiscent of the Old Testament, the Dead Sea Scrolls and Philo, and the seat of human desire in a way reminiscent of Epicurus and his detractors (5:24; compare 5:16-17). See Eduard Schweizer, "σάρξ," in *Theological Dictionary of the New Testament*, ed. Gerhard Kittel and Gerhard Friedrich, 10 vols. (Grand Rapids, Mich.: Eerdmans, 1971), 7:103-14, 121-23; Walter Bauer, *A Greek-English Lexicon of the New Testament and Other Early Christian Literature*, trans. and aug. William Arndt, F. Wilbur Gingrich and Frederick Danker, 2nd ed. (Chicago: University of Chicago Press, 1979), s.v.; and Barclay, *Obeying the Truth*, pp. 185-91. In Galatians, as Barclay observes (*Obeying the Truth*, p. 204; compare Jewett, *Paul's Anthropological Terms*, p. 96), Paul probably exploits these widely diverse and widely recognized semantic connotations to link the physical rite of circumcision, and through it the entire Mosaic law, with the human tendency to sin.

[25]Rudolf Bultmann claims (in *Theology*, 1:232-46, and *Primitive Christianity in Its Contemporary*

Setting [New York: World, 1956], pp. 192-93) that *flesh* in Paul refers to "the sphere of the humanly natural and transitory" (*Theology*, 1:238), not in any fundamental sense to that which inevitably leads humanity into disobedience against God. Life lived according to the flesh, says Bultmann, is sinful in Paul's view because it attempts to attain life without God. This attempt can take the path of the classic sins of the flesh or the path of thinking that by keeping the law or being wise by the standards of the world one can attain life by oneself. Paul's use of the term in Galatians 3:3, says Bultmann, provides evidence that this understanding of his use of *flesh* is correct. See also W. David Stacey, *The Pauline View of Man* (London: Macmillan, 1956), pp. 164-65. Paul's use of the term in 2:16, however, weighs against Bultmann's thesis, since in this verse, as we have seen, the problem is not with an attempt to keep the law in order to be justified but with a stubborn refusal to recognize that the law has not been kept. If these connotations are present in the use of the term in 3:3 as well, then in that verse Paul is stating his amazement that the Galatians are abandoning the era of God's eschatological restoration of his people to step back into the era dominated by the human inability to obey God.

[26]We can assume that the Galatians were more familiar with the Hebrew Scriptures than most Gentiles not only because they were on the verge of becoming Jewish proselytes but because Paul himself, in his original work among them, probably taught them much about the Bible. Where Paul seems to echo the content of his missionary preaching in his letters, the "symbolic world" of the Hebrew Scriptures plays a significant role (Rom 1:2-4; 1 Thess 1:9).

[27]Although this is the view of most scholars (including Bultmann, *Theology*, 1:263), a significant minority do not believe that it is correct. Heinrich Schlier takes the verse to mean that a curse lies on those who ground their existence in the law by striving to achieve life through obedience to it (*Der Brief an die Galater*, 11th ed., Kritisch-exegetischer Kommentar über das Neue Testament 7 [Göttingen, Germany: Vandenhoeck & Ruprecht, 1949], pp. 89-90). Sanders takes the verse and its citation as an ad hoc argument constructed only on terminological grounds (*Paul, the Law and the Jewish People*, pp. 21-22). Thus Paul cites the only passage in the Septuagint that mentions the law in the same breath with the curse and therefore the only possible biblical counterbalance to his claim in 3:8 that Gentile believers are blessed. Paul chose the verse not because of what it meant, Sanders says, but because it contained the right terms. Dunn understands Paul to be saying that the Judaizers violate the law by their nationalistic use of it and so fall under the law's curse (*Paul, the Law and the Jewish People*, pp. 226-27). Stanley claims that 3:10 says only that those who undertake the law *might* not do it and *might* therefore be cursed ("'Under a Curse,'" pp. 481-511). Paul's point is that the Galatians are unwise to take the risk of disobedience and curse.

These explanations, however, are not convincing. Schlier ignores the *not* in the quotation: the curse falls on those who disobey the law, not on those who obey it. Sanders, as Stanley comments ("'Under a Curse,'" p. 485), does not recognize that the curse is not merely a fortuitously negative counterbalance to the blessing of faith but the reason for Christ's death (3:13). Dunn's thesis depends on an implausible limitation of the meaning of the phrases "from works of the law" and "in the law" in 3:10-11 to a misuse of the law. Finally, Stanley's reading cannot account for the definitive nature of the curse from which Christ has redeemed (*exēgorasen*) believers. This curse is not, according to 3:13, merely a possibility but a reality for those who expect justification from the Mosaic law. For a particularly lucid discussion of the exegetical issues in this passage, see Thomas R. Schreiner, "Is Perfect Obedience to the Law Possible? A Re-examination of Galatians 3:10," *Journal of the Evangelical Theological Society* 27 (1984): 151-60, and Schreiner, *Law and Its Fulfillment*, pp. 44-59.

[28]Compare Martin Noth, *The Laws of the Pentateuch and Other Studies* (Edinburgh: Oliver & Boyd, 1966), pp. 108-17. Noth, however, misunderstood this section to be a description only of Israel's plight as a result of disobedience. In Deuteronomy 30:1-5 and 32:36-43 Moses also predicts that God will redeem his people from their plight, a theme Paul echoes in his quotation of Habakkuk 2:4 in Galatians 3:11. See N. T. Wright, *The Climax of the Covenant: Christ*

and the Law in Pauline Theology (Edinburgh: T & T Clark, 1991), p. 146, especially n. 31.

[29]See Thielman, *From Plight to Solution*, pp. 65-72, and Wright, *Climax*, pp. 144-48.

[30]See Thielman, *From Plight to Solution*, pp. 65-72; Wright, *Climax*, pp. 144-51, and especially Schreiner, *Law and Its Fulfillment*, 47-50. If this understanding of Paul's argument is accurate, then Hans Hübner and Sanders are each partially correct in their interpretation of the verse. Hübner is right to accept the majority position that Paul argues for the unfulfillability of the law here (*Law in Paul's Thought*, Studies of the New Testament and Its World [Edinburgh: T & T Clark, 1984], pp. 18-20) but wrong to claim that this position reflects the peculiar view of the school of Shammai in which Paul was educated (ibid., p. 44 n. 16). Sanders is right to deny that Jews believed that membership in the covenant required perfect obedience to the law (*Paul, the Law and the Jewish People*, p. 28) but wrong to deny that Paul believed the law to be unfulfillable (ibid., pp. 17-29). Most Jews knew that the law should be kept and that repentance and atonement were available for those who did not keep it. They also knew, however, that Israel lived under the law's curse because the covenant had been broken. Many apparently believed that their own sins had contributed to this condition (Dan 9:20; Baruch 2:8). Although means of atonement for sin were available to them, then, they nevertheless awaited God's redemption as a final remedy to the plight of sin and curse.

[31]The grammatical possiblility of taking the verse this way is mentioned by Burton (*Critical and Exegetical Commentary on the Epistle to the Galatians*, p. 166) and fully discussed by Hermann Hanse ("ΔΗΛΟΝ [Zu Gal 3.11])," *Zeitschrift für die neutestamentliche Wissenschaft* 34 (1935): 299-303. N. T. Wright first suggested to me in private conversation that the verse could be taken this way. See now Wright, *Climax*, p. 149 n. 42.

[32]There are three important differences between this passage in the Masoretic text and its rendering in the Septuagint: (1) In the Masoretic text the Lord tells Habakkuk to write the prophecy in characters large enough that even someone rushing by on the run could read it, whereas in the Septuagint Habakkuk is instructed to write visions on a courier's tablet so that he might run with the message to its destination, (2) in the Masoretic text the vision of God's deliverance, although it tarries, will surely come, but in the Septuagint this vision becomes an individual for whom the faithful are to wait, and (3) the ambiguous statement that "the righteous shall live by his faith" becomes in one manuscript tradition of the Septuagint "the righteous shall live by my faith," and in another "my righteous one shall live by faith."

[33]In Galatians 3:1 Paul describes his own preaching among the Galatians as the portrayal of Christ crucified. He then asks rhetorically in 3:2 whether the Galatians received the Spirit by works of the law or, literally, "by the preaching of faith" (*ex akoēs pisteōs*, cf. 3:5). The term translated "preaching" (*akoēs*) can mean "the act of hearing" as well as "account, report, preaching" (Bauer, *Greek-English Lexicon*, s.v.). Since Paul has just described his preaching among the Galatians in graphic terms in 3:1, and since his language is probably modeled on Isaiah 53:1 ("Lord, who has believed our report *[akoē]*"; compare Rom 10:16), it is likely that the *akoēs* of 3:2 refers to the act of Paul's preaching. See Schlier, *Brief an die Galater*, p. 81; Bruce, *Epistle to the Galatians*, p. 149; and Richard B. Hays, *The Faith of Jesus Christ: An Investigation of the Narrative Substructure of Galatians 3:1—4:11*, Society of Biblical Literature Dissertation Series 56 (Chico, Calif.: Scholars Press, 1983), pp. 146-48. *Pisteōs* probably refers to the response that Paul's preaching demanded (see Bauer, *Greek-English Lexicon*, s.v. 2b; Schlier, *Brief an die Galater*, p. 82; Sanders, *Paul and Palestinian Judaism*, p. 482; Bruce, *Epistle to the Galatians*, p. 149; and Longenecker, *Galatians*, p. 103), although faith and the gospel, its object, are so closely tied together for Paul that he can refer to the gospel as "the faith" (1:23; 3:14, 23 [2x], 25, 26).

[34]Paul may refer to Jews alone or to both Jews and Gentiles when he uses the first person in 3:13 and 4:5. Bruce (*Epistle to the Galatians*, 166-67), Fung (*Epistle to the Galatians*, pp. 148-49) and Longenecker (*Galatians*, p. 121) claim that the first-person references refer to both groups, and Burton, *Critical and Exegetical Commentary on the Epistle to the Galatians*, p. 169), Lagrange (*Saint Paul Épître*, p. 71), Matera (*Galatians*, p. 120), T. L. Donaldson ("The 'Curse of the Law'

and the Inclusion of the Gentiles: Galatians 3:13-14," *New Testament Studies* 32 [1986]: 94-112) and Wright (*Climax*, pp. 151-52) believe that they refer only to Jews. If Paul was thinking in Deuteronomic terms in this passage, then the first-person references must refer primarily to Israel, but along with most other Jews of his day, he would have assumed that if Israel stood under the law's curse the Gentiles could surely fare no better. Thus the "everyone" (*pas*) in his quotation of Deuteronomy 27:26 in 3:10 and the statement that Scripture enclosed "all things *[ta panta]* under sin" in 4:22 should be understood literally to refer not simply to the Jews but to all people.

[35]See Thielman, *From Plight to Solution*, pp. 70-72, and Wright, *Climax*, pp. 148-51.

[36]Fredriksen observes that hanging on a tree did not itself bring the curse of God either in Deuteronomy 21:23 or in popular Jewish thought during Paul's time ("Judaism, the Circumcision of Gentiles," pp. 551-52). Instead, the curse attached to the crime for which the criminal was hung. Paul, she believes, ignored this distinction and employed Deuteronomy 21:23 for rhetorical reasons. This reading of 3:13, however, misses the point of 3:10-14. Paul's primary point is not the correspondence between Jesus' crucifixion and the mention of hanging in Deuteronomy 21:23, although he probably found that interesting, but in an innocent Messiah's bearing the curse justly pronounced by the law on a guilty Israel. Compare Wright, *Climax*, pp. 151-53.

[37]Compare Donaldson, " 'Curse of the Law,' " pp. 105-6; Wright, *Climax*, pp. 151-55.

[38]On the inclusion of the Gentiles in the final redemption of Israel, see Isaiah 2:2-4; 25:6-10; 56:6-8 (compare 42:6-7); Micah 4:1-4; and Zechariah 8:20-23 (compare Tobit 13:3; 14:5-7; *1 Enoch* 90:30, 33; 91:14; *Psalms of Solomon* 17:31; *Sibylline Oracles* 3:710-23) and the discussions in Donaldson, " 'Curse of the Law,' " pp. 99-100, 110 n. 49, and Fredriksen, "Judaism, the Circumcision of Gentiles," pp. 544-45. On the place of the Spirit in Israel's eschatological restoration see Ezekiel 11:19; 36:26-27; 37:1-14 (compare 18:31; *Jubilees* 1:21, 23).

[39]Many older commentators interpreted Paul's death to the law as a consequence of his inability to keep it, but they generally failed to connect the verse with 3:10. See Martin Luther, *LW* 26:159; John Calvin, *Comm. Gal.* 2:19; William Perkins, *A Commentary on Galatians* (orig. ed. 1617; reprint New York: Pilgrim, 1989), p. 119; Lightfoot, *Saint Paul's Epistle to the Galatians*, p. 118. Compare the more recent comments of Ridderbos, *Epistle of Paul to the Churches of Galatia*, pp. 103-4. Modern commentators usually interpret 2:19 as a condensed form of Paul's statements on death with Christ and to the law in Rom 6:1-11 and 7:1-6 and miss the connection between 2:19 and 3:10. See Lagrange, *Saint Paul Épître*, p. 51; Bruce, *Epistle to the Galatians*, pp. 143-44; and Fung, *Epistle to the Galatians*, pp. 122-23. Franz Mußner recognizes that Paul's inability to do the law and the law's inability to give life to those who disobey it are at issue in 2:19, but he does not bring 3:10 into the discussion (*Der Galaterbrief*, Herders theologischer Kommentar zum Neuen Testament 9 [Freiburg, Germany: Herder, 1974] pp. 179-80).

[40]Compare Hübner, *Law*, p. 153; Räisänen, *Paul and the Law*, p. 95. Some commentators believe that 5:3 implies only that keeping the law is difficult and that, even if kept in its entirety, it is the wrong way to justification (Bruce, *Epistle to the Galatians*, p. 231; Matera, *Galatians*, p. 189). Sanders claims that if Paul implies the unfullfillability of the law in 5:3 as a reason for saying that the law cannot justify (5:4), he ignores the universal Jewish beliefs that the law could be adequately kept and that repentance and atonement were available for those who fell short (*Paul, the Law and the Jewish People*, pp. 27-29; compare Samuel Sandmel, *Judaism and Christian Beginnings* [New York: Oxford University Press, 1978], p. 320). Sanders goes on to argue that Paul is simply reminding the Galatians that if they undertake circumcision they must accept the Jewish way of life in its entirety, something that Paul's opponents may not have yet told them. Galatians 5:3 and 3:10, however, should be interpreted within the same context. In neither does Paul deny that repentance and atonement are available for those who transgress the law; instead he assumes, with many Jews of his time, that Israel has transgressed the law,

stands under its curse and must therefore rely on God's eschatological intervention for justification.

[41] Hübner, *Law,* p. 109; Räisänen, *Paul and the Law,* p. 96; Longenecker, *Galatians,* p. 293. Sanders believes that in 6:13 Paul exploits the quandary in which Jewish Christians like Peter found themselves when socializing with Gentile believers: they wanted to keep the law themselves and lead Gentile believers into observance of it, but doing this sometimes involved relaxing their own observance (*Paul, the Law and the Jewish People,* p. 23). If the understanding of 3:10 and 5:3 presented here is correct, however, the most obvious interpretation of 6:13 is simply that Paul's opponents were acting as if the law could be kept when, in fact, it could not.

[42] This seems to have been the conclusion of the Qumran covenanters. See, for example, 1QS V, where those who enter the community are required to repent and keep all the commandments of the law of Moses.

[43] On the possibility that fear of slipping into idolatry through too much association with Gentiles stood behind the dispute in Antioch, see E. P. Sanders, "Jewish Association with Gentiles and Galatians 2:11-14," in *The Conversation Continues: Studies in Paul and John in Honor of J. Louis Martyn,* ed. Robert T. Fortna and Beverly R. Gaventa (Nashville: Abingdon, 1990), p. 186.

[44] Some interpreters believe that Paul begins a new section of his argument with 3:7 rather than 3:6. On this reading, 3:6 briefly mentions that the Galatians' faith is analogous to the faith of Abraham and, by mentioning Abraham, opens the way for Paul's argument that believers are recipients of the promises to Abraham because they are both "in" him (3:8) and "in" his seed (3:16), who is Christ (3:29). It is best to view 3:6 as a transitional verse, closing the argument of 3:1-5 and introducing the argument of 3:7-29. Such transitions are typical of Paul's method. For a list of examples from Romans, see Nils Alstrup Dahl, *Studies in Paul* (Minneapolis: Augsburg, 1977), pp. 82-83.

[45] Hays (*Faith of Jesus Christ,* pp. 196-212) followed by Donaldson (" 'Curse of the Law,' " pp. 101-2) believes that Paul does not compare the faith of the believing Galatians with the faith of Abraham in 3:6-9 but that in 3:6-9, as in 3:8, 14, 16, 29, Paul asserts that believers are "in Abraham." The link between the phrase "the preaching of faith" in 3:5 (compare 3:2) and Paul's quotation of Genesis 15:6 in 3:6, however, is the semantic similarity between the noun *faith (pistis)* and the verb *believe (pisteuō).* This semantic link shows that Paul's interest in 3:6 is the correspondence between Abraham's faith and that of the Gentile Galatians.

[46] Compare Lagrange, *Saint Paul Épître,* p. 94; Ridderbos, *Epistle of Paul to the Churches of Galatia,* p. 150; Mußner, *Galaterbrief,* p. 266; Betz, *Galatians,* p. 201; Matera, *Galatians,* pp. 143, 147.

[47] Paul uses the singular *promise* (3:17, 18, 22, 29) and the plural *promises* interchangeably (3:16, 21) when speaking of God's commitment to Abraham. See Longenecker, *Galatians,* pp. 130-31.

[48] See the thorough discussion in ibid., pp. 138-39.

[49] See especially Burton, *Critical and Exegetical Commentary on the Epistle to the Galatians,* pp. 195-96, and Luther, *LW* 26:332. Compare Schlier, *Brief an die Galater,* pp. 121-22; Lagrange, *Saint Paul Épître,* p. 88; Ridderbos, *Epistle of Paul to the Churches of Galatia,* pp. 141-42; Mußner, *Galaterbrief,* pp. 252-53; and Fung, *Epistle to the Galatians,* pp. 164-65.

[50] See Norman H. Young, "*PAIDAGOGOS:* The Social Setting of a Pauline Metaphor," *Novum Testamentum* 29 (1987): 156.

[51] David J. Lull believes that the point of comparison between the law and the pedagogue for Paul was that they both restrained those under them from sin (" 'The Law Was Our Pedagogue': A Study in Galatians 3:19-25," *Journal of Biblical Literature* 105 [1986]: 481-98). Young believes that Paul uses the metaphor to evoke notions of the law's restrictive guardianship of God's people, a restrictiveness now removed by the influx of Gentiles into the church ("*PAIDAGOGOS,*" pp. 170-73). T. David Gordon argues that a positive guardianship, or protective role, is in view ("A Note on ΠΑΙΔΑΓΩΓΟΣ in Galatians 3.24-25," *New Testament Studies* 35 [1989]: 153-54). Older commentators, such as Calvin (*Comm. Gal.* 3:24) and Perkins (*Commentary on Galatians,* p. 200) believed that the pedagogue's role as a teacher was uppermost in Paul's mind. Fung claims

that the law's role of enclosing humanity under sin is primarily in view (*Epistle to the Galatians*, p. 169).

[52]On this aspect of the pedagogue's role, see Young, "*PAIDAGOGOS,*" pp. 160-63.

[53]Compare ibid., pp. 174-75, and Gordon, "Note on ΠΑΙΔΑΓΩΓΟΣ," pp. 152-53.

[54]In 3:19-20 Paul probably intends to show that the law was mediated through both angels and Moses and therefore does not represent God's direct dealings with his people. Because it is an indirect way of dealing with God's people, Paul seems to say, the law does not perfectly reflect the unity of God. This in turn implies that the law does not constitute God's permanent means of relating to his people. See Longenecker, *Galatians*, pp. 141-42.

[55]The Greek phrase is *eis Christon*. In this instance, according to Bauer, *Greek-English Lexicon*, s.v. εἰς, the preposition "indicates the time up to which something continues."

[56]Compare Longenecker, *Galatians*, p. 151.

[57]Paul is using conventional language here in a way that shows that his argument in 4:1-6 continues the themes of 3:24-25. As Young has shown ("*PAIDAGOGOS,*" p. 155), the term *epitropos* ("guardian") which Paul uses in 4:2 was sometimes coupled in ancient literature with the term *paidagōgos* when the two terms were used metaphorically. Paul is probably doing much the same in 3:24-25 and 4:1-7. Compare Longenecker, *Galatians*, pp. 162-63; Matera, *Galatians*, p. 153.

[58]A vigorous debate has raged for centuries over the meaning of the phrases "elements of the world" (*stoicheia tou kosmou*, 4:3; cf. Col 2:8 and 20) and "weak and poverty-stricken elements" (*asthenē kai ptōcha stoicheia*, 4:9). Although a wide variety of interpretations have been defended, they fall basically into two categories: (1) those that argue for some connection between the elements and supernatural beings and (2) those that argue that the phrase refers only to elementary stages of development. See Burton, *Critical and Exegetical Commentary on the Epistle to the Galatians*, pp. 510-18, and Matera, *Galatians*, pp. 149, 155. Since the evidence for a connection between "the elements" and supernatural beings is later than the New Testament, explanations that fall into the second category are probably nearer Paul's meaning. See Burton, *Critical and Exegetical Commentary on the Epistle to the Galatians*, pp. 516-18; Gerhard Delling, "στοιχεῖον," in *Theological Dictionary of the New Testament*, ed. Gerhard Kittel and Gerhard Friedrich, 10 vols. (Grand Rapids, Mich.: Eerdmans, 1971), 7:670-87; Matera, *Galatians*, p. 150; *contra* Räisänen, *Paul and the Law*, p. 22 n. 41. In 4:3, where Paul claims that when he and other Jews lived under the law they lived under "the elements of the world," he means simply that in light of the gospel, the law is the "ABCs of religion" (compare Heb 5:12). When he speaks of the Gentile Galatians' former religious practices in 4:8, however, he qualifies the term in a more negative way as "the weak and poverty-stricken ABCs of religion." By making an idol out of the law, then, the Galatians were making the good law, which God had used for his saving purposes among the Jews, equivalent to the idolatrous practices of their own rudimentary religion. Räisänen's claim in *Paul and the Law* (p. 23) that Paul's argument in 4:1-11 logically implies that the former idolatry of the Galatians must, like the Jewish law for the Jews, have been a guardian, steward and tutor of the Gentiles unto Christ—a conclusion from which Paul would recoil—does not recognize the historical dimensions of Paul's argument. The law changes status in Paul's thinking from a positive element in God's redemptive purpose to something that, like an idol, can receive the devotion that belongs to God alone.

[59]See Raymond E. Brown and John P. Meier, *Antioch and Rome: New Testament Cradles of Catholic Christianity* (New York: Paulist, 1983), p. 121. Compare Beker, *Paul the Apostle*, p. 73.

[60]Compare T. J. Deidun, *New Covenant Morality in Paul*, Analecta Biblica 89 (Rome: Biblical Institute Press, 1981), p. 49.

[61]See also ibid., p. 49 n. 158; Deidun observes that not only does 4:6 echo the promise of the Spirit in Ezekiel 36:27 but the theme of knowing God and being known by him in 4:9 is probably indebted to Jeremiah 31:34.

[62]In addition see Micah 7:15, Isaiah 35:6, 41:18, 43:19-20 and 48:21, and the discussion of these texts in Joseph Klausner, *The Messianic Idea in Israel from Its Beginning to the Completion of the Mishnah* (London: George Allen & Unwin, 1956), pp. 63, 74, 97-98, 122-23, 159.

[63]Compare also Deuteronomy 9:16 LXX^A. See Mußner, *Galaterbrief,* p. 53 n. 54, and Longenecker, *Galatians,* p. 14.

[64]Compare 1 Corinthians 10:1-14.

[65]Martin W. Schoenberg, "St. Paul's Notion on the Adoptive Sonship of Christians," *The Thomist* 28 (1964): 53-54. Compare James M. Scott, *Adoption as Sons of God: An Exegetical Investigation into the Background of* ΥΙΟΘΕΣΙΑ *in the Pauline Corpus,* Wissenschaftliche Untersuchungen zum Neuen Testament ser. 2, no. 48 (Tübingen, Germany: J. C. B. Mohr/Paul Siebeck, 1992), pp. 148-49.

[66]See James I. Cook, "The Concept of Adoption in the Theology of Paul," in *Saved by Hope: Essays in Honor of Richard C. Oudersluys,* ed. James I. Cook (Grand Rapids, Mich.: Eerdmans, 1978), pp. 133-44, and Scott, *Adoption as Sons,* pp. 121-86. Paul probably has the status of Israelites as "sons of God" (Ex 4:22-23; *Psalms of Solomon* 17:27; *Jubilees* 1:24-25) in mind also when he describes the Galatians with this phrase in 3:26. See Matera, *Galatians,* pp. 141, 144-45.

[67]Compare Josephus *Antiquities* 4.190.

[68]C. K. Barrett points out that when Paul begins his exegetical work, he simply refers to Hagar and Sarah as "the slave woman" and "the free woman," evidently assuming that the Galatians are familiar with the story (*Essays on Paul* [Philadelphia: Westminster, 1982], pp. 161-62). In addition, he says, a straightforward reading of the story is more congenial to the argument of Paul's opponents than to Paul's own argument, and may indicate that Paul himself did not bring the text into the debate.

[69]Most commentators believe that Paul's allegory contrasts Judaism with Christianity. His use of the term *beget* elsewhere to refer to missionary activity (1 Cor 4:15; Philem 10) and his use of the present tense of this verb in 4:24 to refer to the ongoing activity of those associated with the covenant from Mount Sinai, however, probably mean that his contrast is limited to his own missionary efforts and those of his opponents. See J. Louis Martyn, "The Covenants of Hagar and Sarah," in *Faith and History: Essays in Honor of Paul W. Meyer,* ed. John T. Carroll, Charles H. Cosgrove and E. Elizabeth Johnson (Atlanta: Scholars Press, 1990), pp. 160-92.

[70]At first glance it might seem possible to understand the "two covenants" as the "old covenant" and the "new covenant." On closer inspection, however, the correspondence does not appear likely. Certainly one covenant, the Sinaitic (4:24-25), corresponds to what Paul calls the "old covenant" in 2 Corinthians 3:14, but because he has already used the term *covenant* in 3:17 to refer to God's promises to Abraham, it is best to see the other covenant as God's covenant with Abraham rather than the new covenant of Jeremiah 31:31 and 2 Corinthians 3:6. Paul may have avoided reference to the new covenant in Galatians to prevent confusion over his argument that believers are included in the Abrahamic covenant.

[71]See, for example, Isaiah 41:14; 43:1, 14; 52:3; 54:5; and compare Paul's use of the language of redemption in Galatians 3:13 and 4:4. This concept probably also stands behind Paul's claim that God has rescued believers from "the present evil age" (1:4), a phrase that closely parallels descriptions from his period of the curse of dispersion to which Israel was subject (2 Maccabees 1:5). It may lie behind Paul's claim that the Galatians were "called in freedom" (5:13), a phrase that echoes Hosea's statement that God "called" his son Israel out of Egyptian bondage (11:1).

[72]For Paul's concept of "the world" (*ho kosmos*), see Romans 5:12-13; 1 Corinthians 1:21, 26-28; 4:9, 13; 6:2; 11:32.

[73]Longenecker, *Galatians,* pp. 297-99, and Matera, *Galatians,* pp. 226-27, 232, canvass the exegetical options thoroughly.

[74]Compare Barclay, *Obeying the Truth,* pp. 97-98; Longenecker, *Galatians,* p. 298; and Matera, *Galatians,* p. 232; all three correctly point out that the statement must be interpreted within the context of Paul's strenuous argument in 3:6—4:31 that Gentile believers are part of

Abraham's family. In light of this context, "the Israel of God" must include Gentile believers.

[75]See Matthew 5:43, 19:19, 22:39, Mark 12:31, Luke 10:27 and Philo *On the Special Laws* 2.62-63 (282). Compare Romans 13:9 and James 2:8.

[76]See Räisänen, *Paul and the Law*, pp. 63-64 and Sanders, *Paul, the Law and the Jewish People*, p. 97. Compare Ulrich Wilckens, "Statements on the Development of Paul's View of the Law," in *Paul and Paulinism: Essays in Honour of C. K. Barrett*, ed. M. D. Hooker and S. G. Wilson (Cambridge: Cambridge University Press, 1982), pp. 22-23.

[77]See Dunn, *Jesus, Paul and the Law*, p. 200, and Ridderbos, *Epistle of Paul to the Churches of Galatia*, p. 201.

[78]For a more detailed discussion of this point see Frank Thielman, "The Coherence of Paul's View of the Law: The Evidence of First Corinthians," *New Testament Studies* 38 (1992): 251-52.

[79]Hübner believes that Paul distinguishes between the many commandments of the Mosaic law, which he calls "the whole law" in 5:3, and the law "as a whole," to which he refers in 5:14 (*Law*, pp. 36-41). On this view, although the Mosaic law is obsolete, the law of 5:14, which is a different entity, remains valid for Christians. As Barclay points out, however (*Obeying the Truth*, p. 137), the linguistic distinctions on which Hübner's case is built are not clear enough to warrant his conclusions. *Law* in 5:14 must mean what it means in 5:3 and 5:18—the Mosaic law.

[80]See Betz, *Galatians*, p. 275; Westerholm, *Israel's Law*, pp. 201-5; Longenecker, *Galatians*, pp. 242-43; and Matera, *Galatians*, p. 197. Barclay (*Obeying*, pp. 140-41) and Westerholm (*Israel's Law*, p. 205) believe that Paul chose the term *fulfill* in part because of its ambiguity: it allows him to claim that Christians do what the law commands without imposing on them an exact keeping of the law. By using the term, then, Paul could forestall criticism that Christians did not "do" some requirements of the law at the same time that he refused to give the Mosaic law sovereignty over Christian conduct.

[81]See, for example, Colossians 4:17. Other examples appear in Bauer, *Greek-English Lexicon*, s.v. πληρόω, 4b. C. F. D. Moule correctly says that "to fulfil the law is strictly . . . to accomplish what the law requires" (" 'Fulness' and 'Fill' in the New Testament," *Scottish Journal of Theology* 4 [1951]: 84). The meaning of the word *plēroō* in 5:14 is therefore similar to the meaning of the cognate term *anaplēroō* ("fulfill") in 6:2, where Paul speaks of fulfilling one's obligation to the law of Christ by bearing one another's burdens (compare Bauer, *Greek-English Lexicon*, s.v. 2).

[82]Barclay points out that Paul's use of *plēroō* with *law* is unique within ancient Jewish literature and that Paul himself never speaks of Jewish observance of the law as "fulfilling" the law (*Obeying the Truth*, pp. 138-41). Instead Paul seems to reserve the term for Christian fulfillment of the law (Rom 8:4; 13:8; compare Rom 13:10; Gal 6:2).

[83]Barclay, *Obeying the Truth*, p. 139.

[84]Paul connects the thought of 5:14 with his command in 5:13 using the word *gar* ("because"). Compare Mußner, *Galaterbrief*, p. 369.

[85]A series of important manuscripts, including Codex Sinaiticus, have instead of "you will fulfill the law of Christ" the imperative statement "so fulfill the law of Christ." The difference in Greek is a matter of one letter, *anaplērōsete* or *anaplērōsate*, and the ancient evidence is nearly evenly balanced. The early date and the diverse geographical range of manuscripts that read the future indicative rather than the aorist imperative weigh slightly in favor of the future indicative. In addition, a scribe would have been more likely to try to conform a future indicative before him to the imperative in the previous clause than to change an existing aorist imperative into a less harmonious-looking future indicative. See Bruce Metzger, *A Textual Commentary on the Greek New Testament* (Stuttgart: United Bible Societies, 1971), p. 598. Although this is true, the future indicative retains the force of an imperative, since the term gives the means by which the imperative statement "bear one another's burdens" in the previous clause is to be obeyed.

[86]See also Barclay, *Obeying the Truth*, p. 134, and Matera, *Galatians*, pp. 220-21.

[87]See also C. H. Dodd, "ENNOMOΣ XPIΣTOY," in *Studia Paulina in Honorem Johannis de Zwaan Septuagenarii*, ed. J. N. Sevenster and W. C. van Unnik (Haarlem: Erven F. Bohn, 1953), pp. 135-37.

[88]Compare Barclay, *Obeying the Truth*, pp. 76-83, and Jan Lambrecht, "Transgressor by Nullifying God's Grace: A Study of Gal 2,18-21," *Biblica* 72 (1991): 230-36. Barclay agrees that 2:18 refers to the transgression of a new pattern of behavior but does not see behind the term *transgression* a reference to a new law. Lambrecht argues that in 2:18 Paul must be referring to transgression of the new command to live to God.

[89]Twice the term refers to God's command not to eat of the tree in Eden (Rom 5:14; 1 Tim 2:14).

[90]Other explanations of the "transgression" of 2:18 are (1) that it refers to Paul's previous eating with Gentiles, something that he would admit was transgression if he "rebuilt" the law (so Lagrange, *Saint Paul Épître*, p. 50), (2) that it refers to transgression of the law's actual intention (so Burton, *Critical and Exegetical Commentary on the Epistle to the Galatians*, p. 131) and (3) that it refers to the inevitability of transgression of the law if one lives within the sphere of the law (so Fung, *Epistle to the Galatians*, p. 122). For a thorough treatment of these alternatives see Fung, *Epistle to the Galatians*, pp. 120-22, and Lambrecht, "Transgressor," pp. 231-34.

[91]Paul explains himself more fully in 2:19: "For through the law I have died to the law in order that I might live to God." Paul's ethical guide is no longer the Mosaic law but living in a way that pleases God. Conceptually, this provides a close parallel to his statement in 1 Corinthians 9:21 that although he is no longer under the Mosaic law, he is not "outside the law of God but in the law of Christ."

[92]Barclay observes that sects often attempt to legitimate their existence by attempting to take over the traditions of their parent bodies (*Obeying the Truth*, pp. 96-99). Watson believes this to be a kind of inviolable principle for sectarian societies and assumes that it must be true of Paul's argument in Galatians (*Paul, Judaism and the Gentiles*, pp. 69-72). Paul himself, however, gives no other explanation for his efforts than that he believes Scripture continues to "speak" (4:21).

Chapter 7: Rubbish & Resource

[1]See, for example, Stephen Westerholm, *Israel's Law and the Church's Faith* (Grand Rapids, Mich.: Eerdmans, 1988), pp. 114-15; E. P. Sanders, *Paul, the Law and the Jewish People* (Philadelphia: Fortress, 1983), pp. 43-45; Heikki Räisänen, *Paul and the Law*, Wissenschaftliche Untersuchungen zum Neuen Testament 29 (Tübingen, Germany: J. C. B. Mohr/Paul Siebeck, 1983), pp. 175-76, 106, 230-31; Francis Watson, *Paul, Judaism and the Gentiles: A Sociological Approach* (Cambridge: Cambridge University Press, 1986), pp. 73-80; and Thomas R. Schreiner, *The Law and Its Fulfillment: A Pauline Theology of Law* (Grand Rapids, Mich.: Baker Book House, 1993), pp. 70-71, 112-114.

[2]J. B. Lightfoot, *Saint Paul's Epistle to the Philippians: A Revised Text with Introduction, Notes and Dissertations*, 4th ed., rev. (London: Macmillan, 1885), p. 83; Gerald F. Hawthorne, *Philippians*, Word Biblical Commentary 43 (Waco, Tex.: Word, 1983), p. 19; Moisés Silva, *Philippians*, Baker Exegetical Commentary on the New Testament (Grand Rapids, Mich.: Baker Book House, 1992), pp. 46-47; Peter T. O'Brien, *The Epistle to the Philippians: A Commentary on the Greek Text*, New International Greek Testament Commentary (Grand Rapids, Mich.: Eerdmans, 1991), pp. 61-63. Compare F. F. Bruce, *Philippians*, Good News Commentary (New York: Harper & Row, 1983), p. 9.

[3]Many interpreters believe that the delayed expression of gratitude for the Philippians' gift, the abrupt warning at 3:2, and the mention in Polycarp's letter to the Philippians (3.2) of Paul's "letters" to the Philippians demonstrate that the present letter is a compilation of Pauline letters to the Philippians. See the discussion in Jean-François Collange, *The Epistle of Saint Paul to the Philippians* (orig. ed. 1973; London: Epworth, 1979); David E. Garland, "The Composi-

tion and Unity of Philippians: Some Neglected Literary Factors," *Novum Testamentum* 27 (1985): 44-47; and O'Brien, *Epistle to the Philippians*, pp. 10-14. Weighty arguments against this notion, however, include the lack of any manuscript evidence for it, the difficulty of finding a plausible motive for the hypothetical editor's method of editing, and the thematic unity of the letter. See Robert Jewett, "The Epistolary Thanksgiving and the Integrity of Philippians," *Novum Testamentum* 12 (1970): 362-90; Garland, "Composition and Unity," pp. 147-73; Silva, *Philippians*, pp. 14-16; and O'Brien, *Epistle to the Philippians*, pp. 14-18.

[4]Walter Bauer, *A Greek-English Lexicon of the New Testament and Other Early Christian Literature*, trans. and aug. William Arndt, F. Wilbur Gingrich and Frederick Danker, 2nd ed. (Chicago: University of Chicago Press, 1979), s.v. βλέπω, 1, 4a, 6.

[5]See G. D. Kilpatrick, "ΒΛΕΠΕΤΕ, Philippians 3₂," in *In Memoriam Paul Kahle*, ed. Matthew Black and Georg Fohrer, Beihefte zur *Zeitschrift für die alttestamentliche Wissenschaft* 103 (Berlin: Töpelmann, 1968), pp. 146-48 (compare Bauer, *Greek-English Lexicon*, s.v. 6); G. B. Caird, *Paul's Letters from Prison (Ephesians, Philippians, Colossians and Philemon) in the Revised Standard Version*, New Clarendon Bible (Oxford: Oxford University Press, 1976), pp. 132-33; Hawthorne, *Philippians*, pp. 124-25; Garland, "Composition and Unity," pp. 165-66.

[6]Compare R. P. Martin, *Philippians*, New Century Bible (Grand Rapids, Mich.: Eerdmans/London: Marshall, Morgan & Scott, 1976), p. 124; Bruce, *Philippians*, p. 80; and O'Brien, *Epistle to the Philippians*, pp. 353-54.

[7]Marvin R. Vincent, *The Epistles to the Philippians and to Philemon*, International Critical Commentary (Edinburgh: T & T Clark, 1897), pp. 92-93; J. Hugh Michael, *The Epistle of Paul to the Philippians* (London: Hodder & Stoughton, 1928), p. 134; Robert Jewett, "Conflicting Movements in the Early Church as Reflected in Philippians," *Novum Testamentum* 12 (1970): 362-90; Collange, *Epistle of Saint Paul to the Philippians*, p. 13; Martin, *Philippians*, pp. 22-36, 125; Silva, *Philippians*, p. 169; O'Brien, *Epistle to the Philippians*, pp. 355-56.

[8]Bruce, *Philippians*, p. 79; compare O'Brien, *Epistle to the Philippians*, p. 354.

[9]See Caird, *Paul's Letters from Prison*, pp. 133-34, and Garland, "Composition and Unity," pp. 166-73. Hawthorne argues (*Philippians*, pp. xl-xlvii) that Paul refers to itinerant unbelieving Jews who followed him in order to oppose his preaching of the gospel (compare Acts 14:19; 17:13).

[10]This argument has less force against Hawthorne's thesis, since he holds that the unbelieving Jews in view in 3:2 *are* opposing Paul's preaching of the gospel.

[11]Among the sixteen uses of the word, nine fall into this category: Matthew 9:37, 38; 10:10; Luke 10:2 (2x), 7; 2 Corinthians 11:13; 1 Timothy 5:18; and 2 Timothy 2:15. Compare Dieter Georgi, *The Opponents of Paul in Second Corinthians* (orig. ed. 1964; Philadelphia: Fortress, 1986), p. 40.

[12]Compare 1 Timothy 5:18 and 2 Timothy 2:15.

[13]In this they differ from the "deceitful workers" of 2 Corinthians. Compare Georgi, *Opponents of Paul*, p. 40.

[14]Jewett suggests ("Conflicting Movements," pp. 384-86) that the epithet *dogs* in Paul's warning was not, as is commonly thought, an ironic charge that his opponents were unclean (as in Ex 22:31) but a figurative reference to the Judaizers' practice of intruding into Paul's congregations against the Jerusalem agreement (compare Gal 2:7-9).

[15]See Walter Schmithals, *Paul and the Gnostics* (New York: Abingdon, 1972), pp. 82-83, and Willi Marxen, *Introduction to the New Testament* (Philadelphia: Fortress, 1968), pp. 63-64. Both Schmithals and Marxen believe that Paul's opponents in Philippi belong to the same group as his opponents in Galatia.

[16]See Schmithals, *Paul and the Gnostics*, pp. 82-115.

[17]See the discussion in ibid., pp. 37-40. The troublemakers against whom Paul argues in Colossians appear to have combined circumcision with theosophical speculation (Col 2:8, 11, 18), but this group's strict adherence to the law (Col 2:20-23) separates it sharply from the hypothetical antinomians whom Schmithals describes.

[18]Compare Jewett, "Conflicting Movements," pp. 382-87.

[19]Marxen believes that Paul responded the way he did in 3:2-11 because he misunderstood the nature of the opposition against him (*Introduction to the New Testament*, pp. 63-64; compare Schmithals, *Paul and the Gnostics*, p. 91). The notion that an interpreter nineteen centuries removed from the situation can understand it better than Paul himself, however, seems an unstable foundation on which to build.

[20]Some interpreters who believe that Paul is speaking of common Jews in 3:2 think that his language in 3:19 refers to the same group. On this theory the phrase "their god is their belly" is most frequently attributed to a Jewish fixation on dietary regulations and "their glory is their shame" is often said to refer figuratively either to circumcision (Hawthorne, *Philippians*, pp. xlvii; compare p. 166) or to disgrace at the last judgment (Silva, *Philippians*, p. 210, and O'Brien, *Epistle to the Philippians*, p. 457). Watson believes that both phrases are derisive references to circumcision (*Paul, Judaism and the Gentiles*, p. 76). Helmut Koester argues that Paul's opponents are Jews with a Gnostic tendency toward perfectionism and that his references to them as dogs, evil workers, mutilators, servants of the belly and those who glory in their shame are "reversals of the perfectionistic slogans of the opponents" (*History and Literature of Early Christianity*, vol. 2 of *Introduction to the New Testament*, 2 vols. [Berlin: Walter de Gruyter, 1982], pp. 133-34). The most natural understanding of these references, however, is that they refer to people, such as appear in 1 Corinthians, who freely violate dietary and sexual customs.

[21]Many interpreters believe that Philippians was written after Romans, during a Roman imprisonment (Acts 28:16; Phil 1:13; 4:22) and in close connection with Colossians, Philemon and Ephesians. This is the traditional position, attested as early as the second-century Marcionite prologue to Philippians. A considerable number of scholars, however, believe that the epistle was composed during an otherwise unattested Ephesian imprisonment (although see 2 Cor 1:8-10). Among these scholars, disagreement exists over the precise point at which Philippians was written during Paul's long ministry in Ephesus (Acts 19:8, 10, 22; 20:31). If Paul wrote it after 1 Corinthians but before 2 Corinthians, then the allusions to hardship in 1 Corinthians 15:32 and 16:9 are not to imprisonment but to the trouble that eventually landed him in prison, and Paul's comments in 2 Corinthians 1:8-10 are a retrospective look at the imprisonment out of which Philippians was written. See A. H. McNeile, *An Introduction to the Study of the New Testament*, 2nd rev. ed. (Oxford: Clarendon, 1953), pp. 183-84.

[22]Compare Jewett, "Conflicting Movements," pp. 380-81.

[23]This is confirmed by the Philippians' generous support of Paul's offering for the needy believers in Jerusalem (2 Cor 8:1-5). Some scholars believe that Paul's reference to "as many as are perfect" in 3:15 is an ironic description of a group within the Philippian church whose perfectionistic tendencies he hopes to check. This view does not adequately account for Paul's inclusion of himself among the *teleioi*, however. The term *teleioi* therefore probably means "mature" rather than perfect, and the sentence is not ironic but an encouragement to the Philippians to seek maturity in their faith (compare 1 Cor 2:6; Eph 4:13-15; Col 1:28). See O'Brien, *Epistle to the Philippians*, pp. 435-38.

[24]Compare O'Brien, *Epistle to the Philippians*, p. 366.

[25]Compare Robert Jewett, *Paul's Anthropological Terms: A Study of Their Use in Conflict Settings*, Arbeiten zur Geschichte des antiken Judentums und des Urchristentums 10 (Leiden, Netherlands: Brill, 1971), pp. 117-19.

[26]The phrase "be found in him" (*heurethō en autō*) probably refers to Paul's anticipation of the last day. See O'Brien, *Epistle to the Philippians*, pp. 391-92.

[27]Caird, *Paul's Letters from Prison*, p. 133; Garland, "Composition and Unity," pp 168, 170.

[28]O'Brien, *Epistle to the Philippians*, p. 362.

[29]Ibid., pp. 394-95; compare Bruce, *Philippians*, p. 83.

[30]Mark Seifrid argues persuasively that because Paul lists privileges into which he was born as

well as personal achievements in 3:5-6, it is inappropriate to say that the pre-Christian Paul believed his righteous standing before God was solely a matter of his own efforts (*Justification by Faith: The Origin and Development of a Central Pauline Theme*, Supplements to *Novum Testamentum* 68 [Leiden, Netherlands: Brill, 1992], pp. 173-74).

[31]Ibid., p. 174.

[32]Compare R. H. Gundry, "Grace, Works and Staying Saved in Paul," *Biblica* 66 (1985): 13-14; O'Brien, *Epistle to the Philippians*, pp. 395-96; Seifrid, *Justification by Faith*, pp. 174-75; Schreiner, *Law and Its Fulfillment*, pp. 112-14.

[33]Caird, *Paul's Letters from Prison*, p. 136.

[34]Rudolf Bultmann, *Theology of the New Testament*, 2 vols. (New York: Scribner's, 1951-1955), 1:266-67.

[35]Sanders, *Paul, the Law and the Jewish People*, pp. 43-45, 139-41.

[36]Seifrid, *Justification by Faith*, p. 174.

[37]Luke, for example, comments that Zechariah and Elizabeth "were both righteous before God, living blamelessly within all the commandments and just requirements of the Lord" (1:6), but Zechariah can, nevertheless pray for the redemption of Israel from their enemies (1:71, 74) and say that his son John will "go before the Lord to prepare his ways and to give knowledge of salvation to his people by the forgiveness of their sins" (1:76-77).

[38]The passage reads: "Do not say in your heart when the Lord your God expels these nations from before you, 'On account of my righteous deeds *[dia tas dikaiosynas mou]* the Lord has led me to inherit this good land.' Rather it is on account of the wickedness of these nations that the Lord will utterly destroy them before you. It is not on account of your righteous deeds *[dia tēn dikaiosynēn sou]* nor on account of the uprightness of your heart that you will enter to inherit their land, but on account of the wickedness of these nations that the Lord will utterly destroy them before you, and in order that he should establish his covenant, which he swore to your fathers, to Abraham and to Isaac and to Jacob. And you shall know today that it is not on account of your righteous deeds *[dia tas dikaiosynas sou]* that the Lord your God is giving this good land to you to inherit, because you are a stiff-necked people."

[39]At first Paul's claim in 3:6 to have been "blameless" with respect to the law seems to oppose this interpretation. Sanders, for example, has argued that 3:6 and 3:9 together show that Paul believed righteousness could be maintained by means of the law (*Paul, the Law and the Jewish People*, pp. 43-45, 139-41). The problem, says Sanders, was not that the law was impossible to keep, but simply that in Paul's eyes righteousness by the law was the wrong kind of righteousness but righteousness through faith in Christ was the right kind. "The only thing that is wrong with the old righteousness," he says, "seems to be that it is not the new one; it has no fault that is described in other terms" (ibid., p. 140). The difficulty with this interpretation of 3:6 and 3:9 is that it leaves no room for explaining *why* Paul shifted from one righteousness to the other. A reason for this shift is apparent if we remember that "blameless" conformity with the law, and therefore "righteousness" with respect to the law, included observance of the prescribed sacrifices of atonement for sin (see E. P. Sanders, *Paul and Palestinian Judaism: A Comparison of Patterns of Religion* [Philadelphia: Fortress, 1977], p. 203, and *Judaism: Practice and Belief 63 BCE—66 CE* [London: SCM Press/Philadelphia: Trinity Press International, 1992], pp. 262-78). "The righteousness from God," because it was the ultimate sacrifice of atonement (Rom 3:21-26) and involved the imputation of righteousness to the believer (2 Cor 5:21), atoned for transgression once and for all. This righteousness implied that the "righteousness that comes by the law" was provisional and proleptic.

[40]See Bultmann, *Theology*, 1:285, and Seifrid, *Justification by Faith*, pp. 213-14.

[41]H. Strathmann, "λατρεύω, λατρεία," in *Theological Dictionary of the New Testament*, ed. Gerhard Kittel, 10 vols. (Grand Rapids, Mich.: Eerdmans, 1967), 4:60; and O'Brien, *Epistle to the Philippians*, p. 360 n. 84, provide many other examples of the Septuagint's use of the word *latreuō* in this way.

[42]See Hawthorne, *Philippians,* p. 98; Silva, *Philippians,* p. 134; O'Brien, *Epistle to the Philippians,* p. 276. T. J. Deidun believes that the obedience of Christ and the obedience of the Philippians are not related to one another, since Paul says that the Philippians are to work out their own salvation, not that they should emulate Christ (*New Covenant Morality in Paul,* Analecta Biblica 89 [Rome: Biblical Institute Press, 1981], p. 64). The verbal link between the two passages, however, probably indicates a conceptual link as well.

[43]Compare Lightfoot, *Saint Paul's Epistle to the Philippians,* p. 117; Collange, *Epistle of Saint Paul to the Philippians,* p. 112; Hawthorne, *Philippians,* p. 102; Silva, *Philippians,* pp. 143-45; and O'Brien, *Epistle to the Philippians,* p. 292.

[44]Daniel G. Reid has, in private correspondence, offered the suggestive observation that Paul's language may also echo God's promise to make Abraham's descendants as numerous as the stars of heaven (Gen 15:5; 22:17; 26:4). Compare Romans 4:18.

[45]Compare O'Brien, *Epistle to the Philippians,* p. 294.

[46]See John 7:12; Acts 6:1; 1 Peter 4:9; *Epistle of Barnabas* 3:5; and *Didache* 3:6.

[47]Compare O'Brien, *Epistle to the Philippians,* p. 291, and contrast Silva, *Philippians,* p. 144.

[48]Both phrases have caused considerable consternation among commentators, since here Paul seems to allow human effort some role in salvation and even to speak of divine retribution for not working hard enough. Thus the phrase "with fear and trembling" *(meta phobou kai tromou)* is sometimes explained as a stock expression for "respect and reverence" (Michael, *Epistle of Paul to the Philippians,* p. 102) or "healthy respect" (Martin, *Philippians,* p. 103) and said to refer to the attitude Paul wants the Philippians to have toward one another. Elsewhere in Paul the terms are used together of attitudes among people (1 Cor 2:3; 2 Cor 7:15; Eph 6:5) and in the LXX primarily of the attitude of fear that will come upon Israel's enemies when Israel defeats them (Ex 15:16; Deut 2:25; Is 19:16). Perhaps in a context in which Paul has alluded to the disobedience of Israel in the wilderness, however, the phrase recalls the proper fear of judgment that characterized the disobedient Israelites (Ex 33:5; Num 11:33; 14:10-12, 36-37; 16:31-35, 46; 17:10-13) and serves as a reminder to the Philippians not to presume upon their calling as the new people of God (compare 1 Cor 10:1-5 and especially Rom 11:19-21). Paul denies that this implies human cooperation with God's grace to bring about salvation, however, when he says in 2:13 that both wanting to do God's will and actually doing it are a result of God's work within the believer.

[49]See the references to sacrifice as an *osmēn euōdias* in, for example, Exodus 29:18, 25, 41 and Ezekiel 20:41, and as *dektos* in Leviticus 1:3-4; 17:4; 19:5; 22:19-20; Malachi 2:13; Isaiah 56:7; 60:7; and Jeremiah 6:20. Compare Michael Newton, *The Concept of Purity at Qumran and in Paul,* Society for New Testament Studies Monograph Series 53 (Cambridge: Cambridge University Press, 1985), p. 66, and O'Brien, *Epistle to the Philippians,* p. 541.

[50]The phrase *epi tē thysia kai leitourgia tēs pisteōs hymōn* could be translated "upon the sacrifice and service of your faith." Since Paul is probably reflecting the sacrificial prescriptions of the Mosaic law, however, it is better to take *epi* with the dative in the sense of "in addition to." This meaning appears elsewhere in Paul (such as in 2 Cor 7:13) and corresponds to the pouring out of a libation in addition to other sacrifices in such passages as Numbers 15:1-10. See Bauer, *Greek-English Lexicon,* s.v., II.1.b.β, and O'Brien, *Epistle to the Philippians,* p. 307. The phrase *thysia kai leitourgia,* moreover, describes one concept with two sacrificial terms and so should be rendered "sacrificial service." See O'Brien, *Epistle to the Philippians,* p. 309.

[51]See Lightfoot, *Saint Paul's Epistle to the Philippians,* p. 119, and Vincent, *Epistles to the Philippians and to Philemon,* p. 72.

[52]R. P. Martin observes that Paul had introduced sacrificial notions already in 2:15 with the remark that the Philippians were "blameless"—a quality that, according to Leviticus 1:10 and 22:17-25, should characterize sacrificial animals (*Philippians,* 2nd ed., Tyndale New Testament Commentaries [Grand Rapids, Mich.: Eerdmans, 1987], p. 124).

[53]See the description of the procedure in, for example, Numbers 15:1-10.

[54]It is perhaps also significant that Paul calls Epaphroditus the Philippians' *leitourgos* (2:25) who completed what was lacking in the Philippians' *leitourgia* (2:30) to him. These words were commonly used without cultic connotations to mean, respectively, "servant" and "service." The Septuagint, however, occasionally uses *leitourgos* of temple ministers (2 Esdras 7:24; 20:40) or synonymously with the word *priest* (Is 61:6) and frequently uses *leitourgia* to refer to temple worship (for example, Num 8:22; 16:9; 18:4; 2 Chron 31:2). See Bauer, *Greek-English Lexicon,* s.vv.

[55]See the remarks of Silva, *Philippians,* pp. 134-40.

Chapter 8: The Law of Moses, the Human Plight and the Law of Faith in Romans 1—4

[1]M. -J. Lagrange, *Saint Paul Épître aux Romains,* 3rd ed. (Paris: Librairie Victor Lecoffre, 1922), p. 16; C. E. B. Cranfield, *A Critical and Exegetical Commentary on the Epistle to the Romans,* International Critical Commentary, 2 vols. (Edinburgh: T & T Clark, 1975-1979), 1:87; Ulrich Wilckens, *Der Brief an die Römer,* Evangelisch-katholischer Kommentar zum Neuen Testament 6, 3 vols. (Zurich: Benziger/Neukirchen, Germany: Neukirchener, 1978-1982), 1:77; James D. G. Dunn, *Romans 1-8,* Word Biblical Commentary 38A (Dallas: Word, 1988), pp. 37-38; Joseph A. Fitzmyer, *Romans: A New Translation with Introduction and Commentary,* Anchor Bible 33 (New York: Doubleday, 1993), p. 253.

[2]See, respectively, Charles Hodge, *A Commentary on Romans* (rev. ed. 1864; Edinburgh: Banner of Truth Trust, 1972), pp. 10-11, 191; Philipp Melanchthon, "Römerbrief-Kommentar, 1532," in *Melanchthons Werke in Auswahl,* ed. Robert Stupperich (Gütersloh, Germany: Gerd Mohn, 1965), 5:30; and Anders Nygren, *Commentary on Romans* (Philadelphia: Muhlenberg, 1949), p. 8. For a survey of the scholarly debate over the occasion of Romans see J. Christiaan Beker, *Paul the Apostle: The Triumph of God in Life and Thought* (Philadelphia: Fortress, 1980), pp. 59-69; Karl P. Donfried, "Introduction 1977: The Nature and Scope of the Romans Debate" and "Introduction 1991: The Romans Debate Since 1977," in *The Romans Debate,* ed. Karl P. Donfried, rev. and expanded ed. (Peabody, Mass.: Hendrickson, 1991), pp. xli-lxxii; Neil Elliot, *The Rhetoric of Romans: Argumentative Constraint and Strategy and Paul's Dialogue with Judaism, Journal for the Study of the New Testament* Supplement Series 45 (Sheffield, U.K.: JSOT, 1990), pp. 9-43; and L. Ann Jervis, *The Purpose of Romans: A Comparative Letter Structure Investigation, Journal for the Study of the New Testament* Supplement Series 55 (Sheffield, U.K.: JSOT, 1991), pp. 11-28.

[3]Scholars have often argued that Romans 16 was not originally part of the letter that Paul sent to Rome but was instead sent to Ephesus. T. W. Manson, for example, claimed that Paul sent Rom 1—15 to Rome and then sent a modified form of the same epistle, to which he attached the greetings in Romans 16, to Ephesus ("St. Paul's Letter to the Romans—and Others," in *The Romans Debate,* ed. Karl P. Donfried, rev. and expanded ed. [Peabody, Mass.: Hendrickson, 1991], pp. 3-15). Although Karl Paul Donfried could say in 1970 that there was "a growing consensus" especially among Continental New Testament scholars that Romans 16 was not originally part of Paul's letter to Rome ("A Short Note on Romans 16," *Journal of Biblical Literature* 89 [1970]: 441), the tide of opinion now seems to have changed in favor of including the chapter with the letter. This change is due largely to the argument of H. Gamble Jr., *The Textual History of the Letter to the Romans: A Study in Textual and Literary Criticism,* Studies and Documents 42 (Grand Rapids, Mich.: Eerdmans, 1977).

[4]Compare Beker, *Paul the Apostle,* p. 74; A. J. M. Wedderburn, *The Reasons for Romans* (Minneapolis: Fortress, 1991), p. 13; and Peter Lampe, "The Roman Christians of Romans 16," in *The Romans Debate,* ed. Karl P. Donfried, rev. and expanded ed. (Peabody, Mass.: Hendrickson, 1991), pp. 216-230. Even if, as Francis Watson suggests, only nine people (Prisca, Aquila, Epaenetus, Ampliatus, Urbanus, Stachys, Persis, Rufus and Rufus's mother) were definitely acquaintances of Paul (*Paul, Judaism and the Gentiles: A Sociological Approach* [Cambridge: Cambridge University Press, 1986], p. 99), the link is sufficient to have provided information

about the condition of the Roman church.

[5]Compare Watson, *Paul, Judaism and the Gentiles*, pp. 94-96; Wedderburn, *Reasons for Romans*, pp. 32-34; Mark Seifrid, *Justification by Faith: The Origin and Development of a Central Pauline Theme*, Supplements to *Novum Testamentum* 68 (Leiden, Netherlands: Brill, 1992), p. 205. That Paul addresses a predominantly Gentile congregation seems clear from 1:5-6, 13; 11:13-24; and 15:16.

[6]Compare James D. G. Dunn, *Romans 9-16*, Word Biblical Commentary 38B (Dallas: Word, 1988), p. 795. Scholars have often considered this section to be a general summary of Paul's approach to issues he had faced prior to writing Romans, especially in Corinth. See, for instance, Robert J. Karris, "Romans 14:1-15:13 and the Occasion of Romans," in *The Romans Debate*, ed. Karl P. Donfried, rev. and expanded ed. (Peabody, Mass.: Hendrickson, 1991), pp. 65-84. Watson believes that the weak and the strong did not worship together but formed separate congregations—one Jewish in character and the other Pauline—which Paul sought to bring together (*Paul, Judaism and the Gentiles*, pp. 94-98). Paul therefore intends his letter to be a means of reconciling the two congregations so that the Jewish congregation, a "failed reform-movement," might become a Pauline "sect" (pp. 106-7). If Paul addresses separate congregations, however, it is difficult to understand in what context those who ate meat could injure those who abstained to the point that the vegetarians stood in danger of destruction (14:15). Paul's comment assumes that the two groups had frequent interaction with one another.

[7]Paul may show knowledge of the Roman church in 3:8, 6:1 and 6:15, where he refers to false inferences about his gospel. See Peter Stuhlmacher, "Paul's Understanding of the Law in the Letter to the Romans," *Svensk Exegetisk Årsbok* 50 (1985): 90; Peter Stuhlmacher, *Paul's Letter to the Romans: A Commentary* (Louisville, Ky.: Westminster/John Knox, 1994), pp. 5-6, 51-53, 90-91, 94; and Wedderburn, *Reasons for Romans*, p. 115. It is equally likely, however, that these verses refer to objections raised against Paul's preaching during his missionary efforts in the east. See Fitzmyer, *Romans*, p. 34.

[8]Romans 12:1—13:14 is sometimes considered general ethical advice of little relevance to the situation in Rome (as in Martin Dibelius, *From Tradition to Gospel* [Greenwood, S.C.: Attic, 1971], p. 238, and *James: A Commentary on the Epistle of James*, Hermeneia [Philadelphia: Fortress, 1975], pp. 2, 3, 10). Even if this section of the letter draws on a common stock of ethical instruction, however, Paul must have chosen this particular instruction from the available material for a reason. Compare the criticism of Dibelius's approach to James in Sophie Laws, *The Epistle of James* (New York: Harper & Row, 1980), p. 7; this criticism is also valid for Dibelius's approach to Romans 12 and 13. Wedderburn observes (*Reasons for Romans*, pp. 75-87) that admonitions to be discerning about God's will (12:2), to avoid thinking of oneself too highly (12:3), to be unified (12:4-5), to exercise the gift of service to others (12:7), to cultivate mutual love (12:9-16) and to respond to persecution with love (12:17-21; compare 13:8-10) are relevant to Paul's admonitions in chapters 14 and 15 to accept one another and support his efforts to take the collection to Jerusalem (15:30-31).

[9]See Wolfgang Wiefel, "The Jewish Community in Ancient Rome and the Origins of Roman Christianity," in *The Romans Debate*, ed. Karl P. Donfried, rev. and expanded ed. (Peabody, Mass.: Hendrickson, 1991), pp. 85-101.

[10]The author of this commentary, although unknown, is commonly given the name Ambrosiaster. The translation used here belongs to John Knox, "The Epistle to the Romans," in *Interpreter's Dictionary of the Bible*, ed. George A. Buttrick, 12 vols. (Nashville: Abingdon, 1952-1957), 9:362.

[11]The translation is from the Loeb Classical Library edition of Suetonius's *Lives of the Caesars*.

[12]See Watson, *Paul, Judaism and the Gentiles*, p. 93; Watson believes Suetonius's statement implies that Christ had been preached by Jews and among Jews at least since the beginning of Claudius's reign in A.D. 41.

[13]Priscilla is the diminutive form of Prisca. See Walter Bauer, *A Greek-English Lexicon of the New Testament and Other Early Christian Literature*, trans. and aug. William Arndt, F. Wilbur Gingrich and Frederick Danker, 2nd ed. (Chicago: University of Chicago Press, 1979), s.v. Πρίσκα.

[14]See Lampe, "Roman Christians," pp. 219, 224.

[15]See Cranfield, *Critical and Exegetical Commentary on the Epistle to the Romans*, 2:700. The terms *powerful (dynatoi)* and *powerless (adynatoi)* in 15:1, although they primarily refer to "the strength of superior knowledge and understanding of how God's grace works" (Dunn, *Romans 9-16*, p. 837) may also refer to the positions of social power that each group occupied in the community. Compare Paul's use of the term *weak (asthenēs)* in 1 Corinthians to designate those who were both socially and spiritually weak (1:27; 8:7, 9, 10). On this see Gerd Theissen, *The Social Setting of Pauline Christianity: Essays on Corinth* (Philadelphia: Fortress, 1982), p. 125.

[16]Even these predominantly Gentile churches, however, would have been familiar with the Jewish Scriptures and with Jewish customs. Many Gentile believers in Rome may have been "God-fearers" *(sebomenoi)* or Gentile inquirers into Judaism, prior to believing in Jesus (see Acts 13:50; 16:14; 17:4, 17; 18:7; Josephus *Ant.* 14.110; and "σέβομαι," in *Exegetical Dictionary of the New Testament*, ed. H. Balz and G. Schneider, 3 vols. [Grand Rapids, Mich.: Eerdmans, 1990-1993], 3:236). Paul could assume, therefore, that they would understand his dialogue with Judaism in chapters 1—11 and that they would "know the law" (7:1). See Walter Schmithals, *Der Römerbrief als historisches Problem*, Studien zum Neuen Testament (Gütersloh, Germany: Gerd Mohn, 1975), pp. 63-94, and Beker, *Paul the Apostle*, pp. 76, 91.

[17]See Wiefel, "Jewish Community," pp. 86-89, and N. T. Wright, *The Climax of the Covenant: Christ and the Law in Pauline Theology* (Edinburgh: T & T Clark, 1991), pp. 195 and especially 234.

[18]Compare Willi Marxen, *Introduction to the New Testament* (Philadelphia: Fortress, 1968), pp. 95-104, and Karl P. Donfried, "Romans 16," in *The Romans Debate*, ed. Karl P. Donfried, rev. and expanded ed. (Peabody, Mass.: Hendrickson, 1991), pp. 48-49.

[19]Compare Cranfield, *Critical and Exegetical Commentary on the Epistle to the Romans*, 2:817.

[20]Compare Wedderburn, *Reasons for Romans*, pp. 97-102.

[21]Compare Jervis, *Purpose of Romans*, pp. 163-64, and Seifrid, *Justification by Faith*, pp. 187-210.

[22]Compare Fitzmyer, *Romans*, p. 79. On the possible anti-Semitism of the predominantly Gentile Roman congregations, see also Wright, *Climax*, p. 234, and compare Seifrid, *Justification by Faith*, p. 206. Beker believes that Romans is a rehearsal of the presentation Paul hopes to make of his gospel in Jerusalem (*Paul the Apostle*, p. 72). The intention of the presentation, according to Beker, is to temper the statements about Judaism and the law that appear in Galatians and about which the Jewish Christians in Jerusalem have presumably heard. Paul hopes that in light of these modifications, the gifts he bears to the Jerusalem saints from his predominantly Gentile churches will be acceptable. Passages such as Romans 7:1-6 and 9:6—11:10 would hardly be helpful to such an effort, however, and as Wedderburn observes (*Reasons for Romans*, p. 20), conservative Jewish Christians in Jerusalem would have been offended that Paul sided with the "powerful" in Romans 15:1. Compare Seifrid, *Justification by Faith*, p. 196.

[23]Compare Seifrid, *Justification by Faith*, pp. 207-10.

[24]For a lucid presentation of the difference between the two perspectives see C. E. B. Cranfield, "Giving a Dog a Bad Name: A Note on H. Räisänen's *Paul and the Law*," *Journal for the Study of the New Testament* 38 (1990): 77-85.

[25]See Fitzmyer, *Romans*, pp. 131-32.

[26]Compare E. P. Sanders, *Paul, the Law and the Jewish People* (Philadelphia: Fortress, 1983), pp. 30, 33-35. Sanders believes, however, that the equality of Jew and Gentile is Paul's primary emphasis. He concedes that Paul uses the argument of universal sinfulness extensively in the early chapters of Romans (ibid., p. 35), but he claims that this argument is inconsistent and cannot therefore be Paul's primary concern. Sanders bases this judgment on his belief that in Romans 2:1-29, in a way inconsistent with Romans 3:9, 19-20, Paul claims that some people do keep the law. Jouette M. Bassler advances a similar argument in "Divine Impartiality in

Paul's Letter to the Romans," *Novum Testamentum* 26 (1984): 43-58, and *Divine Impartiality: Paul and a Theological Axiom*, Society of Biblical Literature Dissertation Series 59 (Chico, Calif.: Scholars Press, 1982), pp. 164-66. It is possible to understand Romans 2, however, in a way that is consistent with Paul's summary statements in 3:9 and 19-20 and, in light of that understanding, to give his argument on the universality of sin a much more prominent place in the letter's argument. Beker claims that Paul's argument throughout 1:18—3:20 is designed to address Jewish "ethnic superiority and election pride," not to make a systematic statement about the sinfulness of the whole world (*Paul the Apostle*, pp. 78-83). Although Paul's concern to refute a view of Jewish election that impugned God's impartiality is clear, 3:9 demonstrates that in 1:18—2:29 he was equally concerned to indict Gentiles as transgressors. Compare Heikki Räisänen, *Paul and the Law*, Wissenschaftliche Untersuchungen zum Neuen Testament 29 (Tübingen, Germany: J. C. B. Mohr/Paul Siebeck, 1983), p. 97.

[27]The difficulty is well illustrated in 3:19-22, where the term is used six times to mean Scripture generally, the distinguishing mark of the Jew (twice), good works, or the five books of Moses.

[28]For the translation of *ek pisteōs eis pistin* as "by faith from first to last," compare Psalm 83:8 (LXX)—*poreusontai ek dynameōs eis dynamin* ("they proceed from strength to strength")—and 2 Corinthians 2:16—*hois men osmē ek thanatou eis thanaton, hois de osmē ek zōēs eis zōēn* ("to some a fragrance from death to death, but to others a fragrance from life to life"). See Fitzmyer, *Romans*, p. 263.

[29]Compare Cranfield, *Critical and Exegetical Commentary on the Epistle to the Romans*, 1:105-6, although he believes that the section describes sinful humanity from the perspective of the gospel, not in language with which those outside the faith would necessarily agree. See ibid., 1:104, and Cranfield, "Giving a Dog a Bad Name," pp. 78-79.

[30]Compare Fitzmyer, *Romans*, pp. 270-71. Paul comments in 3:9, moreover, that in the preceding argument he has charged both Jew and Greek with sin. He probably considers 1:18-32 to be his indictment of the Greek.

[31]The term can also mean "righteous deed" (Rom 5:12; Rev 15:4; 19:8) or "justification" (Rom 5:16), neither of which is possible in 1:32. See Bauer, *Greek-English Lexicon*, s.v. δικαίωμα.

[32]It is true, as Cranfield observes, that many of the sins listed in 1:29-31 could not carry the death penalty in any civil code (*Critical and Exegetical Commentary on the Epistle to the Romans*, 1:134). Since Deuteronomy 30:17 envisions obedience from the heart, however, Paul might still have linked the penalty of death referred to in Deuteronomy 30:15, 19 to the sinful attitudes listed in 1:29-31.

[33]Compare Beker, *Paul the Apostle*, p. 80.

[34]It is sometimes said that 2:1-16 has specifically in mind not the Jew but anyone, whether Jew or Gentile, who might have joined in the condemnation of those described in 1:18-32. See especially Stanley Kent Stowers, *The Diatribe and Paul's Letter to the Romans*, Society for Biblical Literature Dissertation Series 57 (Chico, Calif.: Scholars Press, 1981), pp. 110-12, and Elliot, *Rhetoric of Romans*, pp. 119-27, 173-90. Paul names his imaginary reader in 2:17, however, as a Jew and uses the second-person singular to address this reader just as he had in 2:1. For these reasons it seems unlikely that the individual in view in 2:1 is different from the Jewish individual in view in 2:17. Compare Watson, *Paul, Judaism and the Gentiles*, p. 110.

[35]Most commentators take 2:1-2 with 2:4-11 as a single section, and this has considerable merit since, as Cranfield says, the verse "is closely connected with 2:1 and 2, the language of which it echoes" (*Critical and Exegetical Commentary on the Epistle to the Romans*, 1:143). Despite this close linguistic connection, however, 2:2 states a general principle that Paul will spend the rest of chapter 2 proving to be true in the case of the Jew. In a sense, then, verse 2 governs the discussion throughout the chapter and not simply the argument of verses 1-11. Commentators also usually divide chapter 2 into four sections, verses 1-11, verses 12-16, verses 17-24 and verses 25-29. The last two sections, however, should be taken together, since Paul's discussion of circumcision elaborates the point of verses 17-24 that the privileges unique to Jews are

advantageous to them in the final day only if they have obeyed the law. For a division of the chapter that is similar to the one adopted here, see C. K. Barrett, *A Commentary on the Epistle to the Romans* (New York: Harper & Row, 1957), pp. 42, 48, 54.

[36]Amos prophesies against Damascus, Gaza, Tyre, Edom, Ammon, Moab and Judah but then turns his prophecy against Israel as well, eventually asking in 9:7, "Are you not like the Ethiopians to me, O people of Israel? says the LORD." His point is that since the people of Israel have sinned in ways equivalent to the nations, they cannot claim exemption from judgment. See C. H. Dodd, *The Epistle of Paul to the Romans* (orig. ed. 1932; London: Collins, 1959), p. 56.

[37]For the translation of *hoitines* with "by their very nature" see Stanley Porter, *Idioms of the Greek New Testament* (Sheffield, U.K.: JSOT Press, 1992), p. 133.

[38]Compare James M. Scott, "Paul's Use of Deuteronomic Tradition," *Journal of Biblical Literature* 112 (1993): 645-47.

[39]Interpreters often point to another problem. This passage, it is said, like 1:18-32 and 7:14-25, has an unrealistically bleak picture of human inability to do good. See Räisänen, *Paul and the Law,* p. 98, and Sanders, *Paul, the Law and the Jewish People,* pp. 124-25. Paul's charges in 1:18-32 and 2:17-25 are sweeping, but as Stephen Westerholm has shown, they echo similar denunciations in the biblical prophets of large groups of people in light of the heinous transgressions of a few (*Israel's Law and the Church's Faith: Paul and His Recent Interpreters* [Grand Rapids, Mich.: Eerdmans, 1988], pp. 158-59). Westerholm cites Jeremiah 6:28; 8:6; 9:2-6 as examples. Speaking of Romans 2:17-25, Thomas Schreiner has appropriately observed that Paul does not charge every Jew with the particularly objectionable sins that he lists but simply gives "colorful examples" to make his chief point that Jews fail to keep the law. See Thomas R. Schreiner, "Did Paul Believe in Justification by Works? Another Look at Romans 2," *Bulletin for Biblical Research* 3 (1993): 133, and *The Law and Its Fulfillment: A Pauline Theology of Law* (Grand Rapids, Mich.: Baker Book House, 1993), p. 181.

[40]Comapre Räisänen, *Paul and the Law,* pp. 102, 106, and Sanders, *Paul, the Law and the Jewish People,* pp. 123-24.

[41]Räisänen, *Paul and the Law,* p. 106, and Sanders, *Paul, the Law and the Jewish People,* p. 124.

[42]Compare Knox, "Epistle to the Romans," pp. 409, 418; Otto Kuss, *Der Römerbrief übersetzt und erklärt,* 3 parts (Regensburg, Germany: Friedrich Pustet, 1957-1978), 1:64-65. The status of the Gentiles in chapter 2 is hotly contested. In addition to those who believe that Paul contradicts himself in the passage, some interpreters (for example, Cranfield [*Critical and Exegetical Commentary on the Epistle to the Romans,* 1:158-59]) believe that the Gentiles in Romans 2 are Christians whose Spirit-led conduct conforms to the law written on believers' hearts (compare Jer 31:33), some that Paul speaks of Gentiles prior to the age of the gospel who will be justified because of their obedience (for example, Glenn N. Davies, *Faith and Obedience in Romans: A Study in Romans 1-4, Journal for the Study of the New Testament* Supplement Series 39 [Sheffield, U.K.: JSOT Press, 1990], pp. 53-71), some that the obedience of which Paul speaks is not perfect obedience and that he therefore refers to people who obey what they understand of God's will (Klyne R. Snodgrass, "Justification by Grace—to the Doers: An Analysis of the Place of Romans 2 in the Theology of Paul," *New Testament Studies* 32 [1986]: 72-93) and some that whereas Paul refers to Gentile Christians in 2:7, 10, 26-29, he speaks of unbelieving Gentiles in 2:14-15 (Schreiner, "Did Paul Believe in Justification by Works?" pp. 139-55, and *Law and Its Fulfillment,* pp. 179-204).

That Paul intended the reader to see Christians anywhere in the chapter is unlikely, since his purpose is to show that all are sinners (3:9). His reference to Gentiles' doing the law "by nature" in 2:14, moreover, seems to exclude a reference to Christians in 2:14-16. When Paul speaks clearly of believers' fulfilling the law, as Ernst Käsemann points out, they do so by the power of the indwelling Spirit (8:1-11), not "by nature" (*Commentary on Romans* [Grand Rapids, Mich.: Eerdmans, 1980], p. 65). Furthermore, the idea that Paul refers to the salvation of some by their obedience outside faith in Christ seems excluded by the way he phrases his universal indictment in 3:19-20. There his use of the phrase "works of the law" seems calculated to recall the language of 2:6 ("works") and 2:12-16 ("law") in order to deny that the possibilities suggested in those passages have actually happened.

[43]C. H. Dodd observes (*The Bible and the Greeks* [London: Hodder & Stoughton, 1935], p. 36) that Paul's language is close to that of Plutarch *Moralia* 780 and Aristotle *Nicomachean Ethics* 4.8.14 (1128a).

[44]Räisänen concedes that the wording of 2:14 may leave open the possibility that in this verse Paul refers only to Gentiles who occasionally keep the law (*Paul and the Law,* p. 103). He says that no such explanation, however, suits 2:26-27. Sanders lumps both passages together and claims that it is "simply impossible" to understand them hypothetically (*Paul, the Law and the Jewish People,* p. 126).

[45]Compare Schreiner, "Did Paul Believe in Justification by Works?" pp. 146-47, and *Law and Its Fulfillment,* pp. 195-96.

[46]Compare Lagrange, *Saint Paul Épître aux Romains,* p. 56.

[47]As most commentators recognize, 3:1-4 forms a discrete section that discusses the covenant relationship between God and Israel, and 3:5-8 forms another section in which Paul discusses the special problem of whether his gospel leads to antinomianism. See Cranfield, *Critical and Exegetical Commentary on the Epistle to the Romans,* 1:140, 183, and Käsemann, *Commentary on Romans,* pp. 78, 82. Fitzmyer believes that the section ends at verse 9 rather than at verse 8 because the query "What therefore?" *(ti oun)* in verse 1 forms an inclusio with the "What therefore?" *(ti oun)* in verse 9 (*Romans,* p. 325). The "just as" *(kathōs)* that begins verse 10, however, seems to link verse 9 with verse 10 more closely than with what precedes.

[48]The terms *epistēsan* and *apistia* in 3:3, then, refer primarily to Israel's unfaithfulness to the covenant and not, as Cranfield argues, to Israel's lack of belief in the gospel (*Critical and Exegetical Commentary on the Epistle to the Romans,* 1:180).

[49]Ibid., 1:183-87.

[50]See Lagrange, *Saint Paul Épître aux Romains,* p. 65; Nygren, *Commentary on Romans,* pp. 138-39; Franz J. Leenhardt, *The Epistle to the Romans: A Commentary* (Cleveland: World, 1957), p. 92; Barrett, *Commentary on the Epistle to the Romans,* pp. 63-64; and Cranfield, *Critical and Exegetical Commentary on the Epistle to the Romans,* 1:183.

[51]Cranfield, *Critical and Exegetical Commentary on the Epistle to the Romans,* 1:183; Käsemann, *Commentary on Romans,* pp. 78, 82.

[52]Compare Wilckens, *Der Brief an die Römer,* p. 165.

[53]Compare Cranfield, *Critical and Exegetical Commentary on the Epistle to the Romans,* 1:191-95.

[54]See, for example, Rudolf Bultmann, *Theology of the New Testament,* 2 vols. (New York: Scribner's, 1951-1955), 1:263-64, and "καυχάομαι," in *Theological Dictionary of the New Testament,* ed. Gerhard Kittel, 10 vols. (Grand Rapids, Mich.: Eerdmans, 1965), 3:649; Käsemann, *Commentary on Romans,* p. 89. Compare Luther, *LW* 25:30, 234-35, 241-42.

[55]See, for example, Dunn, *Romans 1-8,* pp. 158-60, and Watson, *Paul, Judaism and the Gentiles,* pp. 129-30. Dunn does not claim that "works of the law" refers only to circumcision, dietary observance and sabbath keeping but to the perception by some Jews that the entire law functioned primarily as a barrier between Jews and Gentiles. Circumcision, dietary observance and sabbath keeping were particularly important for making distinctions between Jews and Gentiles but were not the only elements of the law to which Paul refers when he speaks of "works of the law." See Dunn's clarifications in *Jesus, Paul and the Law,* p. 210, in "Yet Once More—'The Works of the Law': A Response," *Journal for the Study of the New Testament* 46 (1992): 100-104, and "Echoes of Intra-Jewish Polemic in Paul's Letter to the Galatians," *Journal of Biblical Literature* 112 (1993): 466.

[56]Räisänen, *Paul and the Law,* pp. 177-91, especially 187-91.

[57]Compare C. E. B. Cranfield, " 'The Works of the Law' in the Epistle to the Romans," *Journal for the Study of the New Testament* 43 (1991): 94, and Douglas Moo, *Romans 1-8,* Wycliffe Exegetical

Commentary (Chicago: Moody Press, 1991), p. 215. Cranfield places particular importance on the phrase "the work of the law" in 2:15 for the interpretation of "the works of the law" in 3:20.

[58]Dunn, "Yet Once More," pp. 104-6.

[59]See Westerholm, *Israel's Law,* pp. 106-9, 114-15, and especially 117-19, and Cranfield, " 'Works of the Law,' " p. 96.

[60]Wedderburn believes that Paul argues his case on presuppositions that only Christian Jews would accept and attempts in the argument to answer certain charges of Christian Jews against his gospel (*Reasons for Romans,* pp. 59, 93, 104-39). The centerpiece of Paul's case that Jews need "a righteousness of God that comes through faith in Jesus Christ" (3:21), however, is that God's judgment will be impartial, something that non-Christian Jews, on the basis of their Scriptures, also believed (2 Chron 19:7; compare Sirach 35:15-16). Beker's comment that "Paul could not have written Rom. 1:18-2:29 without knowing that Jews are indeed aware of sin and boasting" (*Paul the Apostle,* p. 241) seems fully justified.

[61]Compare Westerholm, *Israel's Law,* pp. 120-21, and Dunn, "Yet Once More—" p. 105. Paul's point is thoroughly biblical. Thus the statement that "by works of the law shall no flesh be justified before him" (*ex ergōn nomou ou dikaiōthēsetai pasa sarx enōpion autou*) is itself a paraphrase of Psalm 142:2 (LXX; 143:2 in English versions): "Do not enter into judgment with your servant, because nothing living shall be justified before you" (*ou dikaiōthēsetai enōpion sou pas zōn*) and stands in continuity with his more exact quotation of phrases from Psalm 13:1-3 (LXX; 14:1-3 in English versions) in 3:10-12.

[62]Paul used the term *grace (charis)* in 1:5 and 1:7 and *faith (pistis)* in 1:5, 8, 12, 17, and 3:3. Compare *believe (pisteuō)* in 1:16 and 3:2.

[63]See Dunn, *Romans 1-8,* p. 170.

[64]See Leenhardt, *Epistle to the Romans,* p. 108; Fitzmyer, *Romans,* p. 359; Stuhlmacher, *Paul's Letter to the Romans,* pp. 65-66.

[65]Compare Hans Hübner, *Law in Paul's Thought,* Studies of the New Testament and Its World (Edinburgh: T & T Clark, 1984), pp. 113-16.

[66]Compare Fitzmyer, *Romans,* p. 363. The phrase does not refer to a Jewish misunderstanding of the law, either as a means of seeking reward (Cranfield, *Critical and Exegetical Commentary on the Epistle to the Romans,* 1:220) or as a means of limiting God's redemptive purposes to the Jewish people (Dunn, *Romans 1-8,* p. 186). It accurately describes the Mosaic law as a law that demands obedience.

[67]See Käsemann, *Commentary on Romans,* pp. 102-3, and Dunn, *Romans 1-8,* pp. 186-87.

[68]Compare Moo, *Romans 1-8,* p. 250.

[69]See, for example, Beker, *Paul the Apostle,* pp. 81-83.

[70]Compare Sanders, *Paul, the Law and the Jewish People,* p. 33.

[71]Compare Heikki Räisänen, *Jesus, Paul and Torah: Collected Essays, Journal for the Study of the New Testament* Supplement 43 (Sheffield, U.K.: Sheffield Academic Press, 1992), pp. 48-94; Westerholm, *Israel's Law,* pp. 123-26; and Moo, *Romans 1-8,* p. 253. The word *poiou* in the phrase *dia poiou nomou* can mean either "what kind of" or simply "what." See Bauer, *Greek-English Lexicon,* s.v. ποῖος. Some interpreters (Hübner, *Law,* p. 138; Wilckens, *Der Brief an die Römer,* pp. 245-46; Cranfield, *Critical and Exegetical Commentary on the Epistle to the Romans,* 1:219-20) believe that "the law of faith" is simply the Mosaic law now properly viewed from the perspective of faith. But Räisänen correctly observes that Paul does not speak of what has happened to the law through faith in this passage but of what has happened to boasting through the law of faith (*Paul and the Law,* p. 52). The term *law,* then is not a reference to the Mosaic law, although since it probably signifies the new covenant it is not merely a play on words as Räisänen believes.

[72]Paul seems to have designed this paragraph specifically to recall the primary themes of his previous argument. Abraham, like the Gentiles described in 1:18, is "ungodly" (*asebē;* compare

asebeian in 1:18). And like the Jews in 2:23, he had no legitimate reason to "boast" before God (*kauchēma;* compare *kauchasai,* 2:23), because he could not supply the "works" (*ergōn;* compare *ergōn,* 3:20, 27, 28) necessary to legitimate such a boast (compare 3:27). Therefore his only recourse was to "believe" (*episteusen;* compare *tous pisteuontas,* 3:22) "the one who justifies" (*ton dikaiounta;* compare *dikaiounta,* 3:26) on the basis of "grace" (*kata charin;* compare *tē . . . chariti,* 3:24) and "apart from works" (*chōris ergōn;* compare *chōris nomou,* 3:21).

[73]An example of how Abraham was popularly conceived in Paul's era can be found in the *Testament of Abraham* (probably composed between A.D. 100 and 200). See especially T*estament of Abraham* 4.6.

[74]See, for example, *Testament of Abraham* 10, in which the archangel Michael conducts Abraham on a tour of the world. As Abraham sees people engaged in various sins, he asks Michael to punish them. His requests are fulfilled immediately. At last a voice from heaven is heard to say, "Commander Michael! Stop the chariot and turn Abraham away so that he will not see the whole earth. For if he sees all those engaged in sin, he will destroy everything. For behold, Abraham has not sinned and has no mercy on sinners" (10.14). It is noteworthy, however, that later in the narrative God assures Abraham that his sins have been forgiven (14.14; compare 10.15). See also Prayer of Manasseh 8, Sirach 44:19-21 and *Jubilees* 23:10.

[75]For this understanding of the ambiguous grammar of 4:2, see Cranfield, *Critical and Exegetical Commentary on the Epistle to the Romans,* 1:228.

[76]This, as Käsemann says (*Commentary on Romans,* p. 114), was the position of Paul's Judaizing opponents, "hence the question is important in practice as well as principle." Compare Dodd, *Epistle of Paul to the Romans,* p. 91.

[77]Hübner claims (*Law,* pp. 51-57) that Paul's approach to circumcision in this passage represents a radical change in his view of the law since the writing of Galatians. In Galatians, says Hübner, circumcision was identified with the whole law, and any who accepted it came under the law's curse, but in Romans 4:12 circumcision, coupled with faith, has value. In Galatians, however, Paul opposes not circumcision itself (see Gal 5:6; 6:15) but the circumcision of Gentile believers in order to qualify them for entry into the people of God. Romans 4:12 offers Abraham as a model to Jewish believers who couple their circumcision with faith. Both in Galatians and Romans, then, faith is the crucial entrance requirement.

[78]Here "seed" refers to believers, not, as in Galatians 3:16, to Christ. The thought here is not inconsistent with Galatians 3:16, however, since in Galatians 3:29 those who are incorporated into Christ are also said to be Abraham's "seed."

[79]Compare Cranfield, *Critical and Exegetical Commentary on the Epistle to the Romans,* 1:240-41.

[80]The prefixed preposition *epi* on the term *epignōsis* ("knowledge") in this verse may carry an intensifying force and give the term the connotation of "full knowledge." Compare Dunn, *Romans 1-8,* p. 155.

Chapter 9: Old Covenant Sin & New Covenant Sanctity in Romans 5—15

[1]Chapter 5 is clearly transitional, but its rhetorical features link it more closely with chapters 6—8 than with chapters 1—4. See C. E. B. Cranfield, *A Critical and Exegetical Commentary on the Epistle to the Romans,* International Critical Commentary, 2 vols. (Edinburgh: T & T Clark, 1975-1979), 1:252-54; and Frank Thielman, "The Story of Israel and the Theology of Romans 5-8," in *Society of Biblical Literature 1993 Seminar Papers,* ed. Eugene H. Lovering (Atlanta: Scholars Press, 1993), p. 233 n. 30.

[2]See the discussion in Stephen Westerholm, *Israel's Law and the Church's Faith* (Grand Rapids, Mich.: Eerdmans, 1988), p. 183.

[3]See Cranfield, *Critical and Exegetical Commentary on the Epistle to the Romans,* 1:282. Paul may be alluding, as Joseph A. Fitzmyer suggests, to the concept of heavenly bookkeeping (compare Dan 7:10) when he says that sin was not reckoned when there was no law (*Romans: A New Translation with Introduction and Commentary,* Anchor Bible 33 [New York: Doubleday, 1993],

p. 417 [compare p. 373]). Paul's meaning then is that "sin neither in its grossness nor in its quantity was booked against individuals."

[4] Compare Cranfield, *Critical and Exegetical Commentary on the Epistle to the Romans*, 1:292-94, and N. T. Wright, *The Climax of the Covenant: Christ and the Law in Pauline Theology* (Edinburgh: T & T Clark, 1991), pp. 35-40, 193-200.

[5] See Cranfield, *Critical and Exegetical Commentary on the Epistle to the Romans*, 1:293, and Wright, *Climax*, p. 39. M.-J. Lagrange says that *hou* ("where") should not be translated in a "local" but in a "temporal" sense, although he admits that the term is normally used in a spatial sense (*Saint Paul Épître aux Romains*, 3rd ed. [Paris: Librairie Victor Lecoffre, 1922], p. 113).

[6] See Cranfield, *Critical and Exegetical Commentary on the Epistle to the Romans*, 1:293-94, and Wright, *Climax*, p. 39.

[7] Compare Ulrich Wilckens, *Der Brief an die Römer*, Evangelisch-katholischer Kommentar zum Neuen Testament 6, 3 vols. (Zurich: Benziger/Neukirchen, Germany: Neukirchener, 1978-1982), 2:8-9.

[8] Rudolf Bultmann has argued that the verse is a non-Pauline intrusion into the text ("Glossen im Römerbrief," in *Exegetica: Aufsätze für Erforschung des Neuen Testaments*, ed. Erich Dinkler [Tübingen, Germany: J. C. B. Mohr/Paul Siebeck, 1967], p. 283). Compare Franz J. Leenhardt, *The Epistle to the Romans: A Commentary* (Cleveland: World, 1957), p. 172, and Victor Paul Furnish, *Theology and Ethics in Paul* (Nashville: Abingdon, 1968), pp. 197-98.

[9] C. H. Dodd, for example, believes that Paul's argument here "has gone hopelessly astray" (*The Epistle of Paul to the Romans* [orig. ed. 1932; London: Collins, 1959], p. 120).

[10] Compare Wright, *Climax*, p. 196.

[11] Paul does not merely say that some aspect of the law, such as the law's curse on the disobedient, has ended or that a particular way of viewing the law, such as its legalistic interpretation, has come to an end for the believer, but that the Mosaic law itself has ceased to exercise authority over the believer. See Heikki Räisänen, *Paul and the Law*, Wissenschaftliche Untersuchungen zum Neuen Testament 29 (Tübingen, Germany: J. C. B. Mohr/Paul Siebeck, 1983), pp. 46-47.

[12] See, for example, Ezekiel 36:25-27; compare 11:19; 18:31; 37:14.

[13] The questions the passage poses are legion: Who is the "I" of the passage? Do the past tenses in verses 7-13 refer to Paul's own past, to Israel, to Adam or to something else entirely? Do the present tenses in verses 14-25 mean that the struggle described there is experienced by the believer? Does Paul slip into a dualistic view of good and evil in verses 14-25, portraying sin as a power out of even God's control? Is his view of human nature unconvincingly pessimistic? In order to retain the clarity of the argument, the following discussion will not address these questions directly, although the notes will touch on all of them briefly.

[14] Compare James D. G. Dunn, *Romans 1-8*, Word Biblical Commentary 38A (Dallas: Word, 1988), p. 359; Fitzmyer, *Romans*, p. 457.

[15] The antecedent of the "I" in 7:7-12 is one of the classic problems in the interpretation of Romans. The way Paul describes sin's springing to life with the coming of the law in verse 9 is reminiscent of Adam's experience with the command of God, and the reference to the tenth commandment in verses 7-8, 10 is reminiscent of Israel's encounter with the law of Moses. Probably, then, both stand behind the "I" in the passage (compare 5:12-21) and Wright, *Climax*, p. 197). Paul's sudden shift from first-person plural verbs and pronouns in verses 5-7 to the first-person singular in verses 8-25, however, indicates that he is also speaking in this passage of his own experience as a member of both Adam's race and Israel's. See Mark Seifrid, *Justification by Faith: The Origin and Development of a Central Pauline Theme*, Supplement to *Novum Testamentum* 68 (Leiden, Netherlands: Brill, 1992), p. 148.

[16] Rudolf Bultmann believed that in Paul's use of the commandment "You shall not covet" the term "covet" ("desire" in the English translation of Bultmann's theology) carried the special meaning of attempting to keep the commandment as a means of achieving life (*Theology of the New Testament*, 2 vols. [New York: Scribner's, 1951-1955], 1:245-46, 264-65; compare Ernst

Käsemann, *Commentary on Romans* [Grand Rapids, Mich.: Eerdmans, 1980], p. 194; and Hans Hübner, *Law in Paul's Thought*, Studies of the New Testament and Its World [Edinburgh: T & T Clark, 1984], pp. 69-78). The most apparent meaning of Paul's reference to sin's use of the tenth commandment, however, is simply that Paul found the commandment impossible to observe fully. The frustration to which this led then produced the anguish of 7:13-25. J. Christiaan Beker's understanding of this passage in *Paul the Apostle: The Triumph of God in Life and Thought* (Philadelphia: Fortress, 1980), p. 239, is precisely correct: "Paul argues not that the intent to obey the law is wrong but that Jews have sealed their doom because of their factual transgressions." See also Räisänen, *Paul and the Law*, pp. 111-13; Heikki Räisänen, *Jesus, Paul and Torah: Collected Essays*, Journal for the Study of the New Testament Supplement 43 (Sheffield, U.K.: Sheffield Academic Press, 1992), pp. 95-111; and Seifrid, *Justification by Faith*, p. 229.

[17]Räisänen (*Paul and the Law*, pp. 141-42) argues that Paul's reference to the law in verse 7a cannot be to the law's role in defining sin. Paul's claim that "without the law sin lies dead" in v. 8 (compare v. 9), he says, excludes so passive a role for the law in v. 7a (compare Lagrange, *Saint Paul Épître aux Romains*, p. 168; Francis Watson, *Paul, Judaism and the Gentiles: A Sociological Approach*, Society of New Testament Studies Monograph Series 56 [Cambridge: Cambridge University Press, 1986], p. 150). If verse 7a connects sin and the law at a deeper level than the level of definition, however, it is difficult to see in what sense it responds to the question "Is the law sin?" Paul probably believes that the law defined sin and, by providing a clear definition of what is forbidden, suggested to the "I" of the passage a means of rebelling against God. This is why "sin sprang to life when the commandment came" (v. 9). Compare Cranfield, *Critical and Exegetical Commentary on the Epistle to the Romans*, pp. 348-49; Westerholm, *Israel's Law*, p. 186.

[18]E. P. Sanders argues that in 3:20, 4:15 and 5:20 both sin and the law have stayed within the sphere of God's saving plan—God used the law to bring knowledge of and increase sin so that he might save everyone by grace (*Paul, the Law and the Jewish People* [Philadelphia: Fortress, 1983], pp. 70-74). Sanders believes that in 6:1—7:6, however, sin becomes a power outside God's control. In 7:7-13, then, Paul must give a different account of the relationship between God, the law and sin. Paul claims, in a way incompatible with 5:20, that God gave the law but that sin used the law for its own evil purposes and thus produced "a situation *contrary* to the will of God" (p. 73). Sanders does not, however, give an adequate explanation of 7:13, which appears to be fully compatible with 5:20. Thus "might be shown" *(phanē)* is a divine passive indicating that God's intention lay behind the connection between the law and death. This intention, Paul says, is that "sin might become exceedingly sinful," a phrase that, as Sanders says (p. 71), echoes Paul's statement of the law's intention in 5:20. Compare Westerholm, *Israel's Law*, pp. 191-92.

[19]Some interpreters believe that because Paul has shifted from past- to present-tense verbs in 7:14 and seems to move from confessional language in verse 13 to philosophical language in verse 14, verse 13 closes the first section of 7:7-25 and verse 14 opens the second section. See Michael Winger, *By What Law? The Meaning of* Νόμος *in the Letters of Paul*, Society of Biblical Literature Dissertation Series 128 (Atlanta: Scholars Press, 1992), p. 161; Fitzmyer, *Romans*, pp. 472-73; and compare Seifrid, *Justification by Faith*, pp. 226-44. Dunn is undoubtedly right in saying that 13 is a transitional verse (*Romans 1-8*, p. 376), but Lagrange (*Saint Paul Épître aux Romains*, p. 171) and Cranfield (*Critical and Exegetical Commentary on the Epistle to the Romans*, 1:354) are correct to regard 13 as the beginning of the new section. Lagrange states the reason well: "A new paragraph begins at v. 13 . . . rather than at v. 14 because of the question which stands parallel to that of v. 7. The new idea which is presented is that of death."

[20]Compare Wright, *Climax*, pp. 198-99.

[21]Compare Westerholm, *Israel's Law*, p. 192 n. 54.

[22]Seifrid probably has the correct perspective on the age-old question of whether Paul refers to the believer or to the unbeliever in this passage (*Justification by Faith*, pp. 235-37). He observes

that a close correlation exists between Romans 7:14-25 and ancient Jewish penitential prayers such as Isaiah 63:7-9; Jeremiah 3:22-25; Ezra 9:5-15; Esther 4:17L-Z (LXX); Prayer of Azariah; *Joseph and Asenath* 12:1—13:15; Tobit 3:1-6; Baruch 1:15-3:8; and Prayer of Manasseh. In such prayers the penitents focus on their unworthiness of God's mercy in light of their sinful nature. As in these prayers, Seifrid concludes, Paul's concern is less whether the unworthiness is past or present and more the element of human inadequacy: the "I" in the passage, therefore, "is not what Paul once was: it is what he still is, intrinsically considered" (*Justification by Faith*, p. 237). This is the situation, however, from which God has rescued the believer through Christ (Rom 8:9; Seifrid, ibid., p. 241).

[23]See Räisänen, *Paul and the Law*, pp. 109-13, Sanders, *Paul, the Law and the Jewish People*, p. 80; Winger, *By What Law?* pp. 81-82 n. 74, 183-85; and Fitzmyer, *Romans*, pp. 475-76. Seifrid observes (*Justification by Faith*, p. 239 n. 236) that "the good" in 7:18 and 21 (*[to] agathon* and *to kalon*) does not refer to a single good deed but to "the moral perfection which is contained in the law as a whole" and to which Paul refers when he calls the law "holy" and the commandment "holy and righteous and good" (v. 12; compare Deut 13:19, LXX). Paul does not say in 7:13-25, then, that the person "sold under sin" (v. 14) cannot do a single good deed but that this person cannot achieve the moral perfection the law demands. Thus the passage does not contradict Paul's claim in 2:14-16 that the Gentile can, at times, perform the law's demands.

[24]Compare Lagrange, *Saint Paul Épître aux Romains*, pp. 177-78. Winger believes that verse 23 is an explanation of verse 21 but that in verse 23 Paul refers to four distinct laws, "the law of God," "another law in my members," "the law of my mind," and "the law of sin" (*By What Law?* p. 187). The proliferation of different laws, says Winger (pp. 185-86), allows Paul subtly to relativize the Mosaic law. It seems strange, however, that Paul would have this intention in a passage designed to defend the law as "holy" and the commandment as "holy and righteous and good" (v. 12). It seems better to view Paul's various uses of the term *nomos* in this passage as simple wordplays.

[25]Sanders believes that in 7:14-25 Paul has offered an explanation of the relationship between God, the law and sin that is incompatible with either the one given in 5:20 (compare 3:20; 4:15) or the one given in 7:7-13 (*Paul, the Law and the Jewish People*, pp. 74-81). In 7:14-25 Paul says that God and the law are allies and sin so powerfully controls the self that the self cannot obey the law. It is possible, however, that in 7:13-25 Paul is simply analyzing the connection between sin and the law at a deeper level than he did in 5:20 or 7:7-12. Thus he is showing how sin uses the commandment to provoke sin in the self, although the self knows what is right and, at one level, wants to do it.

[26]Paul thus picks up a theme mentioned but quickly dropped in 7:6. The procedure is reminiscent of Paul's brief mention in 3:20 and 4:15 of aspects of the law which he deals with fully only at a later point in the argument.

[27]The phrase *peri hamartias* in 8:3 should be translated "as a sin offering" and probably refers to the atoning effect of Christ's death (compare Wilckens, *Der Brief an die Römer*, 2:126-28, and Dunn, *Romans 1-8*, p. 422). Wright offers persuasive arguments that not only does Paul's phrase parallel the language of the Septuagint for "as a sin offering" (*peri hamartias*, Lev 9:2), but in the Septuagint one purpose of the sin offering is to cover unwilling sins or sins of ignorance (*Climax*, pp. 220-25). This is precisely the kind of sin Paul describes in 7:13-20, particularly in verse 15.

[28]Dunn argues that Paul refers to the Mosaic law viewed from two different perspectives in 8:2 (*Romans 1-8*, pp. 416-18). Most commentators, however, take the term *law* to mean "order" (Anders Nygren, *Commentary on Romans* [Philadelphia: Muhlenberg, 1949], pp. 311-12), "system" (Dodd, *Epistle of Paul to the Romans*, p. 135), "principle" (Fitzmyer, *Romans*, 482) or even "religion" (C. K. Barrett, *A Commentary on the Epistle to the Romans* [New York: Harper & Row, 1957], p. 155). Räisänen correctly observes that because "the law of the Spirit of life in Christ Jesus" is the subject that effects liberation from "the law of sin and death," it must be a

different entity from "the law of sin and death" (*Paul and the Law*, p. 52, and *Jesus, Paul and Torah*, pp. 63-68).

[29]Compare Räisänen, *Jesus, Paul and Torah*, p. 68: "Paul means God's saving action in Christ when he speaks of the 'saving order' of faith or of the spirit." It is probably significant, however, that Paul used the word *nomos* here. Although the new order is not identical to the old, the two orders have many elements in common. The word *law* indicates this continuity.

[30]Compare Barrett, *Commentary on the Epistle to the Romans*, p. 155; Nygren, *Commentary on Romans*, p. 312.

[31]"The law of sin and of death" in 8:2, therefore, is different from "the law of sin" in 7:23. In 7:23 Paul referred to the "axiom" that sin dominates the self and prevents it from obeying the law completely. In 8:2 Paul refers to the Mosaic law as it was used by sin to incite transgression and so bring about death (7:10-11, 13).

[32]T. J. Deidun believes that "the law of sin and of death" must be identical with "the law of sin that is in my members" in 7:23, a law that the context demonstrates is not identical with the Mosaic law (*New Covenant Morality in Paul*, Analecta Biblica 89 [Rome: Biblical Institute Press, 1981], pp. 194-203). Deidun is correct that "the law of sin" in 7:23 does not refer to the Mosaic law, but Paul's addition of the words "and death" to the phrase in 8:2 show that he is echoing the argument of chapter 7 about the way sin uses the Mosaic law (7:7) to produce death (7:13).

[33]In 8:3 Paul recalls the discussion in 7:7-25 of the relationship between the Mosaic law (v. 7), sin and the flesh. In 8:4 the phrase "the just requirement of the law" echoes Paul's similar reference to "the just requirements of the law" in 2:26, which in its own context refers to the Mosaic law. In addition "the law" in 8:4 must refer to the same entity as "the law of God" in 8:7, and that expression, because it echoes Paul's references to the law of Moses as "the law of God" in 7:22 and 7:25, probably refers to the law of Moses.

[34]Compare Räisänen, *Paul and the Law*, p. 67. Westerholm believes that Paul uses the term *fulfill* in 8:4 in the special sense of doing "what God 'really' requires" (*Israel's Law*, pp. 201-5). If so, the problem of 8:7-9 still stands: in that verse Paul implies that submission to the law is equal with pleasing God and that believers do both.

[35]Compare Räisänen, *Paul and the Law*, pp. 62-73, especially 71, and Westerholm, *Israel's Law*, p. 202.

[36]Compare Richard B. Hays, *Echoes of Scripture in the Letters of Paul* (New Haven, Conn.: Yale University Press, 1989), p. 63.

[37]Wright observes that at some point in the letter each of the privileges Paul attributes to Israel in 9:4-5 is ascribed to believers (*Climax*, p. 237).

[38]Hays describes these chapters appropriately when he says, "While Rom. 9:6-29 and 11:1-32 affirm the unshakable efficacy of God's word and God's elective will, Rom. 9:30-10:21 pauses in mid-course to describe how Israel has temporarily swerved off the track during an anomalous interval preceding the consummation of God's plan" (*Echoes of Scripture*, p. 75).

[39]Cranfield, *Critical and Exegetical Commentary on the Epistle to the Romans*, 1:503-6, and Paul Achtemeier, *Romans* (Atlanta: John Knox, 1985), pp. 167, 172.

[40]James D. G. Dunn, *Romans 9-16*, Word Biblical Commentary 38B (Dallas: Word, 1988), pp. 579, 599-600.

[41]For a more detailed explanation of this understanding of Rom 9:6-13, see Frank Thielman, "Unexpected Mercy: Echoes of a Biblical Motif in Romans 9-11," *Scottish Journal of Theology* 46 (1994).

[42]Compare Robert Badenas, *Christ the End of the Law: Romans 10.4 in Pauline Perspective* (Sheffield, U.K.: JSOT Press, 1985), p. 101.

[43]On the meaning of *righteousness (dikaiosynē)* in this passage as "covenant righteousness, that righteousness defined by the covenant between God and Israel," see Dunn, *Romans 9-16*, p. 580.

[44]Sanders believes that when Paul wrote "law" (*nomos*) he meant "righteousness by faith" (*Paul,*

the Law and the Jewish People, p. 42) and Fitzmyer that he meant "uprightness" (*Romans,* p. 578). Clearly an explanation of the passage that makes sense of the words Paul actually uses, however, is preferable to the claim that Paul invested a common word with a unique meaning. See Cranfield, *Critical and Exegetical Commentary on the Epistle to the Romans,* 2:507.

[45]Compare Badenas, *Christ the End,* pp. 104, 107. Räisänen believes that 10:4 refers to the end of the law (compare 10:5-13) and so contradicts 9:31 (*Paul and the Law,* p. 54). But in light of the athletic imagery that controls the passage, *telos* ("end" or "goal") in 10:4 probably refers to the goal for which the runners compete—a goal that, once obtained, signals the end of the race. Räisänen's charge that the interpretation assigning *telos* the meaning of both "end" and "goal" is "the most dubious of all" (p. 53) is unwarranted.

[46]Wilckens argues (*Der Brief an die Römer,* 2:212) that the verb *ephthasen* ("reached") should be supplied in 9:32 rather than a form of *diōkō* ("pursue"), and T. David Gordon believes that a form of the copula should be supplied ("Why Israel Did Not Obtain Torah-Righteousness: A Translation Note on Rom 9:32," *Westminster Theological Journal* 54 [1992]: 163-66). He argues that the phrase refers not to Israel's pursuit of the law but to the nature of the Sinai covenant, and should be translated "because the Sinai covenant is not identified/characterized by faith." Both suggestions come to grief on the particle *hōs* ("as"). Gordon's translation leaves it out, and taking it with *ephthasen,* as Wilckens does, seems less natural than taking it with some form of the verb *diōkō.*

[47]See Käsemann, *Commentary on Romans,* p. 278; Cranfield, *Critical and Exegetical Commentary on the Epistle to the Romans,* 2:510; Badenas, *Christ the End,* p. 112; Thomas R. Schreiner, "Israel's Failure to Attain Righteousness in Romans 9:30-10:3," *Trinity Journal* n.s. 12 (1991): 214, 216, 219-20; and Thomas R. Schreiner, *The Law and Its Fulfillment: A Pauline Theology of Law* (Grand Rapids, Mich.: Baker Book House, 1993), pp. 104-12.

[48]Although Paul's biblical quotations draw parallels between Israel's past rejection of the message of the prophets and its present rejection of the gospel, his focus is on the present, as his explicit mention of Israel's disobedience to the gospel in 10:16 shows. Watson believes that 10:14-21 refers to the *Gentile* mission (*Paul, Judaism and the Gentiles,* pp. 166-68). Cranfield is correct in his judgment, however, that 9:30—10:21 is concerned with Israel's rejection of the gospel and that since the third-person plurals in 9:32, 10:2 and 10:3 refer to Israel, the third-person plural verb "they shall call" (*epikalesōntai*) in 10:14 probably refers to Israel also (*Critical and Exegetical Commentary on the Epistle to the Romans,* 2:533).

[49]Compare Wilckens, *Der Brief an die Römer,* 2:212-16.

[50]The stumbling stone, then, is Christ as he is preached in the gospel. In *Romans* (p. 579) Fitzmyer helpfully points out the correspondence between 9:32 and 1 Corinthians 1:23.

[51]Interpreters have often noted the parallels between this passage and Paul's description of his own pre-Christian approach to the law as it appears in Philippians 3:4-11. See, for example, Fitzmyer, *Romans,* p. 582, and Peter Stuhlmacher, *Paul's Letter to the Romans: A Commentary* (Louisville, Ky.: Westminster/John Knox, 1994), pp. 154-55. The parallels are impressive. Israel's "zeal for God" (*zēlon theou*) in Romans 10:2 recalls Paul's own "zeal" (*zēlos*) as a persecutor of the church in Philippians 3:6. His claim in Romans 10:3 that Israel's failing is "being ignorant" (*agnoountes*) of the righteousness of God recalls his claim in Philippians 3:8 that when he became a Christian he gained the "knowledge" (*gnōseōs*) of Christ Jesus (compare 3:10). Most important, his statement in Romans 10:3 that Israel seeks to establish its "own righteousness" (*idian dikaiosynēn*) rather than submit to the righteousness of God seems to echo the contrast in Philippians 3:9 between Paul's "own righteousness" (*emēn dikaiosynēn*) and the righteousness that comes from God. These similarities, however, do not mean that he equates his own pre-Christian approach to the Jewish law with that of all unbelieving Jews. Paul's stress in Philippians 3:4 on his confidence in the flesh as an unbeliever is missing from Romans 10:2-3, and therefore Philippians 3:4 cannot be imposed on Romans 10:2-3 in order to argue that most Jews viewed the law "legalistically."

[52]Compare Beker, *Paul the Apostle*, p. 240. Sanders, consistent with his notion that Paul's argument in Romans 1—11 focuses on the equality of Jew and Gentile, argues that Israel's "own righteousness" refers to the righteousness that is accessible only to the Jews and therefore excludes the Gentiles (*Paul, the Law and the Jewish People*, p. 38). See also Wright, *Climax*, p. 241, and Watson, *Paul, Judaism and the Gentiles*, p. 165. If Paul is thinking biblically, however, and the biblical language of 10:5-13 shows that he is, then he is probably echoing Deuteronomy's references to Israel's "own" inadequate "righteousness."

[53]See Henry George Liddell and Robert Scott, *A Greek-English Lexicon*, rev. and aug. Henry Stuart Jones, 9th ed. (Oxford: Oxford University Press, 1940), s.v. 3.2, and compare Badenas, *Christ the End*, 115.

[54]Compare Frank Thielman, *From Plight to Solution: A Jewish Framework for Understanding Paul's View of the Law in Romans and Galatians*, Supplements to *Novum Testamentum* 61 (Leiden, Netherlands: Brill, 1989), pp. 113-14.

[55]The differences between Paul's language and the language of Deuteronomy 30:11-14 stem from his characteristic rearrangements and omissions of certain words as well as from conflations of two other passages with the Deuteronomy section. Paul actually begins his paraphrase with the opening words of Deuteronomy 9:4 (LXX), "Do not say in your heart," and his reference to descent into the abyss to retrieve Christ from the dead is closer to Psalm 106:26 (LXX—a psalm that must have been on Paul's lips often during his missionary travels) than to Deuteronomy 30:13.

[56] Peter J. Tomson believes that the dispute between the "weak" *(asthenēs)* and the "strong" in 14:1—15:13 was between the "delicate" (Tomson's translation of *asthenēs*) who believed that nonabstaining Gentiles were tainted with idolatry and the "strong" who took a more lenient view (*Paul and the Law: Halakha in the Letters of the Apostle to the Gentiles*, Compendia Rerum Iudaicarum ad Novum Testamentum 3/1 [Minneapolis: Fortress/Assen, Netherlands: Van Gorcum, 1990], pp. 236-45). The dispute does not appear to be an intra-Jewish affair over whether association with Gentiles is permissible, however, but a quarrel between Jews (or Judaizing Gentiles) who abstain and Gentiles (or nonobservant Jews) who do not (compare 11:17-24).

[57]The numbering here represents the traditional Protestant scheme rather than the Roman Catholic.

[58]Paul lists the seventh commandment before the sixth and leaves out the ninth, "You shall not bear false witness against your neighbor."

[59]Peter Stuhlmacher comes close to this understanding of the relationship between the old and the new covenant in Romans (*Reconciliation, Law and Righteousness: Essays in Biblical Theology* [Philadelphia: Fortress, 1986], p. 87). Stuhlmacher speaks, however, of the "*transformation* of the law of Moses into the law of Christ," a formulation that in light of 6:1, 14 and 7:6 seems to find too much continuity between the two.

Chapter 10: Old Convictions in New Settings

[1]See Eusebius *Ecclesiastical History* 2.22. In Philemon, which was probably written from the Roman imprisonment to which Acts 28:30 refers, Paul asks Philemon to prepare a guest room for him (v. 22). Since Philemon was located in Colossae (compare Col 4:17 with Philem 2), Paul must have changed his plans to travel to Spain and decided to travel east. Such changes in travel plans were not unprecedented for him (compare 2 Cor 1:12-2:4 and Acts 16:7-8). *First Clement* 5.6-7 claims that Paul reached "the limit of the west," but this may be nothing more than an inference from Paul's statements in Romans 15:24, 28.

[2]Tertius "wrote" Romans (16:22) and may have helped Paul with his other early letters as well. My own convictions about the widespread belief that Colossians, Ephesians, 2 Thessalonians and the Pastoral Epistles are pseudonymous closely parallel those of Luke T. Johnson (*The Writings of the New Testament: An Interpretation* [Philadelphia: Fortress, 1986], pp. 255-57).

Johnson points out the subjectivity of arguments that Paul could not have written these letters because their vocabulary, literary style and theology do not mesh with those of the seven undisputed letters. He argues, for example, that 1 Thessalonians is accepted because it finds such a comfortable place in the narrative of Acts but that in fact it lacks many of the literary and theological features which supposedly confirm the authenticity of Paul's "genuine" letters. Johnson's own acceptance of all thirteen letters as authentic "is based on the persuasiveness of their literary self-presentation, the ability to find plausible places for them in Paul's career, and a conviction that the whole Pauline corpus is one that Paul 'authored' but did not necessarily write."

[3]This is true even of the letter to Titus, which was written to Crete but is connected to Ephesus through its close association with 1 and 2 Timothy. The false teaching addressed by all three Pastoral Epistles appears to be identical, although it seems to have made more progress in Ephesus than on Crete.

[4]On the attractiveness of Judaism among some Gentiles during Roman times and the anti-Semitic response that this situation often prompted in Greek and Roman literature, see John G. Gager, *The Origins of Anti-Semitism: Attitudes Toward Judaism in Pagan and Christian Antiquity* (New York: Oxford, 1985), pp. 35-112. On the history of Pauline Christianity in Asia Minor shortly after Paul's death, see Andrew T. Lincoln, *Ephesians*, Word Biblical Commentary 42 (Dallas: Word, 1990), pp. lxxxi-lxxxvii.

[5]Interesting but different reconstructions of the events that led to the founding of the Colossian church appear in Bo Reicke, "The Historical Setting of Colossians," *Review and Expositor* 70 (1973): 429-38, and F. F. Bruce, *The Epistles to the Colossians, to Philemon and to the Ephesians*, New International Commentary on the New Testament (Grand Rapids, Mich.: Eerdmans, 1984), pp. 13-17.

[6]Paul's statement that the Colossians were circumcised "by the circumcision of Christ" *(en tē peritomē tou Christou)* is probably best understood as a claim that the Colossians have experienced a "Christian circumcision" rather than as a metaphorical reference to Christ's death. See the full discussion in Peter T. O'Brien, *Colossians, Philemon*, Word Biblical Commentary 44 (Waco, Tex.: Word, 1982), pp. 116-18, and for the understanding of the phrase adopted here see N. T. Wright, *Colossians and Philemon*, Tyndale New Testament Commentaries (Grand Rapids, Mich.: Eerdmans, 1986), pp. 105-6.

[7]Compare Morna Hooker, "Were There False Teachers in Colossae?" in *Christ and Spirit in the New Testament* (Cambridge: Cambridge University Press, 1973), pp. 318-19.

[8]Hooker (ibid., p. 317) is probably correct when she translates *tí . . . dogmatizesthe* in 2:20 as "Why subject yourselves?" rather than "Why *do* you subject yourselves?" Hooker's own thesis that no false teachers were present in Colossae does not take sufficient account of the specificity of Paul's warnings, especially in 2:18, but she is correct to observe that Paul's references to the good condition of the church's faith show that it had not succumbed to false teaching.

[9]The term *philosophy* provides no clear information about the nature of the false teaching, since it could be used to describe systems of thought as diverse as Epicureanism and Pharisaism. The term was generally a positive one, and the false teachers themselves may have used it to describe their teaching. If so, Paul's use of it here is ironic, as his characterization of it as "empty deceit" shows. See O'Brien, *Colossians, Philemon*, pp. 109-10.

[10]C. F. D. Moule takes the phrase "This I say in order that . . ." *(touto legō hina)* to refer to what comes after it and paraphrases 2:4 this way: "What I mean is, nobody is to talk you into error by specious words . . ." (*The Epistles to the Colossians and to Philemon*, Cambridge Greek Testament Commentary [Cambridge: Cambridge University Press, 1957]). Persuasive arguments for taking the phrase as a reference to what Paul has just said in 2:3, however, appear in Eduard Lohse, *Colossians and Philemon: A Commentary on the Epistles to the Colossians and to Philemon* (Philadelphia: Fortress, 1971), p. 83 n. 119, and O'Brien, *Colossians, Philemon*, p. 97.

[11]Compare O'Brien, *Colossians, Philemon*, pp. 110-11.

[12]J. J. Gunther lists forty-four different suggestions and claims that this represents a greater variety of proposals than for any of Paul's other letters (*St. Paul's Opponents and Their Background: A Study of Apocalyptic and Jewish Sectarian Teachings*, Supplements to *Novum Testamentum* 25 [Leiden, Netherlands: Brill, 1973], pp. 3-4). Among the most influential theories are that the error was a gnostic form of Judaism, that it was a form of Judaism heavily influenced by pagan religions, that it was a form of mystical Judaism, that it was a form of Judaism whose piety is reflected in the Dead Sea Scrolls and that it was a pagan mystery religion. See Fred O. Francis and Wayne A. Meeks, eds., *Conflict at Colossae: A Problem in the Interpretation of Early Christianity Illustrated by Selected Modern Studies*, rev. ed., Society of Biblical Literature Sources for Biblical Study 4 (Missoula, Mont.: Scholars Press, 1975), the summaries of proposals in Thomas J. Sappington, *Revelation and Redemption at Colossae, Journal for the Study of the New Testament* Supplement Series 53 (Sheffield, U.K.: JSOT Press, 1991), pp. 15-17, and O'Brien, *Colossians, Philemon*, pp. xxx-xxxviii.

[13]For the use of *feast (heortē), new moon (neomēnia)* and *sabbaths (sabbata)* together in the LXX, see 1 Chronicles 23:31; 2 Chronicles 2:3; 31:3; Ezekiel 45:17; Hosea 2:13. G. B. Caird comments that Paul could have made his point in 2:11-12 easily by referring only to the believer's death and resurrection with Christ, but instead he adds a reference to circumcision (*Paul's Letters from Prison [Ephesians, Philippians, Colossians and Philemon] in the Revised Standard Version*, New Clarendon Bible [Oxford: Oxford University Press, 1976], p. 192). The reason for this, Caird says, is that the "philosophers" in Colossae were placing special emphasis on circumcision.

[14]On the exemplary law-observance of the apocalyptic seer, see, for example, Daniel 1:8 and 4 Ezra 6:31-32. Recording angels appear in *2 Enoch* 19:5; *Testament of Abraham*, Recension A, 12:12; 13:9; Recension B, 10:7-16; and *Apocalypse of Zephaniah* 7—8. Compare the discussions in Sappington, *Revelation and Redemption*, pp. 63-65, 100-110.

[15]Tours of heaven with angelic guides appear in, for example, *1 Enoch* 17—36 and *Apocalypse of Abraham* 9—29, scenes of worshiping angels in *1 Enoch* 47:3; 61:6-13; *2 Enoch* 20:3-21:1; 22:2-3; *Apocalypse of Abraham* 17, and seers reverently doing obeisance before an angel believed to be God in *Apocalypse of Zephaniah* 6:11-15; and Revelation 19:10; 22:8-9. See Sappington, *Revelation and Redemption*, pp. 90-94. So whether the ambiguous phrase "the worship of angels" (*thrēskeia tōn angelōn*, 2:18) means that the visionaries worshiped the angels or that they saw angels worshiping God, the apocalyptic literature provides the background against which the phrase can be understood. Compare Fred O. Francis, "Humility and Angelic Worship," in Francis and Meeks, *Conflict at Colossae*, pp. 176-81.

[16]The phrase "not holding fast to the head" (*ou kratōn tēn kephalēn*) may mean either that the false teachers had once held fast to Christ and are now losing their grip on him or that they never have held fast to him and continue not to do so. See Wright, *Colossians and Philemon*, p. 123.

[17]A venerable tradition within New Testament scholarship claims that in Colossians 1:15-20 and 2:3 Paul identifies Christ with the Mosaic law. These passages echo descriptions of Wisdom in the Old Testament (Prov 2:1-8; 8:22-31), and later Jewish tradition identified Wisdom with the Mosaic law (Sirach 24:1-29; Baruch 3:9—4:4). So, the argument runs, Paul identifies Jesus with Torah in these passages. See, for example, W. D. Davies, *Paul and Rabbinic Judaism*, 4th ed. (Philadelphia: Fortress, 1980), pp. 147-76; Hooker, "Were There False Teachers," pp. 329-31; and N. T. Wright, *The Climax of the Covenant: Christ and the Law in Pauline Theology* (Edinburgh: T & T Clark, 1991), p. 118. It is true that Paul's language echoes biblical descriptions of Wisdom, but the crucial link between such language and the Mosaic law is missing from the passage. Compare Jean-Noël Aletti, *Colossiens 1,15-20: Genre et exégèse du texte: Fonction de la thématique sapientielle*, Analecta Biblica 91 (Rome: Biblical Institute Press, 1981), pp. 152-57.

[18]See Caird, *Paul's Letters from Prison*, pp. 171-74; O'Brien, *Colossians, Philemon*, pp. 26-28; and Wright, *Colossians and Philemon*, 61-63. Compare Werner Foerster, "κλῆρος, κτλ.," in *Theological*

Dictionary of the New Testament, ed. Gerhard Kittel, 10 vols. (Grand Rapids, Mich.: Eerdmans, 1965), 3:759-60. Exodus 6:6 uses *rhyomai* ("deliver") and *lytroō* ("redeem") together to describe God's deliverance of Israel from slavery in Egypt much in the way that Paul uses *rhyomai* and *apolytrōsis* ("redemption") in 1:13-14 to describe God's rescue of believers from sin.

[19]See Wright, *Colossians and Philemon*, p. 63.

[20]For "elect" *(eklektos)* see Psalm 105:6 and Isaiah 43:20; 65:9, 15, 22; for "holy" *(hagios)* see especially Exodus 19:6 and Leviticus 11:44; and for "beloved" *(ēgapēmenos)* see Isaiah 5:1. See J. B. Lightfoot, *St. Paul's Epistles to the Colossians and to Philemon*, rev. ed. (London: Macmillan, 1879), p. 221, and O'Brien, *Colossians, Philemon*, pp. 197-98.

[21]Some interpreters point out that the Mosaic law nowhere regulated "drink" as the false teachers in Colossae seemed to do according to 2:16. This is an indication, they claim, that the Colossian error advocated a rigor that went beyond the commands of the Mosaic law. See O'Brien, *Colossians, Philemon*, p. 138, and Caird, *Paul's Letters from Prison*, p. 198. Paul's summary of the false teachers' regulations in the phrase "Do not handle, do not taste, do not touch" (2:21) is often believed to be another reference to the ascetic nature of their practices. See, for example, Lohse, *Colossians and Philemon*, pp. 123-24, and Herold Weiss, "The Law in the Epistle to the Colossians," *Catholic Biblical Quarterly* 34 (1972): 304. Fasting is sometimes viewed in the apocalypses as an appropriate way to encourage visionary experiences (4 Ezra 5:13, 20; 6:35; 9:23-27), but it is more likely that in 2:16, 21 Paul refers simply to the regulations of the Mosaic law. *Letter of Aristeas* 139-69 shows that Jews of Paul's time could interpret the purity laws as symbols of moral qualities. *Letter of Aristeas* 162, moreover, claims that these laws deal with matters of "foods and drink and touch" (compare 142). For a moralistic interpretation of circumcision see, for example, Philo *On the Migration of Abraham* 92.

[22]The phrase "the elements of the world" *(ta stoicheia tou kosmou)* in 2:8 and 20 probably means here what it did in Galatians 4:3 (compare 4:9). It is a reference to the immature religious practices the Colossians left behind when they received Christ Jesus as Lord (2:6). See Lightfoot, *St. Paul's Epistles to the Colossians and to Philemon*, p. 180, and Bruce, *Epistles to the Colossians, to Philemon and to the Ephesians*, pp. 98-100.

[23]Compare O'Brien, *Colossians, Philemon*, p. 150.

[24]The term *handwriting (cheirographon)* typically means "a certificate of indebtedness, bond" (Walter Bauer, *A Greek-English Lexicon of the New Testament and Other Early Christian Literature*, trans. and aug. William Arndt, F. Wilbur Gingrich and Frederick Danker, 2nd ed. [Chicago: University of Chicago Press, 1979], s.v.). In the Coptic text of the *Apocalypse of Zephaniah*, however, the term is transliterated from the Greek seven times to refer to the "manuscript" that the accusing angel consults to find the good and evil deeds of the seer at the time of his judgment. The term probably refers to this kind of record in Colossians 2:14. See the discussion in Sappington, *Revelation and Redemption*, 214-20.

[25]Compare J. Schneider, "σταυρός κτλ.," in *Theological Dictionary of the New Testament*, ed. Gerhard Kittel and Gerhard Friedrich, 10 vols. (Grand Rapids, Mich.: Eerdmans, 1971), 7:577; and Bauer, *Greek-English Lexicon*, s.v. δόγμα. Weiss believes that the term *dogmata* does not refer to the "decrees" of the Mosaic law ("Law in the Epistle," pp. 310-11). The Mosaic law itself, he argues, is not an issue in the letter. He has not taken adequate account, however, of the clear allusions to the false teachers' use of the Mosaic law in 2:11 and 2:16.

[26]Paul does not say explicitly either that Onesimus had run away from Philemon or that Onesimus had taken money from his master. Thus P. Lampe ("Keine 'Sklavenflucht' des Onesimus," *Zeitschrift für die neutestamentliche Wissenschaft* 76 [1985]: 135-37) and S. Scott Bartchy ("Philemon, Epistle to," in *Anchor Bible Dictionary*, ed. David Noel Freedman, 6 vols. [New York: Doubleday, 1992], 5:307-8) believe that Onesimus fled to Paul not as a fugitive slave but because he and Philemon were at odds and he needed Paul to intercede for him. Sara C. Winter suggests that Philemon sent Onesimus to Paul ("Paul's Letter to Philemon," *New Testament Studies* 33 [1987]: 2-5). Compare the suggestion of F. F. Bruce that Philemon

had sent Onesimus to Paul and that Onesimus became so attached to the apostle that he stayed longer than his master intended (*Paul: Apostle of the Heart Set Free* [Grand Rapids, Mich.: Eerdmans, 1977], p. 400). Lohse believes that verse 18 may imply only that by running away Onesimus had deprived his master of the labor that he might have given him during his absence (*Colossians and Philemon*, p. 204).

That Onesimus had both run away and stolen from his master seems clear, however, from Paul's references to Onesimus's past uselessness (v. 11), his request that Philemon receive Onesimus as he would receive Paul himself (v. 17), and his promise to pay any damages (*egō apotisō*) that Onesimus owes to his master (vv. 18-19). See Caird, *Paul's Letters from Prison*, p. 214; Bauer, *Greek-English Lexicon*, s.v. ἀποτίνω; and the comments of John M. G. Barclay, "Paul, Philemon and the Dilemma of Christian Slave-Ownership," *New Testament Studies* 37 (1991): 163-65.

[27]Compare Caird, *Paul's Letters from Prison*, p. 215.

[28]Bruce argues that in verse 13 Paul asks Philemon to send Onesimus back to him (*Epistles to the Colossians, to Philemon and to the Ephesians*, pp. 214-15). As Caird points out, however (*Paul's Letters from Prison*, p. 222), verse 15 seems to mean that Paul is sending Onesimus back to Philemon permanently (compare v. 11).

[29]The passage reads, "Slaves who have escaped to you from their owners shall not be given back to them. They shall reside with you, in your midst, in any place they choose in any one of your towns, wherever they please; you shall not oppress them." The law probably referred to slaves from outside Israel who sought refuge within Israelite territory. For the ancient debate over the significance of this law see Philo *On the Virtues* 124 and the rabbinic discussion canvassed in Peter J. Tomson, *Paul and the Jewish Law: Halakha in the Letters of the Apostle to the Gentiles*, Compendia Rerum Iudaicarum ad Novum Testamentum 3/1 (Minneapolis: Fortress/Assen, Netherlands: Van Gorcum, 1990), pp. 92-94.

[30]Compare Bruce, *Paul: Apostle of the Heart*, p. 400 n. 19.

[31]Compare Paul's use of *parrēsia* in 2 Corinthians 3:12. See Heinrich Schlier, "παρρησία,κτλ.," in *Theological Dictionary of the New Testament*, ed. Gerhard Kittel and Gerhard Friedrich, 10 vols. (Grand Rapids, Mich.: Eerdmans, 1967), 5:883, and Lohse, *Colossians and Philemon*, p. 198. Paul does not use the verb *epitassō* elsewhere in his letters, but when he uses its cognate noun *epitagē*, it always carries the connotation of an authoritative "command" issued by a superior to someone of lesser rank. See Romans 16:26; 1 Corinthians 7:6, 25; 2 Corinthians 8:8; 1 Timothy 1:1; Titus 1:3; 2:15; and O'Brien, *Colossians, Philemon*, p. 288.

[32]See, for example, Romans 6:17; 1 Corinthians 4:17; 11:23; Colossians 2:6-7; and 1 Thessalonians 4:1.

[33]The most critical aspect of the verse for our purposes is the meaning of *pan agathon* ("everything good"). Does it mean "every blessing" or "every good work"? Moule points out (*Epistles to the Colossians and to Philemon*, p. 143) that *to agathon* ("the good") usually refers to something that is done rather than to some possession (as in Rom 14:16), and Peter Stuhlmacher observes that the Septuagint's rendering of the Psalter uses this idiom to refer to God's will (*Der Brief an Philemon*, 3rd ed., Evangelisch-katholischer Kommentar zum Neuen Testament 17 [Zurich: Benziger/Neukirchen, Germany: Neukirchener, 1989], p. 34). See Psalms 33:15; 36:27; 52:2, 4 LXX.

[34]See Stuhlmacher, *Der Brief an Philemon*, p. 34. The term Paul uses to describe Philemon's knowledge, *epignōsis*, refers in the New Testament primarily to religious and moral knowledge (see Bauer, *Greek-English Lexicon*, s.v.). Compare Colossians 1:9.

[35]Paul also indicates in verses 7-8 that his confidence is based on Philemon's past record of helping God's people (compare v. 20). Paul probably regarded Philemon's past record of service as evidence that God was at work in Philemon to show him his will and enable him to do it.

[36]Scholars have often compared Paul's letter to Philemon with Pliny's letters to Sabinianus

(*Epistles* 9.21, 24), and several have observed that whereas Pliny goes straight to the point and asks Sabinianus for clemency on behalf of his freedman, Paul's request to Philemon is indirect. Barclay believes that Paul's reticence is a result of his own indecisiveness in the face of a difficult theological and practical problem ("Paul, Philemon and the Dilemma," pp. 161-86). If the argument presented here is correct, however, Paul knows exactly what Philemon should do—forgive his slave—but does not command him to do it directly because he trusts Philemon's knowledge of God's will and willingness to do what is right.

[37]This seems to be the best explanation for Paul's reference to Tychicus in Ephesians 6:21-22 and for the many verbal reminiscences to Colossians and Philemon contained in Ephesians.

[38]Codex Sinaiticus and Codex Vaticanus, both fourth-century manuscripts, and the Chester Beatty biblical papyrus, from about A.D. 200, do not have "in Ephesus" (*en Ephesō*) in 1:1. The resulting Greek in Codex Sinaiticus and Codex Vaticanus is awkward but not impossible: *tois hagiois tois ousin kai pistois.* Compare Acts 5:17; 13:1; 14:13. The Chester Beatty biblical papyrus leaves out the second definite article, apparently by a mistake of eyesight. See the discussions in Rudolf Schnackenburg, *Ephesians: A Commentary* (orig. German ed. 1982; Edinburgh: T & T Clark, 1991), pp. 40-41, and Lincoln, *Ephesians,* pp. 1-4.

[39]Markus Barth believes that although the church at Ephesus was composed of both Jews and Gentiles, Paul wrote Ephesians only for recent Gentile converts who were not personally acquainted with Paul (*Ephesians 1-3: A New Translation with Introduction and Commentary,* Anchor Bible 34 [New York: Doubleday, 1974], pp. 11, 58, 67). It is clear that the recipients were not personally acquainted with Paul (1:15; 3:2), but the notion that they are recent converts does not cohere well with Paul's desire that his readers remember what God has done for them (2:1-22). See Lincoln, *Ephesians,* pp. xxxvi-xxxvii.

[40]Lincoln, however, believes that a Jewish Christian follower of Paul composed the letter in an attempt to alleviate an identity crisis that occurred among Christians in Asia Minor in the wake of Paul's death (*Ephesians,* pp. lxxiii-lxxxvii).

[41]It is not likely that Paul makes a distinction in 1:1, 1:18 and 2:19 between Jewish Christians, whom he calls "the saints," and the Gentile Christians who now have been added to their number (as, for example, Caird argues in *Paul's Letters from Prison,* pp. 31, 45, 60). Paul's use of the term in 1:15, 3:18, 4:12 and 6:18 (compare 3:8; 5:3) show that it has a wider reference than to Jewish Christians. See Schnackenburg, *Ephesians,* pp. 42-43, and Lincoln, *Ephesians,* pp. 2, 5-6.

[42]Paul's comparison of the church with a bride whom Christ, the groom, sanctifies and washes in order that she might be glorious and beautiful (5:26-27) recalls the imagery of Ezekiel 16:8-14. In that passage the prophet describes God's choice of Israel to be his people as the choice of a bride whom God bathed, clothed in splendor and fed sumptuously. See Lincoln, *Ephesians,* p. 375.

[43]"The saints" (*tōn hagiōn*) in this verse has been variously understood. Some believe that it refers to Jewish Christians, some that it means angels, and some that it designates the total body of other believers. In the rest of the letter, however, Paul characteristically uses the phrase "the saints" for believers generally, and no compelling reason exists for abandoning that meaning here. The readers joined the newly constituted people of God, "the saints," when they became believers and therefore were no longer strangers and resident aliens but fellow citizens with other believers in God's commonwealth. See Schnackenburg, *Ephesians,* p. 121, and Lincoln, *Ephesians,* p. 151.

[44]See Lincoln, *Ephesians,* p. 146.

[45]Markus Barth believes that since Ephesians is addressed to Gentiles, Paul uses the term transgressions (*paraptōmatōn*) in 1:7 in the sense of "lapses" rather than with its normal Pauline sense of offenses against the law (*Ephesians 1-3,* pp. 83-84). But in Romans 1:32 Paul says that Gentiles know "the just requirement of God," and here, in any case, he is alluding to a passage of Scripture that prophesies the rescue of God's people from disobedience to the law. Bruce

believes that the phrase "the Holy Spirit of promise" refers to the promise of future glory which the Holy Spirit represents (*Epistles to the Colossians, to Philemon and to the Ephesians*, p. 265). Most commentators, however, take the phrase as a Semiticism meaning "the promised Holy Spirit." See C. F. D. Moule, *An Idiom-Book of New Testament Greek*, 2nd ed. (Cambridge: Cambridge University Press, 1959), p. 175.

[46]Ephesians 2:17 says that Christ "preached peace" (*euēngelisato eirēnēn*), and Isaiah 52:6-7 (LXX) reads, "Thus shall the people know my name in that day, because I myself am the one who speaks. I am present as a season of beauty upon the mountains, as the feet of one who preaches the good news of peace *[hōs podes euangelizomenou akoēn eirēnēs]*, as one who preaches good news of good things *[hōs euangelizomenos agatha]*, for I will make a declaration of your salvation saying, 'Zion, your God shall reign.' " Compare Ephesians 6:15.

[47]The relevant phrase in the Septuagint's rendering of Isaiah 57:19 is *eirēnēn ep' eirēnēn tois makran kai tois engys ousin*, and in Ephesians 2:17, *tois makran kai ... tois engys*. Peter Stuhlmacher argues perusasively that this biblical background provides the proper context within which to interpret 2:17 rather than, as some have suggested, the world of Gnostic mythology (*Reconciliation, Law and Righteousness: Essays in Biblical Theology* [Philadelphia: Fortress, 1986], pp. 182-91).

[48]Paul's reference to Zechariah 8:16 is nearly an exact quotation of the Septuagint. The only difference is that whereas Paul admonishes his readers to speak the truth "with" (*meta*) one another, the prophet tells his readers to speak the truth "to" (*pros*) one another. Paul's reference to Isaiah 63:10 is less direct. Ephesians 4:30 reads, "Do not grieve the Holy Spirit of God" (*mē lypeite to pneuma to hagion tou theou*), whereas the Septuagint's rendering of Isaiah 63:10 says that Israel "provoked his Holy Spirit [to wrath]" (*parōxynan to pneuma to hagion autou*).

[49]Some commentators believe that when Paul refers to "you" in this passage he means "you Gentiles," and when he refers to "we" he means "we Jews." See, for example, Barth, *Ephesians 1-3*, p. 211, and Caird, *Paul's Letters from Prison*, pp. 49-52. As Lincoln points out, the distinction cannot be maintained and begins to break down in 2:5a, where the author cannot mean "although we [Jews] were dead in our trespasses . . ." (*Ephesians*, p. 88).

[50]The thesis of Karl Martin Fischer that Ephesians moves against the tendency in early Christianity toward a clear separation from Judaism, then, is probably not correct (*Tendenz und Absicht des Epheserbriefes*, Forschungen zur Religion und Literatur des Alten und Neuen Testaments [Göttingen, Germany: Vandenhoeck & Ruprecht, 1973], pp. 79-94; compare Stuhlmacher, *Reconciliation, Law and Righteousness*, pp. 192-93). The argument of 1:3—3:21 is designed to show that the predominantly Gentile church is heir to the promises made to Israel and that whether composed of Jews or Gentiles, it is a new entity. Compare Lincoln, *Ephesians*, p. lxxx.

[51]Compare Colossians 1:12, 26; 3:12.

[52]For the notion that all have sinned and stand under God's wrath, compare Romans 1:18—3:20, Galatians 2:15-16 and 3:10-13, and Philippians 3:9, for example, with Ephesians 2:1-10, 16-18. For the role of the law in this plight and the role of Christ's death in solving it, compare Romans 3:21-26, Galatians 2:19-21 and 3:10-13, and Philippians 3:9-10, for example, with Ephesians 1:7 and 2:13, 16.

[53]Compare Romans 3:22-24, 29-30 and Galatians 2:11-18 and 3:28, for example, with Ephesians 2:11-22.

[54]Compare Ephesians 2:4-9 with Romans 3:20, 28 and Galatians 2:16. Paul's opposition of grace to human effort generally in Ephesians 2:4-9, however, is anticipated in such passages as Romans 4:2, 6; 9:11; and 11:6. On the consistency of Ephesians 2:8-10 with Paul's theology, despite some changes to meet a new situation, see Andrew T. Lincoln, "Ephesians 2:8-10: A Summary of Paul's Gospel?" *Catholic Biblical Quarterly* 45 (1983): 617-30.

[55]See especially Romans 5:9. Paul usually uses the verb *sōzō* ("save") in the future tense (as in Rom 5:9-10; I Cor 3:15), although there are significant exceptions to this custom (for example,

Rom 8:24; 1 Cor 1:18). Ephesians 2:5 and 2:8 provide the only occurrences of the perfect tense of *sōzō* in the Pauline letters. See Lincoln, "Ephesians 2:8-10," p. 620.

[56]This reconstruction of Paul's travels follows the suggestions of Gordon D. Fee, *1 and 2 Timothy, Titus* (New York: Harper & Row, 1984), p. xviii, and George W. Knight III, *The Pastoral Epistles: A Commentary on the Greek Text,* New International Greek Testament Commentary (Grand Rapids, Mich.: Eerdmans, 1992), pp. 9-10.

[57]Not everyone agrees that the false teaching presupposed in the three letters is the same. See, for example, James D. G. Dunn, "Anti-Semitism in the Deutero-Pauline Literature," in *Anti-Semitism and Early Christianity: Issues of Polemic and Faith,* ed. Craig A. Evans and Donald A. Hagner (Minneapolis: Fortress, 1993), pp. 159-64. The description of the false teaching in Titus emphasizes its Jewish origin (Tit 1:10, 14; 3:9). Nevertheless, the role of the false teachers as "teachers of the law" in 1 Timothy 1:7 meshes well with this picture and Paul's consistent description of the false teaching in all three letters as "myths" (1 Tim 1:4; 4:7; 2 Tim 4:4; Tit 1:14) and "empty talk" (1 Tim 1:6; Tit 1:10; 3:9) probably means that a single religious movement stands in the background of the three letters. This false teaching is often identified with a Jewish form of Gnosticism. See the survey of proposals in Philip H. Towner, *The Goal of Our Instruction: The Structure of Theology and Ethics in the Pastoral Epistles, Journal for the Study of the New Testament* Supplement Series 34 (Sheffield, U.K.: JSOT Press, 1989), pp. 21-24.

[58]These "households" *(oikoi)* were probably not merely individual families but the churches that met in their houses as well. The false teachers, then, are moving from house church to house church in an effort to spread false teaching. See Fee, *1 and 2 Timothy, Titus,* p. 133, and Jerome D. Quinn, *The Letter to Titus: A New Translation with Notes and Commentary and an Introduction to Titus, I and II Timothy, the Pastoral Epistles,* Anchor Bible 35 (New York: Doubleday, 1990), pp. 106-7.

[59]In 1 Timothy 5:13 the irresponsible younger widows are charged with "saying what they must not" *(lalousai ta mē deonta),* the same charge that Paul levels against the false teachers in Titus 1:11 *(ha mē dei).* It may also be significant that 1 Timothy 5:16 implies that these widows are living off the beneficence of the church and Titus 1:11 that they are interested in monetary gain. Compare 2 Timothy 3:6 and Jürgen Roloff, *Der Erste Brief an Timotheus,* Evangelisch-katholischer Kommentar zum Neuen Testament 15 (Zurich: Benziger; Neukirchen, Germany: Neukirchener, 1988), p. 298.

[60]T. C. Skeat has argued persuasively that the term *malista* in the Pastorals means not "especially," as it is usually translated, but "that is" or "in other words" (" 'Especially the Parchments': A Note on 2 Timothy IV.13," *Journal of Theological Studies* n.s. 30 [1979]: 173-77). If his case is sound, then Titus 1:10 should read not "For there are many rebellious people, *especially* the circumcision, who speak empty words and are deceivers," but "For there are many rebellious people, *that is* the circumcision, who speak empty words and are deceivers." This translation implies that the false teachers did not merely include some Jews but were entirely Jewish.

[61]Clement, writing in A.D. 96, probably used the Pastorals, and it is virtually certain that Polycarp, whose letter to the Philippians was probably written in A.D. 117, knew them. Evidence for fully developed Gnosticism does not appear, however, until about the middle of the second century.

[62]Compare Towner, *The Goal of Our Instruction,* pp. 21-45.

[63]Some believe that the Colossian error provides a close parallel to the false teaching described in the Pastorals. See, for example, Knight, *Pastoral Epistles,* p. 28. It is true that the false teaching in both situations emphasized esoteric knowledge (Col 2:18; 1 Tim 6:20), and both were apparently interested in the Jewish law (Col 2:11, 14-17, 21-23; 1 Tim 1:7; Tit 2:14; 3:9). But the Colossian false teachers seem to have urged the Colossians to accept circumcision and to come under the yoke of the law as Jewish proselytes (Col 2:11, 16, 21), whereas the false teachers depicted in the Pastorals had no interest in promoting circumcision and were interested in the law primarily as a source-book for "myths," "genealogies," esoteric knowledge and an ascetic approach to food. Compare J. N. D. Kelly, *The Pastoral Epistles,* Harper's New

Testament Commentary (New York: Harper & Row, 1960), p 95.

[64]False teaching does not dominate Titus in the way that it does 1 and 2 Timothy. Explicit references to it occur only in 1:9-16 and 3:9-11. See Fee, *1 and 2 Timothy, Titus*, p. xxiv.

[65]Paul uses the term *law* in only one passage (1 Tim 1:7-9; compare Tit 3:9). "Human commandments" *(entolais anthrōpōn)* in Titus 1:14 is probably not a reference to the Mosaic law but to the ascetic regulations that, according to 1 Timothy 4:3, the false teachers were imposing on the households they had infiltrated. Compare Kelly, *Pastoral Epistles*, p. 236.

[66]See Kelly, *Pastoral Epistles*, pp. 49-50, and Roloff, *Der Erste Brief an Timotheus*, p. 75.

[67]On Paul's use of the term *law* in this passage to refer to the Mosaic law as a subcategory of law in general, see Walter Lock, *A Critical and Exegetical Commentary on the Pastoral Epistles (I & II Timothy and Titus)* (Edinburgh: T & T Clark, 1924), pp. 11-12, and Kelly, *Pastoral Epistles*, pp. 48-49. On Paul's purpose of associating the false teachers with wickedness by means of the vice list in 1:9-10, see Martin Dibelius and Hans Conzelmann, *The Pastoral Epistles*, Hermeneia (Philadelphia: Fortress, 1972), p. 23, and Towner, *The Goal of Our Instruction*, p. 27.

[68]Compare Knight, *Pastoral Epistles*, p. 83.

[69]E. F. Scott claims that this passage provides decisive evidence that Paul could not have written the Pastorals (*The Pastoral Epistles*, Moffatt New Testament Commentary [New York: Harper & Brothers, 1936], pp. 10-11). The author, he says, gives such a poor account of Paul's view of the law that he is himself guilty of not understanding the things on which he insists (compare 1 Tim 1:7). But Scott does not take adequate account of Paul's rhetorical strategy in the passage. Paul is not interested in a theology of the law here but in a rhetorical link between "law" and "the lawless and rebellious."

[70]The sentence reads literally, "I give thanks to God whom I serve, from my ancestors *(apo progonōn)*, with a pure conscience," but in this context *apo progonōn* means "as my ancestors did." See Bauer, *Greek-English Lexicon*, s.v. πρόγονος, and Knight, *Pastoral Epistles*, p. 367.

[71]Compare Ezekiel 37:23 LXX. The motif of the rescue from Egypt and the selection of Israel as God's "special people" *(laos periousios)* is also present in the Septuagint's rendering of Exodus 19:4-6.

[72]This is the view of many students of the Pastorals. See, for example, Rudolf Bultmann, *Theology of the New Testament*, 2 vols. (New York: Scribner's, 1951-1955), 2:185, and Dibelius and Conzelmann, *Pastoral Epistles*, pp. 8-10. For thorough criticisms of this perspective, see Towner, *The Goal of Our Instruction*, and Reggie M. Kidd, *Wealth and Beneficence in the Pastoral Epistles*, Society of Biblical Literature Dissertation Series 122 (Atlanta: Scholars Press, 1990).

[73]Compare Towner, *The Goal of Our Instruction*, pp. 168-99, 253-54.

[74]See ibid., pp. 38-42.

[75]Titus 3:7 does use justification language to refer to salvation in a way that is reminiscent of the earlier letters. God poured out his Spirit on Christians, Paul says, "in order that, having been justified by that grace, we might become heirs in the hope of eternal life" (compare Rom 5:1-2).

[76]Thus it appears in Galatians and Philippians, where Paul is concerned with Judaizers, and in Romans, where he is in dialogue with a Jewish debating partner about, among other things, why believers are no longer "under law" (Rom 6:14-15).

[77]Compare, for example, the language of 1 Corinthians 6:1-11 with Ephesians 5:3, 26, and the echoes of Jeremiah 31:31-34 in 2 Corinthians 3:3-6 with the echoes of the same passage in Colossians 1:14 and Ephesians 1:7.

[78]Compare, for example, Romans 7:6 and 13:8-10 with Ephesians 2:15 and 6:2-3.

Chapter 11: Paul & the Law in Context

[1]Compare Paul Hanson, *The People Called: The Growth of Community in the Bible* (New York: Harper & Row, 1986), pp. 11-12, and W. D. Davies, *Jewish and Pauline Studies* (Philadelphia: Fortress, 1984), pp. 94-95.

[2]A frequent criticism of E. P. Sanders's understanding of the relationship between Judaism and Christianity in first-century Judaism is that it cannot explain why Jews became Christians. See J. Christiaan Beker, *Paul the Apostle: The Triumph of God in Life and Thought* (Philadelphia: Fortress, 1980), pp. 237-38, and Jacob Neusner, *Judaic Law from Jesus to the Mishnah: A Systematic Reply to Professor E. P. Sanders*, South Florida Studies in the History of Judaism 84 (Atlanta: Scholars Press, 1993), p. 295.

[3]This is why Paul's arguments that works of the law do not justify and that the law cannot be obeyed contain no references to the Jewish institutions of atonement and repentance. Paul, like most Jews, took those institutions for granted but looked forward to a time when God would deal conclusively with Israel's disobedience.

[4]Whether Paul conceived of Christ's commands as a new law, as C. H. Dodd ("ΕΝΝΟΜΟΣ ΧΡΙΣΤΟΥ," in *Studia Paulina in Honorem Johannis de Zwaan Septuagenarii*, ed. J. N. Sevenster and W. C. van Unnik [Haarlem: Erven F. Bohn, 1953]) and W. D. Davies (*Paul and Rabbinic Judaism*, 4th ed. [Philadelphia: Fortress, 1980], pp. 136-46) have argued, is difficult to say. Heikki Räisänen correctly criticizes Dodd's terminological argument that *ennomos Christou* and *nomos tou Christou* refer in their own contexts to a body of Jesus' commands (*Paul and the Law*, Wissenschaftliche Untersuchungen zum Neuen Testament 29 [Tübingen, Germany: J. C. B. Mohr/Paul Siebeck, 1983], pp. 78-82). The claim that Jesus' teachings functioned as part of the ethical content of the new covenant, however, is based more on the parallels between the ethical teaching of Paul and Jesus than on Paul's use of the term *nomos*. Although it would be difficult to make a decisive case for a connection, the parallels at least admit the possibility of such a connection.

[5]Stephen Westerholm, *Israel's Law and the Church's Faith* (Grand Rapids, Mich.: Eerdmans, 1988), pp. 143-50.

Bibliography

Aletti, Jean-Noël. *Colossiens 1,15-20: Genre et exégèse du texte: Fonction de la thématique sapientielle.* Analecta Biblica 91. Rome: Biblical Institute Press, 1981.

Attridge, H. W. *The Interpretation of Biblical History in the* Antiquitates Judaicae *of Flavius Josephus.* Harvard Dissertations in Religion 7. Missoula, Mont.: Scholars Press, 1976.

Badenas, Robert. *Christ the End of the Law: Romans 10.4 in Pauline Perspective.* Sheffield, U.K.: JSOT Press, 1985.

Balz, H. "ἔννομος." In *Exegetical Dictionary of the New Testament,* 1:455-56. Edited by H. Balz and G. Schneider. 3 vols. Grand Rapids, Mich.: Eerdmans, 1990-1993.

_____. "παρρησιάζομαι." In *Exegetical Dictionary of the New Testament,* 3:45-47. Edited by H. Balz and G. Schneider. 3 vols. Grand Rapids, Mich.: Eerdmans, 1990-1993.

Barclay, John M. G. "Mirror-Reading a Polemical Letter: Galatians as a Test Case." *Journal for the Study of the New Testament* 31 (1987): 73-93.

_____. *Obeying the Truth: A Study of Paul's Ethics in Galatians.* Studies of the New Testament and Its World. Edinburgh: T & T Clark, 1988.

_____. "Paul, Philemon and the Dilemma of Christian Slave-Ownership." *New Testament Studies* 37 (1991): 161-86.

Barrett, C. K. *A Commentary on the Epistle to the Romans.* Harper's New Testament Commentaries. New York: Harper & Row, 1957.

_____. *Essays on Paul.* Philadelphia: Westminster Press, 1982.

_____. *The First Epistle to the Corinthians.* Harper's New Testament Commentaries. New York: Harper & Row, 1968.

_____. *The Second Epistle to the Corinthians.* Harper's New Testament Commentaries. New York: Harper & Row, 1973.

Bartchy, S. Scott, "Philemon, Epistle to." In *Anchor Bible Dictionary,* 5:305-10. Edited by David Noel Freedman. 6 vols. New York: Doubleday, 1992.

Barth, Markus. *Ephesians 1-3: A New Translation with Introduction and Commentary.* Anchor Bible 34. New York: Doubleday, 1974.

Bassler, Jouette M. *Divine Impartiality: Paul and a Theological Axiom.* Society of Biblical Literature Dissertation Series 59. Chico, Calif.: Scholars Press, 1982.

_____. "Divine Impartiality in Paul's Letter to the Romans." *Novum Testamentum* 26 (1984): 43-58.

Bauer, Walter. *A Greek-English Lexicon of the New Testament and Other Early Christian Literature.* Translated, revised and augmented by William F. Arndt, F. Wilbur Gingrich and Frederick W. Danker. 2nd ed. Chicago: University of Chicago Press, 1979.

Beker, J. Christiaan. *Paul the Apostle: The Triumph of God in Life and Thought.* Philadelphia: Fortress, 1980.

Best, Ernest. *A Commentary on the First and Second Epistles to the Thessalonians.* Harper's New Testament Commentaries. New York: Harper & Row, 1972.

Betz, Hans Dieter. *Galatians: A Commentary on Paul's Letter to the Churches in Galatia.* Hermeneia. Philadelphia: Fortress, 1979.

Bornkamm, Heinrich. *Luther and the Old Testament.* Edited by Victor I. Gruhn. Philadelphia: Fortress, 1969.

Bowler, Maurice Gerald. *Claude Montefiore and Christianity.* Brown Judaic Studies 157. Atlanta: Scholars Press, 1988.

Brown, Raymond E., and John P. Meier. *Antioch and Rome: New Testament Cradles of Catholic Christianity.* New York: Paulist, 1983.

Bruce, F. F. *The Epistle to the Galatians: A Commentary on the Greek Text.* New International Greek Testament Commentary. Grand Rapids, Mich.: Eerdmans, 1982.

_____. *The Epistles to the Colossians, to Philemon and to the Ephesians.* New International Commentary on the New Testament. Grand Rapids, Mich.: Eerdmans, 1984.

_____. *1 & 2 Thessalonians.* Word Biblical Commentary 45. Waco, Tex.: Word, 1982.

_____. *Paul: Apostle of the Heart Set Free.* Grand Rapids, Mich.: Eerdmans, 1977.

_____. *Philippians.* Good News Commentary. New York: Harper & Row, 1983.

Bultmann, Rudolf. "Glossen im Römerbrief." In *Exegetica: Aufsätze für Erforschung des Neuen Testaments.* Edited by Erich Dinkler. Tübingen: J. C. B. Mohr/Paul Siebeck, 1967.

_____. "καυχάομαι κτλ." *In Theological Dictionary of the New Testament,* 3:645-54. Edited by Gerhard Kittel. 10 vols. Grand Rapids, Mich.: Eerdmans, 1965.

_____. *Primitive Christianity in Its Contemporary Setting.* New York: World Publishing, 1956.

_____. *The Second Letter to the Corinthians.* Minneapolis: Augsburg, 1985.

_____. *Theology of the New Testament.* 2 vols. New York: Scribner's, 1951-1955.

Burton, Ernest de Witt. *A Critical and Exegetical Commentary on the Epistle to the Galatians.* International Critical Commentary. Edinburgh: T & T Clark, 1921.

Caird, G. B. *Paul's Letters from Prison: Ephesians, Philippians, Colossians and Philemon in the Revised Standard Version.* New Clarendon Bible. Oxford: Oxford University Press, 1976.

Calvin, John. *The Epistles of Paul the Apostle to the Galatians, Ephesians, Philippians and Colossians.* Grand Rapids, Mich.: Eerdmans, 1965.

Charlesworth, James H. *The Old Testament Pseudepigrapha.* 2 vols. New York: Doubleday, 1983-1985.

Clements, Ronald E. *One Hundred Years of Old Testament Interpretation.* Philadelphia: Westminster Press, 1976.

Collange, Jean-François. *The Epistle of Saint Paul to the Philippians.* Orig. ed. 1973. London: Epworth, 1979.

Collins, Raymond F. *Studies on the First Letter to the Thessalonians.* Bibliotheca Ephemeridum Theologicarum Lovaniensium 66. Leuven, Belgium: Leuven University Press/Uitgeverij Peters, 1984.

Cook, James I. "The Concept of Adoption in the Theology of Paul." In *Saved by Hope: Essays in Honor of Richard C. Oudersluys.* Edited by James I. Cook. Grand Rapids, Mich.: Eerdmans, 1978.

Cranfield, C. E. B. *A Critical and Exegetical Commentary on the Epistle to the Romans.* 2 vols. International Critical Commentary. Edinburgh: T & T Clark, 1975-1979.

_____. "Giving a Dog a Bad Name: A Note on H. Räisänen's *Paul and the Law.*" *Journal for the Study of the New Testament* 38 (1990): 77-85.

_____. " 'The Works of the Law' in the Epistle to the Romans." *Journal for the Study of the New Testament* 43 (1991): 89-101.

Davies, Glenn N. *Faith and Obedience in Romans: A Study in Romans 1-4. Journal for the Study of the New Testament* Supplement Series 39. Sheffield, U.K.: JSOT Press, 1990.

Davies, W. D. *Jewish and Pauline Studies.* Philadelphia: Fortress, 1984.

_____. *Paul and Rabbinic Judaism: Some Rabbinic Elements in Pauline Theology.* 4th ed. Philadelphia: Fortress, 1980.

Deidun, T. J. *New Covenant Morality in Paul.* Analecta Biblica 89. Rome: Biblical Institute Press, 1981.

Deissmann, Adolf. *Light from the Ancient East: The New Testament Illustrated by Recently Discovered Texts of the Graeco-Roman World.* Grand Rapids, Mich.: Baker Book House, 1978.

Delling, Gerhard. "στοιχεῖον." In *Theological Dictionary of the New Testament,* 7:670-87. Edited by Gerhard Kittel and Gerhard Friedrich. 10 vols. Grand Rapids, Mich.: Eerdmans, 1971.

Dibelius, Martin. *From Tradition to Gospel.* Greenwood, S.C.: Attic, 1971.

_____. *James: A Commentary on the Epistle of James.* Hermeneia. Philadelphia: Fortress, 1975.

Dibelius, Martin, and Hans Conzelmann. *The Pastoral Epistles.* Hermeneia. Philadelphia: Fortress, 1972.

Dodd, C. H. *The Bible and the Greeks.* London: Hodder & Stoughton, 1935.

_____. "ΕΝΝΟΜΟΣ ΧΡΙΣΤΟΥ." In *Studia Paulina in Honorem Johannis de Zwaan Septuagenarii.* Edited by J. N. Sevenster and W. C. van Unnik. Haarlem: Erven F. Bohn, 1953.

Donaldson, T. L. "The 'Curse of the Law' and the Inclusion of the Gentiles: Galatians 3.13-14." *New Testament Studies* 32 (1986): 94-112.

Donfried, Karl P. "Introduction 1977: The Nature and Scope of the Romans Debate." In *The Romans Debate.* Edited by Karl P. Donfried. Rev. and exp. ed. Peabody, Mass: Hendrickson, 1991.

_____. "Introduction 1991: The Romans Debate Since 1977." In *The Romans Debate.* Edited by Karl P. Donfried. Rev. and expanded ed. Peabody, Mass. Hendrickson, 1991.

_____. "A Short Note on Romans 16." *Journal of Biblical Literature* 89 (1970): 441-49.

Dunn, James D. G. "Anti-Semitism in the Deutero-Pauline Literature." In *Anti-Semitism and Early Christianity: Issues of Polemic and Faith.* Edited by Craig A. Evans and Donald A. Hagner. Minneapolis: Fortress, 1993.

_____. "Echoes of Intra-Jewish Polemic in Paul's Letter to the Galatians." *Journal of Biblical Literature* 112 (1993): 459-77.

_____. *Jesus, Paul and the Law: Studies in Mark and Galatians.* Louisville, Ky.: Westminster/John Knox, 1990.

_____. "The Justice of God: A Renewed Perspective on Justification by Faith." *Journal of Theological Studies* n.s. 43 (1992): 1-22.

_____. *The Partings of the Ways Between Christianity and Judaism and Their Significance for the Character of Christianity.* London: SCM Press/Philadelphia: Trinity Press, 1991.

_____. *Romans 1-8.* Word Biblical Commentary 38A. Dallas: Word, 1988.

_____. *Romans 9-16.* Word Biblical Commentary 38B. Dallas: Word, 1988.

_____. "2 Corinthians III.17—'The Lord Is the Spirit.' " *Journal of Theological Studies* n.s. 21 (1970): 309-20.

_____. "Yet Once More—'The Works of the Law': A Response." *Journal for the Study of the New Testament* 46 (1992): 99-117.

Dupont, Jacques. *Gnosis: La connaissance religieuse dans les épîtres de Saint Paul.* 2nd ed. Louvain, Belgium: Nauwelaerts/Paris: Gabalda, 1960.

Elliott, Neil. *The Rhetoric of Romans: Argumentative Constraint and Strategy and Paul's Dialogue with Judaism.* Journal for the Study of the New Testament Supplement Series 45. Sheffield, U.K.: JSOT Press, 1990.

Fee, Gordon D. "Εἰδωλόθυτα Once Again: An Interpretation of 1 Corinthians 8-10." *Biblica* 61 (1980): 172-97.

_____. *The First Epistle to the Corinthians.* New International Commentary on the New Testament. Grand Rapids, Mich.: Eerdmans, 1987.

_____. *1 and 2 Timothy, Titus.* New York: Harper & Row, 1984.

Fischer, Karl Martin. *Tendenz und Absicht des Epheserbriefes.* Forschungen zur Religion und Literatur des Alten und Neuen Testaments. Göttingen, Germany: Vandenhoeck & Ruprecht, 1973.

Fitzmyer, Joseph A. *According to Paul: Studies in the Theology of the Apostle.* New York: Paulist, 1993.

_____. *Romans: A New Translation with Introduction and Commentary.* Anchor Bible 33. New York: Doubleday, 1993.

Foerster, Werner. "κλῆρος, κτλ." *Theological Dictionary of the New Testament,* 3:758-69. Edited by Gerhard Kittel. 10 vols. Grand Rapids, Mich.: Eerdmans, 1965.

Francis, Fred O. "Humility and Angelic Worship in Col 2:18." In *Conflict at Colossae: A Problem in the Interpretation of Early Christianity Illustrated by Selected Modern Studies.* Edited by Fred Francis and Wayne A. Meeks. Rev. ed. Society of Biblical Literature Sources for Biblical Study 4. Missoula, Mont.: Scholars Press, 1975.

Fredriksen, Paula. "Judaism, the Circumcision of Gentiles and Apocalyptic Hope: Another Look at Galatians 1 and 2." *Journal of Theological Studies* n.s. 42 (1991): 532-64.

Fung, Ronald Y. K. *The Epistle to the Galatians.* New International Commentary on the New Testament. Grand Rapids, Mich.: Eerdmans, 1988.

Furnish, Victor Paul. "Paul the Theologian." In *The Conversation Continues: Studies in Paul and John in Honor of J. Louis Martyn.* Edited by Robert T. Fortna and Beverly R. Gaventa. Nashville: Abingdon, 1990.

_____. *II Corinthians: A New Translation with Introduction and Commentary.* Anchor Bible 32A. New York: Doubleday, 1984.

_____. *Theology and Ethics in Paul.* Nashville: Abingdon, 1968.

Gager, John G. *The Origins of Anti-Semitism: Attitudes Toward Judaism in Pagan and Christian Antiquity.* New York: Oxford University Press, 1985.

Gamble, H., Jr. *The Textual History of the Letter to the Romans: A Study in Textual and Literary Criticism.* Studies and Documents 42. Grand Rapids, Mich.: Eerdmans, 1977.

Garland, David E. "The Composition and Unity of Philippians: Some Neglected Literary Factors." *Novum Testamentum* 27 (1985): 141-73.

Gärtner, Bertil. *The Temple and the Community in Qumran and the New Testament: A Comparative Study in the Temple Symbolism of the Qumran Texts and the New Testament.* Society for New Testament Studies Monograph Series 1. Cambridge: Cambridge University Press, 1965.

Gaston, Lloyd. *Paul and the Torah.* Vancouver: University of British Columbia Press, 1987.

George, Timothy. *Theology of the Reformers.* Nashville: Broadman, 1988.

Georgi, Dieter. *The Opponents of Paul in Second Corinthians.* Philadelphia. Fortress, 1986.

Goldstein, Jonathan A. *I Maccabees: A New Translation with Introduction and Commentary.* Anchor Bible 41A. New York: Doubleday, 1976.

_____. *II Maccabees: A New Translation with Introduction and Commentary.* Anchor Bible 41A. New York: Doubleday, 1983.

Gordon, T. David. "A Note on ΠΑΙΔΑΓΩΓΟΣ in Galatians 3.24-25." *New Testament Studies* 35 (1989): 150-54.

_____. "Why Israel Did Not Obtain Torah-Righteousness: A Translation Note on Rom 9:32." *Westminster Theological Journal* 54 (1992): 163-66.

Green, Peter. *Alexander to Actium: The Historical Evolution of the Hellenistic Age.* Berkeley: University of California Press, 1990.

Gundry, R. H. "Grace, Works and Staying Saved in Paul." *Biblica* 66 (1985): 1-38.

Gunther, J. J. *St. Paul's Opponents and Their Background: A Study of Apocalyptic and Jewish Sectarian Teachings.* Supplements to *Novum Testamentum* 25. Leiden, Netherlands: Brill, 1973.

Hafemann, Scott. *Suffering and the Spirit: An Exegetical Study of II Cor. 2:14-33 within the Context of the Corinthian Correspondence.* Wissenschaftliche Untersuchungen zum Neuen Testament 2/19. Tübingen: J. C. B. Mohr/Paul Siebeck, 1986.

Hagner, Donald A. "Paul's Quarrel with Judaism." In *Anti-Semitism and Early Christianity: Issues of Polemic and Faith.* Edited by Craig A. Evans and Donald A. Hagner. Minneapolis: Fortress, 1993.

Haight, Roger. *The Experience and Language of Grace.* New York: Paulist, 1979.

Hanse, Hermann. "ΔΗΛΟΝ (Zu Gal 3[11])." *Zeitschrift für die neutestamentliche Wissenschaft* 34

(1935): 299-303.

Hanson, Paul. *The People Called: The Growth of Community in the Bible.* New York: Harper & Row, 1986.

Hawthorne, Gerald F. *Philippians.* Word Biblical Commentary 43. Waco, Tex.: Word, 1983.

Hays, Richard B. *Echoes of Scripture in the Letters of Paul.* New Haven, Conn.: Yale University Press, 1989.

_____. *The Faith of Jesus Christ: An Investigation of the Narrative Substructure of Galatians 3:1-4:11.* Society of Biblical Literature Dissertation Series 56. Chico, Calif.: Scholars Press, 1983.

Hengel, Martin. *The Hellenization of Judaea in the First Century After Christ.* London: SCM Press/Philadelphia: Trinity Press International, 1989.

_____. *Judaism and Hellenism: Studies in Their Encounter in Palestine During the Early Hellenistic Period.* 2 vols. Philadelphia: Fortress, 1974.

_____. *The Pre-Christian Paul.* London: SCM Press/Philadelphia: Trinity Press International, 1991.

Hennecke, Edgar. "Preaching of Peter." In *New Testament Apocrypha,* 2:111-27. Edited by Wilhelm Schneemelcher. 2 vols. Philadephia: Westminster Press, 1963-1964.

Hodge, Charles. *A Commentary on Romans.* Orig. ed. 1835; rev. 1864. Edinburgh: Banner of Truth Trust, 1972.

Hofius, Otfried. "Das Gesetz des Mose und das Gesetz Christi." *Zeitschrift für Theologie und Kirche* 80 (1983): 262-86.

Holtz, Traugott. *Der Erste Brief an die Thessalonicher.* Evangelisch-katholischer Kommentar zum Neuen Testament 13. Zurich: Benziger/Neukirchen, Germany: Neukirchener, 1990.

Hooker, Morna. "Beyond the Things That Are Written? St. Paul's Use of Scripture." *New Testament Studies* 27 (1981): 295-309.

_____. "Were There False Teachers in Colossae?" In *Christ and Spirit in the New Testament.* Edited by Barnabas Lindars and Stephen S. Smalley. Cambridge: Cambridge University Press, 1973.

Horsley, Richard A. "Gnosis in Corinth: 1 Corinthians 8.1-6." *New Testament Studies* 27 (1980): 32-51.

Hübner, Hans. *Law in Paul's Thought.* Studies of the New Testament and Its World. Edinburgh: T & T Clark, 1984.

Hughes, Philip Edgcumbe. *Paul's Second Epistle to the Corinthians.* New International Commentary on the New Testament. Grand Rapids, Mich.: Eerdmans, 1962.

Janz, Denis R. *Luther on Thomas Aquinas: The Angelic Doctor in the Thought of the Reformer.* Veröffentlichungen des Instituts für Europäische Geschichte 140. Stuttgart: Franz Steiner Verlag, 1989.

Jaubert, Annie. *La notion d'alliance dans le Judaïsme aux abords de l'ère Chrétienne.* Patristica Sorbonensia 6. Paris: Éditions du Seuil, 1963.

Jeremias, Joachim. *The Eucharistic Words of Jesus.* London: SCM Press, 1966.

Jervis, L. Ann. *The Purpose of Romans: A Comparative Letter Structure Investigation. Journal for the Study of the New Testament* Supplement Series 55. Sheffield, U.K.: JSOT Press, 1991.

_____. "Conflicting Movements in the Early Church as Reflected in Philippians." *Novum Testamentum* 12 (1970): 362-90.

Jewett, Robert. "The Agitators and the Galatian Congregation." *New Testament Studies* 17 (1971): 198-212.

_____. "The Epistolary Thanksgiving and the Integrity of Philippians." *Novum Testamentum* 12 (1970): 40-53.

_____. *Paul's Anthropological Terms: A Study of Their Use in Conflict Settings.* Arbeiten zur Geschichte des antiken Judentums und des Urchristentums 10. Leiden: Brill, 1971.

Johnson, Luke T. *The Thessalonian Correspondence: Pauline Rhetoric and Millenarian Piety.* Foundations and Facets: New Testament. Philadelphia: Fortress, 1986.

_____. *The Writings of the New Testament: An Interpretation*. Philadelphia: Fortress, 1986.

Karris, Robert J. "Romans 14:1-15:13 and the Occasion of Romans." In *The Romans Debate*. Edited by Karl P. Donfried. Rev. and expanded ed. Peabody, Mass.: Hendrickson, 1991.

Käsemann, Ernst. *Commentary on Romans*. Grand Rapids, Mich.: Eerdmans, 1980.

_____. *Perspectives on Paul*. Philadelphia: Fortress, 1971.

Kelly, J. N. D. *The Pastoral Epistles*. Harper's New Testament Commentaries. New York: Harper & Row, 1960.

Kertelge, Karl. "δικαιοσύνη." In *Exegetical Dictionary of the New Testament*, 1:326-30. Edited by H. Balz and G. Schneider. 3 vols. Grand Rapids, Mich.: Eerdmans, 1990-1993.

Kevan, Ernest F. *The Grace of Law: A Study in Puritan Theology*. Ligonier, Penn.: Soli Deo Gloria, 1993.

Kidd, Reggie M. *Wealth and Beneficence in the Pastoral Epistles*. Society of Biblical Literature Dissertation Series 122. Atlanta: Scholars Press, 1990.

Kilpatrick, G. D. "ΒΛΕΠΕΤΕ, Philippians 3₂." In *In Memoriam Paul Kahle*. Edited by Matthew Black and Georg Fohrer. Beihefte zur *Zeitschrift für die alttestamentliche Wissenschaft* 103. Berlin: Töpelmann, 1968.

Klausner, Joseph. *The Messianic Idea in Israel from Its Beginning to the Completion of the Mishnah*. London: George Allen & Unwin, 1956.

Knight, George W., III. *The Pastoral Epistles: A Commentary on the Greek Text*. New International Greek Testament Commentary. Grand Rapids, Mich.: Eerdmans, 1992.

Koester, Helmut. *Introduction to the New Testament*. 2 vols. Berlin: Walter de Gruyter, 1982.

Kuss, Otto. *Der Römerbrief übersetzt und erklärt*. 3 parts. Regensburg, Germany: Friedrich Pustet, 1957-1978.

Laato, Timo. *Paulus und das Judentum: Anthropologische Erwägungen*. Åbo, Finland: Åbo Akademis Förlag, 1991.

Lagrange, M. J. *Saint Paul Épître aux Galates*. Paris: Librairie Lecoffre, 1950.

_____. *Saint Paul Épître aux Romains*. 3rd ed. Paris: Librairie Victor Lecoffre, 1922.

Lambrecht, Jan. "Transgressor by Nullifying God's Grace. A Study of Gal. 2,18-21." *Biblica* 72 (1991): 217-36.

Lampe, Peter. "Keine 'Sklavenflucht' des Onesimus." *Zeitschrift für die neutestamentliche Wissenschaft* 76 (1985): 135-37.

_____. "The Roman Christians of Romans 16." In *The Romans Debate*. Edited by Karl P. Donfried. Rev. and expanded ed. Peabody, Mass.: Hendrickson, 1991.

Laws, Sophie. *The Epistle of James*. New York: Harper & Row, 1980.

Leenhardt, Franz J. *The Epistle to the Romans: A Commentary*. Cleveland: World Publishing, 1957.

Levine, Baruch A. *The JPS Torah Commentary: Leviticus*. Philadelphia: The Jewish Publication Society, 1989.

_____. "On the Presence of God in Biblical Religion." In *Religions in Antiquity: Essays in Memory of Erwin Ramsdell Goodenough*. Edited by Jacob Neusner. Studies in the History of Religion 14. Leiden: Brill, 1968.

Liddell, Henry George, and Robert Scott. *A Greek-English Lexicon*. Revised and augmented by Henry Stuart Jones. 9th ed. Oxford: Oxford University Press, 1940.

Liebreich, Leon J. "The Impact of Nehemiah 9:5-37 on the Liturgy of the Synagogue." *Hebrew Union College Annual* 32 (1961): 227-37.

Lietzmann, Hans. *An die Korinther I/II*. 5th ed. Handbuch zum Neuen Testament 9. Tübingen: J. C. B. Mohr/Paul Siebeck, 1969.

Lightfoot, J. B. *Saint Paul's Epistle to the Galatians*. 10th ed. London: Macmillan, 1890.

_____. *Saint Paul's Epistle to the Philippians: A Revised Text with Introduction, Notes and Dissertations*. 4th ed. rev. London: Macmillan, 1885.

_____. *St. Paul's Epistles to the Colossians and to Philemon*. Rev. ed. London: Macmillan, 1879.

Lincoln, Andrew T. *Ephesians*. Word Biblical Commentary 42. Dallas: Word, 1990.

_____. "Ephesians 2:8-10: A Summary of Paul's Gospel?" *Catholic Biblical Quarterly* 45 (1983): 617-30.

Lock, Walter. *A Critical and Exegetical Commentary on the Pastoral Epistles (I and II Timothy and Titus)*. Edinburgh: T & T Clark, 1924.

Lohse, Eduard. *Colossians and Philemon: A Commentary on the Epistles to the Colossians and to Philemon*. Hermeneia. Philadelphia: Fortress, 1971.

Longenecker, Richard N. *Galatians*. Word Biblical Commentary 41. Dallas: Word, 1990.

_____. *Paul, Apostle of Liberty: The Origin and Nature of Paul's Christianity*. Grand Rapids, Mich.: Baker Book House, 1976.

Luedemann, Gerd. *Opposition to Paul in Jewish Christianity*. Minneapolis: Fortress, 1989.

Lull, David J. " 'The Law Was Our Pedagogue': A Study in Galatians 3:19-25." *Journal of Biblical Literature* 105 (1986): 481-98.

Lyons, George. *Pauline Autobiography: Toward A New Understanding*. Society of Biblical Literature Dissertation Series 73. Atlanta: Scholars Press, 1985.

McKim, Donald K. "Calvin's View of Scripture." In *Readings in Calvin's Theology*. Edited by Donald K. McKim. Grand Rapids, Mich.: Baker Book House, 1984.

McNeile, A. H. *Introduction to the New Testament*. 2nd ed. Oxford: Oxford University Press, 1953.

_____. *An Introduction to the Study of the New Testament*. 2nd rev. ed. Oxford: Clarendon, 1953.

Malherbe, Abraham J. *Paul and the Thessalonians: The Philosophic Tradition of Pastoral Care*. Philadelphia: Fortress, 1987.

Manson, T. W. *Studies in the Gospels and Epistles*. Philadelphia: Westminster Press, 1962.

Marshall, I. Howard. *Last Supper and Lord's Supper*. Grand Rapids, Mich.: Eerdmans, 1980.

Martin, R. P. *Philippians*. New Century Bible. Grand Rapids, Mich.: Eerdmans/London: Marshall, Morgan & Scott, 1976.

_____. *Philippians*. Tyndale New Testament Commentaries. 2nd ed. Grand Rapids, Mich.: Eerdmans, 1987.

_____. *2 Corinthians*. Word Biblical Commentary 40. Dallas: Word, 1986.

Martyn, J. Louis. "The Covenants of Hagar and Sarah." In *Faith and History: Essays in Honor of Paul W. Meyer*. Edited by John T. Carroll, Charles H. Cosgrove and E. Elizabeth Johnson. Atlanta: Scholars Press, 1990.

Marxen, Willi. *Introduction to the New Testament*. Philadelphia: Fortress, 1968.

Mason, Steve. *Josephus and the New Testament*. Peabody, Mass.: Hendrickson, 1992.

Matera, Frank J. *Galatians*. Sacra Pagina Series Series 9. Collegeville, Minn.: Liturgical Press, 1992.

Melanchthon, Philipp. "Römerbrief-Kommentar, 1532." In *Melanchthons Werke in Auswahl*, vol. 5. Edited by Robert Stupperich. Gütersloh, Germany: Gerd Mohn, 1965.

Metzger, Bruce. *A Textual Commentary on the Greek New Testament*. Stuttgart: United Bible Societies, 1971.

Michael, J. Hugh. *The Epistle of Paul to the Philippians*. Moffatt New Testament Commentary. London: Hodder & Stoughton, 1928.

Moessner, David P. *Lord of the Banquet: The Literary and Theological Significance of the Lukan Travel Narrative*. Minneapolis: Fortress, 1989.

Moffatt, James. *The First Epistle of Paul to the Corinthians*. Moffatt New Testament Commentary. London: Hodder & Stoughton, 1938.

Montefiore, Claude G. "First Impressions of Paul." *Jewish Quarterly Review* 6 (1894): 428-74.

_____. *Judaism and St. Paul: Two Essays*. London: Max Goschen, 1914.

_____. "Rabbinic Judaism and the Epistles of St. Paul." *Jewish Quarterly Review* 13 (1990-1901): 161-217.

Moo, Douglas. *Romans 1-8*. Wycliffe Exegetical Commentary. Chicago: Moody Press, 1991.

Moore, Carey A. "Toward the Dating of the Book of Baruch." *Catholic Biblical Quarterly* 36 (1974): 312-20.

Moore, George Foot. *Judaism in the First Centuries of the Christian Era: The Age of the Tannaim.* 3 vols. Cambridge, Mass.: Harvard University Press, 1927-1930.

Mørkholm, Otto. *Antiochus IV of Syria.* Classica et Mediaevalia, Dissertationes 8. Copenhagen: Gyldendalske Boghandel, 1966.

Moule, C. F. D. *The Epistles to the Colossians and to Philemon.* Cambridge Greek Testament Commentary. Cambridge: Cambridge University Press, 1957.

_____. *An Idiom-Book of New Testament Greek.* 2nd ed. Cambridge: Cambridge University Press: 1959.

Munck, Johannes. *Paul and the Salvation of Mankind.* Atlanta: John Knox, 1959.

Murphy-O'Connor, Jerome. *The Theology of the Second Letter to the Corinthians.* Cambridge: Cambridge University Press, 1991.

Mußner, Franz. *Der Galaterbrief.* Herders theologischer Kommentar zum Neuen Testament. Freiurg, Germany: Herder, 1974.

Neusner, Jacob. *The Idea of Purity in Ancient Judaism.* Studies in Judaism in Late Antiquity 1. Leiden: Brill, 1973.

_____. "Sanders's *Judaism: Practices* [sic] *and Beliefs, 63 B.C.E.-66 C.E.*" In *Judaic Law from Jesus to the Mishnah: A Systematic Reply to Professor E. P. Sanders.* South Florida Studies in the History of Judaism 84. Atlanta: Scholars Press, 1993.

Newton, Michael. *The Concept of Purity at Qumran and in Paul.* Society for New Testament Studies Monograph Series 53. Cambridge: Cambridge University Press, 1985.

Nickelsburg, George W. E. *Jewish Literature Between the Bible and the Mishnah.* London: SCM Press, 1981.

Noth, Martin. *The Laws of the Pentateuch and Other Studies.* Edinburgh: Oliver & Boyd, 1966.

_____. *Leviticus: A Commentary.* Philadelphia: Westminster Press, 1965.

Nygren, Anders. *Commentary on Romans.* Philadelphia: Muhlenberg, 1949.

O'Brien, Peter T. *Colossians, Philemon.* Word Biblical Commentary 44. Waco, Tex.: Word, 1982.

_____. *The Epistle to the Philippians: Commentary on the Greek Text.* New International Greek Testament Commentary. Grand Rapids, Mich.: Eerdmans, 1991.

Parker, T. H. L. *Calvin's New Testament Commentaries.* Grand Rapids, Mich.: Eerdmans, 1971.

Perkins, William. *A Commentary on Galatians.* Orig. ed. 1617. New York: Pilgrim, 1989.

Plummer, Alfred. *A Critical and Exegetical Commentary on the Second Epistle of St. Paul to the Corinthians.* International Critical Commentary. Edinburgh: T & T Clark, 1915.

Porter, Stanley. *Idioms of the Greek New Testament.* Sheffield, U.K.: JSOT Press, 1992.

Provence, Thomas E. " 'Who Is Sufficient for These Things?' An Exegesis of 2 Corinthians ii 15-iii 18." *Novum Testamentum* 24 (1982): 54-81.

Quinn, Jerome D. *The Letter to Titus: A New Translation with Notes and Commentary and an Introduction to Titus, I and II Timothy, the Pastoral Epistles.* Anchor Bible 35. New York: Doubleday, 1990.

Räisänen, Heikki. *Beyond New Testament Theology.* Philadephia: Fortress, 1990.

_____. *Jesus, Paul and Torah: Collected Essays. Journal for the Study of the New Testament* Supplement Series 43. Sheffield, U.K.: JSOT Press, 1992.

_____. *Paul and the Law.* Wissenschaftliche Untersuchungen zum Neuen Testament 29. Tübingen: J. C. B. Mohr/Paul Siebeck, 1983.

_____. "Paul's Conversion and the Development of His View of the Law." *New Testament Studies* 33 (1987): 404-19.

_____. *The Torah and Christ: Essays in German and English on the Problem of the Law in Early Christianity.* Publications of the Finnish Exgetical Society 45. Helsinki: Finnish Exegetical Society, 1986.

Reid, Daniel G. "Triumph." In *Dictionary of Paul and His Letters.* Edited by Gerald F. Hawthorne,

Ralph P. Martin and Daniel G. Reid. Downers Grove, Ill.: InterVarsity Press, 1993.

Richardson, P. "Spirit and Letter: A Foundation for Hermeneutics." *Evangelical Quarterly* 45 (1973): 208-18.

Ridderbos, Herman N. *The Epistle of Paul to the Churches of Galatia.* New International Commentary on the New Testament. Grand Rapids, Mich.: Eerdmans, 1953.

Roloff, Jürgen. *Der Erste Brief an Timotheus.* Evangelisch-katholischer Kommentar zum Neuen Testament 15. Zurich: Benziger/Neukirchen, Germany: Neukirchener, 1988.

Roth, Cecil, and Geoffrey Wigoder, eds. *Encyclopedia Judaica.* 16 vols. Jerusalem: Keter, 1971.

Safrai, S., and M. Stern. *The Jewish People in the First Century: Historical Geography, Political History, Social, Cultural and Religious Life and Institutions.* Compendia Rerum Iudaicarum ad Novum Testamentum 1. Assen, Netherlands: Van Gorcum/Philadelphia: Fortress, 1974.

Sanday, William, and Arthur C. Headlam. *A Critical and Exegetical Commentary on the Epistle to the Romans.* International Critical Commentary. 5th ed. Edinburgh: T & T Clark, 1902.

Sanders, E. P. "The Covenant as a Soteriological Category and the Nature of Salvation in Palestinian and Hellenistic Judaism." In *Jews, Greeks and Christians: Studies in Honor of W. D. Davies.* Edited by R. G. Hamerton-Kelly and Robin Scroggs. Studies in Judaism in Late Antiquity 21. Leiden: Brill, 1976.

_____. "Jewish Association with Gentiles and Galatians 2:11-14." In *The Conversation Continues: Studies in Paul and John in Honor of J. Louis Martyn.* Edited by Robert T. Fortna and Beverly R. Gaventa. Nashville: Abingdon, 1990.

_____. *Jewish Law from Jesus to the Mishnah: Five Studies.* London: SCM Press/Philadelphia: Trinity Press International, 1990.

_____. *Judaism: Practice and Belief 63 BCE-66 CE.* London: SCM Press/Philadelphia: Trinity Press International, 1992.

_____. "On the Question of Fulfilling the Law in Paul and Rabbinic Judaism." In *Donum Gentilicium: New Testament Studies in Honour of David Daube.* Edited by Ernst Bammel, C. K. Barrett and W. D. Davies. Oxford: Oxford University Press, 1977.

_____. *Paul: Past Master.* Oxford: Oxford University Press, 1991.

_____. *Paul and Palestinian Judaism: A Comparison of Patterns of Religion.* Philadelphia: Fortress, 1977.

_____. *Paul, the Law and the Jewish People.* Philadephia: Fortress, 1983.

Sandmel, Samuel. *The Genius of Paul: A Study in History.* Philadelphia: Fortress, 1979.

_____. *Judaism and Christian Beginnings.* New York: Oxford University Press, 1978.

Sappington, Thomas J. *Revelation and Redemption at Colossae. Journal for the Study of the New Testament* Supplement Series 53. Sheffield, U.K.: JSOT Press, 1991.

Schlier, Heinrich. *Der Brief an die Galater.* 11th ed. Kritischer-exegetischer Kommentar über das Neue Testament 7. Göttingen, Germany: Vandenhoeck & Ruprecht, 1949.

_____. "παρρησία, παρρησιάζομαι." In *Theological Dictionary of the New Testament,* 5:871-86. Edited by Gerhard Kittel and Gerhard Friedrich. 10 vols. Grand Rapids, Mich.: Eerdmans, 1967.

Schmidt, K. L. "καλέω." In *Theological Dictionary of the New Testament,* 3:489-91. Edited by Gerhard Kittel. 10 vols. Grand Rapids, Mich.: Eerdmans, 1965.

Schmithals, Walter. *Paul and the Gnostics.* Nashville: Abingdon, 1972.

_____. *Der Römerbrief als historisches Problem.* Studien zum Neuen Testament. Gütersloh, Germany: Gerd Mohn, 1975.

Schnackenburg, Rudolf. *Ephesians: A Commentary.* Orig. German ed. 1982. Edinburgh: T & T Clark, 1991.

Schneider, Bernardin. "The Meaning of St. Paul's Antithesis 'The Letter and the Spirit.' " *Catholic Biblical Quarterly* 15 (1953): 163-207.

Schneider, J. "σταυρός, κτλ." In *Theological Dictionary of the New Testament,* 7:572-84. Edited by Gerhard Kittel and Gerhard Friedrich. 10 vols. Grand Rapids, Mich.: Eerdmans, 1971.

Schnelle, Udo. *Wandlungen im paulinischen Denken*. Stuttgart Bibelstudien 137. Stuttgart: Katholisches Bibelwerk, 1989.

Schoenberg, Martin W. "St. Paul's Notion on the Adoptive Sonship of Christians." *The Thomist* 28 (1964): 51-75.

Schoeps, Hans Joachim. *Paul: The Theology of the Apostle in the Light of Jewish Religious History*. Philadelphia: Westminster Press, 1961.

Schrage, Wolfgang. *Der Erste Brief an die Korinther (1 Kor 1, 1-6, 11)*. Evangelisch-katholischer Kommentar zum Neuen Testament 7/1. Zurich: Benziger/Neukirchen, Germany: Neukirchener, 1991.

Schreiner, Thomas R. "Israel's Failure to Attain Righteousness in Romans 9:30-10:3." *Trinity Journal* n.s. 12 (1991): 209-20.

_____. *The Law and Its Fulfillment: A Pauline Theology of Law*. Grand Rapids, Mich.: Baker Book House, 1993.

_____. " 'Works of Law' in Paul." *Novum Testamentum* 33 (1991): 217-44.

Schrenk, Gottlob. "γράμμα." In *Theological Dictionary of the New Testament*, 1:761-69. Edited by Gerhard Kittel. 10 vols. Grand Rapids, Mich.: Eerdmans, 1964.

Schulze, S. "Die Decke des Moses, Untersuchungen zu einer vorpaulinischen Überlieferung in 2 Cor. iii 7-18." *Zeitschrift für die neutestamentliche Wissenschaft* 49 (1958): 1-30.

Schweitzer, Albert. *The Mysticism of Paul the Apostle*. New York: Seabury, 1931.

Schweizer, Eduard. "σάρξ, κτλ." In *Theological Dictionary of the New Testament*, 7:98-151. Edited by Gerhard Kittel and Gerhard Friedrich. 10 vols. Grand Rapids, Mich.: Eerdmans, 1971.

Scott, E. F. *The Pastoral Epistles*. Moffatt New Testament Commentary. New York: Harper & Brothers, 1936.

Scott, James M. *Adoption as Sons of God: An Exegetical Investigation into the Background of* YIOΘEΣIA *in the Pauline Corpus*. Wissenschaftliche Untersuchungen zum Neuen Testament 2/48. Tübingen: J. C. B. Mohr/Paul Siebeck, 1992.

_____. "Paul's Use of Deuteronomic Tradition." *Journal of Biblical Literature* 112 (1993): 645-65.

_____. "Restoration of Israel." In *Dictionary of Paul and His Letters*. Edited by Gerald F. Hawthorne, Ralph P. Martin and Daniel G. Reid. Downers Grove, Ill.: InterVarsity Press, 1993.

Seifrid, Mark. *Justification by Faith: The Origin and Development of a Central Pauline Theme*. Supplements to *Novum Testamentum* 68. Leiden: Brill, 1992.

Sevenster, J. N. *Do You Know Greek? How Much Greek Could the First Jewish Christians Have Known?* Supplements to *Novum Testamentum* 19. Leiden: Brill, 1968.

Silva, Moisés. "The Law and Christianity: Dunn's New Synthesis." *Westminster Theological Journal* 53 (1991): 349-53.

_____. *Philippians*. Baker Exegetical Commentary on the New Testament. Grand Rapids, Mich.: Baker Book House, 1992.

Skeat, T. C. " 'Especially the Parchments': A Note on 2 Timothy IV.13." *Journal of Theological Studies* n.s. 30 (1979): 173-77.

Snodgrass, Klyne R. "Justification by Grace—to the Doers: An Analysis of the Place of Romans 2 in the Theology of Paul." *New Testament Studies* 32 (1986): 72-93.

Stacey, W. David. *The Pauline View of Man*. London: Macmillan, 1956.

Stanley, Christopher D. " 'Under a Curse': A Fresh Reading of Galatians 3.10-14." *New Testament Studies* 36 (1990): 481-511.

Steck, Odil H. *Israel und das gewaltsame Geschick der Propheten: Untersuchungen zur Überlieferung des deuteronomistischen Geschichtsbildes im Alten Testament, Spätjudentum und Urchristentum*. Wissenschaftliche Monographien zum Alten und Neun Testament 23. Neukirchen, Germany: Neukirchener, 1967.

Stein, Joshua. *Claude Goldsmid Montefiore on the Ancient Rabbis*. Brown Judaic Studies 4. Missoula,

Mont.: Scholars Press, 1977.

Stendahl, Krister. *Paul Among Jews and Gentiles*. Philadelphia: Fortress, 1976.

Stewart, James S. *A Man in Christ: The Vital Elements of St. Paul's Religion*. London: Hodder & Stoughton, 1935.

Stone, Michael E., ed. *Jewish Writings of the Second Temple Period*. Compendia Rerum Iudaicarum ad Novum Testamentum 2/2. Philadelphia: Fortress/Assen, Netherlands: Van Gorcum, 1984.

Stowers, Stanley Kent. *The Diatribe and Paul's Letter to the Romans*. Society of Biblical Literature Dissertation Series 57. Chico, Calif.: Scholars Press, 1981.

_____. *Letter Writing in Greco-Roman Antiquity*. Library of Early Christianity 5. Philadelphia: Westminster Press, 1986.

Strachan, R. H. *The Second Epistle of Paul to the Corinthians*. Moffatt New Testament Commentary. London: Hodder & Stoughton, 1935.

Strack, H. L., and Paul Billerbeck. *Kommentar zum Neuen Testament aus Talmud und Midrasch*. 6 vols. Munich: Beck, 1922-1961.

Strathmann, H. λατρεύω, λατρεία In *Theological Dictionary of the New Testament*, 4:58-65. Edited by Gerhard Kittel. 10 vols. Grand Rapids, Mich.: Eerdmans, 1967.

Stuhlmacher, Peter. *Der Brief an Philemon*. 3rd ed. Evangelisch-katholischer Kommentar zum Neuen Testament 17. Zurich: Benziger/Neukirchen, Germany: Neukirchener, 1989. 34.

_____. *Paul's Letter to the Romans: A Commentary*. Louisville, Ky.: Westminster/John Knox, 1994.

_____. "Paul's Understanding of the Law in the Letter to the Romans." *Svensk Exegetisk Årsbok* 50 (1985): 87-104.

_____. *Reconciliation, Law and Righteousness: Essays in Biblical Theology*. Philadelphia: Fortress, 1986.

Sumney, Jerry L. *Identifying Paul's Opponents: The Question of Method in 2 Corinthians. Journal for the Study of the New Testament* Supplement Series 40. Sheffield, U.K.: Sheffield Academic Press, 1990.

Tasker, R. V. G. *The Second Epistle of Paul to the Corinthians*. Tyndale New Testament Commentaries. Grand Rapids, Mich.: Eerdmans, 1958.

Theissen, Gerd. *The Social Setting of Pauline Christianity: Essays on Corinth*. Philadelphia: Fortress, 1982.

Thielman, Frank. "The Coherence of Paul's View of the Law: The Evidence of First Corinthians." *New Testament Studies* 38 (1992): 235-53.

_____. *From Plight to Solution: A Jewish Framework for Understanding Paul's View of the Law in Romans and Galatians*. Supplements to *Novum Testamentum* 61. Leiden, Netherlands: Brill, 1989.

_____. "The Story of Israel and the Theology of Romans 5-8." In *Society of Biblical Literature 1993 Seminar Papers*. Edited by Eugene H. Lovering. Atlanta: Scholars Press, 1993.

_____. "Unexpected Mercy: Echoes of a Biblical Motif in Romans 9-11." *Scottish Journal of Theology* 46 (1994).

Thompson, J. A. *The Book of Jeremiah*. New International Commentary on the Old Testament. Grand Rapids, Mich.: Eerdmans, 1980.

Tomson, Peter J. *Paul and the Jewish Law: Halakha in the Letters of the Apostle to the Gentiles*. Compendia Rerum Iudaicarum ad Novum Testamentum. Minneapolis: Fortress/Assen, Netherlands: Van Gorcum, 1990.

Towner, Philip H. *The Goal of Our Instruction: The Structure of Theology and Ethics in the Pastoral Epistles. Journal for the Study of the New Testament* Supplements Series 34. Sheffield, U.K.: JSOT Press, 1989.

van Unnik, W. C. " 'With Unveiled Face': An Exegesis of 2 Corinthians iii 12-18." In *Sparsa Collecta: The Collected Essays of W. C. van Unnik*, 1:194-210. 3 parts. Supplement to *Novum*

Testamentum 29-31. Leiden, Netherlands: Brill, 1973-1983.

Vincent, Marvin R. *A Critical and Exegetical Commentary on the Epistles to the Philippians and to Philemon.* International Critical Commentary. Edinburgh: T & T Clark, 1897.

von Harnack, Adolf. *Marcion: The Gospel of the Alien God.* Orig. ed. 1920. Durham, N.C.: Labyrinth, 1990.

Wanamaker, Charles. *The Epistles to the Thessalonians: A Commentary on the Greek Text.* New International Greek Testament Commentary. Grand Rapids, Mich.: Eerdmans, 1990.

Watson, Francis. *Paul, Judaism and the Gentiles: A Sociological Approach.* Cambridge: Cambridge University Press, 1986.

Weber, Ferdinand. *Jüdische Theologie auf Grund des Talmud und verwandter Schriften.* 2nd improved ed. Edited by Franz Delitzsch and George Schnedermann. Leipzig: Dörffling Franke, 1897.

Wedderburn, A. J. M. *The Reasons for Romans.* Minneapolis: Fortress, 1991.

Weiss, Herold. "The Law in the Epistle to the Colossians." *Catholic Biblical Quarterly* 34 (1972): 294-314.

Weiss, Johannes. *Der erste Korintherbrief.* 10th ed. Meyer Kommentar. Göttingen, Germany: Vandenhoeck & Ruprecht, 1925.

Wellhausen, Julius. *Prolegomena to the History of Ancient Israel.* Cleveland: World, 1957.

Westerholm, Stephen. *Israel's Law and the Church's Faith: Paul and His Recent Interpreters.* Grand Rapids, Mich.: Eerdmans, 1988.

_____. "Letter and Spirit: The Foundation of Pauline Ethics." *New Testament Studies* 30 (1984): 229-48.

Wiefel, Wolfgang. "The Jewish Community in Ancient Rome and the Origins of Roman Christianity." In *The Romans Debate.* Edited by Karl P. Donfried. Rev. and expanded ed. Peabody, Mass.: Hendrickson, 1991.

Wilckens, Ulrich. *Der Brief an die Römer.* 3 vols. Evangelisch-katholischer Kommentar zum Neuen Testament 6. Zurich: Benziger/Neukirchen, Germany: Neukirchener, 1978-1982.

_____. "Statements on the Development of Paul's View of the Law." In *Paul and Paulinism: Essays in Honour of C. K. Barrett.* Edited by M. D. Hooker and S. G. Wilson. Cambridge: Cambridge University, Press, 1982.

Windisch, Hans. "ζύμη, κτλ" In *Theological Dictionary of the New Testament,* 2:902-6. Edited by Gerhard Kittel. 10 vols. Grand Rapids, Mich.: Eerdmans, 1964.

Winger, Michael. *By What Law? The Meaning of* Νόμος *in the Letters of Paul.* Society of Biblical Literature Dissertation Series 128. Atlanta: Scholars Press, 1992.

Winter, Sara C. "Paul's Letter to Philemon." *New Testament Studies* 33 (1987): 1-15.

Wolff, Christian. *Jeremia im Frühjudentum und Urchristentum.* Texte und Untersuchungen. 118. Berlin: Akademie Verlag, 1976.

Wright, N. T. *The Climax of the Covenant: Christ and the Law in Pauline Theology.* Edinburgh: T & T Clark, 1991.

_____. *Colossians and Philemon.* Tyndale New Testament Commentaries. Grand Rapids, Mich.: Eerdmans, 1986.

_____. *The New Testament and the People of God.* Minneapolis: Fortress, 1992.

Zimmerli, Walther. *Ezekiel I: A Commentary on the Book of the Prophet Ezekiel, Chapters 1-24.* Hermeneia. Philadelphia: Fortress, 1979.

_____. *Ezekiel II: A Commentary on the Book of the Prophet Ezekiel, Chapters 25-48.* Hermeneia. Philadelphia: Fortress, 1983.